CLASSIC CASES IN
NEUROPSYCHOLOGY

Classic Cases in Neuropsychology

edited by

Chris Code, Claus-W. Wallesch, Yves Joanette
and André Roch Lecours

Psychology Press
Taylor & Francis Group
HOVE AND NEW YORK

First published 1996 by Psychology Press
27 Church Road, Hove, East Sussex BN3 2FA

Simultaneously published in the USA and Canada
by Psychology Press
711 Third Avenue, New York NY 10017

Psychology Press is an imprint of the Taylor & Francis Group, an Informa business

This publication has been produced with paper manufactured to
strict environmental standards and with pulp derived from
sustainable forests.

British Library Cataloguing in Publication Data
A catalogue record for this book is available from the British Library

ISBN 978-0-86377-396-9 (Pbk)
ISSN 0967-9944

Contents

v

Series Preface

From being an area primarily on the periphery of mainstream behavioural and cognitive science, neuropsychology has developed in recent years into an area of central concern for a range of disciplines. We are witnessing not only a revolution in the way in which brain–behaviour–cognition relationships are viewed, but a widening of interest concerning developments in neuropsychology on the part of a range of workers in a variety of fields. Major advances in brain-imaging techniques and the cognitive modelling of the impairments following brain damage promise a wider understanding of the nature of the representation of cognition and behaviour in the damaged and undamaged brain.

Neuropsychology is now centrally important for those working with brain-damaged people, but the very rate of expansion in the area makes it difficult to keep up with findings from current research. The aim of the *Brain Damage, Behaviour and Cognition* series is to publish a wide range of books which present comprehensive and up-to-date overviews of current developments in specific areas of interest.

These books will be of particular interest to those working with the brain damaged. It is the editors' intention that undergraduates, postgraduates, clinicians and researchers in psychology, speech pathology, and medicine will find this series a useful source of information on important current developments. The authors and editors of the books in this series are experts in their respective fields, working at the forefront of contemporary research. They have produced texts which are accessible and scholarly. We thank them for their contribution and their hard work in fulfilling the aims of the series.

C.C. and D.J.M.
Sydney, Australia and Ipswich, U.K.
Series Editors

Brain Damage, Behaviour and Cognition
Developments in Clinical Neuropsychology

Series Editors
Chris Code, University of Sydney, Australia
Dave Müller, Suffolk College of Higher and Further Education, UK

Published titles

Cognitive Rehabilitation Using Microcomputers
Veronica A. Bradley, John L. Welch and Clive E. Skilbeck

The Characteristics of Aphasia
Chris Code (Ed.)

Classic Cases in Neuropsychology
Chris Code, Claus-W. Wallesch, Yves Joanette, and André Roch Lecours (Eds)

The Neuropsychology of Schizophrenia
Anthony S. David and John C. Cutting (Eds)

Neuropsychology and the Dementias
Siobhan Hart and James M. Semple

Clinical Neuropsychology of Alcoholism
Robert G. Knight and Barry E. Longmore

Acquired Neurological Speech/Language Disorders in Childhood
Bruce E. Murdoch (Ed.)

Neuropsychology of the Amnesic Syndrome
Alan J. Parkin and Nicholas R.C. Leng

Clinical and Neuropsychological Aspects of Closed Head Injury
John T.E. Richardson

Unilateral Neglect: Clinical and Experimental Studies
Ian H. Robertson and J.C. Marshall (Eds)

Acquired Apraxia of Speech in Aphasic Adults
Paula A. Square (Ed.)

Cognitive Rehabilitation in Perspective
Rodger Wood and Ian Fussey (Eds)

Preface

More than for any other area of psychology, for neuropsychology the single case has always been of central importance. This was certainly so in the early years of development of the field, but beginning between the wars and continuing up until relatively recently, the single case took a back seat to group studies; for many the single case had no place at all. That is no longer true. The role of the single case is recognised as crucial both in the historical development of the field as well as in its increasing contribution to contemporary work.

Within the last decade or so the importance of detailed examination and theoretical interpretation of data from the single case has been increasingly recognised in neuropsychology. The value of the hypothesis-driven approach is exemplified by a range of recent detailed single case studies in the literature. The aim of this book is to bring together in one volume discussion of the classic cases which have shaped the way we think about the relationships between brain, behaviour, and cognition.

In selecting cases, the editors have been concerned with the important single case. It may be ancient (Broca's case LeBorgne) or modern (Marshall and Newcombe's deep dyslexic G.R.), famous (Phineas Gage) or less well-known (Burckhardt's early psychosurgery cases). But at the same time the book seeks to be comprehensive in its coverage of contemporary neuropsychological issues. While many of the cases are concerned with language (an inevitable reflection of the central position of language break down in the genesis of knowledge in neuropsychology), also represented are classic cases in memory, perception and attention, and praxis. For many cases discussed in this book, the original reports were in German or French. We have taken the opportunity to bring some cases which have been highly influential in their own languages to the attention of the English-speaking world. This means that some of the cases in this book will be new to many readers.

Some of the cases included in this book are rare, and have been seen as *experiments of nature* and in so many instances have acted as catalysts to the development of theory. Some have remained the definitive case, many were the first of their type to be described and gave rise to the development of new syndrome entities. Some are still controversial. In some instances, the cases resulted in major paradigm shifts. Some, while still highly influential, were misinterpreted. But most of them were read only by a few in their original form. All the cases included are, we believe, classics in the sense that they have made a special contribution or are particularly representative. Inevitably, there will be cases that some readers may feel should have been included in this volume. In contrast, we are confident that there is no case that we have included which any reader would want to leave out.

The cases discussed in this book have defied too rigid a classification. To a large extent developments in neuropsychology have been concerned with either (or both) issues of delineation of function or issues relating function to structure. The description and interpretation of single cases have been crucial to these developments. We have chosen to organise the book into two parts to reflect these two central developments. Some cases are concerned most centrally with delineation of function and others with issues of biology of function, although many are concerned with both, with the *interface* between structure and function. We therefore decided to organise the contents into two sections and include chapters in the section which appeared to be the most relevant.

Each chapter highlights the importance or relevance of the case for the development of neuropsychology, describes the particular features of the case that are interesting and rare, and discusses the theoretical implications of the findings. Authors were asked not to shrink from criticism of the case in the light of recent findings and developments and were asked to take particular care to put right any misunderstandings or misconceptions about an historical case that may have influenced neuropsychological development. Authors were encouraged to consider the case they discussed from the perspective of theory development and were asked to impart to the reader an understanding of the place of the case in the development of neuropsychology. We are pleased with the way authors have interpreted our requests. We are indebted to them for their patience, particularly for their fortitude in dealing with an international range of viewpoints on their work. We also want to express our thanks to the reviewers for making useful suggestions on improvements to the book, to Dave Müller who bullied us into getting the book under way, Sonia Sharma and Paul Dukes at Erlbaum (UK) for their patience and support over a long period, and to Gabi Code and Colette Cerny for help with indexing. It has been a pleasure for us to read about the cases that have shaped a science. It is our hope that the reader will share our pleasure.

Chris Code, Sydney
Claus-W. Wallesch, Magdeburg
Yves Joanette and André Roch Lecours, Montréal
January 1995

List of Contributors

Christopher Barry, School of Psychology, University of Wales College of Cardiff, P.O. Box 901, Cardiff CF1 3YG, U.K.

Claudius Bartels, Department of Neurology, University of Magdeburg, Liepziger Str. 44, D-39120 Magdeburg, Germany.

Patrizia S. Bisiacchi, Dipartimento di Psicologia Generale, University of Padova, Piazza Capitaniato 3, Padova, 35139 Italy.

John L. Bradshaw, Department of Psychology, Monash University, Clayton, Victoria 3168, Australia.

Jason W. Brown, Department of Neurology, New York University Medical Center, 66 East 79th Street, New York, NY 10021, U.S.A.

M. Ceccaldi, Service de Neurologie et de Neuropsychologie, C.H.U. Timone, Marseille, France.

Chris Code, Brain Damage and Communication Research, School of Communication Disorders, Faculty of Health Sciences, University of Sydney, East Street, Lidcombe, NSW 2141, Australia.

Jules Davidoff, Department of Psychology, University of Essex, Wivenhoe Park, Colchester CO4 3SQ, U.K.

Ria De Bleser, Institute of Linguistics, Centre for Cognitive Neurolinguistics, Potsdam University, Postfach 601553, D-14415 Potsdam, Germany.

Ennio De Renzi, Clinica Neurologica, Universitá di Modena, Via del Pozzo, 71, Modena, 41100, Italy.

Hadyn D. Ellis, School of Psychology, University of Wales, Cardiff, P.O. Box 901, Cardiff CF1 3YG, U.K.

Elaine Funnell, Department of Psychology, Royal Holloway University of London, Egham TW20 0EX, U.K.

Kenneth M. Heilman, Department of Neurology, Box 100236, University of Florida, Gainesville, Florida 32610, U.S.A.

Glyn W. Humphreys, Cognitive Science Research Centre, School of Psychology, Edgbaston, Birmingham B15 2TT, U.K.

Yves Joanette, Centre de Recherche, Centre Hospitalier Côtes-des-Neiges, 4565 Chemin-de-la-reine Marie, Montréal, Quebec, H3W 1W5, Canada.

Karen Kaplan-Solms, Neurosurgical Unit, London Hospital Medical College, 4th Floor, Alexandra Wing, Royal London Hospital (Whitechapel), London E1 1BB, U.K.

Maryse Lassonde, Groupe de Recherche en Neuropsychologie Expérimentale, Departement de Psychologie, Université de Montréal, C.P. 6128, Succ. A, Montréal, Québec, H3C 3J7, Canada.

André Roch Lecours, Centre de Recherche, Centre Hospitalier Côtes-des-Neiges, 4565 Chemin-de-la-reine Marie, Montréal, Québec, H3W 1W5, Canada and Faculté de Médecine, Université de Montréal, C.P. 6128, Succ. A, Montréal, Quebec, H3C 3J7, Canada.

Malcolm Macmillan, School of Psychology, Deakin University, 221 Burwood Highway, Burwood, Victoria 3125, Australia.

Jason B. Mattingley, Department of Experimental Psychology, University of Cambridge, Downing Street, Cambridge CB4 3EB, U.K. and MRC Applied Psychology Unit, 15 Chaucer Road, Cambridge CB2 2EF, U.K.

John C. Marshall, Neuropsychology Unit, Radcliffe Infirmary, University of Oxford, Woodstock Road, Oxford OX2 6HE, U.K.

Inger Moen, Department of Linguistics, University of Oslo, P.O. Box 1102, Blindern, 0317 Oslo, Norway.

Alan J. Parkin, Laboratory of Experimental Psychology, University of Sussex, Brighton BN1 9QG, U.K.

Michel Poncet, Service de Neurologie et de Neuropsychologie, C.H.U. Timone, Marseille, France.

M. Jane Riddoch, Cognitive Science Research Centre, School of Psychology, University of Birmingham, Edgbaston, Birmingham B15 2TT, U.K.

Leslie J. Gonzalez Rothi, Staff Speech Pathologist-126, Veterans Affairs Medical Center, Gainesville, Florida 32608, U.S.A.

John Ryalls, Department of Communication Disorders, HPB113 University of Central Florida, Orlando, Florida 32816-2215, U.S.A.

Hannelore C. Sauerwein, Groupe de Recherche en Neuropsychologie Expérimentale, Departement de Psychologie, Université de Montréal, C.P. 6128, Succ. A, Montréal, Québec, H3C 3J7, Canada.

Avraham Schweiger, Center for Cognition and Communication, 952 5th Avenue, New York, N.Y. 10021, U.S.A.

Carlo Semenza, Dipartimento di Psicologia Generale, University of Padova, Piazza Capitaniato 3, Padova, 35139 Italy.

Mark Solms, Neurosurgical Unit, London Hospital Medical College, 4th Floor, Alexandra Wing, Royal London Hospital (Whitechapel), London E1 1BB, U.K.

C. Soubrouillard, Service de Neurologie et de Neuropsychologie, C.H.U. Timone, Marseille, France.

Brigette Stemmer, Centre de Recherche, Centre Hospitalier Côtes-des-Neiges, 4565 Chemin-de-la-reine Marie, Montréal, Québec, H3W 1W5, Canada.

Claudia van de Wal, Faculty of Social Sciences, University of Leiden, Wassenaarse-weg 52, 2333 AK Leiden, The Netherlands.

Claus-W. Wallesch, Department of Neurology, University of Magdeburg, Leipziger Str. 44, D-39120 Magdeburg, Germany.

Harry A. Whitaker, Départment de Psychologie, Université du Québec à Montréal, C.P. 8888, Succ. A, Montréal, Québec, H3C 3P8, Canada.

Andrew W. Young, M.R.C. Applied Psychology Unit, 15 Chaucer Road, Cambridge CB2 2EF, U.K.

1 Classic Cases: Ancient and Modern Milestones in the Development of Neuropsychological Science

Chris Code
*Brain Damage and Communication Research, School of
Communication Disorders, University of Sydney, Australia.*

Developments in neuropsychology owe much to the discovery and careful examination of sometimes rare and remarkable individuals. From Broca's first and most famous case Leborgne and the frontal lobe case Phineas Gage, through the commissurotomy, lobectomy, and hemispherectomy cases, right up to the highly influential deep dyslexia cases of contemporary times, the single case—especially the extraordinary case—has provided new directions and improved our understanding of the way mental life is represented in the brain. In some instances, the interpretation of the case has proved nothing less than revolutionary.

Both the older and the more modern classic cases represent milestones in neuropsychology's journey. We owe most of what we know about the brain's control of cognition and behaviour to the damaged brains of a range of often unusual people. Many of these cases have become celebrated and have consequently been established in the annals of neuropsychological history. The patterns of specificity of impairment in these human beings has guided neuropsychology's central quest, comprehension of the nature of the relationship between brain structure and brain function. Consequently, what is often the most significant contribution of a single case might be the way particular functions may be seen to dissociate or fractionate following brain damage with findings informing theory on the organisation of mental processing. For several of the cases in this book, dissociation of function following brain damage has been the focus of interest.

1

The significant role of the single case in neuropsychology no doubt owes much to the fact that the origins of neuropsychology lie in neurology and the founding fathers of the field were medical men; the single case has always played a significant role in the development of medicine. While the case study has been important in neuropsychology from its earliest beginnings, there was a period between the wars and on into the 1960s when the relevance of the case was forgotten as workers attempted to take the field forwards through group research. During this period we saw the development of theories of brain and behaviour based on psychometric models derived from group studies. However, coupled with developments in technology and theory, the single case study has returned and has in recent years once more taken centre stage.

Case studies in neuropsychology vary quite widely. Shallice (1979) observed that the case study can last for just a few clinical sessions or several years (see, for instance, Parkin's Chapter 23 on the bilateral temporal lobectomy H.M. and the continuing studies of that individual's amnesia). Shallice has suggested that, however long the study lasts, it will usually go through four distinct stages. Firstly, the patient will be selected for study because their pattern of deficits and retained abilities are of potential and special interest. Secondly, the patient is, or at least should be, fully assessed using psychometrically controlled tests and the results should allow the patient to be assigned to a provisional syndrome category. Many of the older case reports, while often rich in qualitative information, lacked adequate quantitative specification. The third stage entails detailed quantitative study of the specific deficits that are of particular interest. For novel syndromes, like some of the cases described in this book, this may simply involve describing the history of the syndrome. For other cases assessment would focus on the specific processing domains that are impaired. More complexly, testing might aim to uncover how impaired mechanisms operate. Theories and methodology from cognitive, experimental, or physiological psychology will probably need to be involved during the more complex stages. Results of testing may demonstrate that the original provisional diagnosis was not appropriate and the study will be abandoned. Finally, Shallice suggests, the results need to be statistically analysed. Of course, Shallice's criteria refer mainly to contemporary case study research and were often not considered in many of the earlier classic case studies.

But, even for contemporary study, not everyone agrees with the detail of Shallice's agenda for single case research, particularly in his insistence that quantitative measures be used and that for contemporary study "the psychometric tests performed in clinical assessment are essential baseline tests for any competently conducted case study" (p. 187, 1979), or his suggestion that "the concept of a 'syndrome' is essential to the usefulness of the case study" (p. 189, 1979). Alternative views within cognitive neuropsychology on the value of the syndrome approach (Caramazza, 1984; Ellis, 1987; Schwartz, 1984) and psychometric testing (Byng, Kay, Edmundson, & Scott, 1990) have been expressed with many feeling that the syndrome approach to research has outlived its usefulness. However, syndromes have intuitive appeal, and even in cognitive neuropsychology there are strong arguments for the retention of the syndrome approach (Coltheart, 1987; Shallice, 1979). This book is not so much concerned with issues of design of single case studies; discussion on issues of statistical analysis and single case research design can be found in Caramazza (1984), Miller (1993), Shallice (1979), and Willmes (1990).

This notwithstanding, within all branches of neuropsychology, case studies have been centrally influential in theoretical development. Indeed, for neuropsychology it is almost possible to pinpoint certain major changes in direction or conception with the discovery, description and interpretation of an important individual case. This is true of the classic Leborgne of Broca (Chapter 7 by Ryalls and Lecours), the description of whom is generally considered to have proclaimed the very beginnings of modern neuropsychology and the birth of dominance theory. Right up to contemporary times Leborgne's preserved brain is still capable of generating discussion of theoretical importance (Lecours, Nespoulous, & Pioger, 1987). Although Broca's case represents the, as it were, "authorised" beginnings of neuropsychology, Broca, like many great scientific originals, owed much to those who had gone before, such as Gall and Bouillaud. As De Renzi points out in Chapter 10, "it is a feature of the history of science that for every discovery attributed to an author a forerunner will sooner or later be found". Some famous cases, like Phineas Gage (Macmillan in Chapter 18), have been over interpreted. The neuropsychologically useful information we have on Gage has not curbed the extent to which he has been cited as a basis for research and development.

Another case which had a significant impact and continues to inform development is H.M. (Chapter 23 by Parkin), who heralded new ideas on the role of the temporal lobes in memory. Other classic cases from the rich past of neuropsychology include Wernicke's case of pure agraphia (Chapter 2 by De Bleser), Charcot's case of impaired imagery (Chapter 3 by Young and van de Wal), Bodamer's first cases of prosopagnosia (Chapter 6 by Ellis), Poppelreuter's case of neglect (Chapter 7 by Humphreys, Riddoch, and Wallesch), Liepmann's original cases of apraxia (Chapter 9 by Gonzalez Rothi and Heilman), Lewandowsky's case of object–colour agnosia (Chapter 11 by Davidoff) and Monrad-Krohn's first case of foreign-accent syndrome (Chapter 12 by Moen). Paterson and Zangwill's case of unilateral neglect (Chapter 13 by Mattingley) while not the first represents, as Mattingley puts it, "a paradigm shift towards objectivity, both in the approach to assessment of patients with unilateral neglect, and in the interpretation of their preserved and impaired capacities." In Chapter 10, De Renzi brings together classic cases described by Badal, Balint, and Holmes with attentional and oculomotor disorders to delineate a new entity, Balint–Holmes Syndrome.

But while the classic historical case is a well-known phenomenon, no less important are the modern classics. Cases like G.R., who is the first deep dyslexic in the contemporary literature described by Marshall and Newcombe (1966) (discussed in Chapter 14 by Barry), Warrington and Shallice's (1984) category-specific aphasic case J.B.R. (discussed in Chapter 16 by Semenza and Bisiacchi) and W.L.P. (Schwartz, Marin, & Saffran, 1979), a case which shows that the dissolution of language in dementia can be subject to individual variability and modular deficits can be revealed (discussed in Chapter 15 by Funnell). It is with these contemporary classic cases that the most influential development in recent years began, the advent of cognitive neuropsychology.

A number of cases discussed in this book are concerned with that central quest for much neuropsychology, understanding the nature of the representation of function in structure. The commissurotomy studies of the early 1960s conducted on the Bogen–Vogel series of cases began to have major consequences for how we viewed the lateralisation of language, relationships between the hemispheres, and the very integrity of conscious-ness (Bogen & Vogel, 1962; Gazzaniga, 1988; Gazzaniga, Bogen, & Sperry, 1962). Chapter 21 by Sauerwein and Lassonde discusses some of the earliest "split-brain" cases investigated by Akelaitis in the 1940s. A small range of cases which have caused us to think again about the left hemisphere's dominating role in the control of behaviour, especially language, are those individuals who have had a left hemisphere surgically removed. The left hemispherectomy cases E.C. and N.F. (discussed by Code in Chapter 22) provide us with insights into the role of the right hemisphere in speech production. Schweiger (in Chapter 19) re-examines Bramwell's celebrated crossed aphasia case. He points out that what Bramwell described as crossed aphasia—aphasia in a left-handed adult with left hemisphere damage—is different to what we call crossed aphasia today; that is, aphasia in a right-handed adult with right hemisphere damage. This fact is usually not acknowledged or appreciated in contemporary work on crossed aphasia. Parkin in Chapter 23 outlines the extraordinary and continuing story of H.M., the most celebrated of all amnesic patients, whose impairments in memory resulted from bilateral surgical removal of the temporal lobes. As Parkin's chapter shows, H.M. continues to represent a benchmark for research in amnesia. Gail D. (discussed by Bradshaw in Chapter 24) is one of the deaf aphasic signers studied in recent years at the Salk Institute. This case in particular illustrates that the development of an auditory-sequential language system is not necessary for hemispheric specialisation for language to develop. This unique case appears to show that the left hemisphere may not have an innate predisposition for the core components of language, which is independent of modality.

While the influence of some cases is widely appreciated, many, like those originally described in languages other than English, are recent discoveries for many English readers. The case of Johann Voit (discussed in Chapter 5 by Bartels and Wallesch) is an intensively studied case in the German literature, but relatively little is known of him in English. Likewise, the early psychosurgery cases of Burckhardt (discussed in Chapter 20 by Whitaker, Stemmer, and Joanette) and the possible first case of primary progressive aphasia described in French by Sérieux (Chapter 4 by Ceccaldi, Soubrouillard, Poncet, and Lecours) have received little attention in the past. Similarly, the case of "mind-blindness" described in German by Wilbrand (Chapter 8 by Solms, Kaplan-Solms, and Brown) is little known in English and earlier translations have caused misapprehensions to arise concerning the disorder.

The re-emergency of the single case suggests that in some sense neuropsychology was reinvented about 15 years ago by a group of workers, many of whom were new to neuropsychology. Cognitive psychology and psycholinguistics began at the same time to inform and be informed by neuropsychology. A mutually beneficial relationship was cultivated as cognitive neuropsychology developed. With cognitive neuropsychology a new era of single case research began. An important development in cognitive neuropsychology, and one which has encouraged the re-emergence of the single case to the centre stage, has been a re-examination of the earlier cases within a cognitive neuropsychological theoretical framework. Cognitive neuropsychology figures very widely in this book and a number of contributors discuss cases in terms of their place in contemporary theory. For this reason we will spend a little time below outlining the main features of the theory.

Cognitive neuropsychology brought together the information-processing metaphor, the notion of a mind organised in modules and, significantly, the rediscovery of the view that progress in the scientific investigation of the nature of cognition could be achieved best by careful investigation of individuals with brain damage through a process of hypothesis testing using tests controlled for a range of manipulable variables. Cognitive neuropsychology embraced the traditional single case approach and brought it back in from the cold. A common central view for many workers in the field is that a theory-driven approach to the investigation of individual patients is preferable to attempts to compare heterogenous groups of patients categorised according to classical syndrome models.

The notion of a modular organisation for cognition is a form of faculty psychology going back to Gall's phrenology (Chomsky, 1980; Fodor, 1983). Essential features of modularity which have their origins with Gall are the view that there exist independent, autonomous, domain-specific, and innately specified cognitive subsystems. The neural networks engaged in one faculty, say language, are formally disparate to those networks engaged in other cognitive faculties, such as perception or memory. The psychological processes involved in the encoding and decoding of speech, for instance, are unconscious processes which are unique to language. Cognitive neuropsychology has seen a return of what Head (1926) referred to disparagingly as "the diagram makers" in the form of information processing. The information processing metaphor lies at the centre of the cognitive neuropsychology model. This framework allows for a characterisation of how cognitive representations are related one to another within modules. A central contention of cognitive neuropsychology "is that behavioral observations of brain-damaged subjects can stand on their own in the development of a meaningful cognitive science" (Caramazza, 1992, p. 85). The agenda for cognitive neuropsychology is to determine the nature of the cognitive architecture by testing out these models on brain-damaged people for whom cognitive processes may have fractionated and dissociated in various patterns. Through detailed case studies of brain-damaged individuals the components and subcomponents of cognition can be mapped in terms of the information processing framework made up of units and input–output routes between units. Analysis of performance entails examining the stages and routes involved in such functions as reading single words aloud, recognising objects, or repeating words. Much of the research concentrates on characterising a deficit or constellation of deficits in terms of failure in access to a module or combination of modules and impairment to a module or modules. Within cognitive neuropsychological studies in language impairment, there is current controversy over the extent to which semantic information is categorised within the semantic system in separate subordinate categories (e.g. fruit or vegetables). If there is a modular organisation to language in the brain then we would expect to observe patients with deficits which affect very specific components and subcomponents of the language system. There are reports of cases who have very individual, and rare, forms of impairment apparently limited to specific semantic categories (for discussion of modularity see Semenza and Bisiacchi's Chapter 16 on J.B.R., the case described by Warrington and Shallice, who they claimed had a category-specific anomia, and also Funnell's Chapter 15 on modularity in W.L.P., a patient with dementia, and Bartels and Wallesch's Chapter 5 on the celebrated early German case of Johann Voit).

A further important and basic assumption in cognitive neuropsychology is the *transparency assumption* (Caramazza, 1986, 1992): a functionally lesioned system can explain the observed patterns of performance. Lesions lead only to local changes in the system and new processing structures are not created as a result of the lesion. "That relation (between impaired performance and normal cognition) may be transparent in the sense that the hypothesized modifications of the normal processing system are traceable within the proposed theoretical frameworks" (Caramazza, 1992, p. 82). Thus, brain damage does not result in the creation of new cognitions. The transparency assumption is considered to be crucial to the continuing development of the cognitive neuropsychology enterprise. This fairly resolute position has been termed the *strong*, contrasting with the *weak* (Kosslyn & Intriligator, 1992) or *ultra* (Shallice, 1988), or *radical* (McCloskey, 1993; Robertson, Knight, Rafel, & Shimamura, 1993) variant of cognitive neuropsychology. The transparency assumption may present serious problems for radical variants of cognitive neuropsychology as brain-damaged individuals present with patterns of behaviour which can be interpreted as resulting from functional reorganisation or modification of intact functions at the cognitive level and even the creation of new functions (Kosslyn & Intriligator, 1992; Kosslyn & Van Kleek, 1990).

We mentioned earlier that the development of cognitive neuropsychology can be seen to some extent as a reinvention of neuropsychology. This assertion is supported by the observation that its three major features— modularity, an information processing metaphor, and a single case methodology, are not new. As already mentioned, Fodor's (1983) modularity of mind traces back to Gall's phrenology, the dominant faculty theory abroad at the time of Broca's case descriptions (see Chapter 17 by Ryalls & Lecours). The information-processing metaphor, of course, has its origins in the way digital computers process information (Morton, 1968). However, its application with brain-damaged patients is certainly eased by the similarities it shares with the box and arrow models of the diagram makers epitomised by the Wernicke–Lichtheim models (Lichtheim, 1885). The other major feature of the contemporary approach to research and theory development in neuropsychology is the rediscovery of the value of detailed hypothesis testing with a single case.

Recent developments in connectionist network modelling are having a major impact on cognitive neuropsychology (Hinton & Shallice 1991; McClelland, Rumelhart, & the P.D.P. Research Group, 1986; Patterson, Seidenberg, & McClelland, 1989; see Harley, 1993 for review). Neural networks use ways of processing information diametrically different to the orthodox, serial information-processing method utilised so widely in the past as a basis for explanation in the cognitive sciences and artificial intelligence. Neural networks run on computers, but simulate fairly grossly certain features of mammalian neuronal organisation. They are based on knowledge of the behaviour of real neurones in real neural networks. Whilst conventional computation is serial and linear, neural network models are nonlinear and parallel. Where serial computation is based on logic and syntax, on systems of rules to manipulate symbols, connectionist networks represent knowledge as patterns of activation across neurones in the network. Like real neurones, they can be excitory or inhibitory and are arranged in connected layers. These layers are either input layers, output layers, or "hidden" layers, and form a network of interconnections. These networks have no inbuilt facility to process input as conventional computer programs do, but they learn through training which is accomplished through a process of associative learning and a sort of feedback called "back-propagation". Values of the synaptic weights on neurones can be set or are initially set to random values and determined through back-propagation where actual values are compared to desired values and propagated back from the output layer during training to the input layer to adjust weights. Once it is trained, the network is ready to perform its task.

Brain function is nonlinear and it may be that the conventional linear information-processing framework is unlikely to be an accurate model for cognitive processing (Kosslyn & Intriligator, 1992). The future of neurocognitive research therefore appears to require a continued interaction between a computer metaphor and brain damage, where models of cognitive processing will be developed on computers within a nonlinear connectionist paradigm and tested on brain-damaged individuals.

Because much of neuropsychology is built on the extraordinary case, this should alert us to the fact that theory must attempt to address the common phenomenon in human neuropsychology of the exception to the rule. The description and/or investigation of the single case is not, of course, the only methodology used in neuropsychology even if, as this book celebrates, single case research is back and the dogma that only group research is scientifically respectable in neuropsychology is dead and buried.

None the less, as Millar and Whitaker (1983, p. 102) observe, "from the case history one answers the question 'Is it possible for such and such to occur?' From the case history one does not answer the question 'Does everyone exhibit such-and-such?'" This, the lack of generalisability, is of course the fundamental limitation of the single case. Because these are single cases, because they are individuals, then they cannot be seen as representative of the population as a whole. Indeed, dissociations observed in a specific patient may only reflect the organisation of his or her peculiar cognitive system. Clearly, progress in neuropsychology will come from group as well as single case research. As every budding researcher learns, the research question should come first and it is the research question which should determine the methodology. Nevertheless, the individual with a pattern of impairment which allows an investigator to test some aspect of a model of normal mental processing, and the unusual individual whose patterns of impairments are such that they fly in the face of prevailing theory, will continue to play a central role in the future development of neuropsychology. As this book illustrates, the detailed individual case study continues to be able to instruct theory and stimulate research. Funnell states in her chapter on W.L.P. (Chapter 15) that the genuine classic case should, if possible, raise questions for the future too. Many of the cases discussed in this book do just that, and the questions they raise are still there to be answered.

REFERENCES

Bogen, J.E., & Vogel, P.S. (1962). Cerebral commissurotomy in man. *Bulletin of the Los Angeles Neurological Societies, 29*, 169–172.

Byng, S., Kay, J., Edmundson, A., & Scott, C. (1990). Aphasia tests reconsidered. *Aphasiology, 4*, 67–91.

Caramazza, A. (1984). The logic of neuropsychological research and the problem of patient classification in aphasia. *Brain and Language, 21*, 9–20.

Caramazza, A. (1986). On drawing inferences about the structure of normal cognitive processes from patterns of impaired performance: The case for single-patient studies. *Brain and Cognition, 5*, 41–66.

Caramazza, A. (1992). Is cognitive neuropsychology possible? *Journal of Cognitive Neuroscience, 4*, 80–95.

Chomsky, N. (1980). *rules and representations*. New York: Columbia University Press.

Coltheart, M. (1987). Functional architecture of the language-processing system. In M. Coltheart, G. Satori, & R. Job (Eds.), *The cognitive neuropsychology of language*. Hove, U.K.: Lawrence Erlbaum Associates Ltd.

Ellis, A. (1987). Intimations of modularity, or, the modality of mind: Doing cognitive neuropsychology without syndromes. In M. Coltheart, G. Sartori, & R. Job (Eds.), *The cognitive neuropsychology of language*. Hove, U.K.: Lawrence Erlbaum Associates Ltd.

Fodor, J. (1983). *The modularity of mind*. Cambridge, MA: MIT Press.

Gazzaniga, M.S. (1988). Brain modularity: Towards a philosophy of consciousness. In A.J. Marcel & E. Bisiach (Eds.), *Consciousness in contemporary science*. Oxford: Oxford University Press.

Gazzaniga, M.S., Bogen, J.E., & Sperry, R. (1962). Some functional effects of sectioning the cerebral commissures in man. *Proceedings of the National Academy of Sciences, 48*, 1765–1769.

Harley, T.A. (1993). Connectionist approaches to language disorders. *Aphasiology, 7*, 221–249.

Head, H. (1926). *Aphasia and kindred disorders of speech*. Cambridge: Cambridge University Press.

Hinton, G.E., & Shallice, T. (1991). Lesioning an attractor network: Investigations of acquired dyslexia. *Psychological Review, 98*, 74–95.

Kosslyn, S.M., & Intriligator, J.M. (1992). Is cognitive neuropsychology plausible? The perils of sitting on a one-legged stool. *Journal of Cognitive Neuroscience, 4*, 96–106.

Kosslyn, S.M., & Van Kleek, M.H. (1990). Broken brains and normal minds: Why Humpty-Dumpty needs a skeleton. In E.L. Schwartz (Ed.), *Computational neuroscience*. Cambridge, MA: MIT Press.

Lecours, A.R., Nespoulous, J.-L., & Pioger, D. (1987). Jacques Lordat or the birth of cognitive neuropsychology. In E. Keller & M. Gopnik (Eds.), *Motor and sensory processes of language*. Hillsdale, NJ: Lawrence Erlbaum Associates Inc.

Lichtheim, L. (1885). On aphasia. *Brain*, *7*, 433–484.

Marshall, J.C., & Newcombe, F. (1966). Syntactic and semantic errors in paralexia. *Neuropsychologia*, *24*, 5–24.

McClelland, J.L., Rumelhart, D.E., & the P.D.P. Research Group. (1986). *Parallel distributive processing: vol 2. Foundations*. Cambridge, MA: MIT Press.

McCloskey, M. (1993). Theory and evidence in cognitive neuropsychology: A "radical" response to Robertson, Knight, Rafel, and Shimamura (1993). *Journal of Experimental Psychology: Learning, Memory and Cognition*, *19*, 718–734.

Millar, J.M., & Whitaker, H.A. (1983). The right hemisphere's contribution to language: A review of the evidence from brain-damaged subjects. In S.J. Segalowitz (Ed.), *Language functions and brain organization*, London: Academic Press.

Miller, E. (1993). Dissociating single cases in neuropsychology. *British Journal of Clinical Psychology*, *32*, 155–167.

Morton, J. (1968). Grammar and computation in language behaviour. In J.C. Catford (Ed.), *Studies in language and language behaviour* (C.R.L.L.B. Progress Report No. VI). Ann Arbor: University of Michigan.

Patterson, K., Seidenberg, M.S., & McClelland, J.L. (1989). Connections and disconnections: Acquired dyslexia in a computational model of reading processes. In R.G.M. Morris (Ed.), *Parallel distributive processing: Implications for psychology and neurobiology*. Oxford: Clarendon Press.

Robertson, L.C., Knight, R.T., Rafel, R., & Shimamura, A.P. (1993). Cognitive neuropsychology is more than single-case studies. *Journal of Experimental Psychology: Learning, Memory and Cognition*, *19*, 710–717.

Schwartz, M.F. (1984). What the classical aphasia categories can't do for us, and why. *Brain and Language*, *21*, 3–8.

Schwartz, M.F., Marin, O.S.M., & Saffran, E.M. (1979). Dissociations of language function in dementia: A case study. *Brain and Language*, *7*, 277–306.

Shallice, T. (1979). Case study approach in neuropsychological research. *Journal of Clinical Neuropsychology*, *1*, 183–211.

Shallice, T. (1988). *From neuropsychology to mental structure*. Cambridge: Cambridge University Press.

Warrington, E., & Shallice, T. (1984). Category specific semantic impairments. *Brain*, *107*, 829–853.

Willmes, K. (1990). Statistical methods for single-case approach to aphasia therapy research. *Aphasiology*, *4*, 415–436.

FUNCTION AND STRUCTURE

2 Wernicke's (1903) Case of Pure Agraphia: An Enigma for Classical Models of Written Language Processing

Ria De Bleser
Institute of Linguistics, Potsdam University, Germany.

This paper discusses the treatment of pure agraphia in classical models of written language processing. At the transition from the 19th to the 20th century, the syndrome of isolated agraphia was not accepted by all aphasiological authors. A crucial issue in the debate was the unit of analysis in graphemic processing, the letter or the word. Closely related to this were questions of localisation, in particular whether specialised cortical centres should be postulated for reading and writing or whether these functions were subserved by more general optic and motor areas. Following from a decision on this question, some authors adopted a unilateral left-hemispheric representation of graphemic units whereas others assumed bilateral processing.

In this article, particular attention will be paid to a case of apparently pure agraphia published by Carl Wernicke in 1903. This paper and related articles demonstrate how cautious Wernicke was in localising higher psychological functions. Furthermore, Wernicke's final interpretation of the patient's impairment as a consequence of some mild disorder of inner speech exemplifies how negative evidence may be logically eliminated in order not to relinquish a deductively derived model. The resulting theory only recognised total modality-specific impairments of reading, i.e. pure alexia, or of reading and writing, i.e. alexia with agraphia. It excluded selective modality-specific impairments of writing, i.e. pure agraphia, as well as subtotal unimodal impairments of reading and writing such as are now known under the labels of surface, phonological, and deep dyslexia or dysgraphia. Under the influence of Wernicke's model, it was not until Marshall and Newcombe (1973) that aphasiologists could start to observe subtotal modality-specific impairments and discuss them with reference to alternative models of written language processing.

INTRODUCTION

Carl Wernicke (1848–1905) was without a doubt the leading German aphasiologist at the end of the last century. He is best known for his discovery of sensory or Wernicke's aphasia and for the development of a deductive theory of language impairments based on Meynert's anatomical insights. This was published as a monograph in 1874 when Wernicke was 26 years old. It was entitled "The Symptom Complex of Aphasia: A Psychological Study on an Anatomical Basis" (Wernicke, 1874, English translation in Cohen & Wartowfsky, 1966–1968). P. Broca (1861) had described a frontal centre for speech production. Wernicke referred to this as the centre **b** (**M** in Lichtheim) and he added a centre for speech comprehension, **a** (**A** in Lichtheim), in the first temporal convolution. An impairment of this centre gave rise to sensory ("Wernicke's") aphasia as opposed to motor ("Broca's") aphasia with an impairment of **b**. A third form of aphasia, conduction aphasia, would result from an interruption of the transcortical fibres connecting these two centres (see Fig. 2.1).

At the age of 37, Wernicke was appointed professor of neurology and psychiatry in Breslau. Other major neuropsychological theories were also a product of his clinic, e.g. Freund's (1889) theory of optic aphasia, Lissauer's (1890) agnosia theory, and Liepmann's (1900) apraxia theory. These

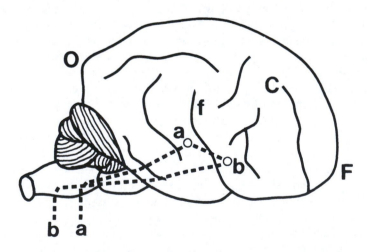

FIG. 2.1 Wernicke's (1874) neuropsychological model of the sound structure of language. Centre b (M in Lichtheim) = speech production (Broca's centre); centre a (A in Lichtheim) = speech comprehension (Wernicke's centre).

theories underwent modifications by other famous Wernicke-trained neurologists such as Bonhoefer, Forster, Goldstein, Heilbronner, and Kleist. They dominated aphasiological research until the Second World War and had a tremendous influence on post-war American neuropsychology.

This chapter will discuss a little-known case of isolated agraphia without alexia published by Wernicke in 1903. The article is of particular interest because the patient presented apparent counter-evidence to the theory of written language processing Wernicke first proposed in 1886b. This case of apparently isolated agraphia caused Wernicke to question his assumptions on written language processing against the background of the French school as represented by Charcot (1883), Pitres (1884), and Déjerine (1884, 1891, 1892).

For readers less familiar with Wernicke's aphasia theory, the development of his theory of oral language processing will be briefly introduced in the next section.

WERNICKE'S MODEL OF SPOKEN LANGUAGE

In contemporary neuropsychology, Wernicke's publications on aphasia following his first and most famous monograph (Wernicke, 1874) are not very well known. Substantial developments in his theory may be found in the review papers he wrote regularly for the journal *Fortschritte der Medicin*. His views on spoken language processing, for example, underwent a modification in 1886a in the review article of Lichtheim's (1885a) paper "Aphasie" ("On Aphasia") who, following Kussmaul (1877), included an object concept centre **B** in Wernicke's 1874 model (see Fig. 2.2). Wernicke's review article provides a clear exposition of the concept of "concept", differentiating between the concept of objects and the concept of words or symbols. The former is an association network of a variety of sensations (e.g. tactile, auditory, visual, gustatory) which are each localised in a different brain area. It follows that their association in the object concept can not be a single localisable centre but that this association process is subserved by the cerebral hemispheres as a whole. On this point, Wernicke thus deviates from authors like Kussmaul and Lichtheim, who adopted a single object concept centre. Following are some excerpts from this paper (Wernicke, 1886a, pp. 371–372):

> I have to explain to the reader what I understand by the "concept" of an object.... How should one, for instance, imagine the process of understanding the word "Bell" and of speaking it spontaneously? If it is to be understood, the telegram arriving in **a** must arouse in us the "concept" of the bell, i.e. the different memory images of the bell deposited in the cortex and localized in accordance with the sensory organs involved in their development. These are (i) acoustic images, resulting from the sound of the bell, (ii) optic images, derived from the form and color of the bell, (iii) tactile images, obtained by

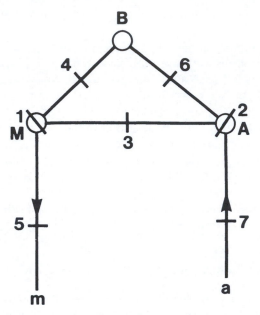

FIG. 2.2 Lichtheim's (1885a) model of language including semantics. Centre M (b in Wernicke) = speech production; centre A (a in Wernicke) = speech comprehension; centre B (after Kussmaul) = centre of concepts ("Begriffe").

skin perceptions, and finally (iv) motor images, acquired by scanning movements of the fingers and the eyes. Due to the steady reoccurrence of the essential features for each bell, a fixed association has been built among these memory images, so that the arousal of each one separately is communicated to the others and they constitute a functional unit. Such units are the "concepts" of concrete objects, in our example, of the bell. If a spoken word is understood and stimulates thoughts, these units are so to speak a second station in the overall activity of the hemispheres which is still accessible to our conscious perception, and conscious perception must be part of the process if the spoken word should not resound uncomprehended at our ears. If the word "Bell" should be spoken spontaneously, that is, probably as a result of very complicated processes in our consciousness, the same station is used. First, the object concept of a bell surfaces, then this process of arousal is conducted onto the corresponding motor memory image in **b**, the place of the telegram dispatches. The example chosen could be schematically represented somewhat like in the next figure [Fig. 2.3 here], where **B** indicates the concept of the object "bell".

A similar diagram may be found in Lichtheim's article. If we want to construct the concept of a word or "symbol"—as the names of concrete objects are often called—for example, of the word "bell", we find that it consists of the firmly associated memory images in **a** and **b**. This concept of the word is thus

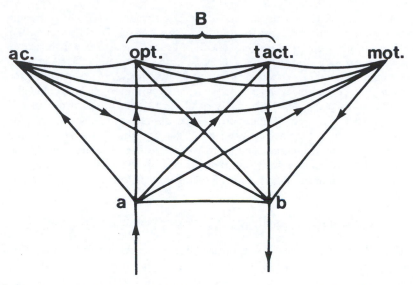

FIG. 2.3   Wernicke's (1886a) model of object concepts and word concepts. B = Object concept ("Begriffe") = association of sensory images; ac. = acoustic images; opt. = optic images; tact. = tactile images; mot. = motor images; ab = Word concept consisting of a (auditory word form) and b (motor word form).

analogous to the concept of the object itself, which is also an association of memory images.

It may be helpful to bear in mind that more precisely two activities must be differentiated in language comprehension. In the first step, the concept of the word is activated, in the second one, the concept of the corresponding object. The process is similar in spontaneous speech, but in the reverse order, so that first the concept of the object arises and then that of the word.

In contrast to his earlier papers, in which he emphasised the complete independence of the motor and sensory speech centres, Wernicke (1886a) still defends the relative anatomical and psychological independence of the two centres **a** and **b** against a growing number of critics, but he now grants that they are not absolutely autonomous, and that spoken language production relies to some extent on the auditory word form for the purpose of speech monitoring. He expresses this as follows (pp. 372–374):

We will have to examine to what extent these word concepts are indivisible units. Two kinds of data from pathology must be considered here. If center **b** is destroyed, language comprehension may remain intact. The sound image of the word in **a** is thus by itself sufficient to activate the concept of the actual object. If, on the other hand, center **b** is also shown in that spontaneous speech remains possible, although the words are not always chosen correctly and there is the symptom of word substitution or paraphasia. The retention of the entire word concept (**a** + **b**) is consequently of more importance for the active part of the speech process than for the passive one. Translating this in terms of our brain diagram, the association of word sound image and concrete object image is fixed and independent, but that between the object image and the word motor image is less fixed and is insufficient to guarantee correct speech all by itself. For spontaneous speech, the entire word concept must be available.... For this reason, I assume that the centrifugal innervation of the word concept by the object concept involves two different routes, namely, the simple route **Bb** and the complicated one **Bab**. If the latter is blocked at some point, the incomplete innervation of the word concept gives rise to word substitutions.

WERNICKE'S MODEL OF WRITTEN LANGUAGE

In 1885, Wernicke reviews a number of recent publications on aphasia, among others Charcot (1883), Pitres (1884), and Déjerine (1884). In this review article, Wernicke still considered it plausible that written language would be stored and processed in complete analogy to spoken language. He expressed this as follows (pp. 827–828; see Fig. 2.4):

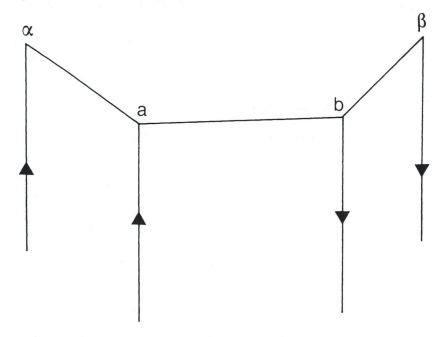

FIG. 2.4 Wernicke's (1885) model of spoken and written language. α = centre for visual graphemic words (cf. **a** = auditory words); β = centre for motor graphemic words (cf. **b** = spoken words).

A further step which has been made everywhere is that attempts are made to explain the disorders of reading and writing very often observed in aphasic patients by assuming two further centers in complete analogy to the centers already observed. Analogous to the center of language comprehension in the acoustic area, there is one for reading comprehension in the optic cortical area; analogous to the center of language movements, there is a center of writing movements, and the symptoms of alexia and agraphia (to retain the generally accepted names) are explained by a loss of these centers.

Take α to be the locus of the optic memory images of the graphemic signs, β the locus of the writing movement representations, a diagram like the following [Fig. 2.4 here] would result, and a loss of α would cause alexia analogous to sensory aphasia, a loss of β agraphia analogous to motor aphasia.

In 1885, Wernicke thus still shares the ideas of independent reading and writing centres entertained by his French colleagues Charcot (1883) and Pitres (1884). In Charcot's model (Fig. 2.5), for example, there is a special optic word centre ("centre visuel des mots: CVM") in addition to a general optic centre ("centre visuel commun: CVC") and likewise a special motor centre for writing ("centre du langage écrit: CLE"). With respect to writing, for example, it was predicted (Pitres, 1884, p. 872) that "aphasia and agraphia are symptoms which often cooccur but are not subordinated either by a causal relationship or by a common etiology."

Pitres, for example, distinguishes three forms of agraphia, the third type being modality specific:

1. Agraphia as a consequence of word blindness (alexia), with impaired copying but preserved spontaneous writing and writing to dictation. This would be caused by a lesion in the left hemispheric optic memory centre in the angular gyrus.

2. Agraphia as a consequence of word deafness (sensory aphasia) with preserved copying and spontaneous writing but impaired writing to dictation. This would be caused by a lesion in the left hemispheric auditory memory centre in the first temporal convolution.

3. Pure motor agraphia, in which all three abilities are impaired (copying, writing spontaneously, and to dictation), and which would be due to a lesion of the graphemic memory centre in the second frontal convolution of the left hemisphere.

Whereas in 1885, Wernicke states that "only clinical experience can decide whether the assumption of such special centers (for reading and writing) is justified" (p. 828), he substantially changes his views in 1886b in his review of Grashey's (1885) paper and now disagrees fully with Charcot and Pitres, not on the basis of clinical experience but under the impression of Grashey's

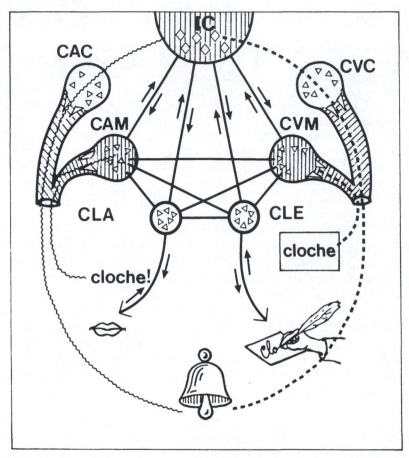

FIG. 2.5   Charcot's (1883) model of spoken and written language. CLA = Centre du langage articulé (motor words, cf. **b**/M); CAM = Centre auditif des mots (auditory words, cf. **a**/A); CAC = centre auditif commun (general auditory centre); IC = Ideation commun (concept center, cf. **B**); CVC = Centre visuel commun (general visual centre); CVM = Centre visuel des mots (visual graphemic words, cf. α); CLE = Centre du langage écrit (motor graphemic words, cf. β).

article, which he considers "the most significant contribution to aphasiology in the last ten years" (p. 467). (See De Bleser, 1989b, for an English translation of Grashey, 1885; and De Bleser, 1989a, for Wernicke's 1886b review of Grashey.) Grashey's paper was important for at least two reasons. It demonstrated the existence of a functional, non-localisable form of anomic aphasia, and it proposed that the single letter was the unit of analysis in graphemic and oral processing. Grashey's patient Voit (see also Chapter 5) presented the unusual phenomenon that he could find the names of objects only as long as he could actually see them, and even this was possible only if he wrote them down letter by letter. Through writing, he could achieve what his memory could no longer manage, namely, that the first letter remained fixed while he was producing the second one. Wernicke (1886b) states that he gained a crucial insight from this paper, namely, that reading and writing always proceed letter by letter. He disagrees with Grashey, however, that oral language processing would also be done on a sound-by-sound basis (1886b, pp. 465–469):

> The optic memory images of graphemic signs deposited in α and the motor images deposited in β both consist of single letters. On the other hand, the word concept always consists of at least one syllable (equivalent to the morpheme for Wernicke), more often of several syllables.... The word as a whole can only be read in the usual manner, i.e. letter-by-letter, a fact which has become established beyond any doubt by Grashey's observations. When I read half a page of printed material quickly, I required approximately the same amount of time per letter as Grashey reported, namely, 0.03 seconds. I must therefore correct my earlier view that a practised reader can race over complete sentences and grasp the contents of whole words without spelling.

Due to his assumption of a letter-by-letter procedure for reading and writing, in contrast to a word procedure for speech and comprehension, Wernicke now emphasises the dependence of written language on oral language. For reading, letter chains have to be converted into spoken words by way of inner speech; for writing, spoken words must be transformed into the corresponding letter chains. Since there was no provision for whole word lexical reading or writing, there could be no modality-specific subtotal forms of written language impairment. Semantic or phonological paralexias and paragraphias were merely considered paraphasias in reading and writing, in other words, they were attributed to a primary disorder of spoken language and were qualified as "verbal". Accordingly, modality-specific disorders of written language would always be total, i.e. already affecting the level of the individual letter, and they were qualified as "literal" alexia and agraphia. Furthermore, Wernicke rejected specialised graphemic centres in the optic or the motor areas since there were only 25 [sic] letters, which he did not consider sufficient psychological material to justify the assumption of special cortical centres. Their neuroanatomical basis would not be essentially different from that of other optic or motor representations, which were generally taken to be bilateral.

Déjerine (1891, 1892) disagreed with Wernicke's view and proposed a unilateral left-hemispheric centre for reading in the angular gyrus to account for cases of pure alexia and alexia with agraphia. In pure alexia without agraphia, the optic word centre itself would be preserved but disconnected from the visual input in the optic radiations. In alexia with agraphia, the lesion would extend to include the optic word centre in the angular gyrus. Both Wernicke (1885; 1996b) and Déjerine (1892) rejected a specialised centre of writing images assumed by Charcot (1883) and Pitres (1884) and supposedly localised in the left second frontal convolution ("Exner's centre"). They considered writing to be a mere copying of the optic-graphemic stimuli in the unilateral left-hemispheric optic word centre according to Déjerine, or the bilateral optic letter centres according to Wernicke.

In subsequent years, Wernicke did not alter his views on written language processing, and the posthumously published treatise on the aphasic symptom complex (Wernicke, 1906) essentially repeats the position he developed in 1886b. Of the different forms of unimodal disorders of graphemic processing, Wernicke recognised pure alexia with agraphia in a cortical and a transcortical form and pure isolated alexia without agraphia or subcortical alexia. Furthermore, he rejected isolated forms of agraphia on a theoretical basis (see De Bleser & Luzzatti, 1989).

Crucial to Wernicke's rejection of an impairment like "pure agraphia" was the assumption of the bilateral representation of optic letter images on which letter writing was based. Given the bilaterality assumption, it was unlikely for anatomical reasons that the full picture of isolated agraphia, i.e. the inability to write with either hand in the face of preserved reading and speech, could ever occur. This would mean that the optic centres in both hemispheres would be disconnected from the motor areas for writing in either hemisphere, although the connection to the motor speech area should be preserved for reading. Such strategic lesions would most likely occur unilaterally only, disconnecting one optic area from the ipsilateral motor area. According to Wernicke, the only pure form of agraphia one could expect to observe for anatomical reasons would thus be a unimanual form of so-called "conduction agraphia" restricted to one hand, as had been reported by Pitres (1884). However, this was not the usual definition of pure agraphia, which was generally proposed to be bimanual. Wernicke thus concludes in 1886b that there can be no agraphia (in the sense of bimanual agraphia) without alexia for theoretical anatomical reasons, and he repeats this statement in 1906.

Surprisingly, in 1903, Wernicke himself presented a case of bimanual pure agraphia without alexia, which according to his theory should not have been expected to occur. It motivated him to analyse other cases in the literature, to re-examine his own views in light of Charcot's and especially Déjerine's theory of reading and writing, and in general to reconsider the functional characteristics of writing and the neuroanatomical substrate of written language.

WERNICKE'S (1903) CASE OF PURE AGRAPHIA

To recapitulate, Wernicke's model of written language processing was based exclusively on a letter-by-letter procedure. His French colleagues Charcot (1883) and Déjerine (1892) adopted the word as well as the letter as a unit of processing for written language. Furthermore, Charcot adopted a centre of writing movements for words in the second frontal convolution (Exner's centre), which was rejected by both Wernicke and Déjerine. These last two authors, however, disagreed whether optic-graphemic images were contained in a special centre strictly localised and lateralised in the left hemispheric angular gyrus (Déjerine) or whether they were bilateral like other optic representations (Wernicke). Wernicke (1903) describes a patient with bimanual pure agraphia without alexia and without obvious aphasic symptoms. It thus provided apparent counter-evidence against his own theory. Following are some relevant excerpts of this remarkable case report:

Subject:
The 46 year old tailor's wife Martha W., always in good health so far, has two adult children and had one still-birth. Her husband admits gonorrhoea but disavows syphilis. Beginning of January 1900, the patient noticed a progressive weakness of the right hand. At the end of March when waking up early in the morning, there was a complete paralysis of both right-sided limbs, the arm was bent on the breast, the face and language were said to be unimpaired. Eight days later, again early when awakening, the mouth was distorted and language had fully disappeared. Allegedly, the patient could understand what was spoken to her but she could not answer one sound. After four days, she could answer questions with "yes" and "no". For weeks, she was totally unable to speak spontaneously. The condition then improved until the beginning of October, when it deteriorated again after a slow influenza. Since then the present condition. Never unconsciousness. Never headaches, vomiting, dizziness, difficulty in swallowing.

On October 19, 1900, the following brief report was made: typical right-sided hemplegia with preserved ability to walk and predominant paralysis of the predilection muscles. Severe stiffness of the right leg, patellar and foot clonus. Toe stretching reflex. Sensitivity weakness in the entire right body half in all qualities. Sensitivity for posture and touch nearly fully lost in the right hand, complete tactile paralysis of the right hand. No hemianopia. Isolated agraphia. A detailed report was constructed in the following weeks based on several examinations. With the exception of fluctuations in the patient's general state of well-being and the consequent differences of fatigue, the condition remained unchanged. . . .

Language impairment:
Spontaneous speech: There is moderate anarthria corresponding best to the concept of syllable stumbling and most outspoken for difficult words. Fatigue has a strong influence, speech is then slowed down, often halting, otherwise

with unlimited vocabulary. Only mild signs of paraphasia: the patient seldom produces a meaning-unrelated or distorted word but she tries to correct it in often multiple attempts. For example, once she says spontaneously: "Here it also does not yet hurt" and when questioned she corrects "yet" and points to her forehead. Difficulties in spontaneous speech are subjectively severe. Asked to tell coherently about her illness, she repeats that she cannot do it, and when insisted upon she once says: "I can say it only in short paragraphs". Asked about the reason for this, she makes the remarkable statement: "I forget it here" while pointing to the middle of her forehead.

Repetition: unimpaired except for anarthria, also for words which sound very strange like e.g. "andra moi ennepe musa" etc. All isolated speech sounds, vowels as well as consonants, are repeated without error.

Reading is fluent and unimpaired, also naming and understanding numbers. Recognition and naming of objects and pictures of objects is unimpaired. Reading aloud from a newspaper shows some paraphasic word distortions and comprehension is incomplete.

The following particulars are noteworthy. The single letters of words which she always reads correctly cannot always be named correctly, for example the C and K of "Zucker" (sugar), the D of "Bild" (image). The same letters are named perfectly in other trials, so that performance is not constant and it is also unrelated to the frequency of the letters.

Number reading is impaired for numbers of more than two digits. In three-digit numbers, the last two are usually permutated, for example, instead of 741, 653, 264 she read 714, 635, 246, four-digit letters cannot be read with the exception of the full thousands, so that e.g. 1000, 2000, etc. are read correctly.

Word comprehension is grossly preserved. It always suffices to lead a normal conversation, but in more detailed examinations it is often impaired. For example, the patient is given the task of pointing with a finger to the nose, ear, left index finger, right elbow, right knee, hair, eye brows, chin, left ear lobe, spine, left shoulder, table, couch, floor, lamp, thermometer, ball, spoon, brush, book—and she makes six errors on the whole, two of them apparently because of perseveration of the preceding correctly understood sounds. Shortly afterwards, she is given 11 commands and makes only one error (nr. 2) which is corrected, however, when repeated at the end of the examination. The error again reflected the influence of the perseveration: 1) lift the right arm— correct. 2) Close your eyes—lifts the right arm in front of the eyes. There is thus a disorder of comprehension although it is only relatively mild.

The major impairment is an *almost complete agraphia*. In the course of time, and apparently as a result of the many examinations, the patient learns to write a few letters to dictation. Spontaneous writing remained totally abolished, also for her own name, for which she can write a German "M" (Martha) to dictation. In letter dictation, she can at first only write the German "a", in number dictation she once wrote 2, 3 and 4, but this was exceptional since she could usually not write any. Letters or numbers can only be copied with effort, and if they are erased, the patient cannot copy them from memory except for one occasion when she produced "h", "n", "a", "v" correctly. Attempts at writing were first conducted with the left hand only because the right hand could not be used, later on a writing aid (Soenecke's writing ball) was used for right-handed writing but there was always the same negative result. Never an indication of mirror writing in the trials with the left hand.

Writing tasks were always done reluctantly, with massive self-conquest, fatigue always set in very quickly and the patient complained about headaches. . . .

Postscript:

I could see and reexamine the patient only after two years, on January 11, 1903. The hemiplegic symptoms and the tactile paralysis of the right hand had remained the same. As before, the patient's reading ability was unimpaired, she could repeat absolutely correctly, and the agraphia was just about complete. Obviously, writing had not been trained any further, and the investigations caused the same feelings of disinclination as they used to. Still, when insisted upon to write the word "der" to dictation, the patient wrote the small German "d" followed by an "a", then she failed and she could not write any number either. When forced to draw a pin, she did not know whether the head had to be at the bottom or on top. For a colon, she made two dots next to each other horizontally instead of vertically. She was unable to indicate the number of syllables of polysyllabic words produced by the examiner. She was also unable to compose the words "but" (aber), "always" (immer), "and" (und), even if only the three, four or five letters composing the words were given in another order. The general condition of the patient was satisfactory, her facial expression even more vivid than before, with full concentration. As in the earlier examination, spontaneous speech was produced only when encouraged and haltingly, but with a good vocabulary. No obvious signs of hemianopia. No occurrence of an attack. The patient had always participated in the management of the household, supported by a daughter, and she was considered intelligent and with good judgment by her family members.

Summarising the essential features of Wernicke's 1903 case of apparently pure bimanual agraphia (pp. 241–245):

After several stroke-line incidents, one of which was accompanied by aphasia for several days, there was a lasting and severe impairment of sensitivity and somewhat less disturbed motility of the right body part. This not infrequent deficit is accompanied by a disorder which is seldom seen in such purity and specificity, namely, isolated agraphia.

It has been stated above that the purity and isolation of the deficit is not absolute and must be qualified. At any rate, we find a striking contrast between reading and speaking, which are hardly disturbed, and the ability to write, which is totally lost even with the otherwise perfectly usable left hand.

This case thus presents the mirror image of the relatively more frequent cases of so-called pure word blindness or "subcortical alexia" as I proposed to call it. It is a case of true agraphia in the sense we use it, because writing is also impossible with the undamaged left hand. . . .

As I explained in my earlier article (1886b), this deficit can only be understood if we assume that the optic cortical area in which we believe that the letter memory images are represented is still capable of functioning but the connection (by means of conduction fibres) to the motor centers mediating the images of writing movements is lost. Such a disconnection can most easily be expected to occur unilaterally, which naturally involves a modification of the concept of agraphia. A case of Pitres (1884) of so-called pure motor agraphia could then easily be explained, an agraphia which only applied to one extremity (the right hand). At that time, I considered it impossible that the multiple routes connecting the optic images with all motor centers would altogether be interrupted without an impairment of the locus of the optic memory images of letters itself. Nevertheless, my present case forces me to this interpretation, and this makes it so important—unless it can be explained in a totally different way.

This is indeed what Wernicke does after reviewing the cases and arguments in the literature. Following is the interpretation he finally provides for the data (1903, pp. 261–265).

In our case of pure agraphia, the preserved ability to read seems to prove that the route necessary for decomposing a word into its letters is preserved (i.e. the connection between the language area and the optic images). . . . Nevertheless, we find a disorder of "inner speech" (i.e. the language area) demonstrated by the fact that the patient cannot combine the letters known to her into words and that she cannot indicate the syllable number of polysyllabic words. This observation seems to lead me into a contradiction, because above I defended the position that such impairments should appear in reading as well as in writing. I therefore have to go into this issue in some more detail. First, I must mention that our patient's reading shows some mild impairment: longer and more complex sentences cause difficulties of comprehension. . . . Furthermore, I must draw attention to the distinction which generally holds between impressive and expressive components of the language process: the latter always suffers more easily because it is the most complicated task and requires undisturbed processing of the impressive part. If writing is undisturbed, as in subcortical alexia, we can without hesitation conclude that all these preliminary stages are unaffected but not the reverse. We must, therefore, take the possibility into account that reading remains almost undisturbed—approximately like in the cases discussed here—notwithstanding a certain disorder either of the word concept itself or of the route which is responsible for the decomposition of words into letters. . . .

With respect to our patient, this brings us back to a symptom which is only unilateral, namely, the impairment of "inner speech", of the word concept itself, or of the possibly also unilaterally trained route which serves the association between the word concept and the letter. The most simple and natural conclusion is that pure literal agraphia with completely intact "inner speech" only occurs unilaterally, as in Pitres's case. If, however, the literal form is bilateral, as in mine, Pick's, Bastian's case and finally the three cases of brain tumor summarized above, it is linked to a certain, albeit not severe, impairment of inner language. . . .

In conclusion, we come to the result which Déjerine already uttered on the basis of his observation: a really pure agraphia without any impairment of the "word concept" only occurs in the form of "agraphie motrice pure" described by Pitres and restricted to one hand, but it is this unilaterality which contradicts the concept of agraphia. Approximately pure cases like ours, which satisfy the concept of agraphia because of their bilaterality, always show some disorder of the "word concept" also or of the route which allows the decomposition of the word concept into letters. This disorder can be functional and only present in a particular stage of the illness. Although the lesion is unilateral in these cases (namely, of the word concept), they prove the unilaterality of an optic word center as little as the unilateral autopsy reports in so-called pure word blindness or subcortical alexia.

SUMMARY AND CONCLUSION

After a case report of apparently pure isolated agraphia, a review of the published cases, and an analysis of explanations on the nature of graphemic processing proposed by other authors, Wernicke (1903) concludes that his own case as well as other apparently pure isolated bimanual agraphias were in fact not pure cases but they also involved some lesion of the language system. Thus, they did not provide negative evidence to his theory of bilateral letter processing and the consequent impossibility of a really isolated bimanual agraphia. According to his theory, this would have to involve an anatomically very unlikely disconnection of the optic fields from the motor areas. In his later general treatise on aphasia, Wernicke (1906) repeats his views on reading and writing, which he considered to be fully dependent on spoken language, always proceeding letter by letter, with letters being bilaterally represented in the optic areas and transformed into motor movements for writing. He considers his views superior to the theory of his French colleague, Charcot, who assumed two left-hemispheric graphemic word centres, one for reading and one for writing, and also to Déjerine's theory, who rejected a special word motor centre but advocated a left-hemispheric optic word centre in the angular gyrus.

Contemporary cognitive neuropsychological research on reading and writing has proved Wernicke to be wrong on several points. First, the processes of reading and writing do not rely exclusively on a letter-by-letter procedure. Such a sublexical procedure is intrinsically inadequate and leads to regularisation of irregular forms, as is shown by the patterns of performance of patients with so-called "surface dyslexia" (Patterson, Coltheart, & Marshall, 1985) and "surface dysgraphia" (Beauvois & Dérouesné, 1981; Hatfield, 1982; Hatfield & Patterson, 1983). Second, correct word reading and writing require lexical processing, i.e. graphemic word representations which directly address the corresponding phonological word representations in reading and the reverse in writing. This is evidenced by the good word reading in patients using such a direct lexical route with so-called "phonological dyslexia" (Beauvois & Dérouesné, 1979; Caramazza, Miceli, Silveri, & Laudanna, 1985; Funnell, 1983) and by the near-preserved word writing in parallel cases of "phonological agraphia" (Shallice, 1981). For such patients, however, non-word processing is selectively impaired due to a disrupted sub-lexical procedure for reading or for writing. Third, a second (indirect) lexical route has generally been adopted in modern work which accesses phonology from print via semantics in reading and similarly print from phonology via semantics in writing. The assumption of a lexical-semantic route for reading can explain why patients with so-called "deep dyslexia" (Coltheart, Patterson, & Marshall, 1980), who process print exclusively via this route, are unable to read non-words, and produce semantic paralexias to words. A similar performance pattern has been observed in the writing of patients with so-called "deep dysgraphia" (Bub & Kertesz, 1982; Hatfield, 1982; Hatfield & Patterson, 1984). Wernicke's letter-based model of reading and writing provided neither a direct nor an indirect semantic lexical route and thus excluded modality-specific subtotal impairments or preservations of graphemic processing causally unrelated to the aphasia. He modified them as "verbal" to emphasise their dependence on the aphasic disorder.

Present-day models of oral and written language processing bear more resemblance to Charcot's diagram with independent graphemic and phonological input and output lexical systems than to Wernicke's oral language-centred model. Like Wernicke's (1903) case of pure agraphia, modern cases of agraphia without aphasia or alexia (Ellis, 1988) as well as cases of selective preservations of writing over speech (Hier & Mohr, 1977) provide evidence for a specialised graphemic system Wernicke rejected on logical-neuroanatomical grounds. On the other hand, the topic that seemed to be most vulnerable already in Wernicke's days, namely, the bilaterality rather than the unilaterality of reading, has gained support again in modern hypotheses on the role of the right hemisphere in processing graphemic stimuli (Patterson, Vargha-Khadem, & Polkey, 1989).

REFERENCES

Beauvois, M.F., & Dérouesné, J. (1979). Phonological processes in reading: Data from alexia. *Journal of Neurology, Neurosurgery and Psychiatry, 42*, 1125–1132.

Beauvois, M.F., & Dérouesné, J. (1981). Lexical orthographic agraphia. *Brain, 104*, 21–29.

Broca, P. (1861). Remarques sur le siège de la faculté du langage articulé, suivies d'une observation d'aphémie. *Bulletin de la Société d'Anatomie, 36*, 330–357.

Bub, D., & Kertesz, A. (1982). Deep agraphia. *Brain and Language, 17*, 146–165.

Caramazza, A., Miceli, G., Silveri, C., & Laudanna, A. (1985). Reading mechanisms and the organisation of the lexicon: Evidence from acquired dyslexia. *Cognitive Neuropsychology, 2*, 81–114.

Charcot, J.B. (1883). Des différentes formes de l'aphasie. De la cécité verbale. *Progrès médicale, 11*, 441–469.

Cohen, R.S., & Wartowfsky, M.W. (Eds.). (1966–1968). *Boston studies in the philosophy of science: Proceedings of the Boston colloquium for the philosophy of science* (Vol. 4). (Translation of C. Wernicke, 1874.) Dordrecht: Reidel.

Coltheart, M., Patterson, K., & Marshall, J.C. (Eds.). (1980). *Deep dyslexia*. London: Routledge.

De Bleser, R. (1989a). Translation of C. Wernicke (1886b). *Cognitive Neuropsychology, 6*, 547–569.

De Bleser, R. (1989b). Translation of H. Grashey (1885). *Cognitive Neuropsychology, 6*, 515–546.

De Bleser, R., & Luzzatti, C. (1989). Models of reading and writing and their disorders in classical German aphasiology. *Cognitive Neuropsychology, 6*, 501–513.

Déjerine, J. (1884). De l'aphasie et de ses différentes formes. *Semaine Médicale, 44*, 47.

Déjerine, J. (1891). Sur un cas de cécité verbale avec agraphie, suivi d'autopsie. *Compte Rendu de la Société de Biologie, 3*, 197–201.

Déjerine, J. (1892). Contribution à l'étude anatomoclinique et clinique des différentes variétés de cécité verbale. *Mémoires de la Société de Biologie, 4*, 61–90.

Ellis, A.W. (1988). Modelling the writing process. In G. Denes, C. Semenza, & P. Bisiacchi (Eds.), *Perspectives on cognitive neuropsychology*. Hove, U.K.: Lawrence Erlbaum Associates Ltd.

Freund, C.S. (1889). Über optische Aphasie und Seelenblindheit. *Archiv für Psychiatrie und Nervenkrankheiten, 20*, 372–416.

Funnell, E. (1983). Phonological processes in reading: New evidence from acquired dyslexia. *British Journal of Psychology, 74*, 159–180.

Grashey, H. (1885). Über Aphasie und ihre Beziehungen zuer Wahrnehmung. *Archiv für Psychiatrie und Nervenkrankheiten, 16*, 654–688.

Hatfield, F.M. (1982). Diverses formes de désintégration du langage écrit et implications pour la rééducation. In X. Seron & C. Laterre (Eds.), *Rééduquer le cerveau*. Brussels: Mardaga.

Hatfield, F.M., & Patterson, K. (1983). Phonological spelling. *Quarterly Journal of Experimental Psychology, 35A*, 451–468.

Hatfield, F.M., & Patterson, K. (1984). Interpretation of spelling disorders in aphasia: Impact of recent developments in cognitive neuropsychology. In F.C. Rose (Ed.), *Advances in neurology: Vol. 42. Progress in aphasiology*. New York: Raven Press.

Hier, D., & Mohr, J.P. (1977). Incongruous oral and written naming: Evidence for a subdivision of the syndrome of Wernicke's aphasia. *Brain and Language, 4*, 115–126.

Kussmaul, A. (1877). *Die Störungen der Sprache*. Leipzig: Vogel.

Lichtheim, L. (1885a). Über Aphasie. *Deutsches Archiv für Klinische Medizin, 36*, 204–268.

Lichtheim, L. (1885b). On aphasie. *Brain, 7*, 433–485.

Liepmann, H. (1900). Das Krankheitsbild der Apraxie (motorischer Asymbolie). *Monatschrift für Psychiatrie und Neurologie, 8,* 15–44, 102–132, 182–197.

Lissauer, H. (1890). Ein Fall von Seelenblindheit nebst einem Beitrage zur Theorie derselben. *Archiv für Psychiatrie und Nervenkrankheiten, 21,* 222–270.

Marshall, J.C., & Newcombe, F. (1973). Patterns of paralexia: A psycholinguistic approach. *Journal of Psycholinguistic Research, 2,* 175–199.

Patterson, K.E., Coltheart, M., & Marshall, J.C. (Eds.). (1985). *Surface dyslexia.* Hove, U.K.: Lawrence Erlbaum Associates Ltd.

Patterson, K.E., Vargha-Khadem, F., & Polkey, C.E. (1989). Reading with one hemisphere. *Brain, 112,* 39–63.

Pitres, A. (1884). Considération sur l'agraphie: A propos d'une observation nouvelle d'agraphie motrice pure. *Revue médicale de Paris, 4,* 855–873.

Shallice, T. (1981). Phonological agraphia and the lexical route in writing. *Brain, 104,* 413–429.

Wernicke, C. (1874). *Der aphasische Symptomencomplex: Eine Psychologische Studie auf Anatomischer Basis.* Breslau: Cohn & Weigert.

Wernicke, C. (1885). Nervenheilkunde: Die neueren Arbeiten über Aphasie. *Fortschritte der Medicin, 3,* 824–830.

Wernicke, C. (1886a). Nervenheilkunde: Die neueren Arbeiten über Aphasie. (Review of Lichtheim, 1885.) *Fortschritte der Medicin, 4,* 371–377.

Wernicke, C. (1886b). Nervenheilkunde: Die neueren Arbeiten über Aphasie. (Review of Grashey, 1885.) *Fortschritte der Medicin, 4,* 463–482.

Wernicke, C. (1903). Ein Fall von isolierter Agraphie. *Monatschrift für Psychiatrie und Neurologie, 13,* 241–265.

Wernicke, C. (1906). Der aphasische Symptomencomplex. In E. von Leyden & F. Klemperer (Eds.), *Die Deutsche Klinik am Eingange des Zwanzigsten Jahrhunderts in akademischen Vorlesungen: Vol. VI. Nervenkrankheiten.* Berlin: Urban & Schwarzenberg.

3 Charcot's Case of Impaired Imagery

Andrew W. Young
M.R.C. Applied Psychology Unit, Cambridge, U.K.

Claudia van de Wal
Faculty of Social Sciences, University of Leiden, The Netherlands.

UN PEU D'HISTOIRE

The 1880s marked the zenith of Charcot's fame and influence (Ellenberger, 1970; Guillan, 1959; Harris, 1991b). In the years following his appointment as head physician at the Salpêtrière in 1862, he had managed to secure the facilities needed to transform the hospital into an internationally recognised centre for clinical neurological research (Charcot, 1889b). Many of Charcot's interns and students went on to make significant contributions of their own, including Babinski, Cotard, de la Tourette, Marie, and Raymond. Foreign neurologists, such as Bechterev and Freud, came to work with him, and he also collaborated with the psychiatrist Magnan and the psychologists Binet and Janet. He developed a lucrative private practice to which wealthy patients were referred from all over the world, and his Tuesday lecture demonstrations at the Salpêtrière had become fashionable dramatic events which drew considerable public crowds. In 1882 his eminence was publicly recognised when he was appointed Professor of Diseases of the Nervous System in the Faculty of Medicine of Paris; a post that had been specially created for him.

As well as the more showy Tuesday public lectures, Charcot lectured and presented cases to medical audiences. The most important of these were recorded by his students and published in *Le Progrès Médical*, a journal which promoted the secular, scientific approach to mental disease. This secular background was of great importance in the 19th century, when discoveries in neurology were often seen as direct or indirect attacks on organised religion; studies ranging from examination of the effects of brain lesions to demonstrations of non-conscious mental activity could be considered to undermine the concept of free-will promulgated by the Catholic church. Charcot's work was clearly aligned with this anti-clericalist position, and he did not shrink from pointing out that religious experiences could show isomorphisms with hysterical phenomena (Charcot, 1889e). This helps to explain some of the extraordinary public interest in his findings.

The case we discuss here was that of Monsieur X., presented as a sudden loss of visual imagery. A version of the lecture was edited by Bernard, and published in *Le Progrès Médical* (Charcot & Bernard, 1883). It was sufficiently important to be translated into English by Savill as part of a series of Charcot's lectures (Charcot, 1889a, 1889d), and has recently been reprinted (Harris, 1991a).

MONSIEUR X.

Monsieur X. was an educated man, born in Vienna, who was a native speaker of German and Spanish, and also spoke French. He was fluent in Latin and ancient Greek, and knew enough modern Greek to use it for correspondence in his business as a merchant.

Like other members of his family, M. X. had previous enjoyed a remarkably good visual memory. He claimed that his mental images had the clarity and intensity of normal vision, that after reading something two or three times he could recite it by reading it in his mind's eye, and that he could revisualise places he had been in his travels in order to sketch them from memory. In contrast, his auditory memory was less important and effective for him.

The events which led M. X. to seek Charcot's help began some 18 months before, when he had a number of worries connected with his business. One day he noted a profound change in himself; the things around him appeared new and strange, and his visual memories of shapes and colours had disappeared completely. M. X. was led to doubt his sanity, but was somewhat reassured by noting that he could still see shapes and colours even though he could not remember them. Moreover, he realised that he could continue to direct his business affairs by relying on other forms of memory.

Ocular examination by Dr Parinaud had revealed nothing which could account for M. X.'s problems, though he was noted to be myopic and to have suffered a slight loss of sensitivity to colour. Charcot stated that no somatic symptom had been noted to precede, accompany, or follow M. X.'s loss of mental vision.

The impact on M. X.'s life was dramatic, and several anecdotes were given. Every time he returned to his home city of A. he felt as if he was in an unknown place, with all of the monuments, streets, and buildings appearing to him as if he had arrived there for the first time. When asked to describe the main square of A., he could remember nothing about its appearance. Similarly, he could not remember the appearance of his wife or children, and even when they were before him they seemed unfamiliar. These problems extended to his own appearance; M. X. had even found himself standing in someone's way in a public gallery, and then stopping to offer his excuses to a mirror. The problems were also as evident for material learnt in childhood as for more recent things; he could remember nothing about the appearance of the house in which he was brought up, though he had recalled it often in the past.

There was also a loss of ability to remember material for which M. X. had claimed to rely on support from visual imagery; he could only remember the first lines of the *Iliad*, whereas he had apparently been able to 'read' it from an image of the page before. Instead, M. X. found himself having to rely on auditory memory and 'inner speech', which was for him a novel experience. Even his dreams had become entirely verbal.

There was, however, evidence of some language impairment. Monsieur X. could still speak French fluently, but said that he did not think directly in French any longer, and had to translate his thoughts from Spanish or German (the first languages he had learnt as a child). When asked to write the Greek and German alphabets he left out several letters. These letters were traced out in front of him, but he could only recognise them by tracing them himself and then carefully comparing them to each other. Similar problems occurred in reading Greek words containing these letters, when he again had to write them himself before he could recognise them. More generally, his reading seems to have become somewhat slow and laborious, with much recourse to internal speech and articulatory movements of his tongue and lips. Charcot attributed these findings of moderate 'word-blindness' to M. X.'s compensating for his loss of visual memory by using manual or verbal memories.

When performing mental calculations M. X. now proceeded slowly, pronouncing the figures he was adding in a low voice. Previously, he had only needed to look at the columns of figures and the answer would come to him straightaway, without any need for detailed calculation.

As part of the lecture, Charcot produced a letter written by M. X. at his request. This summarised the main points of his case, and gave a few additional details. In the letter, M. X. pointed out that he was no longer able to form any visual images at all, even for things he could still recognise ("if you were to ask me to image the towers of Notre Dame, a grazing sheep or a ship in distress in the open sea, I would answer that, although I know perfectly well how to distinguish these three very different things and know very well what they are about, they have no meaning for me in terms of internal vision"). He also reported that his emotional reactions were reduced, and seemed to attribute this to his lack of imagery ("today I am calm, cold, and my imagination cannot lead me astray" [ma fantaisie ne peut plus m'égarer]). Because of its interest, we include a translation of M. X.'s letter as an Appendix to this Chapter.

THE SIGNIFICANCE OF MONSIEUR X.'S CASE

Monsieur X.'s case has often been regarded as one of the earliest descriptions of prosopagnosia, a neurological deficit in which the ability to recognise familiar faces is lost (Ellis, 1983; Ellis & Florence, 1990; Hécaen, 1981; Hécaen & Angelergues, 1962; Jeeves, 1984). Certainly it contains observations that were later repeated in many reports of prosopagnosic patients, including the combination of retrograde and anterograde problems, the failure to recognise even his own image in a mirror, and the hint of visual hypoemotionality (Bauer, 1982) in M. X.'s letter.

At the time, there were a small number of related reports, though they were not widely known and Charcot did not refer to them. Wigan (1844, p. 170) had briefly described a man with an "utter inability to remember faces. He would converse with a person for an hour, but after an interval of a day could not recognise him again. Even friends, with whom he had been engaged in business transactions, he was unconscious of ever having seen." According to Wigan (1844, p. 170), "He was quite incapable of making a mental picture of anything, and it was not till he heard the voice, that he could recognise men with whom he had constant intercourse."

In addition to Wigan's (1844) case, a particularly interesting study by Quaglino and Borelli (1867) has recently been brought to more general notice by Benton (1990a, 1990b), and there were also cases described by Hughlings Jackson (1872, 1876).

Quaglino and Borelli's (1867) patient showed a left visual field defect, loss of colour vision, impaired spatial orientation, and severely defective facial recognition; a combination of symptoms which has since proved highly characteristic in studies of prosopagnosia (Damasio, Damasio, & Van Hoesen, 1982; Meadows, 1974). They argued for the presence of a right hemisphere lesion, noting that he had earlier had a left hemiplegia which disappeared within a month of his stroke. His visual acuity was excellent, and he could read without difficulty, yet even the most familiar faces were not recognised. There is a hint that he did not initially complain of a loss of imagery for faces, but Benton (1990b) points out that Quaglino and Borelli specifically mention that he had forgotten the facades of houses, and included "loss of memory of the configuration of objects" in the title of their paper.

Hughlings Jackson's (1872) first case had left hemiplegia and an inability to recognise places and persons; "at one time he did not know his own wife" ... "and having wandered from home was unable to find his way back" (p. 513). From this pattern, Hughlings Jackson hypothesised a defect in "the sensori-motor processes concerned in the *recognition* of objects (not in *seeing* objects), and in putting images of things in 'propositional order', so to speak," and diagnosed a lesion affecting posterior areas of the right cerebral hemisphere. He was able to put this knowledge to use in diagnosing a right posterior tumour (confirmed at autopsy) in his second case, who presented with gradual onset of impaired recognition ("she often did not know objects, persons and places" [p. 148]) and left hemiplegia (Hughlings Jackson, 1876). He formed the view that the posterior lobes "are the seat of visual ideation, for most of our mental operations are carried on in visual ideas ... the right posterior lobe is the 'leading' side, the left the more automatic" (p. 148).

Although Charcot did not cite Hughlings Jackson's work, there are some similarities in their ideas. However, whilst Hughlings Jackson's descriptions emphasised the importance of 'visual ideation', he did not report observations on imagery *per se*.

Charcot himself saw the significance of M. X.'s case as being its confirmation of the importance of visual imagery, and its implication of a separation between visual images of familiar objects from other types of memory and imagery (such as auditory memory, and especially the motor representations needed for speech articulation or for writing). We will consider these two points separately.

First, the importance of visual imagery. Here, Charcot related his observations to Galton's recently published work (Galton, 1883), and pointed out that the fact that the ability was so highly developed in M. X. and his family was consistent with Galton's general position.

Perhaps not unreasonably, M. X. had experienced a pervasive sense of things being new and strange. This sense of strangeness was also a prominent feature in a delusion that had recently been described by Charcot's pupil, Cotard (1882), in which patients thought that people and things had ceased to exist or they were themselves dead (le délire des négations). Noting this parallel, Cotard (1884) thought that a loss of mental vision might therefore be involved in this delusion, and indeed found that some of his patients were unable to visualise absent objects in their thoughts. Cotard (1884) considered that this was more than a coincidence, and suggested that this delusion could have its origins in a misinterpretation of an underlying perceptual deficit. ("On ne peut s'empêcher de supposer qu'il y a là, en effet, autre chose qu'un coïncidence fortuite. Si la perte de la vision mentale était un fait ordinaire chez les anxieuses chroniques, on serait invinciblement entraîné à considérer la négation systématisée, comme un délire greffé sur le trouble psycho-sensoriel, comme une interprétation maladive du phénomène [p. 348].) This use of loss of visual imagery to account for a psychiatric delusion gives some idea of the general importance attached to visual imagery in Charcot's group.

We do not know of any earlier reports that focused so clearly on loss of visual imagery, and in that respect Charcot's description of M. X. is strikingly original. Although imagery deficits were noted in some subsequent studies, and occasionally formed a primary focus of interest (Brain 1954; Humphrey & Zangwill, 1951; Nielsen, 1955), it was only some 100 years later that they were again considered to have the fundamental importance Charcot had so readily assumed (Basso, Bisiach, & Luzzatti, 1980; Ehrlichman & Barrett, 1983; Farah, 1984; Farah, Levine, & Calvanio, 1988; Levine, Warach, & Farah, 1985).

The second point Charcot considered important was the separation of visual images (impaired for M. X.) from other forms of memory and imagery that were relatively intact. In the introduction to his lecture Charcot quoted Ribot (1881), who had argued that if different forms of memory are relatively independent in the normal state then "it is only natural that in the morbid state, one form may be lost, while the others remain intact. It is a fact which must now appear simple, requiring no other explanation, because it results from the nature of memory itself." Charcot contrasted this with the idea of memory as a single faculty, and argued that the issue of single or multiple memory systems should be resolved empirically. This is still a beautifully clear and cogent introduction to one of the central issues in the neuropsychology of memory.

THINGS ARE NEVER QUITE THE WAY THEY SEEM

There are some unusual or puzzling features of M. X.'s case which require further comment. Indeed, the interpretations placed on the case have varied considerably. For example, Nielsen (1936) regarded M. X. as closely similar to a case described by Wilbrand (1887, 1892, discussed in Chapter 8) and referred to them as the "Charcot–Wilbrand syndrome", whereas Brain (1954) explicitly rejected this parallel. Hence we need to distinguish M. X.'s putative significance at different times from the significance he has for us now.

Since there was no direct evidence of neurological disease, and M. X. had clearly had business worries for some time, it is surprising that Charcot did not use his lecture to address the issue of whether or not his deficit was hysterical in origin. This was a question to which he usually attached considerable importance (Charcot, 1889b, 1889f). Brain (1954) thought that the possibility of hysteria had to be seriously considered for his own cases of loss of visual imagery, but rejected it because both had suffered head injuries. Wigan (1844, p. 171) had also noted that for his patient there was "no appearance of that morbid vanity which induces a person to affect peculiarities of constitution, but on the contrary a strong desire to conceal his defect from the world." Other studies have confirmed that similar deficits can follow brain injury, but it would have been interesting to know Charcot's views on the aetiology.

What about the idea that this was one of the earliest descriptions of prosopagnosia? As we have seen, there were points in common between Charcot's description of M. X. and later reports of prosopagnosic patients. However, the case reports which predate Charcot's are in some ways closer to the norm for modern descriptions of prosopagnosia, especially Quaglino and Borelli's (1867). As a prosopagnosic, M. X. was relatively unusual in not having a left visual field defect, and in having a less severe impairment of colour perception (achromatopsia) than is often noted. Although modern cases without marked achromatopsia or left visual field defects have been described (de Haan, Young, & Newcombe, 1991; Sergent & Poncet, 1990), they are rare among what is itself a rare defect (Damasio et al., 1982; Meadows, 1974). Of course, it is now thought that there are different forms of prosopagnosia (De Renzi, Faglioni, Grossi, & Nichelli, 1991; Hay & Young, 1982; Hécaen, 1981), and cases without field defects or achromatopsia might correspond to a distinct subtype. Interestingly, neither of these recently reported patients was able to form mental images of the faces of familiar people (de Haan et al., 1991; Sergent & Poncet, 1990).

In thinking of Charcot's patient as an early example of prosopagnosia, we should not lose sight of these unusual features. On the basis of his own investigation Charcot obviously saw no reason to emphasise the loss of ability to recognise faces as a discrete deficit, since M. X. could not revisualise places, colours and other visual material as well. In addition, in the same lecture Charcot briefly mentioned what he considered a second case, in which an accomplished painter lost his powers of visual imagery and found that he could no longer copy things from memory; nothing was said about this patient's recognition abilities (Charcot & Bernard, 1883). Charcot's account thus proposed a relatively non-specific loss of visual imagery, and it was not until the much later work of Bodamer (1947; Ellis & Florence, 1990) that prosopagnosia was generally accepted as a discrete entity. Even though the existence of prosopagnosia is no longer disputed, it is only in exceptionally rare cases that it is only face recognition that is compromised (De Renzi, 1986; De Renzi et al., 1991). Most prosopagnosic patients, like M. X., fail to recognise buildings and other stimuli which come from visual categories in which there are several members with high similarity to each other (Damasio et al., 1982; Ellis & Young, 1989).

A striking feature of M. X.'s case was the parallel loss of recognition and imagery for faces and places; he was not only unable to image faces and places, but he also could not recognise them either. From Charcot's perspective, recognition was considered as involving some form of matching of a percept to a mental image, so that this parallel impairment of recognition and imagery was unsurprising: "this complete suppression of internal vision ... prevents M. X. from picturing anything to himself ... to such an extent that things and faces he has seen many times always appear new to him" (p. 570). More modern studies have also noted parallel impairments of imagery and recognition, though they tend to reverse the explanatory emphasis by arguing that the visual representations involved in recognition are also needed in forming mental images (Farah, Hammond, Mehta, & Ratcliff, 1989; Levine et al., 1985).

However, the studies of parallel impairments of imagery and recognition emphasise that in such cases imagery is intact for material that can still be recognised (Farah et al., 1989). It is therefore anomalous that M. X. should have lost *all* visual imagery, including that for objects he could apparently recognise without difficulty. In fact, later cases with loss of visual imagery without any noticeable impairment of visual recognition have been described (Brain, 1954; Riddoch, 1990).

To reconcile such observations, modern studies tend to consider that some cognitive processes are specific to imagery whilst others are shared by imagery and perception. In particular, they distinguish the process of generating an image from accessing the stored material which may be needed to form a particular image of something familiar (Brain, 1954; Riddoch, 1990). From this perspective, the cases with generally impaired imagery and intact recognition involve deficits in image generation, whereas the cases with parallel deficits of imagery and recognition of particular materials (such as faces) involve damage or loss of access to a certain type of previously stored material. The important point here is that M. X. is difficult to interpret cleanly because he seems to show a combination of both types of deficit. Conceivably, then, M. X. was not a perfectly pure case, and actually showed a combination of loss of ability to generate visual images and a variant of prosopagnosia.

AFTERMATH

With the benefit of more than 100 years' hindsight, M. X. seems to have suffered both a loss of ability to generate visual images and a form of prosopagnosia. In Brain's (1954, p. 290) view, "loss of visualisation is usually found in association with other forms of higher visual disability," so it is not surprising that the first clearly documented case should be of a hybrid type. But it has created some confusion in the literature, since it has allowed different authors to emphasise M. X.'s recognition impairment or his loss of visual imagery and thus arrive at rather different conclusions.

It is an impressive tribute to Charcot's clinical acumen that, despite the novelty of the case, so many of his observations have been repeated in other patients. However, some of the seeds of the later confusion can be found in Charcot's theoretical presentation. In particular, he was too keen to account for all of M. X.'s complex pattern of problems with a single underlying cause, in the form of a loss of visual imagery.

Looking for a single potential cause is a useful first tactic, especially with a unique case. But M. X. was not unique for Charcot, since he gave a brief description of a second case in the same lecture (the painter who could not copy from memory); yet Charcot showed no interest in reporting whether this second case also involved recognition impairments, or in other potential contrasts between them. Moreover, Charcot even tried to relate M.X.'s reading impairments to the loss of visual imagery, despite the fact that he had studied other cases of 'word-blindness' and knew that this could form a separate impairment in which imagery and recognition of other visual stimuli were well preserved (Charcot, 1889c).

Why, then, did Charcot not see M. X. as having more than one problem? There are probably two main reasons. First, the method of fractionating syndromes by looking for evidence of dissociable deficits was not well developed. Although Charcot had cited with approval Ribot's point that different forms of memory will be differentially affected by brain injury if they are relatively independent in the normal state, the corollary of placing more emphasis on dissociations than associations as pointers to different types of mental ability was not fully appreciated. Indeed, for some of the purposes of 19th-century neurology, it was important to focus on associations rather than dissociations. Without neuro-imaging techniques, the pattern of symptoms formed an important source of information on the localisation of lesions for diagnosis. This could be very effective, as in Hughlings Jackson's diagnosis of a right posterior tumour in his second case of 'imperception' (Hughlings Jackson, 1876). But to make such diagnoses accurately, it was often useful to seek syndromes involving striking patterns of co-occurring symptoms. This emphasis on association of symptoms for diagnosis was in tension with the importance of dissociations in providing insight into different types of mental ability.

The second reason relates to Charcot's particular theoretical position. Like Galton (1883), he thought that individual differences were funda-mental, and had an especial interest in the idea that some people are more visual-minded, others auditory-minded. Charcot valued highly his own visual sensibility (Harris, 1991b), which must have given a particular fascination to knowing what it might be like to lose it. Hence, he not only thought that M. X. had lost his mental vision, but that this would have affected him differently than it might affect someone whose powers of visual imagery had in the first place been less developed; in effect, M. X.'s symptoms might be different from those of a less visually minded person with the same brain lesion. For example, he discusses the idea that some people rely more on evoking the visual equivalent of a word in reading, others on evoking its auditory equivalent. The symptoms of alexia might then differ according to an individual's pre-morbid predilection. Later studies have not supported this view, and other cases show M. X.'s problems without having had exceptional pre-morbid mental imagery.

On the evidence of his letter, M. X. seemed to share Charcot's opinion that all his problems arose from a common deficit in the form of a loss of mental imagery. But here we come face to face with concerns about Charcot's methods. His lectures and demonstrations involved cases that had been carefully 'worked up', both by himself and by his assistants, and in the course of these investigations the patients would have the opportunity to discover Charcot's views and theories. In the field of hysteria, this was to damage his reputation. As Ellenberger (1970) explains, because of "Charcot's paternalistic attitude and his despotic treatment of students, his staff never dared contradict him; they therefore showed him what they believed he wanted to see. After rehearsing the demonstrations, they showed the subjects to Charcot, who was careless enough to discuss their cases in the patients' presence. A peculiar atmosphere of mutual suggestion developed between Charcot, his collaborators, and his patients" (p. 98). Although this type of problem was obviously much more serious in the investigation of hysteria, it means that M. X.'s letter may be less objective than it at first appears.

Where does this leave us? There is always a danger of simply selecting from the past those aspects that are congruent with what we now want to see. Over the years, the much-discussed case of M. X. has been particularly susceptible to this; the complex and probably hybrid nature of his impairment has allowed different authors to emphasise different aspects. Charcot's own description also shows that at times he tried hard to get his observations to fit his own general theoretical position. We all do this, and neuropsychology advances when one position is found to account for the observations more successfully than another. But this method will only work to the extent that clinicians and researchers can elicit and report the key details of cases they have investigated. What is therefore so impressive about Charcot's description of M. X. is that, despite the changes in theoretical perspective since the 1880s, so many of the fundamental observations have been repeated with other cases. This is why it has remained a classic in the early history of neuropsychology.

APPENDIX: MONSIEUR X.'S LETTER

I hasten to reply to your letter, and I hope you will excuse my imperfect knowledge of the French language, which makes it a little difficult to express exactly what I want to tell you.

As I have told you, I used to have a great ability to picture to myself [représenter intérieurement] persons who interested me, colours and objects of every kind, in a word everything that is presented to the eye.

Let me bring to your notice that I used this ability in my studies: I read what I wanted to learn and when I closed my eyes I could clearly see again the letters in great detail; it was the same for the appearance of people, or countries and cities I have visited in my long journeys, and, as I just mentioned, for every object I had seen with my eyes.

All of a sudden this mental imagery [vision intérieure] has disappeared completely. Today, no matter how much I want to, I cannot image [représenter intérieurement] the features of my children, of my wife, or any everyday object. So, having established that I have completely lost my mental imagery, you will understand that my impressions have changed absolutely.

No longer being able to form visual images [me répresenter ce qui est visible], and having completely kept my abstract memory, I experience daily astonishment at seeing things I must have known for a long time. With my sensations, or rather my impressions, being indefinitely novel, it seems to me that a complete change has come over my existence and of course my personality [caractère] has changed notably. I used to be impressionable, enthusiastic, and I had a vivid imagination; today I am calm, cold, and my imagination cannot lead me astray [ma fantaisie ne peut plus m'égarer].

With this loss of visual mental imagery [représentation intérieure], my dreams are correspondingly changed. Now I only dream in *words*, whereas in the past I always had visual perception in my dreams.

As a more convincing example: if you were to ask me to image the towers of Notre Dame, a grazing sheep or a ship in distress in the open sea, I would answer that, although I know perfectly well how to distinguish these three very different things and know very well what they are about, they have no meaning for me in terms of internal vision.

A remarkable consequence of the loss of this mental ability is, as I have said, the change in my personality and my impressions. I am much less affected by sorrow or grief. I can tell you that after losing one of my relatives, with whom I was very close, I experienced a much less intense grief than if I had still been able to image the features of that relative, the stages of the illness he went through, or especially if I had been able to picture to myself [voir intérieurement] the outward effect of this untimely death on the members of my family.

I don't know if I explain clearly what I experience; but I can tell you that this mental imagery that I lack today used to be possessed by me in no ordinary degree, and that it is still possessed by my brother, professor of law in the

University of X., by my father, an oriental specialist known in the scientific world, and by my sister, a very talented painter.

In conclusion, I would like you to note that I now have to *say to myself the things I want to remember, whereas in the past I would only have to photograph them by sight.*

Paris, 11th July 1883.

ACKNOWLEDGEMENTS

We thank Andy Calder and Deborah Hellawell for helpful discussion of several points.

REFERENCES

Basso, A., Bisiach, E., & Luzzatti, C. (1980). Loss of mental imagery: A case study. *Neuropsychologia, 18*, 435–442.

Bauer, R.M. (1982). Visual hypoemotionality as a symptom of visual–limbic disconnection in man. *Archives of Neurology, 39*, 702–708.

Benton, A.L. (1990a). Facial recognition 1990. *Cortex, 26*, 491–499.

Benton, A.L. (1990b). The fate of some neuropsychological concepts: An historical inquiry. In E. Goldberg (Ed.), *Contemporary neuropsychology and the legacy of Luria* (pp. 171–179). Hillsdale, NJ: Lawrence Erlbaum Associates Inc.

Bodamer, J. (1947). Die Prosop-Agnosie. *Archiv für Psychiatrie und Nervenkrankheiten, 179*, 6–53.

Brain, R. (1954). Loss of visualization. *Proceedings of the Royal Society of Medicine, 47*, 288–290.

Charcot, J.-M. (1889a). *Clinical lectures on diseases of the nervous system, delivered at the infirmary of La Salpêtrière by Professor J.-M. Charcot* (T. Savill, Trans.). London: New Sydenham Society. [Reprinted in Harris, 1991a.]

Charcot, J.-M. (1889b). Introductory (Lecture I). In T. Savill (Ed.), *Clinical lectures on diseases of the nervous system, delivered at the infirmary of La Salpêtrière by Professor J.-M. Charcot* (pp. 1–19). London: New Sydenham Society.

Charcot, J.-M. (1889c). On a case of word-blindness (Lecture XI). On word-blindness (continued) (Lecture XII). In T. Savill (Ed.), *Clinical lectures on diseases of the nervous system, delivered at the infirmary of La Salpêtrière by Professor J.-M. Charcot* (pp. 130–140, 141–150). London: New Sydenham Society.

Charcot, J.-M. (1889d). On a case of sudden and isolated suppression of the mental vision of signs and objects (forms and colours) (Lecture XIII). In T. Savill (Ed.), *Clinical lectures on diseases of the nervous system, delivered at the infirmary of La Salpêtrière by Professor J.-M. Charcot* (pp. 151–163). London: New Sydenham Society.

Charcot, J.-M. (1889e). Spiritualism and hysteria (Lecture XVI). In T. Savill (Ed.), *Clinical lectures on diseases of the nervous system, delivered at the infirmary of La Salpêtrière by Professor J.-M. Charcot* (pp. 198–206). London: New Sydenham Society.

Charcot, J.-M. (1889f). A case of hysterical mutism in a man (Lecture XXVI). In T. Savill (Ed.), *Clinical lectures on diseases of the nervous system, delivered at the infirmary of La Salpêtrière by Professor J.-M. Charcot* (pp. 360–373). London: New Sydenham Society.

Charcot, J.-M., & Bernard, D. (1883). Un cas de suppression brusque et isolée de la vision mentale des signes et des objets (formes et couleurs). *Le Progrès Médical, 11*, 568–571.

Cotard, J. (1882). Du délire des négations. *Archives de Neurologie, 4*, 152–170, 282–295. [Reprinted in Cotard, 1891.]

Cotard, J. (1884). Perte de la vision mentale dans la mélancolie anxieuse. *Archives de Neurologie, 7*, 289–295. [Reprinted in Cotard, 1891.]

Cotard, J. (1891). *Études sur les maladies cérébrales et mentales.* Paris: Baillière.

Damasio, A.R., Damasio, H., & Van Hoesen, G.W. (1982). Prosopagnosia: Anatomic basis and behavioral mechanisms. *Neurology, 32,* 331–341.

de Haan, E.H.F., Young, A.W., & Newcombe, F. (1991). Covert and overt recognition in prosopagnosia. *Brain, 114,* 2575–2591.

De Renzi, E. (1986). Current issues in prosopagnosia. In H.D. Ellis, M.A. Jeeves, F. Newcombe, & A. Young (Eds.), *Aspects of face processing* (pp. 243–252). Dordrecht: Martinus Nijhoff.

De Renzi, E., Faglioni, P., Grossi, D., & Nichelli, P. (1991). Apperceptive and associative forms of prosopagnosia. *Cortex, 27,* 213–221.

Ehrlichman, H., & Barrett, J. (1983). Right hemispheric specialization for mental imagery: A review of the evidence. *Brain and Cognition, 2,* 55–76.

Ellenberger, H.F. (1970). *The discovery of the unconscious: The history and evolution of dynamic psychiatry.* London: Allen Lane, The Penguin Press.

Ellis, H.D. (1983). The role of the right hemisphere in face perception. In A.W. Young (Ed.), *Functions of the right cerebral hemisphere* (pp. 33–64). London: Academic Press.

Ellis, H.D., & Florence, M. (1990). Bodamer's (1947) paper on prosopagnosia. *Cognitive Neuropsychology, 7,* 81–105.

Ellis, H.D., & Young, A.W. (1989). Are faces special? In A.W. Young & H.D. Ellis (Eds.), *Handbook of research on face processing* (pp. 1–26). Amsterdam: North Holland.

Farah, M.J. (1984). The neurological basis of mental imagery: A componential analysis. *Cognition, 18,* 245–272.

Farah, M., Hammond, K.H., Mehta, Z., & Ratcliff, G. (1989). Category-specificity and modality-specificity in semantic memory. *Neuropsychologia, 27,* 193–200.

Farah, M.J., Levine, D.N., & Calvanio, R. (1988). A case study of mental imagery deficit. *Brain and Cognition, 8,* 147–164.

Galton, F. (1883). *Inquiries into human faculty and its development.* London: Macmillan.

Guillan, G. (1959). *J.-M. Charcot, 1825–1893: His life—his work.* (P. Bailey, Trans.). London: Pitman.

Harris, R. (1991a). *Clinical lectures on diseases of the nervous system, by J.-M. Charcot.* Reprint of Charcot, 1889, with an introduction by R. Harris.) London: Tavistock/Routledge.

Harris, R. (1991b). Introduction. In R. Harris (Ed.), *Clinical lectures on diseases of the nervous system, by J.-M. Charcot* (pp. ix–lxviii). London: Tavistock/Routledge.

Hay, D.C., & Young, A.W. (1982). The human face. In A.W. Ellis (Ed.), *Normality and pathology in cognitive functions* (pp. 173–202). London: Academic Press.

Hécaen, H. (1981). The neuropsychology of face recognition. In G. Davies, H. Ellis, & J. Shepherd (Eds.), *Perceiving and remembering faces* (pp. 39–54). London: Academic Press.

Hécaen, H., & Angelergues, R. (1962). Agnosia for faces (prosopagnosia). *Archives of Neurology, 7,* 92–100.

Hughlings Jackson, J. (1872, 4th May). Case of disease of the brain—left hemiplegia—mental affection. *Medical Times and Gazette,* 513–514.

Hughlings Jackson, J. (1876). Case of large cerebral tumour without optic neuritis and with left hemiplegia and imperception. In J. Taylor (Ed.) (1958), *Selected writings of John Hughlings Jackson: Vol. 2* (pp. 146–152). London: Staples Press.

Humphrey, M.E., & Zangwill, O.L. (1951). Cessation of dreaming after brain injury. *Journal of Neurology, Neurosurgery, and Psychiatry, 14,* 322–325.

Jeeves, M.A. (1984). The historical roots and recurring issues of neurobiological studies of face perception. *Human Neurobiology, 3,* 191–196.

Levine, D.N. Warach, J., & Farah, M. (1985). Two visual systems in mental imagery: Dissociation of "what" and "where" in imagery disorders due to bilateral posterior cerebral lesions. *Neurology, 35*, 1010–1018.

Meadows, J.C. (1974). The anatomical basis of prosopagnosia. *Journal of Neurology, Neurosurgery, and Psychiatry, 37*, 489–501.

Nielsen, J.M. (1936). *Agnosia, apraxia, aphasia: Their value in cerebral localization* (1st edn.). Baltimore: Waverly Press.

Nielsen, J.M. (1955). Occipital lobes, dreams and psychosis. *Journal of Nervous and Mental Disease, 121*, 50–52.

Quaglino, A., & Borelli, G.B. (1867). Emiplegia sinistra con amaurosi—guarigione—perdita totale della percezione dei colori e della memoria della configurazione degli oggetti. *Giornale d'Oftalmologia Italiana, 10*, 106–117.

Ribot, T. (1881). *Les maladies de la mémoire*. Paris. [Cited in Charcot & Bernard, 1883.]

Riddoch, M.J. (1990). Loss of visual imagery: A generation deficit. *Cognitive Neuropsychology, 7*, 249–273.

Sergent, J., & Poncet, M. (1990). From covert to overt recognition of faces in a prosopagnosic patient. *Brain, 113*, 989–1004.

Wigan, A.L. (1844). *The duality of the mind: Proved by the structure, functions, and diseases of the brain, and by the phenomena of mental derangement, and shown to be essential to moral responsibility*. London: Longman, Brown, Green, & Longmans.

Wilbrand, H. (1887). *Die Seelenblindheit als Herderscheinung und ihre Beziehungen zur homonymen Hemianopsie, zur Alexie, und Agraphie*. Wiesbaden: J. Bergmann.

Wilbrand, H. (1892). Ein Fall von Seelenblindheit und Hemianopsie mit Sectionsbefund. *Deutsche Zeitschrift für Nervenheilkunde, 2*, 361–387.

4

A Case Reported by Sérieux: The First Description of a "Primary Progressive Word Deafness"?

M. Ceccaldi, C. Soubrouillard, and M. Poncet
Service de Neurologie et de Neuropsychologie, C.H.U. Timone, Marseille, France.

André Roch Lecours
Centre de Recherche, Centre Hospitalier Côtes-des-Neiges, Montréal, Canada and Faculté de Médecine, Université de Montréal, Canada.

On 18th December, 1893, during a session of the French Society of Biology, Déjerine and Sérieux reported the data provided by the autopsy of a female patient who died in March 1895 at the age of 55, whose symptoms had started as early as 1887.

This right-handed patient had a clinical history which Déjerine and Sérieux divided in two parts. The first part going over a five-year period (from 1887 to 1892) was accurately described in the clinical report initially published by Sérieux in the French *Revue de Medecine* in 1893, as a case of "pure word deafness". The second part covered the last two years of this patient's life which were characterised by the development of a gradually worsening sensory aphasia, associated with a considerable lowering of her other cognitive functions.

This clinical report is generally considered as one of the first published cases of primary progressive aphasia (Mesulam, 1982; Mesulam & Weintraub 1992). Today, when so much emphasis is placed on the neuropsychological aspects of progressive focal atrophies, it is of interest to proceed to a close examination of Déjerine and Sérieux's papers.

A CASE OF PURE WORD DEAFNESS ... WITH ADDITIONAL SYMPTOMS!

In his 1893 paper, Sérieux described this patient's (patient B) symptomatology with careful attention (p. 735): this patient "is perfectly able to hear when one speaks to her, but ... can't understand the meaning of the words." From a clinical point of view, her problems were in short (p. 748): "1) loss of spoken language comprehension, of capacity to repeat words and sentences, and of the capacity to write down dictated words and sentences, 2) maintenance of the capacity of self initiated language, of self initiated writing, of reading comprehension, of reading aloud and of written transcription of a text."

The fact that this patient could talk, read aloud, and even write was underlined by Sérieux. According to the idea that the visual and motor centres were subordinated to the auditory word centre (i.e. "a lesion of that center would inevitably bring about paraphasia and reading impairment"), he proposed that the symptoms of this patient indicated preservation of the auditory word centre. The patient, indeed, was not deaf: in spite of a right ear cophosis, she could hear the ticking of a watch and react to all kinds of sounds, even the faintest ones. In addition, it was also quite easy to communicate with her with the help of written language, and her spontaneous speech was fluent, without any dysarthia or syntactic mistakes. At the most, Sérieux could detect in this patient some morphological paraphasia and some word-finding difficulties.

The dissociations observed between the major problems of oral language comprehension and, on one hand the retention of auditory acuity and on the other hand the retention of inner language (as witnessed by the capacity of spontaneous language and the comprehension of written language) classified this aphasia in the category of "subcortical aphasias". This was actually a type of aphasia fitting the seventh type of aphasia described by Lichtheim (1885), that is, a "conductibility" aphasia, subsequent to a fibre's interruption from both ascending auditory projections to the left auditory word centre.

It is interesting to discuss the assumption made by Sérieux in his first paper on the topic of hypothesised localisation of the cerebral lesion. He believed (1893, p. 750) that it must have been located "outside the auditory word centre, in the cortex or in the white matter, thus interrupting part of its connections with the rest of the brain ... isolating the auditory word centre from the rest of the auditory centre." We can speculate that, in connection to Lichtheim's model, Sérieux must have assumed that this right-handed patient had a lesion located in the left temporal lobe. However, four years later, while proceeding to the macroscopic examination of this patient's brain, Déjerine and Sérieux noticed an atrophy of both temporal lobes. This atrophy was predominantly located in the anterior regions of the superior temporal gyri leaving "the insula exposed" on both sides. From this, they concluded that this subcortical aphasia was caused by a "purely cortical" and bilateral lesion. They also postulated (p. 4) that, since the lesion was lying in the auditory temporal cortex, it could not be the result of a "separation of the common auditory centre from the word auditory centre, but rather was a weakening of the common auditory centre's functions."

It is of course easy to rewrite history after it has happened, but one could imagine that, had all the symptoms of the patient been really taken into consideration, Sérieux could have formulated a hypothesis in his first paper which would have been closer to the actual result of the autopsy. The fact is that in his analysis of the case, Sérieux abided so closely to Lichtheim's model that he neglected what was not predictable in, or explainable by that model. Indeed, in the beginning of his case report, it is clearly noted that "there is no complete recognition of the sounds and the noises in so far as they are related to their cause; the same is true for melodies ... she [the patient] cannot recognize the most popular tunes that she consistently confuses with religious chants ... she does not clearly distinguish between bird chirping and human voice." Therefore it is clear that the deficit of the auditory recognition of patient B., which was obvious in the case of verbal material, was also extended to other familiar noises as well as to melodies. This word deafness was therefore part of a larger concept of auditory agnosia.

More recent research has demonstrated that the term word deafness actually refers to two different concepts (Albert & Bear, 1974; Auerbach, Allard, Naeser, Alexander, & Albert, 1982; Tanaka, Yamadori, & Mori, 1987). The first one is based on the hypothesis of a specific deficit of phonological discrimination where "perceptive" components such as the temporal resolution or the tonal discrimination are unimpaired. This type of deficit may follow a left unilateral lesion. As a matter of fact it might be a "fragment" of Wernicke's aphasia (Wernicke, 1874). The second type of word deafness is believed to follow a disturbance located at a pre-phonemic level, which would be linked in particular to a supra modal flow of temporal analysis resulting from bilateral lesions in the temporal lobes. We find this second type of word deafness which may be described as appreciative auditory agnosia (Vignolo, 1969), to be closer to the case related by Sérieux.

WAS IT A CASE OF PRIMARY PROGRESSIVE APHASIA?

Sérieux's patient is often cited as one of the first cases of reported progressive aphasia in the context of a degenerative disease (Mesulam & Weintraub, 1992). According to Mesulam's definition, primary progressive aphasia meets the following criteria: progressive language disturbance without other significant cognitive disorders, nor attention deficit, nor signs pointing to a more generalised dementia for at least two years, while the existence of systemic disorders or of any other cerebral disease which could create language impairment is ruled out.

In the case described by Sérieux and Déjerine there was no other significant cognitive abnormality besides pure word deafness during the five years following the onset. Indeed, the patient was well aware of her disorder, and it is only during the last two years of her life that the situation worsened and evolved toward a Wernicke-type aphasia with considerable lowering of her intellectual capacities.

However, we must point out that the most frequent clinical characteristics of primary progressive aphasia is a progressive loss of word retrieval being part of non-fluent aphasia or of fluent and "logopenic" aphasia (Mesulam & Weintraub, 1992). The diagnosis of word deafness applies only to this patient of Déjerine and Sérieux and to one of the personal cases reported by Mesulam in his 1982 paper. However, Mesulam admitted that this later case was particular, since the patient was a young woman who had presented a very early clinical onset at the age of 17, whereas the average age for the onset of primary progressive aphasia is 60 years $+/-$ 8 years (Mesulam & Weintraub, 1992).

We feel that there are also other reasons which should rule out the inclusion of Déjerine and Sérieux's case in the group of primary progressive aphasia.

The first reason is that, as discussed earlier, the clinical pattern of that case suggested a syndrome of word deafness being part of a larger auditory apperceptive agnosia. Some authors prefer to use the term verbal auditory agnosia rather than word deafness (Ulrich, 1978). This point of view seems to be substantiated by modern research which regards pure word deafness as being a problem of perception, affecting particularly—although not exclusively—language material because of its auditory nature. We could therefore consider that this was not a primary progressive aphasia, but rather a primary progressive auditory agnosia.

The second reason, as mentioned by Mesulam and Weintraub (1992), is that 65% of the progressive primary aphasia published since 1982 show neuroradiological signs suggesting the existence of an asymmetrical atrophy more prominent in the left frontal perisylvian region. However, as previously mentioned, the autopsy of patient B. had revealed the presence of an atrophy symmetrically affecting the two temporal lobes, which differentiates this case from the class of syndromes correlated with an asymmetrical cortical degeneration (Caselli & Jack, 1992).

Finally, there is a last point: even though it seems clear that during the first phase of her medical history, patient B. was not suffering any cognitive disturbance, we can't necessarily exclude possible behavioural disturbances.

In fact, in 1891, Sérieux wrote that this patient had become "emotional, irritable and violent" and that she occasionally suffered ideation of persecution.

WHAT KIND OF DISEASE WAS IT?

In their review of primary progressive aphasia cases, Mesulam and Weintraub noticed that seven cases out of thirteen in which a post-mortem brain examination had been conducted showed a non-specific neuronal loss with evidence of gliosis and of some spongioform changes. In addition, in the quasi-totality of the cases in which an autopsy had been conducted, the left frontal perisylvian areas were the most affected. All the authors seem to recognise the etiological diversity in primary progressive aphasia. However, they most often hypothesise a focal cortical degeneration which would fit the category of a specific spongioform dementia (Caselli & Jack, 1992).

What Kind of Data Did Examination of Patient B.'s Brain Provide?

Before going any further, we must locate the data of the autopsy in the scientific context of the time. Alzheimer had not yet written about the neuropathological characteristics of the disease which later bore his name (1907). Pick had just recently reported the unusual case of a patient who had suffered a progressive deterioration which had evolved over a three-year period. This case had been essentially characterized by language disturbances and the autopsy later carried out by Chiari revealed a lobar atrophy which affected the frontal and temporal lobes (Pick, 1892). It was only in 1911 that Alzheimer emphasised the importance of data provided by histology, in particular the acute neuronal loss as well as cortical and subcortical glioses in atrophic regions. Later, in 1926, Onari and Spatz introduced the eponym of Pick's disease (Neumann, 1949).

The macroscopic examination of B.'s brain revealed a symmetrical atrophy in both temporal lobes which, to some extent, had spared the most posterior regions of these lobes.

Déjerine and Sérieux stressed the fact that the atrophy was circumscribed to the temporal lobe region and that "all the rest of the hemispheres were strictly unaltered." This type of macroscopic description resembles those found in certain cases of Pick's disease in which the atrophy only strikes the temporal lobes and in which the frontal lobes are spared (Jakob, 1969). Moreover, when there is a lesion in the temporal lobes in the case of Pick's disease, it is typical to see the anterior third of the temporal superior gyrus more affected by some atrophy than the posterior part (Tomlinson, 1992).

If the macroscopic characteristics of B.'s brain were close to those just described, the histological examination is less convincing. The more striking characteristic was a massive neuronal loss in the most superficial layers of the temporal cortex ("chronic polioencephalitis") without focal lesions. This neuronal loss was accompanied by a substantial amount of cortical gliosis ("the molecular layer contains no longer any neurones, but only microglial cells and a concentration of nuclei which far exceeds the typical concentration in a normal state"). Apparently Sérieux and Déjerine had not noticed any swollen cells, even though they made 800 or 900 serial sections for each hemisphere, which far exceeds the usual practice for contemporary neuropathologists. Nor did they observe any abnormal neuronal inclusion; we must remember, however, that no argentophilic staining was being used at that time.

Based on this relatively skimpy description, we should not absolutely exclude the type of Pick's disease which does not entail any neuronal pathognomonic abnormality (Neumann, 1949; Tissot, Constantinidis, & Richard, 1975).

We must bring up here another important point. In his original paper, while describing this patient's clinical history, Sérieux mentioned (p. 734): "the existence of an old spinal affliction: progressive muscular atrophy, interosseus atrophy, thenar space and hypothenar space atrophy, shoulder muscles atrophy, the presence of lordosis, cramps, pain, lower limb paresis, hyperreflexia, spinal trepidation more noticeable on the right side, asymmetry of the pupils." It is too bad that this original clinical data has been left out in the second paper where no information was given about a possible post-mortem examination of the spinal cord. Now, these symptoms would suggest a spinal cord degeneration affecting more predominantly the anterior horn and the lateral tracts. In the light of these symptoms, it is quite tempting to speculate a motor neuron disease. Actually, according to modern research, the median life span for patients suffering an amyotrophic lateral sclerosis with progressive muscular atrophy is of 10 years (Mortara, Chio, Rossi, et al., 1984), and the earlier the onset of the disease the more favourable the prognosis is in terms of life expectancy. In addition, some authors have reported lateral amyotrophic sclerosis cases concurrent with a genuine Pick's disease (Brion, Psimaras, Chevalier, Plas, Masse, & Jatteau, 1980).

It would be erroneous to diagnose B. with Pick's disease, based solely on the data provided by the post-mortem brain examination that Sérieux and Déjerine performed. But it would be equally wrong to diagnose a spongioform focal atrophy. The literature in neurology from the beginning of the century is quite rich with observations of exceptions which deserve to be scrupulously examined by modern researchers. It would certainly be tempting to label Sérieux and Déjerine's case as an example of primary progressive aphasia before its time, if it were not in fact a case of primary auditory agnosia. This case could have stood as an example of progressive focal degeneration, and even illustrated the new concept of progressive focal atrophy, if a careful reading of the autopsy report had not led us towards more classical diagnostic assumptions. In any case it looks like the solution is certainly not to be found on paper, but maybe it lies on some old lab shelf?

ACKNOWLEDGEMENTS

The authors thank Dr Danielle Gambarelli and Brigitte Soubrouillard for helpful comments.

REFERENCES

Albert, M.L., & Bear, D. (1974). Time to understand: A case study of word deafness with reference to the role of time in auditory comprehension. *Brain, 97*, 373–384.

Alzheimer, A. (1907). Über eine eigenartige Erkrankung der Hirnrinde. *Allgemeine Zeitschrift für Psychiatrie, 64*, 146–148.

Alzheimer, A. (1911). Über eigenartigen Krankheitsfälle des späteren Alters. *Zentralblatt für die gesamte Neurologie und Psychiatrie, 4*, 365–385.

Auerbach, S.H., Allard, T., Naeser, M., Alexander, M.P., & Albert, M.L. (1982). Pure word deafness: Analysis of a case with bilateral lesions and a defect at the prephonemic level. *Brain, 105*, 271–300.

Brion, S., Psimaras, A., Chevalier, J.F., Plas, J., Masse, G., & Jatteau, O. (1980). L'association maladie de Pick et sclérose latérale amyotrophique. *Encéphale, 6*, 259–286.

Caselli, R.J., & Jack, C.R. (1992). Asymmetric cortical degeneration syndrome: A proposed clinical classification. *Archives of Neurology, 49*, 770–779.

Déjerine, J., & Sérieux, P. (1897). Un cas de surdité verbale pure terminée par aphasie sensorielle, suivi d'autopsie. *Mem. Soc. Biol., 49*, 1074–1077.

Jakob, H. (1969). Klinisch-anatomische Aspekte bei "reinen" Schläfenlappenfällen Pickscher Krankheit und der basale Neocortex. *Deutsche Zeitschrift für Nervenheilkunde, 196*, 540–568.

Kondo, K. (1978). Motor neuron disease: Changing population patterns and clues for etiology. In B. Schoenberg (Ed.), *Neurological epidemiology: Principles and clinical applications* (pp. 509–543). New York: Raven Press.

Lichtheim, L. (1885). On aphasia. *Brain, 7*, 433–484.

Mesulam, M.-M. (1982). Slowly progressive aphasia without generalized dementia. *Annals of Neurology, 11*, 592–598.

Mesulam, M.-M., & Weintraub, S. (1992). Primary progressive aphasia: Sharpening the focus on a clinical syndrome. In F. Boller, F. Forette, Z. Khachaturian, M. Poncet, & Y. Christen (Eds.), *Heterogeneity of Alzheimer's disease* (pp. 43–66). Springer-Verlag.

Mortara, P., Chio, A., Rossi, M.G., et al. (1984). Motor neuron disease in the province of Turin, Italy, 1966–1980. *Journal of Neurological Sciences, 66*, 165–173.

Neumann, M.A. (1949). Pick's disease. *Journal of Neuropathology and Experimental Neurology, 8*, 255–282.

Onari, K., & Spatz, H. (1926). Anatomische Beiträge zur Lehre von der Pickschen umschriebenen Grosshirnrindenatrophie (Picksche Krankheit). *Zeitschrift für die gesamte Neurologie und Psychiatrie, 101*, 470–511.

Pick, A. (1892). Über die Beziehungen der senilen Hirnatrophie zur Aphaise. *Prager Medicinische Wochenschrift, 17*, 165–167.

Sérieux, P. (1893). Sur un cas de surdité verbale pure. *Revue de Médecine, 13*, 733ff.

Tanaka, Y., Yamadori, A., & Mori, E. (1987). Pure word deafness following bilateral lesions: A psychophysical analysis. *Brain*, *110*, 381–403.

Tissot, R., Constantinidis, J., & Richard, J. (1975). *La maladie de Pick.*, Paris: Masson.

Tomlinson, B.E. (1992). Ageing and the dementias. In J.H. Adams & L.W. Duchen (Eds.), *Greenfield's neuropathology* (pp. 1284–1410). Edward Arnold.

Ulrich, G. (1978). Interhemispheric functional relationships in auditory agnosia: An analysis of the preconditions and a conceptual model. *Brain and Language*, *5*, 286–300.

Vignolo, L.A. (1969). Auditory agnosia: A review and report of recent evidence. In A.L. Benton (Ed.). *Contributions to clinical neuropsychology* (pp. 172–208). Chicago: Aldine.

Wernicke, C. (1874). *Der aphasiche Symptomenkomplex*. Breslau: Cohn & Weigert.

5

Nineteenth-century Accounts of the Nature of the Lexicon and Semantics: Riddles Posed by the Case of Johann Voit

Claudius Bartels and Claus-W. Wallesch
Department of Neurology, University of Magdeburg, Germany.

The beer brewer Johann Voit is probably the most intensively investigated individual in the classical German neuropsychological literature. Two habilitation and at least two doctoral theses have been based on his case. Publications on him span the period from 1884 to 1907. The amount of discussion concerning Voit is equalled only by that conducted about Goldstein's and Gelb's case Schn., in whom the re-evaluation by a commission more than 20 years later suggested that he probably had feigned or exaggerated symptoms in order to gain compensation as a veteran (Jung, 1949).

To a broader neurological public, Voit was first presented in 1885 in the *Archiv für Psychiatrie* by H. Grashey, Professor of Psychiatry at Würzburg University, as a case of "functional aphasia".[1] This paper had considerable influence and led to the acknowledgement of "Grashey's aphasia" as a syndromal entity. The article and comments by Wernicke (1889) were translated for the journal *Cognitive Neuropsychology* by De Bleser (1989).

On 14th November, 1883, the 26-year-old Johann V. suffered a skull fracture when falling from a staircase and was taken to the surgical department of the Juliusspital in Würzburg. He was reported to have suffered from hypacusis for low-pitched tones and tinnitus on the right ear and to have lost the senses of taste and smell. With his right eye he was able to see only hand movements, on the left his visual acuity was two-thirds, but there was a gross concentric visual field reduction. He exhibited right peripheral facial and central hypoglossal nerve palsy and a right sensorimotor hemiparesis. Language disturbance was noted when V. regained consciousness. It was reported that initially he was unable to understand questions. A more detailed assessment made on 28th November was described as follows (Morian, 1885, p. 904ff.):

> The patient required great effort to produce the initial sound in repetition, and when he was able to do so, he got stuck for some time or perseverated, either the initial sound or a whole syllable, continuing until he was able to utter the target word, e.g. "sch—iessen", "F—enster" or "K—K—Kirche", "her—her—herunter", "ad—adieu". Speaking was unimpaired when reading aloud. The patient was almost unable to name object pictures, but could often state the object's function after some consideration (e.g. "it's used for shooting" for a cannon or "it's used for digging" for a spade). In conversation, he suffered from word-finding impairment and resorted to circumlocution. Writing was impaired in a similar way to speaking. Interestingly, he seemed to find words more quickly when writing. When he had written a word up to about its middle, he was frequently able to name it orally. Paraphasias and paragraphias were extremely rare.

In early March 1884 after a failed trial to treat him as an outpatient, Voit was admitted to the psychiatric ward of the Juliusspital, as "the traces of dementia gradually came to light" (Morian, 1885, p. 907). The resident psychiatrist confirmed the language pathology, but in addition found impairments of memory and intelligence. Voit was unable to remember words and commands for more than half a minute. He could perform arithmetical operations only with small numbers, could not read numbers of more than three digits or write numbers of more than five. He was unable to handle money except that he could discern the various coins.

Grashey focused his attention upon Voit's strategy of word finding by writing, still present in August 1884. He studied the patient in August and September. Grashey established that Voit could recognise objects. Without the aid of writing, however, he could neither produce name nor function, nor adjectives relating to properties. "He is able to talk coherently, uses pronouns, modal verbs, prepositions without any difficulties, also some full verbs and adjectives, occasionally even a noun, e.g. after being able to report that he had been to church he was unable to name a picture of a church although easily recognizing the object." (P. 657.)

In most instances, however, Voit used the filler "Dingsda" (that thing) for nouns. Grashey explicitly stated that V. now was unable to name orally function or properties. On the other hand, the patient was able to find the name easily from a number of alternatives in a multiple-choice setting.

Grashey interprets Voit's symptoms on the basis of the model shown in Fig. 5.1. Voit's ability to indicate the name of an object from a multiple-choice array is considered as proof that the centre for object representation (B) must be intact and either the centre for auditory word representations

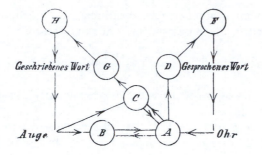

In demselben bedeutet:

A das Centrum für Klangbilder,
B   »   »   » Objectbilder,
C   »   »   » Symbole, d. h. für geschriebene oder ge-
    druckte Buchstaben, Worte und Zahlen,
D das Centrum für die Bewegungsvorstellungen der Sprache,
F die Kerne der Phonations- und Articulationsnerven,
G das Centrum für die Bewegungsvorstellungen des Schreibens,
H Die Kerne der beim Schreiben fungirenden motorischen
    Nerven.

FIG. 5.1   Grashey's (1885, p. 656) model of language processing.

(A) or their mutual connection must be damaged. The intactness of the auditory word centre could easily be demonstrated by the patient's intact comprehension and repetition (he was even able to repeat what nowadays would be labelled "pseudowords"). If, now, both centres A and B must be considered intact, then, in this case, the transmission from A to B would be functional, whereas B to A would be disconnected. Otherwise, a deficit of comprehension would have to be present. Grashey rejects this conclusion and searches for other explanations.

Grashey postulates from considerations concerning written language acquisition a further centre C for symbols such as letters or numbers that is not directly connected with B. Written naming therefore requires transmission from B via A to C. Grashey regards centre C in Voit's case as basically intact, as Voit was able to read words and sentences fluently and with ease, no matter whether he knew the words or not; furthermore, he could match sounds and letters. However, matching spoken with written words was found only possible when the word was constantly repeated, either by the patient or the examiner.

Grashey explains Voit's deficits as resulting from an abnormally rapid decay of sensory perceptions. Therefore, the patient can hold object concepts, auditory or symbolic representations only for short periods of time. This assumption was based on the following findings:

1. Voit could not identify an object as recently seen when it was covered briefly.
2. Spoken words or written letters were instantly forgotten unless permanently repeated.
3. Voit could not assemble words from a sequence of written letters or spoken sounds or recognise object pictures that were presented in successive parts.
4. Voit was able to write spontaneously and to dictation only when permanently repeating the words orally.

Voit's strategy of naming by writing could also be explained on the basis of the rapid decay of images. When confronted with an object he could not name, he looked at the object, wrote down the first letter, looked again, wrote the next one or two letters until he had completed or almost completed the name, and could then produce it orally. If writing material was lacking, he wrote with his fingers in his palm. He could not write the name of an object when it was only briefly presented or when the initial letter he had already written down was covered.

Grashey argues that the sound-by-sound generation of the auditory image of a word would take about 0.06 seconds per letter, whereas the generation of the perceptual object image takes considerably less. If, now, the auditory image decays rapidly, then a word image is never completed. According to Grashey this accounts for V.'s difficulties in number reading as well, because similar to object images (multi-digit) numbers are "momentary images", the parts of which do not correspond to the elements of the auditory or visual word images. On the other hand, an auditorily perceived word image can instantly generate an object image. In naming by writing, the rapid decay of images is compensated for by the external representation.

In conclusion, Grashey argues that repetition, reading, and even spontaneous speech are generally performed by rapid spelling. In more modern terms, Grashey might be interpreted as suggesting that the content of phonemic and graphemic output buffers is processed sequentially from left to right (compare e.g. Marcel, 1980, for the concept of a left–right parser).

According to Grashey, the further course was as follows: Word finding improved by the end of December 1884, and within a fortnight aphasia cleared completely. Simultaneously, the duration of sensory percepts returned to normal.

Wernicke (1886) was much impressed by Grashey's findings and interpretation (De Bleser, 1989, p. 551):

In our consideration on isolated disorders of reading and writing, we have tacitly assumed so far that the word concept itself was unimpaired, in contrast to those cases treated in my earlier contribution on the different types of aphasia. It is now necessary to go into more detail about the word concept and its relation to the letter concept. I was given the most essential insights into this by Grashey's article, and I have no hesitation to claim that it constitutes the most significant contribution to aphasiology in the last ten years. Grashey introduces an entirely novel and—as his work proves—very fruitful element, namely, the time period necessary for the formation of a word as well as for reading and writing it. All these processes require a specific amount of time, and aphasia may be the result of such a reduction of memory that objects or concepts arising via association can no longer be named because they cannot be fixed in memory long enough.

The frequently misused name of amnesic aphasia would seem quite appropriate in this case, since its dependence on a memory deficit has been clearly established. This completely new form of amnesic aphasia will probably not be restricted to the specific symptomatology of this case but is likely to occur in different varieties. (P. 552.)

To summarize. I believe that this remarkable observation should be explained as follows: Grashey's patient has complete preservation of the word concept. He still has access to the object concept as well, but this does not have sufficient intensity long enough to activate the entire word concept, so that only the first temporal component gets activated. (P. 553.)

In the following, Wernicke recounts Grashey's explanation (p. 554):

There are many more aspects of crucial importance in Grashey's case report which should at least be mentioned here, even though the author himself did not pay any further attention to them. When several objects or letters are presented one after the other, the patient always forgets the first one when processing the second. The same patient is able to read fluently, understands everything said to him, and can write words down to dictation. In order to understand a word or sentence, the sounds of several letters or, in the case of sentences, the sounds of several words must remain long enough in the patient's memory for him to grasp their contents. Obviously, the sound images have a much longer duration than the optic images, and in a sense the memory impairment is thus localized insofar as it seems to have predominantly affected the optic region.

Grashey's case leads Wernicke to a revision of his formerly held position, that at least people with a higher educational background were able to understand written words without any mediation of single letters and sounds or auditory word images (Wernicke, 1874, pp. 25–26). He now believes that the cognitive basis for reading and writing is the letter, although he does not accept Grashey's theory of speaking on a sound-by-sound (rapid spelling) basis. This doctrine was widely accepted until the beginning of the 20th century, refuted only by some, e.g. Löwenfeld (1892), who developed an early two-route model for reading and writing. (For a further discussion of Wernicke's state of the art report on German aphasiology of those times see De Bleser & Luzzatti, 1989.)

Voit's symptoms and their interpretation by Grashey were also critically discussed by Sigmund Freud in a separate chapter of his book *Zur Auffassung der Aphasien* (1891). After describing in detail Grashey's findings, Freud gives his own explanation (pp. 41–42):

> For an explanation of Grashey's case, we must assume a localized disturbance, which has to be localized in the centre for auditory word representations, in addition to the general memory impairment. This corresponds to Bastian's second stage of reduced excitability, i.e. a centre does not respond to the normal ("intentional") mode of activation, but is still functional in response to associations and sensory activations. In Grashey's case, the centre for auditory word representations cannot be activated directly from object associations, but still transmits excitations to the reading image (visual word representation) associated with the auditory representation. This representation recognizes the first part (letter) during the short time span the excitation from the seen object is effective. This sequence of actions is repeated until the assembled letters activate the word representation which could not be accessed from the object associations.

Despite his different interpretation Freud awards Grashey's study a "continuing value" (p. 44): "... finally it has irrevocably stated the right point of view for the consideration of disorders of reading by proving that one never reads in a different way but spelling." Almost as a second thought, Freud continues with a reservation (p. 44): "It is probable that with certain ways of reading (at least for certain words) the object image of the whole word contributes to its recognition. This explains that persons who are completely letter-blind, may be able to read their name or a very common word in print (the name of a town, the hospital etc)..."

In 1891, Voit was the object of further investigations when his case was studied extensively by Sommer for his habilitation thesis (Sommer, 1891a). Sommer reports that Voit had meanwhile recovered well and resumed work as a beer brewer. He states (1891a, p. 4) that Voit "had received no compensation from accident insurance for the principal reason that he was not injured at work, so that he would not gain from exaggerations of his condition." Sommer's detailed assessment of Voit gave the following results:

1. Voit still suffers from memory impairment for visual and phonetic perceptions (p. 5). (Sommer, 1891b gives details of the memory

impairment: Voit was found unable to retain visual material for more than a few seconds.)
2. Voit reads with ease (p. 12).
3. Voit still relies on writing movements for naming.

With regard to the third point (p. 6): "These [movements] are usually performed with the right hand on the table. It is of no importance whether or not he looks at his hand. When standing, he writes with his right index finger on his thigh.... If the right hand is restrained, he writes with the left, if both are held, he draws the letters with his feet, always in the common left to right order." Under total restraint of his limbs, Voit was observed to perform writing movements with his tongue. When he had to extend the tongue in addition, Voit was unable to find the target word, state the number of syllables, decide whether a sequence of sounds or syllables belonged to the target, or indicate the initial from a number of alternatives. The last observation is especially important, as Grashey's theory would have predicted that the patient was able to state the initial.

Instead, Sommer assumes a disconnection between the centre of visual object representations and the centre of auditory word representations (p. 9):

> Only via the centre of movement representations there is an indirect connection between the optic centre and the auditory centre. One has to assume further, that the connection from the centre for auditory representations via the centre for script representations to the centre for graphomotor representations is functional in the reverse direction, as Voit gets access to speech sounds by writing.

On the other hand, Voit could judge semantic proximity under restraint, although he was able to find words for the semantic relation only when unbound (Sommer, 1891b). Sommer gives an interpretation of the case that is based on a theory of functional anatomy (p. 22):

> In the optic sphere ... we assume three separate regions for letter, object and digit representations—with corresponding separate acoustic regions for the respective sounds and sound combinations (letter sounds, object names, numbers). The connection between the letter centre and the speech sound centre is preserved, as the patient is able to read fluently. The connection between the centre for object representations and the centre for names is severed, whereas the reverse and supposedly anatomically separate connection from the name centre to the centre for object representations is preserved, because Voit is able to indicate the object for a given name.... It is apparent that [Voit's condition] is basically a very restricted disconnection between the optic and the acoustic sphere.

Sommer points out that, according to the case notes as published by Morian (1885), on the 14th day after injury Voit was observed to produce a word orally with great delay before he wrote. Therefore, Sommer explains the strategy of naming by writing as an act of functional compensation.

In summary, Sommer refutes Grashey's theory of rapid memory decay and proposes a partial explanation on the basis of localisation theory, although being careful to state that the then present localisation theory was unable to explain the symptoms fully.

At the annual conference of the Society of German Psychiatrists in Weimar, 1891, Sommer had the opportunity to discuss the case and his criticism of the recent doctrines of aphasia. With both Grashey and Wernicke being present, Sommer argued in favour of the introduction of psychophysical measurements to aphasiology and the independence of topic diagnosis of brain lesions from explanatory theories of their results (Moeli, 1891). In reply, Grashey pointed out the importance of Voit's transient full recovery for his interpretation and refrains from discussion of Sommer's views, whereas Wernicke turned against the centres and connections postulated by Sommer and questioned the validity of rare single cases for the construction of theories. Wernicke accepts, however, that "there is no causal connection between the massive memory impairment and Grashey's aphasia" (Moeli, 1891, p. 493).

In a note of discussion on Sommer's paper, Pick (1892) argues that the symptoms described by Sommer did not contradict localisation theory but rather strongly supported it. Pick points out that the French literature contains other cases of "moteurs graphiques" in whom the graphomotor image plays a decisive role in the word representation, and also draws attention to the "suppleance fonctionelle" of the French literature, namely that if one component of the word concept is lost, another can replace it, which occasionally may be the graphomotor image.

Voit was again presented to the scientific public in an even more detailed study in 1897 by Wolff, who does not state when he investigated him. Wolff confirms Sommer's finding that Voit was unable to decide whether word fragments belonged to the name of a visually presented target or indicate the initial letter when he was restrained. Wolff advances further support for Sommer's theory that Voit accomplishes word access via writing and rejects Grashey's view that writing is used to preserve an (auditory) word representation (pp. 7–8):

> If Grashey's assumption was correct, namely, if Voit's writing was nothing else than a medium to preserve ... acoustic images, then Voit could only put down what he hears internally. Letters that are not acoustically represented, would be lacking.... Under Grashey's hypothesis, Voit would have to be uncertain about the initial letter when seeing a bird (Vogel), a fish (Fisch) or a

photograph (Photographie); all three objects would result in the same initial acoustic representation. As Voit is claimed not to know the emerging word, he would have no hint as to whether he would have to represent the internally heard sound as an F, a V or a Ph.

As a new aspect of Voit's disturbance, Wolff describes an impairment of imagery (p. 10):

> When asked 'what is the colour of a meadow?', he cannot find it by writing the word 'green'. The question 'what is the colour of sugar?' led to the same result. 'How many legs does a horse have?'. No reply. The same occurs with all visual features or verbally presented objects; he could never give the correct answer.

\Voit also fails to indicate the appropriate alternatives in a multiple-choice array. The patient was unable to state the acoustic, tactile, gustatory, or olfactory properties of a named object. However, Voit had developed strategies to circumvent his deficits (p. 13):

> When asked about the colour of leaves, he goes to the window and tries to look at a tree. This accomplished, he is able to write down the word 'green'. He obviously knows what is required, however, he lacks the sensory image. It is no help for him to see other green objects, he must see green leaves.

> Most impressive was the following example, which demonstrates that the patient knows what is required and how well he understood the target word, but how dependent he is upon sensory perception in order to be able to describe sensory properties. Once I asked him about the colour of blood. He pondered for a long time, looked around, then squeezed out a small pimple until he saw a drop of blood, and now could write down the answer "red". (Pp. 14–15.)

Nonsensory properties were less and only inconsistently impaired ("Does God live in hell?"—'No.'—"Where does he live then?"—"In heaven."—"Does the devil live in heaven?"—"Yes").

Voit is unable to describe nonvisual properties of seen objects. He cannot state the taste of a piece of sugar that is placed on the table unless he puts it in his mouth nor the temperature of boiling water unless by touch.

Naming objects perceived by touch and manipulation only or in response to characteristic noises was markedly impaired. Voit could not even name his own ear when those of all other persons in the room were covered. "However, that the bell tolls, the alarm-clock rattles, he could only state on the basis of auditory perceptions. The word 'thunder' could only be produced on the basis of auditory [perception], the words 'hot' and 'warm' on tactile experience." (Wolff, 1904, p. 6.)

Wolff explains Voit's symptomatology as resulting from a general weakness in the reproduction of images from memory (pp. 32–33):

> It is remarkable that in the case of our patient with respect to all things (we have found only very few exceptions), one sense always plays a predominant role. Only this sense can trigger word access. By the other senses, as we saw, the object can be recognized to a certain extent, but not named. Usually, i.e. for most objects, the visual is this predominant sense. This results from the dominant role of the visual sense in our perception. That the images of various objects are determined to various extents by the various senses, seems conclusive. The image of the rose includes form and colour features, i.e. optic and acoustic images, its scent, an olfactory image, but it contains no acoustic features. The image of a clock includes optic, tactile and acoustic elements ... but no olfactory or gustatory properties. Thus, most object representations contain sensory partial images [sinnliche Teilvorstellungen], each of which suffices in the normal subject to reproduce the complete representation including representations from memory of the other sensory features of the object.... It seems conclusive that the various sensory partial images are not equally important for the representation of the whole object, but that some qualities are more prominent than others depending on the characteristics of the object.

> It is unknown whether a sensory partial image can directly elicit the name representation or whether the other sensory images must be evoked first, or whether one among the partial images is necessary for access to the name and only this one has to be called up from memory, if not perceptually present. (P. 33.)

As Voit is unable to evoke sensory images from memory, he depends on the presence of a sensory perception of the dominant sensory partial image for access to the name.

Analogously, Wolff tries to explain Voit's naming strategy. He argues that, when Voit wrote the words he was searching for in order to gain the images necessary for naming, he got access to sensory perceptual information as well. Therefore, the question arises whether the sensorimotor or the optical image was critical for his oral naming ability. Carefully considering findings in normals and Voit when (mirror) writing under different conditions (such as on his forehead), Wolff concludes that it was probably the image of the writing movement which mediated the oral naming.

Finally (as far as we know), 24 years after his accident, Voit was physically presented to the Wanderversammlung Südwestdeutscher Neurologen und Irrenärzte (an annual conference of psychiatrists) at Baden-Baden in 1907 by Weygandt (Bumke & Rosenfeld, 1907). Weygandt gives reference to a statement of von Monakow, who gave an explanation of the case as one of functional aphasia of traumatic-hysterical origin. The demonstration surprisingly revealed a number of new aspects. Voit appeared physically well, neurological examination revealed a right facial palsy and a brisker knee-jerk on the right. Voit stated that he could speak well except for mild difficulties when excited. He was able to use the public telephone with ease. Occasional word-finding difficulties with empty phrases and filler words ("Dingsda"—that thing) were observed. Speech was accompanied by some facial and hand movements, but writing movements were not detected. Reaction time measurements revealed some slowing. Voit could name sensory properties, superordinates, and could calculate well (e.g. annual profit of 400.–Marks at an interest rate of 4.5%).

Voit described that he had experienced speech deficits initially, so that he had to write down everything, which improved with time and deteriorated again after a second accident in 1895. He also stated that he had used writing with his fingers only when in fear, such as during medical examinations. The town of Würzburg would not have given him burgher's rights in 1889 if he had been incapacitated. A number of witnesses and his work record ("Arbeitsbuch") confirmed that he performed competently at work.

In January 1895, Voit suffered another severe accident when he was hit by a railroad car with fractures of the left arm and a number of ribs on the right, and right lung puncture. According to Voit, the language deficit reappeared and he tried to get compensated from the railroad company. This case was still pending when Voit was demonstrated in Baden-Baden.

Word-finding deficits accompanied by hand and finger movements were still described at a medical examination in 1904. It is pointed out that, as no claims for compensation could be advanced for the first accident, Voit had an interest in minimising the lasting consequences of the first accident. The Baden-Baden conference reached the conclusion that varying combinations of organic impairment and mental (psychologically determined) inhibition could best account for the time course of Voit's symptoms.

DISCUSSION

In an attempt to clarify the issue of Voit, we will take into account the following aspects:

1. Initially, Voit had great difficulty with naming objects and was nonfluent when able to do so. He could often state the function of the target. Reading aloud was preserved. Writing was impaired similarly to speaking, but it was noted that word access tended to be more rapid with writing (Grashey, 1885).
2. According to Grashey, Voit's conversational speech resembled nominal aphasia. Naming of objects, their functions, and properties was highly deficient.

3. In object naming, Voit relied upon graphomotor performance, writing one or two letters at a time and being able to produce the name orally when close to completion (Grashey, 1885).

4. At Grashey's 1884 investigation, a number of findings suggested a rapid decay of perceptions: inability to identify an object as recently seen, rapid forgetting of heard words and letter names, inability to synthesise sequential information. These observations were confirmed by Sommer (1891a) when he investigated Voit five years later.

5. When Sommer investigated the patient (probably 1889 or 1890), Voit was unable to give the name of a target nor give the number of syllables, the initial letter, or state whether a sequence of sounds belonged to the target word when limb and mouth movements were restrained. His findings were confirmed by Wolff (1897). On the other hand, Voit was able to judge semantic proximity when immobilised (Sommer, 1891b).

6. Wolff (1897) pointed out that Voit was able to find the correct among graphemic alternatives related to the same phoneme and that he included letters in writing that were acoustically not represented.

7. Wolff also noted a peculiar reduction of semantic associations. Frequently, only one sensory modality was able to trigger word access.

8. When demonstrated to the Baden-Baden conference in 1907, Voit exhibited mild symptoms of nominal aphasia. He recalled that he had to rely upon writing for word access only when excited.

Voit's symptoms were analysed in various ways, each interpretation biased by the theoretical convictions of its author. The most biased and most influential consideration was Grashey's. His theory is based on three pillars:

● The presence of centres and connections as in Wernicke's (1874) and Lichtheim's (1885) models.

● The acceptance of the letter and the speech sound as the basic units for reading, writing, hearing, and speaking.

● The time course of the generation of mental representations as a possible cause of symptoms of higher mental dysfunction.

The merit of Grashey's contribution lies in the third assumption. He can convincingly demonstrate that Voit indeed suffers from a rapid decay of perceptions. Grashey thus introduces a third mechanism of higher mental dysfunction after Broca's lesion of centres and Wernicke's lesion of connections between centres, which was shortly to be followed by a fourth, Bastian's (1887) concept of diminished excitability. Limited capacity and rapid decay of information transiently stored in buffers or working memory are theoretical concepts related to Grashey's view that are quite popular today (e.g. Caramazza, Miceli, Villa, & Romani, 1987; Ellis, Miller & Sin, 1983).

Grashey's assumption of the central role of the letter in reading and writing had quite devastating effects for mainstream German aphasiology, mainly because it was adopted by Wernicke. Besides observations in written language acquisition and introspection, Voit was the only empirical basis for this theory. Criticisms, such as Löwenfeld's (1892) and in fact the whole French literature in this field went quite unheard. This situation did not improve when the empirical value of Grashey's clinical findings was undermined by Sommer (1891a, 1891b). Contrary to what would be predicted under Grashey's theory, Voit was unable to produce partial information such as the initial when immobilised.

Using the framework of modern theories of language processing, Grashey's interpretation of the speech sound or letter forming the basis of language processing could be specified to apply to the level of phonemic/graphemic input and output buffers, where linear and sequential modes of processing have been suggested (e.g. Caramazza et al., 1987).

Sommer's own interpretation follows the line of the Wernicke–Lichtheim and related models. It contains the interesting possibility that Voit may have established the strategy of naming by writing as a compensatory route, which preempts later concepts mainly of the Soviet school of neuropsychology (e.g. Luria, Naydin, Tsvetkova, & Vibarskaya, 1969). In his discussion of Sommer's interpretation, Pick (1892) draws attention to cases in the French literature of patients with better preserved written than oral naming, a finding re-established repeatedly in the modern literature (e.g. Bub & Kertesz, 1982; Hier & Mohr, 1977).

Besides confirming Sommer's findings, Wolff observed additional deficits of imagery and of modality-specific semantic access. Voit could not describe sensory properties of objects named to him or nonvisual properties of seen objects. He seemed to lack the ability to elaborate a polymodal sensory image related to object representations held in the semantic lexicon. This finding fits well into the literature on mental imagery from Charcot (1883) to Farah (1984).

Naming could be accomplished only when the object was presented to the dominant sensory channel. Wolff's theory is related to modern explanations for category-specific semantic disorders (e.g. Semenza & Bisiacchi, this volume; Warrington & McCarthy, 1983, 1987; Warrington & Shallice, 1984). In fact, Wolff's findings with Voit add another dimension to more recent theories of the representation of semantic concepts. Extending an argument dating back to Lissauer (1890), Warrington and McCarthy conclude that the existence and types of category-specific semantic access deficits indicate the foundation of semantic concepts on differently weighted polymodal sensory associations. Fractionations along prevailing sensory properties are held to explain that only certain categories, e.g. those that include dominant sensorimotor or gustatory features, are affected. In Voit's case, the published data do not indicate category-specific naming problems. His deficits, as described by Wolff, are rather modality-specific access deficits. Assuming extremely weak or even lacking (or rapidly fading?) associations among the different sensory aspects of an object, Wolff's interpretation has considerable theoretical impact. If this speculation on Voit is considered valid, his findings together with modern data on category-specific semantic impairments would strongly support connectionist network models of semantic representations. Modern neuropsychology should look for another Johann Voit.

As the main heuristics used in research on category-specific semantic deficits are word–picture matching, picture naming, and verbal definition tasks, the crossmodal aspects of cases like Voit may escape notice. Perhaps consequently, a comparable case has not been described in the modern literature. In consideration of the potential theoretical importance of a symptom configuration as described by Wolff in Voit's case, future neurolinguistic studies aiming at semantic organisation should include naming tasks across different modalities and/or visual naming combined with controlled cues from other modalities.

Was Voit a malingerer? His 1907 statement that he relied upon writing for word finding only when in fear is plausible. Most aphasics experience symptom aggravation under stress. Voit rather supports Sommer's assumption that writing was used as a compensatory strategy. Both Sommer and Wolff state that Voit's symptoms were most prominent with naming, and that his conversational speech was circumlocutory but functional. We see no contradiction in the acceptance of a mildly aphasic but obviously professionally highly competent beer brewer as a Würzburg burgher in 1889. Also, it is important to note that Voit's 1883 accident was not covered by any insurance and that his symptoms were of little if any consequence for his everyday life as documented by his work record.

In view of their subtle character, it is also highly unlikely that Voit's deficits were caused by hysteria, which may precipitate symptoms at medical examinations as documented in Charcot's cases (Harrington, 1987). However, fear of reproach by or disappointment of the socially vastly superior investigator may have influenced Voit's responses.

All these considerations hamper rather more the validity of the results obtained in the bizarre experiments with the completely immobilised patient and much less Wolff's casual but detailed observations on imagery and semantic access. This today, however, turns out to be the more salient aspect of Voit's symptomatology.

NOTE

1. In the relevant 19th-century German literature the term "functional" in connection with aphasia has quite discordant meanings and connotations. On the one hand in the writings of authors like Kussmaul (1881), Wernicke (cf. Moeli, 1891), or Freud in his aphasia article for the *Handwörterbuch der gesamten Medizin* (Villaret, 1888) it is used to denote dissociative disorders of voice and speech like psychogenic aphonia or mutism, clearly not aphasic disorders *per se*. On the other hand some authors termed cases and symptoms of aphasia as "functional" that did not fit the connectionist schemata developed in these times, and postulated the observed symptoms to be sequels of primarily not language-related disturbances. One example for this use of the term is Grashey, who tries to explain Voit's symptoms by an underlying memory disorder. Others like Störring (1897), refer to "functional aspects" for the explanation of some of Voit's symptoms by assuming a pre-existing physiological disequilibrium between two faculties, which in case of disturbances of both results in a functional dissociation of the subserved functions. One last meaning of "functional" in the literature of those days relates to the effects of a lesion in remote areas as in von Monakow's (1914) concept of diaschisis, which in our days is demonstrated by "functional" imaging methods.

REFERENCES

Bastian, C. (1887, 29th October, 5th November). On different kinds of aphasia. *British Medical Journal*.

Bub, D., & Kertesz, A. (1982). Evidence for lexicographic processing in a patient with preserved written over oral single word naming. *Brain*, *105*, 697–717.

Bumke, O., & Rosenfeld, M. (1907). 32. Wanderversammlung der Südwestdeutschen Neurologen und Irrenärzte in Baden-Baden am 1. und 2. Juni 1907. *Archiv für Psychiatrie*, *43*, 1317–1355.

Caramazza, A., Micheli, G., Villa, G., & Romani, C. (1987). The role of the graphemic buffer in spelling: Evidence from a case of acquired dysgraphia. *Cognition*, *26*, 59–85.

Charcot, J.-M. (1883). Un cas de suppression brusque et isolée de la vision mentale des signes et des objets (formes et coleurs). *Progrès Medical*, *11*, 568–571.

De Bleser, R. (1989). Neurology: Recent contributions on aphasia [Trans. of C. Wernicke, "Nervenheilkunde: Die neueren Arbeiten über Aphasie", *Fortschritte der Medizin* (1886), *4*, 463–482]. *Cognitive Neuropsychology*, *6*, 547–569.

De Bleser, R., & Luzzatti, C. (1989). Models of reading and writing and their disorders in classical German aphasiology. *Cognitive Neuropsychology*, *6*, 501–513.

Ellis, A.W., Miller, D., & Sin, G. (1983). Wernicke's aphasia and normal language processing: A case study in cognitive neuropsychology. *Cognition*, *15*, 111–144.

Farah, M.J. (1984). The neurological basis of mental imagery: A componental analysis. *Cognition*, *18*, 245–272.

Freud, S. (1891). *Zur Auffassung der Aphasien*. Leipzig/Vienna: Deuticke.

Grashey, H. (1885). Über Aphasie und ihre Beziehung zur Wahrnehmung. *Archiv für Psychiatrie und Nervenkrankbeiten*, *16*, 654–688. R. De Bleser. Trans. (1989). On aphasia and its relations to perception. *Cognitive Neuropsychology*, *6*, 515–546.

Harrington, A. (1987). *Medicine, mind, and the double brain*. Princeton: Princeton University Press.

Hier, D.B., & Mohr, J.P. (1977). Incongruous oral and written naming: Evidence for a subdivision of the syndrome of Wernicke's aphasia. *Brain and Language*, *4*, 115–126.

Jung, R. (1949). Über eine Nachuntersuchung des Falles Schn. von Gelb u. Goldstein. *Psychiatrie, Neurologie und Medizinische Psychologie*, *1*, 353–358.

Kussmaul, A. (1891). *Die Störungen der Sprache* (2nd edn.). Leipzig: Vogel.

Lichtheim, L. (1885). Über Aphasie. *Deutsches Archiv für Klinische Medizin, 36*, 204–294.

Lissauer, H. (1890). Ein Fall von Seelenblindheit nebst einem Beitrag zur Theorie derselben. *Archiv für Psychiatrie, 21*, 220–270.

Löwenfeld, L. (1892). Über zwei Fälle von amnestischer Aphasie nebst Bemerkungen über die centralen Vorgänge beim Lesen und Schreiben. *Deutsche Zeitschrift für Nervenheilkunde, 2*, 1–41.

Luria, A.R., Naydin, V.L., Tsvetkova, L.S., & Vibarskaya, E.N. (1969). Restoration of higher cortical function following local brain damage. In P.J. Vinken, & G.W. Bruyn (Eds.), *Handbook of clinical neurology (vol. 3)* (pp. 369–433). Amsterdam: North Holland.

Marcel, G. (1980). Surface dyslexia and beginning reading: A revised hypothesis of the pronunciation of print and its impairments. In M. Coltheart, K. Patterson, & J.C. Marshall (Eds.), *Deep dyslexia*. London: Routledge & Kegan Paul.

Moeli. (1891). Gegenwärtiger Stand der Aphasiefrage. *Allgemeine Zeitschrift für Psychiatrie, 48*, 489–495.

Morian. (1885). Zwei Fälle von Kopfverletzungen mit Herdsymptomen. *Langenbeck's Archiv für Chirurgie, 21*, 898–914.

Pick, A. (1892). Bemerkungen zum Aufsatz von Dr. Sommer "Zur Psychologie der Sprache". *Zeitschrift für Psychologie und Physiologie der Sinnesorgane, 3*, 48–54.

Sommer, R. (1891a). *Ein seltener Fall von Sprachstörung*. Würzburg: Stahl.

Sommer, R. (1891b). Zur Psychologie der Sprache. *Zeitschrift für Psychologie und Physiologie der Sinnesorgane, 2*, 143–163.

Störring, G. (1897). Über den Brashey-Sommerschen Aphasiefall. *Archiv für Psychiatrie, 28*, 607–608.

Villaret, A. (Ed.) (1888). *Handwörterbuch der gesamten Medizin*. Stuttgart: Ferdinand Enke.

Von Monakow, C. (1914). *Die Lokalisation im Grosshirn und der Abbau der Funktion durch kortikale Herde*. Wiesbaden: Bergmann.

Warrington, E.K., & McCarthy, R. (1983). Category specific access dysphasia. *Brain, 106*, 859–878.

Warrington, E.K., & McCarthy, R. (1987). Categories of knowledge: Further fractionations and an attempted integration. *Brain, 110*, 1273–1296.

Warrington, E.K., & Shallice, T. (1984). Category specific semantic impairments. *Brain, 107*, 829–854.

Wernicke, C. (1874). *Der aphasische Symptomencomplex*. Breslau: Cohn & Weigert.

Wernicke, C. (1886). Nervenheilkunde: Einige neuere Arbeiten über Aphasie. *Fortschritte der Medizin, 3*, 824ff.; *4*, 463–482. R. De. Bleser. Trans. (1989). Neurology: Recent contributions on aphasia. *Cognitive Neuropsychology, 6*, 547–569.

Wolff, G. (1897). Über krankhafte Dissoziation der Vorstellungen. *Zeitschrift für Psychologie und Physiologie der Sinnesorgane, 15*, 1–70.

Wolff, G. (1904). *Klinische und kritische Beiträge zue Lehre von den Sprachstörungen*. Leipzig: Veit & Comp.

6

Bodamer on Prosopagnosia

Hadyn D. Ellis
School of Psychology, University of Wales College of Cardiff, U.K.

INTRODUCTION

As Young and van de Wal point out in Chapter 3, studies of patients with a profound inability to recognise previously familiar faces were reported at intervals throughout the 19th century by Wigan (1844), Hughlings Jackson (1872), Charcot and Bernard (1883), and Wilbrand (1892). It was not until 1947, however, that a unique label for this condition was provided. In that year Joachim Bodamer reported his observations made on three brain-injured German soldiers whom he had treated a few years earlier. All three patients revealed pronounced impairments in ability to process facial information and Bodamer gave his paper the title "Die Prosopagnosie", derived from classical Greek and meaning agnosia for faces. Indeed he believed that he had isolated a new subcategory of agnosia—one which was confined to recognising faces. I shall return to this issue later but first let me describe the three cases described in detail by Bodamer. (More complete descriptions are given in the English translation of his paper which Melanie Florence and I published in 1990; Ellis & Florence, 1990.)

Case 1

S. a 24-year-old, was completely blind for a few weeks after his brain injury. When his sight gradually recovered he was found to be achromatopsic. He was also agnosic for some objects and revealed signs of simultagnosia with complex pictures. In addition the patient S. was found to be alexic. His most notable deficit, however, was prosopagnosia, which Bodamer defined as "a disorder of the recognition of faces and, in a wider sense, of expressions". S. revealed what Bodamer believed to be the crucial dysfunction, namely integrating the separate facial features to form the whole physiognomy.

Interestingly S.'s prosopagnosia only became obvious after some time and it required formal tests to confirm it because he had quickly developed compensatory strategies, such as voice recognition, that meant he had no need to identify people by their faces. Presumably, in the restricted hospital setting, an inability to recognise faces was less problematic than it would have been outside. When Bodamer discovered the patient's problem he was able to establish that S. could tell that certain objects were faces, but not to whom they belonged—indeed he was unable to read facial expressions or even distinguish men from women, except by using hair or hat clues. When confronted with his own face in a mirror, S. could not recognise it—nor even be certain of its gender. This inability remained unaltered despite months of exposure to his mirror image. He failed, too, to learn others' faces, apart from occasions where he could use paraphernalia such as glasses or uniform. In fact, when shown a picture of a man's face drawn by Dürer he was only able to recognise it a few days later by the man's cap; when this was obscured on another occasion S. was unable to recognise the face.

Bodamer made another interesting observation when S. was found to be unable to recognise a famous general—yet claimed to be able to generate a clear image of his face, as he said he could for others' faces. Bodamer's tests, however, did not extend beyond noting S.'s assertions that he could visualise faces in fine detail.

S. was found to be unable to distinguish human from animal faces: a dog's face, for example, appeared to him to be that of a human with "funny hair". Not surprisingly, he had difficulties in distinguishing among different animals, such as horses and cows.

On some occasions faces became quite strange—snow white in colour with black areas signifying eyes, mouth, and nostrils and rather two-dimensional in appearance. At other times S. reported related perceptual phenomena. On one occasion the world suddenly became foggy, followed by a brief period when he saw everything more or less as well as he had before his injury—all, that is, except faces.

Case 2

The second of Bodamer's cases was A., who suffered a number of neuropsychological disorders apart from prosopagnosia. These included transient aphasia, slight agnosia, simultagnosia, some loss of colour vision, problems of orientation, apraxia, failure to perceive motion, and problems of appreciating where parts of his body were.

Like S., A. quickly learned to use non-facial clues to identify people—so efficiently, in fact, that he and others were unaware for some time that he could not recognise faces. All faces seemed blurred, except for the eye region, and A. relied upon paraphernalia to recognise people, such as Bodamer himself. Expressions posed the same problem for A. as they had for S.

Although in every respect A. was profoundly prosopagnosic, he was able immediately to identify a photograph of Adolf Hitler, using the moustache and hair parting to do so: a nurse was identifiable by her unusually white teeth. These instances reveal A.'s ability to discern facial details, despite his insistence that apart from the eyes they were all a blur. Moreover, he was able to appreciate configural aspects such as the asymmetry of his own face seen in a mirror.

Case 3

Bodamer's third case, B., was quite different from the first two. A month after his injury, for about eight days, B. reported that all faces were distorted in some way, e.g. the mouth was squint, one eyebrow too high or the nose turned several degrees. Despite these distortions, however, B. was able to recognise people's faces, without fail. His own face was also perceived as being physically altered but the rest of the world seemed quite normal. Thus, the metamorphopsia displayed by the patient B. was specific to faces and, as such, was viewed by Bodamer as reinforcing his belief in the specificity of prosopagnosia to the processing of facial information.

Unfortunately he did not report whether the distortions tended to affect only one half of the face, for, as we shall see, subsequent work on what Critchley (1953) called "prosopometamorphopsia" has generally found the effect confined to the left half of the face (from the viewer's perspective).

PROSOPAGNOSIA POST-BODAMER

Bodamer's observations provided a critical stimulus to 20th-century interest in the phenomena of prosopagnosia and, therefore, we may justifiably consider his 1947 paper to have been seminal. Ironically, it would seem that Bodamer himself was rather less impressed with his achievements: His own subsequent work was spent in psychiatric clinical practice where he developed ideas on existentialism and problems relating to technology. Though he lived until 1985 he was possibly unaware of the impact of his work on prosopagnosia and probably ignorant of the scores of papers on this topic that have been published in the last 46 years, most of which have confirmed his basic observations, and some that have extended them in ways he could not imagine. Moreover, the existence of prosopagnosic patients, rare though they are, has helped to the development of models to account for normal face processing (Bruce & Young, 1986; Ellis, 1986; Hay & Young, 1982).

One of the crucial defining features of prosopagnosia is its specificity: It is a disorder in the ability to recognise faces. Unlike amnesic states, people can be identified by other means: voice, gait, dress, paraphernalia, etc. Two of Bodamer's cases satisfy this criterion: The third, of course, was not prosopagnosic. Though not apparent from these two, it is now thought that there are various categories of prosopagnosia. The most commonly held classification is that first offered by Hécaen (1981). He suggested that there are two types of prosopagnosic: apperceptive and amnesic (cf. De Renzi, Faglioni, Grossi, & Nichelli, 1991). This division can be further refined (Ellis, 1985) but, clinically, there seems little point. Both of Bodamer's prosopagnosics would now be classified as apperceptive because each reported problems with the perception of faces and, in the case of S., transient occasions when all faces assumed the appearance of flat white objects with very dark areas representing internal features.

Because of the perceptual nature of the prosopagnosia revealed by cases S. and A. it is unlikely that either would have shown any covert face recognition. Following, for example, the work of Bauer (1984), Tranel and Damasio (1985), and de Haan, Young, and Newcombe (1987) it is clear that some prosopagnosic patients process facial information to a level below the threshold of awareness. According to Sergent and Signoret (1992a) the capacity of patients to display covert face recognition is inversely related to the severity of their perceptual deficit. Since both S. and A. manifested quite severe perceptual problems it is unlikely they would have been capable of covert face recognition.

Each of Bodamer's prosopagnosic patients complained of being unable to interpret facial expressions. Not surprisingly, he concluded that this ability was coincident with the processes involved in face recognition. We know now, however, that they dissociate and that it is possible for the two deficits to occur independently. Moreover, other aspects of face processing may also dissociate, including lip reading (Campbell, 1989), and the ability to determine where others are looking (Perrett, Hietanen, Oram, & Benson, 1992).

It is worth mentioning that, following the third case, B., who was not prosopagnosic but showed a transient face-specific metamorphosia, there have been a few related cases reported. Grüsser and Landis (1991) described one patient who saw first the left side of her husband's face appear to become swollen and distorted and then her own face in the mirror appeared distorted on the left side. Another of their patients also saw left-sided facial distortions. Related observations were made by Young, de Haan, Newcombe, and Hay (1990) who reported a patient who, when asked to make facial composites using features drawn on acetate sheets, made up faces with obvious left-sided distortions. He also had great difficulty in recognising the left half of either normal or chimeric faces but not for other objects, including car fronts.

Bodamer concluded that all three of his patients presented evidence for the specificity of the mechanisms supporting face processing. This view has been echoed by some (e.g. Ellis, 1981; Ellis & Young, 1989) but denied by others including Damasio, Damasio, and Van Hoesen (1982), who instead prefer to consider prosopagnosia as a problem of within-class discrimination/recognition. It would be inappropriate here to rehearse the arguments for and against the idea of a face-specific processing system, except to point out: (1) it is a fundamental predicate to at least one model of its functional architecture (Ellis, 1986); and (2) there have been reports of fairly "pure" prosopagnosia—i.e. patients whose problems are either virtually confined to faces (e.g. De Renzi, 1986) or who can perform quite amazing feats of within-class recognition such as models of cars while being totally unable to identify faces (e.g. Sergent & Signoret, 1992b). It has to be said, however, that some of the data showing exclusive face recognition deficit may be questioned (Sergent & Signoret, 1992b) and that most cases appear to have additional agnosic problems (Ellis, 1975). On the other hand, the associated difficulties vary from patient to patient and, anyway, one would expect lesions to affect more than one modular system in the brain, making the probability of finding a patient with only loss of face recognition ability almost zero.

Bodamer, understandably, was unable to give precise anatomical details of his patients' injuries. He did report, however, that S. and A. each suffered bilateral injuries in the occipital area. For some considerable time thereafter the received wisdom was that bilateral lesions in the medial occipito-temporal region were necessary for prosopagnosia to occur (e.g. Meadows, 1974; Damasio et al., 1982). More recently, however, various authorities have argued that right hemisphere lesions alone may be sufficient (e.g. Landis, Cummings, Christen, Bogen, & Imhof, 1986; Sergent & Signoret, 1992b). Sergent and Signoret (1992c) also presented PET (position emission tomography) evidence with normal subjects indicating the predominance of right hemisphere activity in most stages of face processing.

The patient S., it was claimed by Bodamer, while unable to recognise faces, none the less could visualise them. The problem with this interesting claim is that no formal tests were made to check the accuracy of his images. When Levine, Warach, and Farah (1985) did test a prosopagnosic patient's claim to be able to visualise faces they found them to be inaccurate: Descriptions from the images often failed quite dramatically to match the real faces. This is consistent with the notion that perception and imagery share common internal representation and that damage to one implies similar problems with the other (Farah, 1988). But, as Behrmann, Winocur, and Moscovitch (1992) have shown, it is possible neurologically to dissociate imagery and perception. They described C.K., a case of severe agnosia with normal imagery capacity as evidenced from his ability to draw objects from memory. Interestingly, C.K. had no trouble recognising faces, even though he could not distinguish visually a dart from a feather duster. As Gurd and Marshall (1992, p. 591) comment, "This pattern of performance constitutes strong evidence for a dedicated face recognition module"—an idea, of course, central to Bodamer's thinking.

In this short chapter I have only been able to outline some of the contents of Bodamer's rather long, dense paper. I have not mentioned, for example, his ideas on the "ocula" or eye region and its role in primitive levels of face processing because there has been little follow-up to this and many of the other ideas he touched upon. In expanding the salient points of his paper I have attempted briefly to show how they have been subsequently developed and, in some cases, shown to be incomplete or plainly wrong. There can be no doubting, however, that Bodamer's paper not only gave us the term prosopagnosia but also showed us the theoretical potential in studying patients with a profound acquired inability to recognise faces.

REFERENCES

Bauer, R.M. (1984). Autonomic recognition of names and faces in prosopagnosia: A neuropsychological application of the guilty knowledge test. *Neuropsychologia, 22*, 457–469.

Behrmann, M., Winocur, G., & Moscovitch, M. (1992). Dissociation between mental imagery and object recognition in a brain-damaged patient. *Nature, 359*, 636–637.

Bodamer, J. (1947). Die Prosop-Agnosie. *Archiv für Psychiatrie und Nervenkrankheiten, 179*, 6–54.

Bruce, V., & Young, A.W. (1986). Understanding face recognition. *British Journal of Psychology, 77*, 305–327.

Campbell, R. (1989). Lipreading. In A. Young & H. Ellis (Eds.), *Handbook of research on face processing*. Amsterdam: North-Holland.

Charcot, J.-M., & Bernard, D. (1883). Un cas de suppression brusques et isolée de la vision mentale des signes et des objets (formes et coleurs). *Le Progrès Médical, 11*, 568–571.

Critchley, M. (1953). *The parietal lobes*. New York: Hafner.

Damasio, A.R., Damasio, H., & Van Hoesen, G.W. (1982). Prosopagnosia: Anatomical basis and behavioural mechanisms. *Neurology, 32*, 331–341.

de Haan, E.H.F., Young, A., & Newcombe, F. (1987). Face recognition without awareness. *Cognitive Neuropsychology, 4*, 385–415.

De Renzi, E. (1986). Current issues in prosopagnosia. In H. Ellis, M., Jeeves, F. Newcombe, & A. Young (Eds.), *Aspects of face processing*. Dordrecht: Nijhoff.

De Renzi, E., Faglioni, P., Grossi, D., & Nichelli, P. (1991). Apperceptive and associative forms of prosopagnosia. *Cortex, 27*, 213–221.

Ellis, H.D. (1975). Recognising faces. *British Journal of Psychology, 66*, 409–426.

Ellis, H.D. (1981). Theoretical aspects of face recognition. In G. Davies, H. Ellis & J. Shepherd (Eds.), *Perceiving and remembering faces*. London: Academic Press.

Ellis, H.D. (1985). Disorders of face recognition. In K. Poeck, H.-J. Freund, & H. Gänshirt (Eds.), *Neurology*. Berlin: Springer-Verlag.

Ellis, H.D. (1986). Processes underlying face recognition. In R. Bruyer (Ed.), *The neuropsychology of face perception and facial expression*. Hillsdale, NJ: Lawrence Erlbaum Associates Inc.

Ellis, H.D., & Florence, M. (1990). Bodamer's (1947) paper on prosopagnosia. *Cognitive Neuropsychology*, 7, 81–105.

Ellis, H.D., & Young, A.W. (1989). Are faces special? In A. Young and H. Ellis (Eds.), *Handbook of research on face processing*. Amsterdam: North-Holland.

Farah, M.J. (1988). Is visual imagery really visual? Overlooked evidence from neuropsychology. *Psychological Review*, 95, 307–317.

Grüsser, O.-J., & Landis, T. (1991). *Visual agnosias and other disturbances of visual perception and cognition*. Basingstoke: Macmillan.

Gurd, J.M., & Marshall, J.C. (1992). Drawing upon the mind's eye. *Nature*, 359, 590.

Hay, D.C., & Young, A.W. (1982). The human face. In A. Ellis (Ed.), *Normality and pathology in cognitive functions*. New York: Academic Press.

Hécaen, H. (1981). The neuropsychology of face recognition. In G. Davies, H. Ellis, & J. Shepherd (Eds.), *Perceiving and remembering faces*. London: Academic Press.

Hughlings Jackson, J. (1872, 4th May). Case of disease of the brain—left hemiplegia—mental affection. *Medical Times and Gazette*, 513–514.

Landis, T., Cummings, J.G., Christen, L., Bogen, J.E., & Imhof, H.-G. (1986). Are unilateral right posterior cerebral lesions sufficient to cause prosopagnosia?: Clinical and radiological findings in six additional patients. *Cortex*, 22, 243–252.

Levine, D.N., Warach, J., & Farah, M. (1985). Two visual systems in mental imagery: Dissociation of "what" and "where" in imagery disorders due to bilateral posterior cerebral lesions. *Neurology*, 35, 1010–1018.

Meadows, J.C. (1974). The anatomical basis of prosopagnosia. *Journal of Neurology, Neurosurgery and Psychiatry*, 37, 489–501.

Perrett, D.I., Hietanen, J.K., Oram, M.W., & Benson, P.J. (1992). Organization and functions of cells responsive to faces in the temporal cortex. *Philosophical Transactions of the Royal Society*, B335, 23–30.

Sergent, J., & Signoret, J.-L. (1992a). Implicit access to knowledge derived from unrecognized faces in prosopagnosia. *Cerebral Cortex*, 2, 389–400.

Sergent, J., & Signoret, J.-L. (1992b). Varieties of functional deficits in prosopagnosia. *Cerebral Cortex*, 2, 375–388.

Sergent, J., & Signoret, J.-L. (1992c). Functional and anatomical decomposition of face processing: Evidence from prosopagnosia and PET study of normal subjects. *Philosophical Transactions of the Royal Society*, B335, 55–62.

Tranel, D., & Damasio, A.R. (1985). Knowledge without awareness: An autonomic index of facial recognition by prosopagnosics. *Science*, 228, 1453–1454.

Wigan, A.L. (1844). *The duality of the mind*. London: Longman.

Wilbrand, H. (1892). Ein Fall von Seelenblindheit und Hemianopsie mit Sectionsbefund. *Deutsche Zeitschrift für Nervenheilkunde*, 2, 361–387.

Young, A.W., de Haan, E.H.F., Newcombe, F., & Hay, D.C. (1990). Facial neglect. *Neuropsychologia*, 28, 391–415.

7 Poppelreuter's Case of Merk: The Analysis of Visual Disturbances Following a Gunshot Wound to the Brain

Glyn W. Humphreys and M. Jane Riddoch
Cognitive Science Research Centre, School of Psychology, University of Birmingham, U.K.

Claus-W. Wallesch
Department of Neurology, University of Magdeburg, Germany.

INTRODUCTION[1]

Over the past ten years, there has been a dramatic increase in neuropsychological research concerned with understanding visual object recognition in general, and the role of visual attention in object recognition in particular. One reason for this increase has been the development of more fully specified theories of visual object recognition and attention than hitherto, plus also the parallel development of neurophysiological research dealing with the properties of visual processing in the brain. Surprisingly perhaps, prior to this more recent expansion of work, there had been few attempts to discuss neuropsychological disturbances of vision in terms of theories of vision and attention, and little discussion of patients who might have been informative for vision theories, apart from the early classic studies carried out at the beginnings of modern neuropsychology. Poppelreuter's report of his patient, Merk, is one such early case that highlights the importance of the interaction between visual attention and recognition for everyday life. The complexity of this case also illustrates the importance of having well-articulated theories in order to understand the interrelated patterns of disturbance that can arise after damage to the visual recognition–attention system.

THE CASE OF MERK

Merk was injured by a gunshot wound to the back of his head in September 1914. The bullet damaged areas of occipito-parietal cortex bilaterally, leaving Merk with several visual and cognitive impairments. He had no marked signs of aphasia (though a minor problem in producing proper names for capital cities and countries is noted), and no problems in memory are discussed. However, he had a severe visual disorientation, finding it extremely difficult to locate and identify almost any visual stimulus. He also had problems in copying, drawing from memory, writing, reading, and in arithmetic operations. Of these problems, we will discuss only those that seem directly related to vision in detail, attempting to locate the impairments in terms of more recent accounts of visual object recognition and attention, and to discuss this case in relation to others documented in the more recent literature.

PROBLEMS IN VISUAL RECOGNITION

Tested by letter chart, Merk had reduced acuity of one-fifth for both eyes. This, however, fails to account for the marked problems he had in almost all visually mediated tasks, including those requiring visual object recognition and those requiring use of visual information to guide behaviour. For example, in tests of simple shape recognition he had problems discriminating between rectangles, squares, and circles, stating only that he saw the shapes as blobs. These problems extended also to difficulties in recognising real objects by sight. He described a cigarette as "something oblong and white ... it could be paper, steel, wood"; he differentiated a man from a woman on the basis of a frock, and described his watch as "I hear the watch and see something white and something like numbers and something like lines." These same difficulties were also apparent in picture recognition. For instance, given a picture of a heart, he named it an apple, saying that it was rounded. Filled-in line drawings seemed to be easier to identify than black and white drawings. Object recognition was also strongly affected by reducing the exposure time, perhaps because it prevented Merk from using some of the non-visual coding strategies discussed later.

Tactile object recognition seemed relatively better than visual object recognition. Thus, when shown a folding rule in vision alone, he said only that it was something long and wooden. Presented tactilely, recognition was immediate. Moreover, recognition often seemed to be achieved by transferring visual information into a motoric code, for example, by tracing his finger, head, or eyes along the contours of an object. Indeed, Merk stated that when tracking along the contour of an object he had to "follow with the tip of his nose." Having tracked the shape of an object, he was sometimes then able to identify it.

These last aspects of the case suggest that Merk not only had problems in visual recognition, but also in visually localising and marking the location of stimuli from vision alone. Normally, we can localise up to about four separate stimuli in the visual field at a glance—an ability termed "subitisation" (e.g. Mandler & Shebo, 1982), and we do not need to make elaborate head or hand movements to track visual locations. We consider these problems in localisation next.

Localisation

Poppelreuter noted that, especially early-on following his lesion, Merk was extremely poor at localising visual stimuli. Poppelreuter described Merk taking 21 seconds to localise and then to discriminate a single vertical line presented at the centre of his visual field. Part of this difficulty was in localising the line in the first place, the other part was in tracing its contour once it had been localised. In another task, Merk was asked to search and to discriminate the number of dots forming an irregular shape (just five dots were present). This took an enormously long time (over 32 seconds), and could not be performed accurately. Merk located one dot after eight seconds, but, having found others present, failed to mark their locations and re-counted elements that he had already counted.

This deficit in localisation was also apparent when Merk attempted to reach to objects under visual guidance. Visually guided reaching was slow, and when Mark was forced to hurry, errors occurred. Also, peripheral stimuli tended to be localised towards the centre of the field.

Visual Fields

Given Merk's deficits in even the simplest visually mediated tasks, it is clearly important to assess whether he has some residual field deficits that prevent him from detecting visual stimuli normally. Several perimetric tests were conducted, with somewhat variable results. Four "zones" of space were separated, according to the types of information Merk could detect. In a central, small zone, Merk was able to detect discrete objects. In a second zone (actually the complete upper halves of both visual fields), shapes were discriminated only as diffuse lights. In a third zone (the upper right quadrant), Merk was described as being able to detect movement without a stable ability to detect stationary targets. In this region of field, Merk was able to identify whether the investigator drew a square or a circle, whilst being unable to perform the same discrimination when shown the same static stimuli. In a fourth zone (upper left quadrant), movement was perceived only as "glitter", and static shape discrimination was also poor.

One of the difficulties in conducting visual tests with neuropsychological patients is in knowing whether any problems are due to a true loss of field, or whether the poor ability to detect visual stimuli is itself a secondary consequence of another deficit. In particular, since in field testing patients may be required to fixate another object in addition to the one they are asked to detect, it is possible that poor performance could be due to the fixated stimulus affecting detection of the non-fixated stimulus rather than being due to poor visual fields per se. For example, recent studies have shown that detection can be improved by removing a fixation point a little time before the presentation of the peripheral visual stimulus (whilst making sure that the patient remains fixated; see Walker, Findlay, Young, & Welch, 1991). As we outline in the next section, Merk had especial difficulties in visual discrimination when presented with competing stimuli within his visual fields. The effects of such competition on the measures of Merk's visual fields should not be discounted.

Visual Attention

Perhaps the most important aspect of the case of Merk was that he showed what has now come to be known as "extinction to double simultaneous stimulation." This represents one of the first cases of "extinction" to be documented. Poppelreuter noticed that, although Merk was able to detect a single object presented either to his left or to his right field, Merk reported that the right field stimulus "disappeared" when a second object was presented simultaneously to his left field. Extinction of the right field stimulus occurred even though, in terms of the identification of individual objects, Merk tended to be better with right field presentations; Poppelreuter also noted that the right field was more amblyopic. It is also interesting for, for Merk, there was extinction of the right-field object, since the subsequent studies have linked extinction to unilateral visual neglect, which shows a left-field/right hemisphere dominance.

Colour Vision

Although Merk appeared to have had normal colour vision prior to his injury, he was reported as having subsequently lost colour vision. He sorted colours according to brightness rather than according to hue.

Depth Perception

One aspect of Merk's visual performance that was noted as remaining relatively good was his depth perception. This was tested simply by asking Merk to make judgements about which of two objects was placed nearer to him (having the objects about 10cm apart, and viewed from about 1m). Although perhaps a little slow (Poppelreuter states that Merk could take between 10 and 15 seconds to make such decisions), performance was accurate. The task was less secure when Merk was asked to carry out monocular judgements.

Drawing and Copying

One frequently used clinical measure of visual perception is to have patients copy drawings of objects they cannot identify. Visual memory for objects can also be tested by having patients draw objects from memory (e.g. Humphreys & Riddoch, 1987a, 1987b). Merk's drawing from memory was extremely limited. He drew only a few primitive shapes (a circle, a rectangle, straight lines), and he was unable to produce an accurate rendition of a cigar. Though his copying was a little better, it was still very limited and cannot be considered normal.

Alexia

Visual disturbances of reading typically go under the heading of alexia which, in extreme cases, can involve patients failing to recognise any visually presented words. This seemed to be true of Merk. Poppelreuter noted that Merk was unable to name even single letters. However, if Merk was allowed to trace around the letters, he was often able to identify the word. For tracing to facilitate identification, Merk also had to move his own hand actively to benefit; there was no improvement from passive movement.

Writing

Similar to his reading, Merk's writing was severely impaired. He was noted only as being able to write his signature, and even then became stuck in the middle of the name and was unable to proceed. Interestingly, he did better if he wrote his name with his eyes closed.

Acalculia

As we shall discuss below, many of the above problems can be linked to impairments of the visual recognition and attention systems. One additional problem experienced by Merk, that does not seem related to any residual visual or attention defect, was acalculia: Merk was severely impaired at making any numerical calculations. Merk failed to write numbers to dictation correctly, for example writing 10,000 as 1000. He could not divide a circle into four, nor could he write down three-digit numbers (writing 326 as 362).

SOME OBSERVATIONS

Consequent on his brain injury, Merk clearly had severe deficits within several areas of cognition, including visual object recognition and attention, reading, writing and mathematical operations. Many of these problems can likely be related to a primary visual disturbance associated with what might be termed visual disorientation and agnosia. From the details provided, it is less easy to be certain about the relations between the visual recognition and attentional disturbances and problems such as poor writing and mathematical operations, though the observation that writing was worse under visual guidance is suggestive of the visual problems playing a causative role even here. It is unfortunate that further testing of spelling (e.g. using oral spelling tests) and of mathematical abilities was not undertaken. Even so, the visual recognition and attentional deficits are important in pointing to the crucial relations between recognition and attention. In addition, some of the dissociations apparent in Merk's ability to process some forms of visual input selectively provide some of the first documented evidence for the modularity of early visual processing in the brain.

VISUAL RECOGNITION, ATTENTION, AND OTHER DISORDERS OF VISION

Normally, visual object recognition takes place within complex environments, in which the visual system has to solve problems of assigning common perceptual features to individual objects. This is a serious computational problem (see, e.g. Marr, 1982), and necessitates that recognition processes co-operate closely with processes that select parts of the image for high-level processing (e.g. Humphreys & Riddoch, 1993); that is, recognition takes place in co-operation with visual attentional processes.

The interaction between visual object recognition and attention remains poorly understood however (e.g. see Humphreys, Riddoch, Donnelly, Freeman, Boucart, & Muller, 1993). In a case such as Merk, we witness some of these complex interactions. Merk may be diagnosed as having a deficit within the sphere of visual attention, since his recognition of visually presented objects was dramatically impaired when two objects were presented simultaneously, relative to when they were presented successively. He cannot be understood as simply having poor perception on one side of space, since, as Poppelreuter noted, single object identification tended if anything to be worse on the left than the right, yet right-field stimuli were extinguished. This observation is important, and enabled Poppelreuter (we believe correctly) to argue that attentional effects on visual processing can be dissociated from poor visual perception per se. Thus, because there exist distinct object recognition and visual attentional systems, problems in visual attention (associated with right field presentations) can be distinct from those involved in object recognition (associated with left-field items).

Several ways of understanding attentional disturbances of vision have been suggested. One, due to Posner and his colleagues (e.g. Posner, Walker, Friedrich, & Rafal, 1984) is that patients can have problems disengaging their attention once attention has been captured by an object. In Merk's case, we may presume that he has difficulty in disengaging attention from left-field stimuli in order to detect stimuli simultaneously present on the right. An alternative is that there is competition between simultaneously presented stimuli in order that one is selected as the object for action (Allport, 1987). Right-field stimuli may be less effective in attracting attentional resources to themselves, relative to left-field stimuli, and so suffer extinction (cf. Bundesen, 1990; Duncan & Humphreys, 1989). Such accounts remain difficult to disentangle to this day, though some attempts have been made by, for example, independently varying the salience of stimuli presented either in isolation in each visual field or simultaneously in both (Humphreys & Riddoch, 1993).

Since Merk's case was first documented, we have also learned an enormous amount about the neurophysiology of the visual system. One distinction that has had a considerable influence over theories in the last 10 years was drawn up by Ungerleider and Mishkin in 1982. They proposed that, within the cortex, two different visual "routes" could be separated: one, running from the occipital to the temporal cortex, concerned with pattern recognition; one running from the occipital to the parietal cortex, and concerned with spatial localisation. Ungerleider and Mishkin termed these the "what" and the "where" systems. Given the site of Merk's lesions, we can expect him to have a problem within the "where" system. This is consistent with his behaviour and, in particular, with his severe problems in visual localisation. However, it is difficult to know the extent to which poor spatial localisation interacts with the attentional deficit apparent in this case. For example, in tasks requiring Merk to locate a series of dots, it is possible that there was extinction due to competition between at least some of the dots, rendering localisation difficult.

Attention also interacts with object recognition. When the limits of normal performance are explored, it has been consistently found that people fail to identify more than one object at a time (e.g. Duncan, 1984). Thus, inputs into the object recognition system appear to be influenced by attentional operations that constrain the amount of information to be dealt with at any one time. One exception to this apparent limit on identifying more than one thing at a time is subitisation, the ability to count up to four or so items with little cost to performance. Yet even here there is evidence suggesting that performance depends on recognising the patterns made by the stimuli. With up to four items, the relations between the items can be described in terms of a simple and discriminable shape (a triangle, a square, etc.); when larger sets of items are consistently presented in regular and discriminable patterns, subitisation can be shown to occur across the larger sets (Mandler & Shebo, 1982). Interestingly, we noted in the case report that Merk was impaired at subitisation. It is conceivable that such problems may be related to abnormal attentional effects on visual pattern recognition. For example, due to competition even between the different parts of simple visual stimuli, Merk's attention could be drawn to small parts of an object, making it then difficult for him to perceive the object's identity. Alternatively, Merk might also have a primary disturbance in visual object recognition, in addition to the impairment in visual attention. In 1968, Efron documented the case of a patient who, following brain damage due to carbon monoxide poisoning, had severe impairments in visual object recognition. These deficits were characterised by poor shape identification, although other aspects of visual processing, such as colour perception, were intact. Efron devised a test requiring shapes to be matched, with shapes on different trials still being matched for brightness (e.g. subjects would have to discriminate between two squares and a square and a rectangle, which covered the same overall area). He reported that his patient was specifically impaired on shape matching, although the patient could report the basic dimensions of the shape. This same deficit has been reported in several subsequent agnosic patients (e.g. Warrington, 1985), and has been interpreted as being due to a basic deficit in shape processing, which, in turn, generates visual agnosia for objects. Merk's problems in identifying very simple shapes such as squares, circles, and rectangles, might today be interpreted in terms of a fundamental deficit in shape perception. The extent to which this holds true may be ascertained by examining shape perception under conditions which vary both the attentional demands of performance plus the shape discrimination requirements (e.g. using shapes presented in isolation and simultaneously).

One reason for suspecting a difference between Merk and the so-called "shape agnosic" patients (cf. Humphreys & Riddoch, 1987b; Warrington, 1985) is that shape agnosic patients, typically with brain damage following carbon monoxide poisoning, have nearly all shown intact colour perception (Benson & Greenberg, 1969; Campion, 1987). Cases of cortical achromatopsia are relatively rare, and in many cases there can be higher-level deficits in object and face perception (Meadows, 1974), though this is by no means always the case (Heywood, Wilson, & Cowey, 1987). Merk's case illustrates that brain damage can lead to selective losses in colour perception, with the patients then responding to brightness rather than to hue. By association, it also suggests that Merk's problem in simple shape perception was unrelated to the deficit in colour perception since, in other, similar patients, the two problems can dissociate.

Holmes (1918) also noted cases of visual disorientation in soldiers in World War I who had suffered gunshot wounds bilaterally to posterior parts of the brain. Holmes noted that such patients were typically grossly impaired in negotiating their visual environments, and in reaching to and avoiding unsuitable objects. However, they also differed from Merk in at least one important respect. Holmes reported these patients as having grossly impaired depth perception. He noted that such patients were typically unable to carry out even simple tasks such as those involving same–different discrimination between shapes varying only in distance (such as those reported with Merk). This was not confined to computing depth from monocular depth cues since, in Holmes's cases, the interpretation of all forms of visual depth cue seems to be impaired. Merk, in contrast, performed relatively well with binocular cues. Merk's case shows that impaired depth perception does not necessarily occur in cases of visual disorientation, nor is impaired depth perception necessarily linked to other visual recognition or attentional impairments. Impairments in depth perception can be dissociated from problems in visual recognition, attention, localisation, and even colour perception. This is consistent with early visual processes being modular for these different forms of visual computation (for colour, depth, location, and so forth).

One other fact apparent in Poppelreuter's study of Merk is the dissociation between impaired detection of static stimuli in certain parts of his visual field, along with good perception of movement. A similar dissociation was first documented by Riddoch in 1917, again with gunshot-wound victims. Subsequently, this and other effects have been reported as phenomena characteristic of "blindsight" (Weiskrantz, 1980, 1986). The term blindsight is used to refer to patients who have a field defect when measured used static perimetric procedures, typically due to a lesion of the primary occipital cortex. Despite this, and despite denying that stimuli presented to their "blind" field create any sort of conscious experience, such patients can be shown to discriminate certain visual properties within the blind field. In particular, they can discriminate movement. They are typically also able to discriminate the location of stimuli, pointing correctly to the location of targets even whilst concurrently claiming that they are guessing. We note the good localisation of stimuli presented in the blind field for such patients by way of a contrast with Merk who, as we have already remarked, showed poor localisation. In other patients with visual disorientation, however, it has been noted (Holmes, 1918) that localisation (measured by pointing) can be better when under proprioceptive than under visual guidance. A patient may be able to point reasonably accurately to their own nose, but show gross mislocalisation when asked to point to the nose of an examiner sitting directly opposite them. Although not noted with localisation, in other aspects of Merk's case it is apparent that performance is better without relative to with vision (e.g. in writing). Paradoxical though it may appear, it is possible that, if Merk had been required to point without conscious visual guidance, his performance might have improved. In blindsight cases, it is often argued that, despite the loss of cortical vision in one area of field, the patients have an intact subcortical visual route, involving pathways from the retina to the superior colliculus. Collicular cells can be used to discriminate movement and to localise visual stimuli. If Merk had had an intact collicular visual pathway, then localisation might have taken place in conditions where his behaviour was not determined by what appeared to be a grossly deficient cortical (presumably occipito-parietal) pathway.

READING, WRITING, AND ARITHMETIC

As we noted earlier, the relations between Merk's visual disturbances and other aspects of his case are more difficult to evaluate. In other patients with visual disorientation, a range of reading behaviours have been apparent. In some, the reading of single words has appeared to be intact (Coslett & Saffran, 1991). In others, reading appears to operate at a single letter level (Price & Humphreys, in press). From this range of behaviours, it is tempting to conclude that there is no consistent relationship between disorders of visual object recognition and attention and visual aspects of reading. However, such a conclusion would be premature, since the precise disturbances of object recognition and attention in at least some of these patients has been shown to differ. For some, visual processing seems limited when multiple elements are present in the field, leading to deficits with both word and object recognition. The identification of individual letters, however, may be relatively unaffected. If, on the other hand, the problem is one of attentional disengagement, then patients may identify single objects relatively well (including single words), but are then poor at identifying more than one object (this would include the letters making up the word). To understand fully the relations between object and word processing requires more detailed studies, which focus on whether object and word processing are affected in similar ways by common variables (such as exposure duration).

For the reported problems in writing and arithmetic, it seems more plausible to conclude that there is no relation with the impairments of object recognition and attention. At least in part, this judgement is based on the lack of computational relations between the different tasks, as well as on dissociations between patients. Nevertheless, there are clearly circumstances in which writing (and also copying and drawing) depends on visual feedback, and Merk's case illustrates that performance may be particularly disordered under that circumstance. Visual disturbances can pervade everyday life in numerous ways.

ACKNOWLEDGEMENTS

This work was supported by grants from the Human Frontier Science Programme and from the Medical Research Council, U.K.

NOTE

1. The case of Merk is reported in Poppelreuter, W. (1923) Zur Psychopathologie und Pathologie der optischen Wahrnehmung. *Zeitschrift fur die gesamte Neurologie und Psychiatrie, 83*, 86–152. Poppelreuter's main work has been published in translation in Poppelreuter, W. (1917/1990). *Disturbances of lower and higher visual capacities caused by occipital damage.* (J. Zihl with L. Weiskrantz Trans.). Oxford: Clarendon Press.

REFERENCES

Allport, D.A. (1987). Selection for action: Some behavioural and neurophysiological considerations of attention and action. In H. Heuer & A.F. Saunders (Eds.), *Perspectives on perception and action.* Hillsdale, NJ: Lawrence Erlbaum Associates Inc.

Benson, D.F., & Greenberg, J.P. (1969). Visual form agnosia. *Archives of Neurology, 20*, 82–89.

Bundesen, C. (1990). A theory of visual attention. *Psychological Review, 97*, 523–547.

Campion, J. (1987). Apperceptive agnosia: The specification of constructs and their use. In G.W. Humphreys & M.J. Riddoch (Eds.), *Visual object processing: A cognitive neuropsychological approach.* Hove, U.K.: Lawrence Erlbaum Associates Ltd.

Coslett, H.B., & Saffran, E. (1991). Simultanagnosia: To see but not two see. *Brain, 114*, 1523–1545.

Duncan, J. (1984). Selective attention and the organization of visual information. *Journal of Experimental Psychology: General, 113*, 501–517.

Duncan, J., & Humphreys, G.W. (1989). Visual search and stimulus similarity. *Psychological Review, 96*, 433–458.

Efron, R. (1968). What is perception? *Boston Studies in Philosophy of Science, 4*, 137–173.

Heywood, C.A., Wilson, B., & Cowey, A. (1987). A case study of cortical colour "blindness' with relatively intact achromatopic discrimination. *Journal of Neurology, Neurosurgery and Psychiatry, 50*, 22–29.

Holmes, G. (1918). Disturbances of vision by cerebral lesions. *British Journal of Ophthalmology, 2*, 353–384.

Humphreys, G.W., & Riddoch, M.J. (1987a). *To see but not to see: A case study of visual agnosia.* Hove, U.K.: Lawrence Erlbaum Associates Ltd.

Humphreys, G.W., & Riddoch, M.J. (1987b). *Visual object processing: A cognitive neuropsychological approach.* Hove, U.K.: Lawrence Erlbaum Associates Ltd.

Humphreys, G.W., & Riddoch, M.J. (1993). Interactions between object and space vision revealed through neuropsychology. In D.E. Meyer & S. Kornblum (Eds.), *Attention and performance (Vol. 14).* Hillsdale, N.J.: Lawrence Erlbaum Associates Inc.

Humphreys. G.W., Riddoch, M.J., Donnelly, N., Freeman, T.A.C., Boucart, M., & Muller, H.M. (1993). Intermediate visual processing and visual agnosia. In M.J. Farah & G. Ratcliff (Eds.), *The neuropsychology of high-level vision.* Hillsdale, NJ: Lawrence Erlbaum Associates Inc.

Mandler, G., & Shebo, B.J. (1982). An analysis of its component processes. *Journal of Experimental Psychology: General, 111*, 1–22.

Marr, D. (1982). *Vision.* San Francisco: W.H. Freeman.

Meadows, J.C. (1974). Disturbed perception of colours associated with localised cerebral lesions. *Brain, 97*, 615–632.

Posner, M.I., Walker, J.A., Friedrich, F.J., & Rafal, R.D. (1984). Effects of parietal injury on covert orienting of visual attention. *Journal of Neuroscience, 4*, 1863–1874.

Price, C.J., & Humphreys, G.W. (in press). Reading in simultanagnosia. *Neuropsychologia.*

Riddoch, G. (1917). Dissociation of visual perceptions due to occipital injuries, with especial reference to appreciation of movement. *Brain, 40*, 15–57.

Ungerleider, C.G., & Mishkin, M. (1982). Two cortical visual systems. In J. Ingle, M.A. Goodale, & R.J.W. Mansfield (Eds.), *Analysis of visual behavior.* Cambridge, MA: MIT Press.

Walker, R., Findlay, J.M., Young, A.W., & Welch, J. (1991). Disentangling neglect and hemianopia. *Neuropsychologia, 29*, 1019–1027.

Warrington, E.K. (1985). Agnosia: The impairment of object recognition. In J.A.M. Frederiks (Ed.), *Handbook of clinical neurology: Vol. 1. Clinical neuropsychology.* Amsterdam: Elsevier Science.

Weiskrantz, L. (1980). Varieties of visual experience. *Quarterly Journal of Experimental Psychology, 32*, 365–386.

Weiskrantz, L. (1986). *Blindsight: A case study and implications.* Oxford: Oxford University Press.

8

Wilbrand's Case of "Mind-blindness"

Mark Solms and Karen Kaplan-Solms
Neurosurgical Unit, London Hospital Medical College, Royal London Hospital (Whitechapel), U.K.

Jason W. Brown
Department of Neurology, New York University Medical Center, U.S.A.

INTRODUCTION

In this chapter we present an English translation of Wilbrand's (1887) celebrated case report of "mind-blindness" and discuss its implications for contemporary neuropsychology. Following the observations of Ferrier (1876) and Munk (1878, 1881), only a handful of human cases of "mind-blindness" had been described by the time Wilbrand published this report (Charcot, 1883; Finkelnburg, 1870; Hughlings Jackson, 1872, 1876; Mauthner, 1881; Quaglino & Borelli, 1867; von Monakow, 1885; Wigan, 1844). In addition to the purely historical interest which therefore attaches to this case, the rationale behind the present chapter is the following.

Due to the development of the concepts of agnosia (Freud, 1891; Lissauer, 1890), topographical agnosia (Paterson & Zangwill, 1945), and prosopagnosia (Bodamer, 1947), and due also to an error in an abridged translation of Wilbrand's case report (Critchley, 1953), a misapprehension as to the essential nature of the disorder in this case has arisen in the literature. This has resulted in an error in contemporary nosography which stands in need of correction. Furthermore, it was widely recognised in the early literature that Wilbrand's case contradicted a fundamental premise of Munk's (1881) theory of mind-blindness. This development has since been forgotten, partly as a result of the nosographic error mentioned above, and partly because the critical case report is not accessible to English-speaking readers. Discredited aspects of the older theory have therefore found their way back into the modern literature. These oversights have contributed to a number of interrelated misconceptions in contemporary theory, which now requires critical re-evaluation.

TRANSLATION OF WILBRAND'S 1887 CASE REPORT

Fräulein, G., a 63-year-old, very intelligent gentlewoman, had previously been in good health. In particular, she was always in possession of good visual capacities.

On 8th March, 1881, suddenly and without prodromal signs, as she stood up, the patient collapsed unconscious. When she came to, several hours later, she found herself in a curious state about which she is unfortunately no longer able to give precise information. Nothing can be learned from her social milieu either, nor from the attendant physicians, for all the people who were in close contact with her at that time have unfortunately died in the interim. All that she is aware of is that she lay in bed for several weeks in a state of fevered agitation, that she was unable to recognise her physician during that period, and that she was regarded as blind by all those around her. She was, however, quite aware that she was not completely blind, "for when people stood at my bedside and spoke with pity of my blindness, I thought to myself: you can't really be blind because you are able to see the table-cloth over there, with the blue border, spread out on the table in the sick-room."

Furthermore, she knows with certainty that after she recovered consciousness she understood everything that people around her were saying, both to her and to each other, and that no hemiplegic symptoms or disturbances of facial musculature or speech were present.

When this—in other respects highly intelligent—lady got up, she found herself in a curious state of not seeing and yet being able to see, which she called a dream-state and which she could only sketch in vague terms. However, she remembers clearly that her field of vision was severely restricted (as, indeed, it continued to be for several years); on the whole, she could only recognise things straight ahead of her and upwards whilst nothing at all could be perceived to the right, sideways to the left and left-downwards. Whereas the loss of vision in the left visual hemi-field persisted, the visual field on the right side was to recover gradually over a period of two years.

In addition, the patient also mentions an occasion during the first weeks of her convalescence when she mistook a dog for the physician that was treating her at the time, and an occasion when the maid-servant called her to eat while she was sitting in the garden, and she said to her company: "there comes the dinner table." This sort of mistake is said to have been a frequent occurrence at that time. From then to the present day, our patient's topographical memory for the city of Hamburg (where she was born and raised), for its streets and squares, even for her own home in places, has been severely defective. Still today she is moved when she recalls her first excursion after the stroke; how absolutely different and completely strange the city appeared to be, and how extremely distressed and shaken she felt when she was led by her attendant for the first time over the Jungfernstieg and the Neuenwell to the Stadthaus, and how the attendant indicated afresh to her the buildings and streets that were usually so familiar. She reports her reaction to the woman that was her escort at the time as being: "if you say that that is the Jungfernstieg, and that the Neuenwall, and this the Stadthaus, then I suppose it must indeed be so, but I do not recognise them." However, her recollection of that period is very poor and it was only possible to gather together the individual fragments of memory from that period by persistent questioning and frequent conversations.

Currently our patient is less disturbed by the restriction of her visual field than by the striking, strange alteration in the impression that is made by old and familiar retinal images. She knows the places of old and yet they are completely strange to her; and because she is no longer able to find her own way around the streets of her home-town, she lives a very secluded life, leaving her home but seldom and never without an escort. Four years after the apoplectic attack, from 10th February, 1885 onwards, her status was recorded as follows.

Female patient; a 64-year-old, slightly stooped, intelligent gentlewoman, provides precise details about her *present* condition. At the moment, she corresponds extensively and, moreover, in several foreign languages. She has always applied herself passionately to the study of foreign languages and especially to correspondence therein. She speaks German, French, English and Danish, and understands Spanish. She has always had a vivid fantasy-life. She could picture to herself entire fairy-tales and stories, and these so vividly that during the fantasies she was "often afraid of going mad." She was told as a child that she grew on a tree and was picked by the stork. Still today, these optical images derived from her childish fantasies appear before her eyes with the greatest vivacity. Before her illness she dreamt a great deal in pictorial images, now she dreams almost not at all anymore. Recently however she once again saw the image of her late sister in a dream.

She is still today able to recite all the poems that she learned in her childhood. She was not particularly talented in drawing, but she could sew well and produced fine embroidery.

Neither motor nor sensory paralyses can be demonstrated at present. Her speech is perfectly clear and correct.

Here we wish to reproduce verbatim the following account of the history of her illness, provided by the patient herself, still unadulterated by my questions:

On 8th March 1881 I arose in, to my mind, perfectly good health. As I went to the washing-basin, I collapsed; I wanted to stand up again, but was no longer capable of doing so. I collapsed again and became completely unconscious; I regained consciousness again, after an indeterminate period of time, lying on my bed, surrounded by my entire domestic staff. How I came to be in bed, and who helped me on to it, I do not know. I was told that I was ill and that the physician was on his way. I do not remember seeing the doctor at the time, nor during the ensuing weeks when he visited daily. For several weeks I lay in a state of high fever, recognising no-one and fantasizing constantly. However I know this only from hear-say. I know that I later mistook animals for people and my maid-servant for a dinner-table, but I do not know when it was that this occurred. Then follows a long period of time about which, again, I no longer have any knowledge. The first event thereafter that I am able to recall concerns a short stroll that I undertook on the arm of my attendant. Thus I improved gradually, but my recollection is very patchy. By the summer of 1882 I was reasonably well, about that I am quite certain, and from then onwards things slowly improved up to my present state.

The specific dates in the history of her illness do not occur to her spontaneously, but still she provides good information—to the extent that she is able—if one aids her memory by putting questions to her.

Investigation of the eyes, conducted on 10th February, 1885, yielded bilaterally normal ophthalmoscopic findings, bilaterally normal visual acuity and normal sense of colour recognition. Together with this, however, there existed a left-sided incomplete homonymous hemianopia, as well as a hemianopic defect in the inferior octants of both right visual hemi-fields (see Fig. 8.1). Within the defective left visual hemi-field there was a zone in which luminosity only, and neither form nor colour, could be recognised. In the upper defective region of both left visual hemi-fields, sensation of light was in every respect absent. The pupils were equal and reactive to light; no restrictions of movement in the ocular musculature could be demonstrated.

Visual acuity was normal bilaterally. The patient could read script and print accurately and fluently with the aid of a pair of convex glasses. She wrote faultlessly to dictation. In the transcription of numbers, from 1 to 100 (without dictation), and in transcribing the alphabet, the figures and letters were produced without omissions and in the appropriate order. However, since the stroke she frequently omits individual words within the sequence of a sentence in her letters, or writes them down twice—for example: "I would like to see you, to see you," or "I would like—[to see you]." What is most

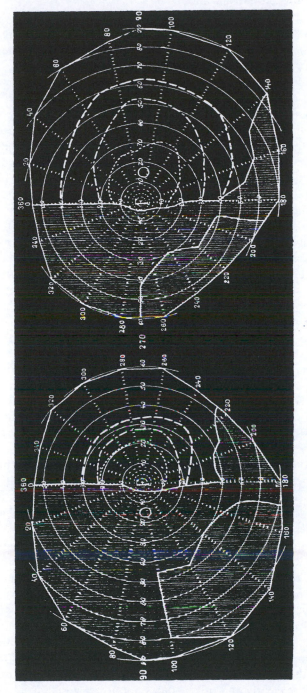

FIG. 8.1 (Reproduced from the 1892 version of Wilbrand's paper.)

93

distressing to her is the circumstance that, since her illness, she repeats out loud all that she thinks in silence. Yet, in reading and writing she does not follow the words with articulatory movements of the lips.

She can identify accurately the meaning of individual gestures—for example, that of the flautist.

She is unable to say whether or not aphasic phenomena were present during the initial period following the stroke, nor is she able to specify when she regained the ability to read and write. In general, she now finds it much easier to make herself understood by writing than by the spoken word (but this is not noticeable objectively). Although the mobility of her hands and fingers leave nothing to be desired, and although she proudly draws attention to the ease with which she is able to write, she has by contrast lost completely the ability to sew and produce needlework. "When I sew nowadays," she says, "my work looks as if it was produced by a child; the stitches are irregular, I insert the needle in places that I shouldn't, etc."

Despite the fact that the patient was born in Hamburg, and that in her healthy days she had a detailed knowledge of its topography, today it is impossible for her even to find her approximate bearings in the street. "I could ([she wrote on] 17th June, 1885) bring a good many streets to mind—for example, I recently went with my escort along X. Street, and I knew that Dr. Y. lived there, but to find my way independently to that street, or even to have said where one begins and where one ends up, was an impossibility for me."

The image of her later paternal home, in which she lived for a good 25 years, has disappeared completely from her mind, whereas the representation of the house in which she lived long ago during her childhood is preserved completely. On the whole, her childhood impressions are still very much alive to her.

In earlier times she travelled frequently and she had occasion often to be in Copenhagen. "If I close my eyes now and cast myself back to Copenhagen, I see the streets quite clearly before me, and I see in my mind the castles on the mountains along the Rhine—but now when I stand with open eyes and survey any city or any neighbourhood, then I have no idea where I am. I could quite well walk through Hamburg in my mind, and with my eyes closed, but when I actually stand in the street I don't know which way to turn again. With my eyes shut I see my old Hamburg in front of me again, or at least I see a good part of many streets."

To her, everything that she sees has "taken on an unfamiliar, strange character." Even the individual pieces of furniture in the room in which she presently lives appear to her to be different than before, "to me it is no longer the familiar impression that they make, it's a strange one." What it is that creates the awareness of this difference she cannot say, for she sees everything quite clearly and often boasts about her good visual capacities.

The following circumstance often gives rise to great concern about madness: when she enters her room from out of doors, her own room appears so strange and curiously odd to her that she believes she has come upon a strange space that belongs to somebody else. At one point, so she says:

> I said to my physician: "The conclusion may be drawn from my condition that man sees more with the brain than with the eye, the eye is but the vehicle for sight; because I see absolutely anything quite clearly and lucidly, but I do not recognise it, and frequently I do not know what the thing that I am seeing could be."—"At that time I saw everything in my room, and I even knew, for example, that that display cabinet over there was the cabinet that I inherited, for it stands in precisely the right place in my room and my staff tell me that it is my old display cabinet; but in my head I just will not accept it, it makes such a strange impression on me. Indeed, even I myself look different in the mirror than before, I just do not look familiar to myself anymore. I swear to you, when I look at myself in the mirror I cannot believe that that could be *me*, I just do not look familiar. However, people say that they still recognise me and that my appearance has not changed; I cannot fathom it—it seems I am going quite mad."
>
> I detect little or no distinction in the physiognomies of people I knew previously. And people whom I have got to know since my illness leave absolutely no pictorial impression in my memory anymore. When I encounter them in the street in the morning, I do not recognise them.

Asked about the persistence of auditory impressions, she answers as follows: "I am quite able to recall to mind the sound of voice or the dialect of my visitors and could easily recognise them thereafter." Her lady friends report that in the initial period after she fell ill, too, before she had been up again for very long, she recognised nobody when they entered the room. However, if she asked "who's there?", and heard just one sound from the caller, then she recognised her visitor immediately. Still today she will often fail to notice someone if they linger in her room (homonymous hemianopia!).

> It has often struck me that, since my illness, I have a sharper and more reliable sense of hearing than before. My hearing really has improved noticeably.
>
> In regard to the sense of time, I find that I am still unsure. Something which has apparently happened 10 minutes ago, feels to me as if it occurred three hours ago or more already. On one occasion, when my sister had not visited me for eight days, I reproachfully asked her why she had not once looked me up in six weeks; I could not pass the time, everything seemed to be carrying on into infinity. If you have just been with me, I would not know after the passage of an hour whether it was today, yesterday or the day before yesterday that I had received you.

Optical images were evoked promptly by specific stimuli from the realm of the other senses, at least in so far as individual, everyday objects were concerned. Thus, my pencil, when placed in her hand with the eyes closed, immediately evoked the pictorial image of the same, and the smell of petroleum evoked the pictorial-image of her lamp.

If one asks the patient about a route, the direction and the streets which are to be passed from her home in order to reach a designated place in the city, she replies: "That I do not know, that I cannot do, I have tried so often in vain."

When she closed her eyes, it was as if it was easier for her to orientate herself in her mind, "then everything is as it was before; reality (the sight of the environment) confuses me, I am able to live better in ideas than in reality"—and in fact she did orientate herself better if she would close her eyes and then describe a route to somebody.

Since the stroke, she is unable to find her way around her chest of drawers and her linen cupboard. She is bewildered by the sight of a large number of things on the table—for example, bottles, glasses and a basket of breadrolls. The sight of her open wardrobe or laundry basket bewilders her. She is in fact able to see the individual pieces of laundry in the cupboard perfectly well, and yet she still needs to call her maid to help if she wishes to find something in it. This bewilderment is also provoked by stepping onto the street and by the sight of a large number of people—as if, in general, by the total effect of different and simultaneous retinal impressions on the eye.

As a result of this bewilderment, and the "anxiety" that it gives rise to, the patient avoids attending concerts, churches, theatres, and receptions. She tells of an occasion, long ago, at a wedding in a church, when the sight of such a large number of people bewildered her so much that she found it necessary to close her eyes.

She always goes down stairs backwards, because she becomes bewildered and dizzy at the sight of the large number of steps when she descends with her vision directed in front of her.

The patient reports further that she frequently suffers from states which she calls "inverted thoughts". Thus, the idea occurred to her, and gripped her fleetingly, that the street was in the place of her bedroom, adjoining her sitting-room. Also, for example, when she had just been rummaging through her wardrobe in her bedroom, had locked it, and had resumed sitting in her usual place near the window in the sitting-room, she was possessed by the idea, something like as if her wardrobe was in the street and it is plainly quite pointless to lock it because it is just in the street. These phenomena of "inverted thoughts" made her fearful of going mad.

Now, the place at the window of the living-room that she occupies all day long overlooks a wide street, leading into the main road that runs past the front of the house. Now she emphasises how good her vision is and how she is even able to see the small children playing at the top end of the street. However, it frequently happens while she is looking out over the street that something frightens her greatly. Thus, just yesterday, she stared in wonder out of the window at a thing moving down the street on wheels, with a human figure in it; but it only became clear to her after a considerable period that it was a butcher's van. "If I walk out my front door," she complains, "I find myself in a foreign world which confuses me; that is why I seldom venture out and am unhappy to do so without my escort."

Once recently, while she was sitting quietly at the window, the idea came to mind that she would like to look at a very valuable flower-vase that she has in her possession. This vase has a conspicuous shape, is large and colourful, and is placed in her display-cabinet in such a way that it would have to strike her as soon as she glanced into the cabinet. Now she searched in the cabinet for it on several occasions but didn't find it until her lady-friend came and showed it to her with the words, "My God, there it is right in front of you." She is currently able to recognise it again and is able to find it after a quick search.

When she rearranges her cabinet, or puts something away somewhere so as to have it close at hand in case she needs to use it again soon, she is usually unable to find it again and becomes ever more bewildered as she searches for it. The maid-servant (who is summoned) then usually has to show her the thing that is sought, which only all too often is right in front of her and could not have escaped her view.

She complains also that the following circumstance in regard to her correspondence frequently agitates and bewilders her. When, for instance, she has written a letter and left it on the writing-table in order to be able to find it easily afterwards, it often happens that she returns to the table later and looks and searches about but cannot find the letter. "I search and search but cannot find it, I become quite bewildered, and in the end it is lying right in front of me—I did not recognise it, although I read splendidly, after all, and can see perfectly well in other respects" (hemianopia).

On the whole, she has particular places in the room to which she must return every thing that leaves her hands if she is to be able to find it again later. Should she forget this place, then it becomes impossible to find the thing (for example, her reading-glasses) that she has put away.

Since her illness she has become excitable and nervous, whereas before she would not have known at all "what nerves are". In other respects, she has not noticed any change in her character.

At present the patient suffers frequently from "explosion-like experiences" (without there being any bang in the head) linked to a sudden experience of light. The patient underwent a strychnine treatment, takes arsenic as well, and complies with the prescription that she should walk as much as possible; she strolls around the city, reliant upon her own strength, with great diligence.

She has gradually lost the visual-field defect that was previously present in the lower octants of the right visual hemi-fields; the left visual hemi-fields—apart from a small, barely perceptible island in the left upper quadrants—display approximately the same form as at the previous examination, apart from the fact that the defect no longer stretches as far as the periphery. The preserved part of the left visual hemi-fields does not have the sharp delimitation indicated in the figures, but rather indicates the region within which the patient noticed "something bright" with rapid to and fro movements of the white object used for the examination (Fig. 8.2). The capacity to perceive brightness, therefore, was apparently preserved, whereas neither form nor colour were recognised.

17th April, 1885. A further consequence of the strychnine treatment, and one for which the patient was thankful, consists in the cessation of the "inverted thoughts." Gradually the things in her room also lost their "foreign character." Also, for the first time, she could now find her way independently to my consulting rooms; she could also describe the route correctly from memory. Along the way, a particular locality (the neighbourhood of the Kunsthalle and the Boat House of the Rowing Club) made a familiar impression on her. When this locality came into view, she was reassured that she had taken the correct route to my rooms. The memory-image for this locality had apparently been preserved in the left visual sphere.

28th April, 1885. If one gets the patient to close her eyes and then names various things for her, she is able to imagine them pictorially. Also, in regard to the topography of Hamburg, she is able to picture images of certain streets, certain squares and certain vantage-points in the city, but others only vaguely, and still others not at all. According to her, if she fell from Heaven into a well-known Hamburg street she would well be able to recognise where she was, but it is still impossible for her to find the way to one of its specified locations.

16th May, 1885. The "inverted thoughts" have stopped. Likewise, the "foreign character" of her furniture has disappeared and she no longer stares at things in the street from her window without recognising them,

> but still, even now at night I take any old object from the table and think; my God, what sort of thing is this then?, and only after protracted and repeated looking at it and palpating of it does it become clear to me what it is meant to be. I can imagine to myself a large number of streets but with the best will in the world I cannot find my way to them; I do not know where the individual streets begin and where they end. If I fell from Heaven into a street, I would well be able to recognise it but the sight of it bewilders me and if I go too far into it I get a headache.

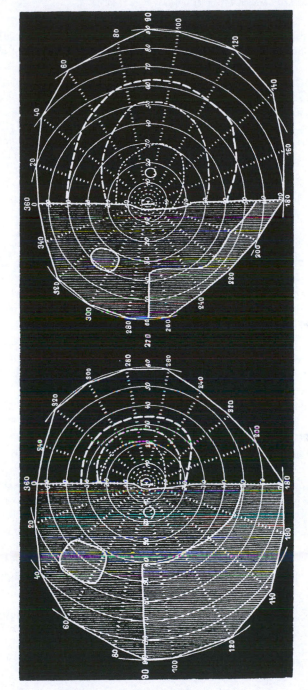

FIG. 8.2 (Reproduced from the 1892 version of Wilbrand's paper.)

99

To my objection that she nevertheless found the route independently to the home of her lady-friend (who lives in the Oberaltenstift) she replied:

> I know that I have to proceed from here, from my house, left at the corner, until I reach the Steindamm, around which I have to take but a few steps before I reach one of the shopkeepers who has befriended me, whom I have visited often. Once I have reached this place, I proceed confidently straight ahead because I know I am on the correct route. I carry on until, oh God, I reach that square with the large number of red and white painted coaches; then I'm done for, then I have to ask directions every three steps of the way if I don't want to get lost. People laugh at me because when I have just asked one passer-by, I have to ask the way of the next one again. Then I don't know whether I'm coming or going.

She is able to find the way from her home to a few other localities, too, but then she is unable to return on her own—that is without asking—to find the same route back.

After repeated visits to her lady-friend in the Oberaltenstift (a barracks-like building with domes on top of the main structures) the circumstance struck her that these structures, which had initially made such an extraordinary impact on her, now made a much smaller impression. "On the whole, nowadays everything comes across as being more condensed."

She sometimes has ringing in the left ear, but otherwise she hears distinctly. The sense of smell is intact.

The so-called explosions without a bang in the head (sensation of the crack of the blast) are currently far more muted, and now are usually experienced at sleep-onset in the form of a short, slight blast.

Up to 10th September, 1885 the condition of our patient improved greatly, "it won't be long yet before my sight and visual impressions are as before the illness." She declares that currently she is "living a mechanical life," a state that she attempted to illustrate by the following example:

> If for instance I wish to put myself to bed at night—then I think, you must still put this and that right and get everything in order. Then, when I enter my bedroom, I am amazed to see that I have already taken care of everything. Everything is in perfect order, in its place, but I have completed it mechanically and I do not realise that the work has already been done.

> At night before I go to sleep I think through my activities of the following day and resolve to get this and that in order: with that I am able to imagine pictorially to myself how I will complete the thing. However, should I wish to execute my intentions in the morning, then it's as if I am stupid and I cannot.

To the question: "Can you imagine to yourself the map of England?" she answers "yes". "Can you draw its contours on this piece of paper?" She does so and produces a sketchy drawing with approximately appropriate proportions of the contours of England and Ireland. She designates correctly the various maps shown to her in an atlas, and is also able to find on them very swiftly the major cities in the countries concerned.

She is able to interpret correctly the individual details in a picture (belonging to the poem *Der Alpenjäger* by Schiller) that is presented to her, but without being able to indicate the poem which is suited to this illustration. To the question: "When reading that poem, can you imagine the individual situations pictorially?" she answers "yes."

When directed to designate individually by name the following objects without touching them (cigar, pencil, knife, matchbox, steel nib, salt-cellar, stone, pottery fragment, blackcurrant berry, ring, button, matchstick, 10-Pfennig coin, cork, key, postage stamp) she recognises and names them promptly and correctly. If these articles are placed together on a plate and she is directed to remove a particular item from it, she swiftly and easily finds the designated article. If one gets her to close her eyes and feel these objects with her hand, and asks her if she is able to imagine them pictorially, she answers "yes." Also, shortly after these experiments she is able to enumerate without omission most of the objects that were presented to her.

In recent weeks her legs became weak suddenly and she collapsed, without loss of consciousness. This weakness and dizziness persisted for four days. Thereafter, when she wished to read the newspaper it struck her that she was quite able to read word-for-word but unable to grasp the meaning of what she read. This condition, too, recovered a few days later.

Among the manifestations of the (apoplectiform) insult in this case we have, at the onset of the symptoms, a bilateral homonymous hemianopia, which is sure to have been complete initially in both left visual hemi-fields, and incomplete on the right.

Together with these focal symptoms, other manifestations of mind-blindness appeared in our patient, the presence of which could still be established four years later. This condition manifested itself principally in a loss of topographical sense and in a peculiar foreignness of the impressions made by old, familiar retinal images. Together with the impossibility—despite normal visual acuity and normal colour sense—of finding her way outside of her home, was the striking manner in which orientation in imagery with closed eyes was much better, as was the persistence of the capacity to visualise any optical memory-image with closed eyes. Together with these manifestations, our patient was also disturbed by the symptom of "inverted thoughts"; that is, the state during which the thought suddenly comes to her that her bedroom is in the street, or that her wardrobe is in the street, etc. Due to the fact that she is bewildered by the sight of a large number of things, this in other respects independent 67-year-old spinster restricts her personal company to one old woman who is far beneath her intellectually, and she leaves her home extremely seldom and usually only for a short distance. As a result of strychnine injections the right visual hemi-field recovered completely, and there were two insular zones on the left within which only the sensation of brightness was preserved.

Gradually, by taking frequent and unaccompanied walks, she learned how to find her way around again, in the direction from her home towards other localities at least; she could only find her way back again with great difficulty and by asking for directions very frequently.[1]

DISCUSSION

Discussion of Wilbrand's case in the secondary literature has traditionally focused upon the visual imagery and dreams. In classical nosography, this case is grouped together with Charcot's famous patient (Charcot, 1883; see Chapter 3) and classified under the heading of "Charcot–Wilbrand syndrome."

Pötzl (1928, p. 306) defined this syndrome as "mind-blindness with disturbance of optic imagination." Nielsen (1946, p. 74) defined it as "visual agnosia plus loss of ability to revisualise images." Critchley's (1953, p. 311) definition is the one most commonly cited today: "The term 'Charcot–Wilbrand syndrome' refers to the symptom whereby a patient loses the power to conjure up visual images or memories, and furthermore, ceases to dream during his sleeping hours."

Critchley considered loss of visual imagery to be the primary symptom of the complex. Loss of dreaming ("or at least, an alteration in the vivid visual component of the dreaming state"; Critchley, 1953, p. 311) was considered to be a secondary consequence of the imagery deficit. Prosopagnosia and topographical amnesia were listed as other necessary sequelae of the primary deficit. Critchley disputed the view that visual object agnosia was an essential part of the syndrome, as had been suggested by Adler (1944, 1950), Gloning and Sternbach (1953), Grünstein (1924), and Nielsen (1946). Brain (1950, 1954) confirmed Critchley's distinction. The syndrome was attributed to "occipital or occipito-parietal lesions, usually bilateral" (Critchley, 1953, p. 314).

The concept of the Charcot–Wilbrand syndrome is retained in current nosological usage (Botez, 1985; Botez, Olivier, Vézina, Botez, & Kaufman, 1985; Epstein, 1979; Peña-Casanova, Roig-Rovira, Bermudez, & Tolosa-Sarro, 1985; Murri, Arena, Siciliano, Mazzotta, & Murarorio, 1984). The disorder is considered rare (Botez, 1985; Murri et al., 1984) but it is well established and relatively non-controversial. A recent definition (Murri et al., 1984, p. 185) reads: "the association of loss of the ability to conjure up visual images or memories and loss of dreaming ... [indicating] a lesion in an acute phase affecting the posterior regions."

Critique of the Charcot-Wilbrand Syndrome

A closer look at the original literature exposes serious flaws in this nosographic concept. A careful reading of Charcot and Wilbrand's reports reveals that their cases differed fundamentally with regard to the cardinal elements of the syndrome. Critchley wrote (1953, p. 313, italics added) that Wilbrand's patient "*could not visualise* the streets of Hamburg where she had been brought up." This was an error. The original report stated only that her "topographical memory" was defective, and it described a deficit that we would totally call topographical *agnosia* (this chapter, p. 91, italics added): "She reports her reaction … as being: 'if you say that that is the Jungfernstieg, and that the Neuenwall, and this the Stadthaus, then I suppose it must indeed be so, *but I do not recognise them.*"

Numerous other instances of topographical and other forms of misrecognition and misperception were contained in the report, but these were specifically and repeatedly contrasted with the preservation of imagery. For example (this chapter, p. 94): "If I close my eyes now and cast myself back to Copenhagen, I see the streets quite clearly before me, and I see in my mind the castles on the mountains along the Rhine—but now when I stand with open eyes and survey any city or any neighbourhood, then I have no idea where I am."

Evidently Wilbrand's case lacked the primary symptom of the Charcot–Wilbrand syndrome; she suffered an abnormality of visual recognition and perception (and perhaps memory) but not one of imagery.

The deficit in Charcot's case was quite different. He clearly described an absence of mental imagery (Savill's translation, 1889, p. 158; italics added): "Now, even with the strongest desire in the world, *I cannot picture to myself* the features of my children or my wife, or any other object of my daily surroundings." The alteration in this patient's visual object perception and recognition was for the most part limited to a sense of strangeness and unfamiliarity (jamais vu), although the original report of the case does also suggest some topographical agnosia and possible prosopagnosia (p. 154; italics added): "In every instance the visual memory of forms and colours had completely disappeared, *yet he could perceive them when present without difficulty*, and the knowledge of this somewhat reassured him as to his mental condition."

Wilbrand himself drew attention to the distinction between his and Charcot's cases in respect of their visual imagery, as did many other early commentators (Brain, 1954; Lange, 1936; Müller, 1892; Pötzl, 1928).

These facts undermine the essential basis of the Charcot–Wilbrand syndrome. In the conventional definition, the second essential element of the syndrome, cessation of dreaming, is considered to be consequent upon the primary loss of visual imagery. But Wilbrand's case did not have an imagery deficit. This reveals a second fundamental distinction between the two prototypical cases, which is also discernable in the original reports. Charcot's patient described his dream-deficit as follows (Savill's 1889 translation, p. 158; italics added): "The faculty of picturing objects within myself being absolutely wanting, my dreams are correspondingly modified. At the present time *I dream simply of speech, whereas I formerly possessed a visual perception in my dreams.*"

Wilbrand described something different: "Before her illness she dreamt a great deal in pictorial images, *now she dreams almost not at all anymore.* Recently however she once again saw the image of her late sister in a dream." (This chapter, p. 91, italics added.)

Evidently, Wilbrand's patient lost completely the faculty of dreaming for a period of time and then regained it, or alternatively she dreamed far less frequently than before. In either event her symptom was a global one; there was no mention of verbal or nonvisual dreams, which is what Charcot's patient described. This distinction was confirmed in 1892, when Müller documented a third case. Müller's patient "had *no further dreams* since her illness, whereas previously she not infrequently had vivid dreams and saw all manner of things in them" (p. 868, italics added). This is an unequivocal description of total cessation of dreaming. The distinction persisted in subsequently reported cases of Charcot–Wilbrand syndrome, as is demonstrated by the following problematic observation recorded in the recent literature (Murri et al., 1984, p. 185, italics added): "Curiously enough, the earliest case reports [of Charcot–Wilbrand syndrome] frequently noted a loss of *visual* dream content, while subsequent authors reported a *total* loss of dreaming."

In short, the Charcot-Wilbrand syndrome, as conventionally defined, does not exist. The primary symptom of the complex, loss of visual imagery, was absent in Wilbrand's case. The second essential symptom—supposedly caused by the imagery deficit—was present in Wilbrand's case in the absence of an imagery deficit. Moreover, the latter symptom assumed two different forms in the two prototypical cases—a distinction that has been confirmed by subsequent case reports (Doricchi & Violani 1992; Solms, in press).

Implications for Contemporary Neuropsychology

The conflation of Charcot's and Wilbrand's cases in the modern literature arose, in the first instance, from the ambiguity of the term "memory" in the classical "mind-blindness" concept. It was originally assumed that visual recognition disorders resulted from a loss of underlying "optical memory-images". The situation was complicated further by the fact that topographical symptoms were prominent in both cases. Before the concept of topographical agnosia was developed and distinguished from topographical amnesia (Paterson & Zangwill, 1945) such symptoms were always conceived of in terms of memory. The same applies to facial recognition (cf. Bodamer, 1947; Hoff & Pötzl, 1937). Critchley's (1953) mistranslation was merely indicative of these pre-existing conceptual and terminological ambiguities.

The assumption that visual recognition depended upon the activation of visual memory-images was derived from Munk's (1881) work. However, this assumption was abandoned early in classical neurology. It was widely recognised that the dissociation of visual imagery and visual recognition in Wilbrand's case disproved the original theory. Thus, Claparède (1900) distinguished asymbolia with and without loss of the underlying images, and Pick spoke of "asymbolia with preservation of the memory-images and disturbance of recognition caused by interruption of associations, as opposed to asymbolia with loss of memory-images" (Brown, 1972, p. 211). Pötzl (1928) and Nielsen (1946) reached similar conclusions. The reasoning behind the abandonment of the original theory was explained by Lange (1936, p. 59, Brown's 1988 translation): "It is apparent from the original observations of Charcot and Wilbrand, that Munk's simple and brilliant assumption to the effect that psychic blindness is based on the loss of optic memory could not be true in such a simple sense."

These facts have been overlooked by contemporary cognitive theorists (e.g. Farah, 1989a, 1989b) who believe that visual imagery and visual perception differ from one another only in terms of the direction of flow of the process that activates the representations ("top-down" versus "bottom-up"). This influential theory is barely distinguishable from Munk's "simple and brilliant assumption". Farah (1984) acknowledges that numerous cases of visual imagery deficit without visual object agnosia have been reported (i.e. cases of the Charcot type). This might appear to contradict her reduction of both recognition and imagery to the activation of common underlying representations, but she explains the anomaly by postulating a separate module for the generation of images (cf. Kosslyn, 1980). Damage to this "image generation" module (which she localised to the left parietal region) would result in impaired imagery without affecting the underlying representations themselves (which are localised to the occipital region). However, this theory fails to account for cases with the opposite pattern of deficits (i.e. cases of the Wilbrand type), and thereby overlooks the facts that demolished Munk's theory in the first place.

The extent of the historical oversight is illustrated by a recent letter published in *Nature* (Behrmann, Winocur, & Moscovitch, 1992), reporting a case with the same dissociation that Wilbrand described in 1887 as if it were a new and unexpected discovery. The authors of this letter conclude (p.637) that "these data contradict the prevailing view that a deficit in perception of central origin arises from a loss of the mental representations and the neural structures that mediate them." Wilbrand's dissociation was in fact repeatedly confirmed throughout the present century, but this, too, has been overlooked by contemporary theorists (see Brain, 1941; Brown, 1972; Jankowiak, Kinsbourne, Shalev, & Bachman, 1992; Schanfald, Pearlman, & Greenberg, 1985; Solms, in press). These facts undermine the modern theory that perception and imagery depend upon the activation of a shared representational module, and they demonstrate that the same theory was proposed and disproved over 100 years ago.

Contemporary cognitive scientists use this same model to explain the link between loss of visual imagery and dreaming. Dreaming is equated with image generation and thereby reduced to top-down activation—by the (left parietal) image-generation module—of the (occipital) visual-representation module (Farah, 1984, 1989a; Greenberg & Farah, 1986).

This extension of the theory is contradicted not only by the fact that dream and image generation were dissociated in Wilbrand's case, but also by the fact that two distinct forms of "loss of dreaming" exist. Every case of so-called Charcot–Wilbrand syndrome reveals the same dissociation; in some patients *nonvisual* dreaming persists, in others *global* cessation of dreaming is reported (Doricchi & Violani, 1992; Solms, in press). Interestingly, loss of visual imagery is a regular correlate of the first (nonvisual) type but not of the second (global) type of "loss of dreaming" (Solms, in press). Also, these two types of "loss of dreaming" correspond to different sites of lesion. Most cases of the nonvisual type have occipital lobe lesions whereas most cases of the global type have parietal lobe lesions (Solms, in press). The two types could therefore be equated with Farah's distinction between (occipital) image representation and (left parietal) image generation. However, global cessation of dreaming occurs with parietal lesions of either hemisphere, and a significant subgroup of the latter type has been identified in which the lesion is deep bifrontal rather than occipital or parietal (Solms, in press). Dreaming apparently is a more complicated process than the prevailing cognitive theory suggests.

SUMMARY AND CONCLUSIONS

Developments in the agnosia concept and a translation error by Critchley (1953) have resulted in misapprehensions in the modern literature as to the essential nature of the deficit in Wilbrand's celebrated (1887) case report. Wilbrand's case is traditionally coupled with Charcot's (1883) report of loss of visual imagery and dreaming, under the heading of Charcot–Wilbrand syndrome. This syndrome is retained in current nosological usage. Loss of dreaming is considered to be a necessary consequence of loss of imagery. However, Wilbrand's original report reveals that his patient did not in fact suffer an imagery deficit. Also, the dream deficit was qualitatively different from that reported by Charcot's patient. These facts undermine the very basis of the Charcot–Wilbrand syndrome.

The significance of the dissociation between imagery and perception in Wilbrand's case was recognised early this century. It was acknowledged that the difference between Charcot's and Wilbrand's cases contradicted Munk's (1881) theory, which predicts that visual perception and visual imagery rely upon the activation of the same underlying representations. These facts have been overlooked by contemporary cognitive theorists who advance models of perception and imagery similar to Munk's. Also, the classical reports of Charcot and Wilbrand—supported by subsequent observations—contradict prevailing cognitive models of dreaming. These facts do not contradict the more fundamental view that dreams and imagery involve the same neural substrate as perception; but they raise serious questions for the prevailing conception of that process (cf. Brown, 1989; Solms, in press).

NOTE

1. In 1892, following the death of this patient, Wilbrand reprinted the case report (very slightly modified) together with autopsy findings and a new discussion. The only substantial variation in the second version of the case report was that the final paragraph above was deleted and replaced by the following addendum:

    Unfortunately, in the final years of her life the patient withdrew from my further observation; however she was to remain free from any further attacks of illness. According to her domestic staff, right up to her death the complaint was always the same: she seees nothing and yet everything. She ventured out only infrequently and lived in a very secluded way, but was still of very sound mind right to the end. Following an apoplectic attack, she passed away within a few hours without ever regaining consciousness.

    The brain was removed from the skull 24 hours after death and placed in Müller's fluid. Our colleague Herr Eisenlohr was kind enough to carry out the fixation of the sections.

    Autopsy report. Right hemisphere (Fig. 8.3): The lobus fusiformis has subsided deeply to form a limp, membranous sack extending to the pole of the occipital lobe. From above the entire occipital lobe appears to have subsided, with somewhat narrow convolutions but a surface that is nowhere softened. The posterior half of the cuneus is greatly reduced and softened. Its tip is contiguous with the focus in the fusiform lobe observed on the inferior surface. There is a slight change in the cortex of the fissura calcarina; the precuneus is normal, as is the lateral surface of the occipital lobe and all parietal convolutions.

    Left hemisphere: In the white radiation of the second occipital convolution, and a few millimetres underneath the grey cortex, in the depths of the fissure separating the first and second occipital convolutions, there is a small cavity that adjoins a softened zone at its frontal end (old focus). This softened zone gradually merges anteriorly into a fresh soft focus which has destroyed completely the central white matter of the hemisphere.

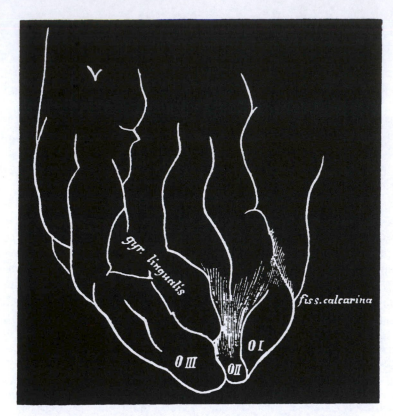

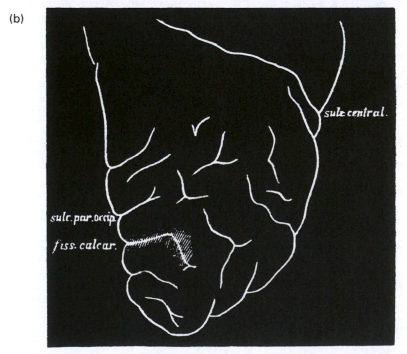

FIG. 8.3 (a) Ventral surface of the right occipital lobe; (b) dorsal surface of the right occipital lobe.

REFERENCES

Adler, A. (1944). Disintegration and restoration of optic recognition in visual agnosia: Analysis of a case. *Archives of Neurology and Psychiatry, 51*, 243–259.

Adler, A. (1950). Course and outcome of visual agnosia. *Journal of Nervous and Mental Diseases, 111*, 41–51.

Behrmann, M., Winocur, G., & Moscovitch, M. (1992). Dissociation between mental imagery and object recognition in a brain-damaged patient. *Nature, 359*, 636–637.

Bodamer, J. (1947). Die Prosop-Agnosie. *Archiv für Psychiatrie und Nervenkrankheiten, 179*, 6–53.

Botez, M. (1985). [In collaboration with T. Botez & M. Olivier.] Parietal lobe syndromes. In P. Vinken, G. Bruyn, H. Klawans, & J. Frederiks (Eds.), *Handbook of clinical neurology, 45: Clinical neuropsychology*, 63–85. Amsterdam & New York: Elsevier.

Botez, M., Olivier, M., Vézina, J.-L., Botez, T., & Kaufman, B. (1985). Defective revisualization: Dissociation between cognitive and imagistic thought. Case report and short review of the literature. *Cortex, 21*, 375–389.

Brain, R. (1941). Visual object-agnosia with special reference to the Gestalt theory. *Brain, 64*, 43–62.

Brain, R. (1950). The cerebral basis of consciousness. *Brain, 73*, 465–479.

Brain, R. (1954). Loss of visualization. *Proceedings of the Royal Society of Medicine, 47*, 288–290.

Brown, J.W. (1972). *Aphasia, apraxia, agnosia: Clinical and theoretical aspects.* Springfield, IL: Thomas.

Brown, J.W. (1988). *Agnosia and apraxia: Selected papers of Liepmann, Lange and Pötzl.* Hillsdale, NJ: Lawrence Erlbaum Associations Inc.

Charcot, J.-M. (1883). Un cas de suppression brusque et isolée de la vision mentale des signes et des objets (formes et couleurs). *Progrès Médical, 11*, 568–571.

Claparède, E. (1900). Revue generale sur l'agnosie. *Revue Annuale de Psychologie, 6*, 74–143.

Critchley, M. (1953). *The parietal lobes.* London: Arnold.

Doricchi, F., & Violani, C. (1992). Dream recall in brain-damaged patients: A contribution to the neuropsychology of dreaming through a review of the literature. In J. Antrobus & M. Berini (Eds.), *The neuropsychology of sleep and dreaming.* Hillsdale, NJ: Lawrence Erlbaum Associates Inc.

Epstein, A. (1979). Effect of certain cerebral hemispheric diseases on dreaming. *Biological Psychiatry, 14*, 77–93.

Farah, M. (1984). The neurological basis of mental imagery: A componential analysis. *Cognition, 18*, 245–272.

Farah, M. (1989a). The neuropsychology of mental imagery. In F. Boller & J. Grafman (Eds.), *Handbook of neuropsychology (Vol. 2)* (pp. 395–413). Amsterdam & New York: Elsevier.

Farah, M. (1989b). The neuropsychology of mental imagery. In J. Brown (Ed.), *Neuropsychology of visual perception.* Hillsdale, NJ: Lawrence Erlbaum Associates Inc.

Ferrier, D. (1876). *The functions of the brain.* London: Dawsons.

Finkelnburg, F. (1870). Niederrheinsche Gesellschaft in Bonn: Medicinische Section. *Berliner klinische Wochenschrift, 7*, 449–450, 460–461.

Freud, S. (1891). *Zur Auffassung der Aphasien: Eine kritische Studie.* Leipzig & Vienna: Deuticke.

Gloning, K., & Sternbach, I. (1953). Über das Träumen bei zerebralen Herdläsionen. *Wiener Zeitschrift für die Nervenheilkunde, 6*, 302–329.

Greenberg, M., & Farah, M. (1986). The laterality of dreaming. *Brain and Cognition, 5*, 307–321.

Grünstein, A. (1924). Die Erforschung der Träume als eine Methode der topischen Diagnostik bei Großhirnerkrankungen. *Zeitschrift für die gesamte Neurologie und Psychiatrie, 93*, 416–420.

Hoff, H., & Pötzl, O. (1937). Über eine optische-agnostische Störung des "Physiognomie-Gedächtnisses. *Zeitschrift für die gesamte Neurologie und Psychiatrie, 159*, 367.

Jackson, J. Hughlings (1872, 4th May). Case of disease of the brain—left hemiplegia—mental affection. *Medical Times and Gazette*, 513–514.

Jackson, J. Hughlings (1876). Case of large cerebral tumour without optic neuritis and with left hemiplegia and imperception. *Royal London Ophthalmic Hospital reports, 8*, 434.

Jankowiak, J., Kinsbourne, M., Shalev, R., & Bachman, D. (1992). *Journal of Cognitive Neuroscience, 4*, 119–131.

Kosslyn, S. (1980). *Image and mind*, Cambridge, MA: Harvard University Press.

Lange, J. (1936). Agnosien und Apraxien. In O. Bumke & O. Förster (Eds.), *Handbuch der Neurologie (Vol. 6)* (pp. 807–960). Berlin: Springer.

Lissauer, H. (1890). Ein Fall von Seelenblindheit nebst einem Beitrag zur Theorie derselben. *Archiv für Psychiatrie und Nervenkrankheiten, 21*, 222–270.

Mauthner, L. (1881). *Gehirn und Auge*. Wiesbaden: Bergmann.

Müller, F. (1892). Ein Beitrag zur Kenntniss der Seelenblindheit. *Archiv für Psychiatrie und Nervenkrankheiten, 24*, 856–917.

Munk, H. (1878). Weitere Mittheilungen zur Physiologie der Grosshirnrinde. *Archiv für Anatomie und Physiologie, 2*, 161–178.

Munk, H. (1881). *Über der Funktionen der Grosshirnrinde: Gesammelte Mittheilungen aus den Jahren 1877–80*. Berlin: Hirschwald.

Murri, L., Arena, R., Siciliano, G., Mazzotta, R., & Murarorio, A. (1984). Dream recall in patients with focal cerebral lesions. *Archives of Neurology, 41*, 183–185.

Nielsen, J. (1946). *Agnosia, apraxia, aphasia: Their value in cerebral localization*. New York & London: Hoeber.

Paterson, A., & Zangwill, O. (1945). A case of topographical disorientation associated with a unilateral cerebral lesion. *Brain, 68*, 188–211.

Peña-Casanova, J., Roig-Rovira, T., Bermudez, A., & Tolosa-Sarro, E. (1985). Optic aphasia, optic apraxia, and loss of dreaming. *Brain and Language, 26*, 63–71.

Pötzl, O. (1928). *Die Aphasielehre vom Standpunkt der klinischen Psychiatrie: Vol. 1. Die optisch-agnostischen Störungen (die verschiedenen Formen der Seelenblindheit)*. Leipzig & Vienna: Deuticke.

Quaglino, A., & Borelli, G. (1867). Emiplegia sinistra con amarousi; guaragione; perdita totale della percezione dei colori e della memoria della configurazione degli oggetti. *Giornale d'Oftalmologia Italiano, 10*, 106–117.

Savill, T. (Trans.). (1889). *Clinical lectures on diseases of the nervous system (Lecture 3)* by J.-M. Charcot. London: The New Sydenham Society.

Schanfald, D., Pearlman, C., & Greenberg, R. (1985). The capacity of stroke patients to report dreams. *Cortex, 21*, 237–247.

Solms, M. (in press). *The neuropsychology of dreams: A clinico-anatomical study*. Hillsdale, NJ: Lawrence Erlbaum Associates Inc.

von Monakow, C. (1885). Experimentelle und pathologisch-anatomische Untersuchungen über die Beziehungen der sogenannten Sehsphäre zu den infracorticalen Opticuscentern und zum N. opticus. *Archiv für Psychiatrie und Nervenkrankheiten, 16*, 151–199, 317–352.

Wigan, A. (1844). *The duality of the mind: Proved by the structure, functions, and diseases of the brain, and by the phenomena of mental derangement and shown to be essential to moral responsibility*. London: Longman, Brown, Green & Longmans.

Wilbrand, H. (1887). *Die Seelenblindheit als Herderscheinung und ihre Beziehung zur Alexie und Agraphie*. Wiesbaden: Bergmann.

Wilbrand, H. (1892). Ein Fall von Seelenblindheit und Hemianopsie mit Sectionsbefund. *Deutsche Zeitschrift für die Nervenheilkunde, 2*, 361–387.

9

Liepmann (1900 and 1905): A Definition of Apraxia and a Model of Praxis

Leslie J. Gonzalez Rothi
Staff Speech Pathologist, Veterans Affairs Medical Center, Gainesville, Florida, U.S.A. and Associate Professor, Departments of Neurology, Communication Processes and Disorders, and Clinical and Health Psychology, University of Florida, U.S.A.

Kenneth M. Heilman
Neurology Service, Veterans Affairs Medical Center, Gainesville, Florida, U.S.A. and Professor, Departments of Neurology, and Clinical and Health Psychology, University of Florida, U.S.A.

INTRODUCTION

Despite ... statements scattered over four decades, despite an occasional inability to perform this or that purposeful movement which was entered in the case history of aphasics as a curiosity, despite also disorders of mimetic movements of aphasics which were interpreted as disorders in the language of gestures, in the last [19th] century there was no true comprehension of the whole area nor was it incorporated with our knowledge of neurology and brain pathology. The brief references to apraxia ... were only rediscovered to some extent after 1900; in any case, they did not make their way into the general knowledge of professionals. And those few who did give some attention to the problem did not recognize the phenomena in their enormous extent and variety; they did not subdivide and comprehend them clinically or psychologically or physiologically, nor did they understand them as being anatomically rooted in the brain. (Brown, 1988, p. 4.)

At the close of the 19th century the inability to correctly perform purposeful movements in response to command had been only superficially described as an aside in cases of aphasia. While the term apraxia had been coined by Steinthal as early as 1871, the presumed mechanism was really quite different than our understanding today. That is, it was assumed in the late

111

1800s that the reason a patient may fail correctly to perform purposeful movements was that they were unable to recognise or fully appreciate the object/tool associated with the desired movement. That is, the movement failure in apraxia was assumed to result from motor "agnosia" or motor manifestations of asymbolia. How this would create an inability to move purposefully to command in the former explanation or to be unable to imitate gestures in the latter explanation is unclear but this was the conception commonly held at the time Hugo Liepmann presented his first paper on the topic of apraxia in 1900. It is cases described in this paper of 1900 and one that followed in 1905 that serve as the focus of this chapter.

LIEPMANN, 1900: APRAXIA IS A DISORDER OF MOTOR PROGRAMMING AND NOT A DISORDER OF SYMBOLIC BEHAVIOUR

Influenced by his mentor Carl Wernicke when describing the case of Mr T., a 48-year-old "senior civil servant", it was clearly Liepmann's intent to establish apraxia as a disorder of motor planning rather than a manifestation of asymbolia or recognition disorder (agnosia), explanations that had dominated the scientific community for at least 30 years. Liepmann stated that the case presentation needed no justification as the patient's deficits were so extraordinary, the importance of the case would be readily evident.

Liepmann saw this case for the first time some two months post onset of "apoplexy, mixed aphasia, dementia". Though he focused on the behavioural examination, Liepmann's notes indicated that the patient's physical examination revealed no hemiplegia. Through hours of observation in which the patient "failed in almost everything" Liepmann noted that Mr T. seemed to fail to understand (as though "cerebrally deaf") and he produced "bizarre and distorted movements" with his right upper limb; the limb that the patient exclusively used to respond during the period of observation. Wondering whether these "bizarre" movements related to the suspected "inability to comprehend" (consistent with the asymbolia notion of apraxia), Liepmann suggested that his patient's "apraxia" should occur on all commands. However, the patient was noted to respond correctly and promptly to whole-body commands such as "walk to the window". In addition, if the patient's apraxia was the result of asymbolia, Liepmann suggested that it should occur equally on both sides of the body. However, when the patient was prevented from using the right side of the body (arm or leg) and thus forced to respond with the left, he responded promptly and accurately to commands. Assessing other behaviours such as reading and writing, similar findings were noted. This led Liepmann to conclude that the patient's difficulty with purposive movement with the right side of his body ("unilateral apraxia") could not be explained as "cerebral deafness" or asymbolia (what he termed "sensory apraxia"), but rather "from a disturbance in his control of motor communication" (for which he used the restrictive term "motor apraxia"). Liepmann continued that this stricter terminology ("motor apraxia") was more consistent with the literal meaning of the term apraxia as a deficit of motor planning exclusive of sensory-specific difficulties.

Through extensive testing and observation Liepmann described a number of findings in his case that were new and unique notions about apraxia. One such finding that Liepmann (1900) noted was that the relative inability of Mr T. to use his right side was apparent when the stimulus input crossed all modalities as well as varying forms of information content. For example he was unable to point with his right hand to the location of a ringing bell, to respond to written commands, to imitate seen gestures, to scratch a tickle in his right ear, to point to objects when named, and so forth. In contrast, the patient rarely failed to respond to these same items and tasks when using his left side.

Additionally, Liepmann noted that Mr T. was satisfied with his error responses. However, speaking against an indifference reaction, Liepmann noted that the patient became embarrassed when mistakes were pointed out. One hypothesis that this finding may suggest is that if this "motor apraxia" was the result of the motor planning failure, the mechanism that allowed motor planning in non-brain-damaged subjects may be important for "on-line" error monitoring. In contrast, "off-line" error awareness did not need this representation of motor planning.

Another interesting finding that Liepmann noted was that the right-sided movement errors of Mr T. were not random nor could they be explained as an elemental movement disorder. For example, when the patient was asked to pick up an object from an array with his right hand, Liepmann recorded what object the patient selected in the array. One finding was that it was common for the patient erroneously to pick up an object immediately contiguous with the target, attesting to the lack of randomness in his errors. In addition, Liepmann removed all of the objects except one. Placing the target in various places on the table, he showed that the patient was able to reach quickly and accurately for the item on command in each location when there was no competition from contiguous objects, thus ruling out "faulty movement projection" as an explanation for these errors.

Finally, Liepmann discussed the competition and conflict that can occur between hands on bimanual tasks. For example, when Mr T. was asked to pour water from a jug held in his left hand to a glass held in the right, the left hand attempted to pour but the right hand simultaneously lifted the empty glass to his mouth. When the glass was held by another person, the patient successfully poured with the left hand.

Thus, the greatest contribution made by Liepmann in his paper of 1900 was more strictly to refine the term apraxia to include those disorders of purposeful movement that are not explained by object recognition deficits, asymbolia, or primary motor dysfunction. This definition still stands today. The conclusion that could be drawn from this refinement in the definition of apraxia was that planned, purposeful movement must have a representation in the brain that can be selectively impaired by cerebral damage.

Additional support for this notion of a representation for movement was that errors were not random, motor production accuracy was not influenced by differing modalities of input, and not all forms of error awareness were impaired in this case. But there were many problems with the case Liepmann reported in 1900. For example, the patient's hand preference was not clearly defined, the patient had syphilis, and the loci of lesions that induced this patient's defects were unknown.

LIEPMANN, 1905: APRAXIA REPRESENTS A HETEROGENEOUS GROUPING OF DISORDERS IMPLYING A MULTICOMPONENT REPRESENTATION OF PRAXIS

In the five years between the 1900 case study and the 1905 paper reported on in this section, Liepmann clearly further pondered the nature of the skilled movement system. Unlike the case study report of his 1900 paper, Liepmann asked questions about the laterality of praxis processing that could only be answered using a group study design.

In this 1905 report Liepmann reviews the data of 83 cases classified as either left- or right-hemisphere lesioned on the basis of side of hemiplegia. He asked each case to perform (with their non-paralytic hand) gesture imitation, transitive pantomime, intransitive gesture, and actual object use tasks. In addition, he carefully studied six cases who had aphasia without hemiplegia and one case who was only apraxic.

A translation of Liepmann's description of praxis performance of the group of 42 left-paralytic (right-hemisphere lesioned) patients was thus (p. 20): "... it rarely happened that one or the other of the given tasks was not promptly solved; and that a larger number of them could not be performed, never occurred. The testing of these left paralytics was always astoundingly quickly completed, the movements were performed 'like clockwork'...."

Though he did not deny that he found instances of praxis item failure, Liepmann did not find the syndrome of apraxia in any one member of this group of 42 right-hemisphere lesioned patients. In contrast, when Liepmann described the performance of the 41 right hemiplegics with left-hemisphere lesions, he reported (p. 21) that "definite disturbances in completion of the

respective tasks with the left ... showed up in no less than 20 of them."
Thus, Liepmann concluded that the syndrome of apraxia resulted from left-
hemisphere lesions and not from right-hemisphere lesions.

The role of the left and right cerebral hemispheres (and the relationship,
one to the other) in movement programming was of interest to Liepmann:
"A part of what the left hand can do is not a property borrowed from the
right hemisphere. The right-sided hand centre, which has generally learned
all the more advanced activities after the left, remains throughout life in a
certain dependence on the left hemisphere." (P. 34.); "Our results show that
even that which the left hand can do is for the most part not its own
property (with respect to the right hemisphere), but it is borrowed from the
right hand (via the left hemisphere)." (P. 35.); "... the right-brained arm
centre remains constantly in a certain dependence on the left, and that the
latter, through the mediation of the corpus callosum, is the leader of the
right." (P. 38.)

Liepmann described the "vertical schema" of limb praxis depicted in Fig.
9.1. In this conceptualisation, the left sensorimotor cortex dominates the
right regarding movement control for both hands. It does this via the corpus
callosum such that a lesion of the left sensorimotor cortex (Lesion 4) would
produce a right hemiplegia and apraxia of hands/arms on both sides. A
lesion sparing the left sensorimotor cortex but involving the inflow to the
corpus callosum from the left sensorimotor cortex (Lesion 2) or of the body
of the corpus callosum (Lesion 1) would produce only a left hand/arm
apraxia. A lesion of the right sensorimotor cortex (Lesion 5) would produce
only a left hemiplegia. A lesion of the internal capsule (Lesion 3) would
produce only a hemiplegia on the side opposite the lesion.

While Liepmann concluded that the left hemisphere contributes more to
the process of movement planning for both hands than does the right
hemisphere, he did not completely exclude the potential contribution of the
right hemisphere for action planning. He simply stated that the left
hemisphere was dominant. That the right hemisphere contributes to action
planning has, in fact, been suggested by recent investigators but the nature
of this contribution to movement planning remains unspecified (Haaland &
Flaherty, 1984).

In addition to proposing and providing evidence for the hypothesis that
there is a system dedicated to skilled motor planning that exists in the left
hemisphere of the human brain, Liepmann also posited that this action
system had certain distinct elements or components. In the remaining part
of the 1905 paper Liepmann suggested (by discussing different types of
"apraxic cases") that these "elements or components" could be differentially damaged by left-hemisphere lesions. The components of the action
system included: (1) the movement formula (space–time sequences of
familiar movements); (2) the ability to realise a movement's innervation; and

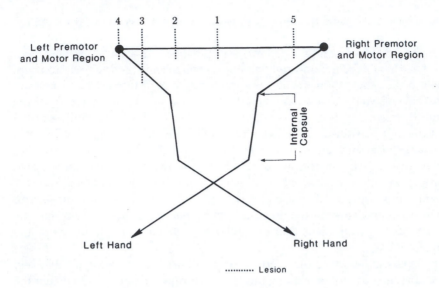

FIG. 9.1   Reconstruction of Liepmann's (1905) vertical schema of praxis representation based on a drawing in Kimura's (1980) translation.

(3) kinetic memories for overlearned movements. Each of the components will be discussed separately.

The Movement Formula

Liepmann described this formula as "... space–time sequences". He defined them as "... general knowledge of the course of the procedure to be realised." Though sensory in nature and most commonly visual, this knowledge could also be represented in other sensory modalities when inherently necessary to the target action. At one point Liepmann referred to a previous presentation in which he suggested that the left supramarginal gyrus supported this formula but no specific information about that particular reference is given. In this 1905 paper, however, Liepmann referred to disorders of the movement formula and suggested that they resulted from left posterior lesions that involved the temporal–parietal interface.

The Innervatory Pattern

Acquired through practice, Liepmann described the contribution of the innervatory pattern system as providing an "increasing ability" to "transform ... movement formula promptly and precisely into innervation" allowing one to "... position the limbs according to directional ideas". Liepmann stated that this is actually accomplished by "... co-operation of innervatory and extra-innervatory areas" of the brain. Though Liepmann did state that this system was not one disturbed by posterior lesions, he did not state what localisation was responsible for failure of this innervatory system. Because Liepmann felt that failure of the innervatory patterns was characteristic of the "motor apraxia" seen in frontal lesions, it is presumed (though not explicitly stated) that the innervatory patterns were considered part of the frontal lobe, praxis system.

The Kinetic Memories

Suggesting that kinetic memories were (p. 44) "... properties of the senso-motorium", Liepmann defined them as "... a functional linkage tak[ing] place between innervations ... which runs its course without intervention from orientation and visual images, through short-circuiting." An obvious obligation of this portion of the praxis system is that these memories require highly practised and familiar movement associations. Therefore, the kinetic memory portion of the praxis system may or may not contribute to the implementation of any particular action plan depending on the plan's component parts.

With the description of these three component parts of a proposed action planning system, Liepmann sets forth principles that remain today. In a cognitive neuropsychological model of action planning that we recently proposed, the three basic components of praxis processing proposed by Liepmann (1905) and their relationship one to another (see Fig. 9.2) remain embedded in a significantly more complex multicomponent model (see Fig. 9.3; Rothi, Ochipa, & Heilman, 1991).

Specifically we have not changed the original description of the innervatory patterns and have assumed that the kinesthetic memories are incorporated in the system referred to late in this cognitive neuropsychological praxis model as "motor systems". However, the "movement formula" of Liepmann (1905) has undergone a great deal of scrutiny and change. We have functionally separated that portion of Liepmann's movement formula which deals with the meaning of actions (e.g. action semantics) from that portion of the movement formula which deals with an action's physical attributes (e.g. action lexicons). (See the Summary and Conclusion section of this chapter for more on this point.) In addition, we have suggested (Rothi et al., 1991) the possibility that information relative to a code about the physical attributes of a "perceived-action" is inherently different to a code about the physical attributes of a "to-be-performed action". For this reason (and other reasons described in Rothi et al., 1991), we have suggested that the action lexicon be split into an Action Input Lexicon (e.g. primarily afferent) and an Action Output Lexicon (e.g., primarily efferent). Finally, we also proposed that there is a system that

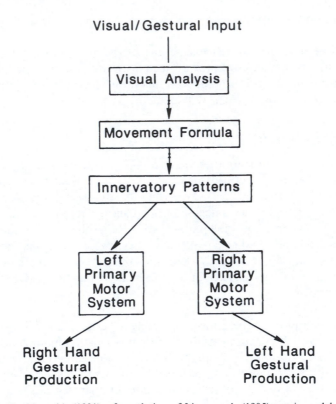

Visual/Gestural Input

Visual Analysis

Movement Formula

Innervatory Patterns

Left Primary Motor System

Right Primary Motor System

Right Hand Gestural Production

Left Hand Gestural Production

FIG. 9.2   Rothi et al.'s (1991) reformulation of Liepmann's (1905) praxis model.

allows one to imitate gestures that does not use any action memory or "movement formula" but instead is performed segmentally by direct access to the innervatory patterns after viewing the performed gesture. This we call the "nonlexical route" of praxis imitation.

As with our own model, Liepmann based his description of the basic praxis components (e.g. movement formula, innervatory patterns) on dissociations of praxis performance in a variety of apraxic patients. For example, Liepmann pointed out that some of his apraxic patients were not able to imitate gesture; a task that should not tax language or symbolic behaviour. Liepmann continued that a few of his patients were able to imitate but not gesture to command. He discussed the notion that his patients were most characteristically unable to gesture "from memory" while a quarter of them were unable to manipulate objects correctly. Thus, Liepmann repeatedly emphasised the need to test gesture imitation, gesture to command, and actual object use, in order to understand the contribution of the various components of action planning.

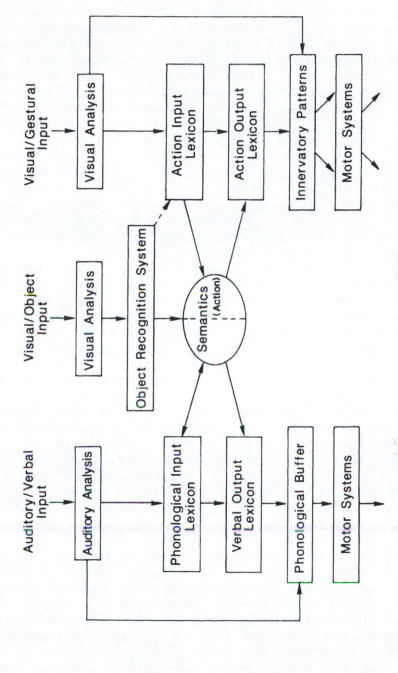

FIG. 9.3 Rothi et al.'s (1991) cognitive neuropsychological model of limb praxis; an elaboration of Liepmann's (1905) basic schema.

119

In conjunction with these behavioural dissociations Liepmann also attempted to extrapolate the nature of the component that was dysfunctional in any particular case. Using information gleaned from the type of errors made by patients, he realised that patients with apraxia may demonstrate a variety of praxis error types (e.g. perseveration of whole movements or aspects of movements, movement substitution, spatial disorganisation, movement delay or protraction, movement "incompleteness", or movement distortion involving such things as errors in hand formation). In addition to making assumptions relating to the nature of the underlying mechanism of the disorder on the basis of error type, Liepmann suggested anatomic-functional relations as well. For example, he suggested that the further posterior a lesion goes, the more likely that error types will reflect misselection of the movement memory with sparing of gesture imitation while more anterior lesions will produce more "amorphic movements" (i.e. mutilations of the correctly selected movement plan) in conjunction with impaired gesture imitation.

Based on these behavioural dissociations and error type distinctions, Liepmann (1905) described several apraxia syndromes (callosal apraxia, motor apraxia, motor or innervatory apraxia, and ideational apraxia) and many of these terms are still used today. For example, Watson and Heilman (1983) described a case of left-hand, callosal apraxia from an ischemic lesion restricted to the body of the corpus callosum. This was precisely consistent with Liepmann's prediction (Liepmann & Maas, 1907) of what a lesion in this anatomic region would produce. But in some cases the terms suggested by Liepmann have been expanded and revised from his initial definition. For example, in his original conceptualisation of ideational apraxia Liepmann did not functionally separate memories of the physical features of an act's movement from its meaning. He collapsed disorders of an action's ideation (e.g. its meaning), disorders of praxis production which result from a loss of the movement formula itself, and disorders of praxis production that reflect disorganisation of the sequences of action components organised in a single item of the movement formula. Ochipa, Rothi, and Heilman (1992) have, in contrast, expanded this class of disorders to distinguish the terms conceptual apraxia and ideational apraxia to refer to the first and third disorders described as features of Liepmann's ideational apraxia respectively. The second disorder Liepmann (1905) described as a feature of ideational apraxia (e.g. as stated above, disorders of praxis production which result from a loss of the movement formula itself) has been termed the "destruction form of ideomotor apraxia" (Heilman, Rothi, & Valenstein, 1982) or a "degraded action memory trace" by Rothi et al. (1991).

In summary, the initial terms originally used by Liepmann led others to begin to consider terms that offer at least some precision in definition when compared to those used previously and this syndrome disambiguation continues to be an important clinical tool in the process of lesion localisation. But one of the problems current readers may have with Liepmann's work is the direct link he made between the symptom complex of a syndrome and its underlying psychological mechanism. Naturally Liepmann was using the terms of his day in application to a model that has subsequently been greatly elaborated but it is clearly helpful to the modern reader to read Liepmann's work without being distracted by the syndromic terms used.

CONCLUSIONS

Liepmann went counter to the norm of his day by stating that disorders of skilled movement planning could not be accounted for by asymbolia or object agnosia. He went on to posit that there was a mechanism in the left hemisphere that guided both sides of the body in skilled movement planning and that this was a multicomponent system; the components of which could fractionate with brain damage. Not only did Liepmann advocate separating apraxia from agnosia and asymbolia, but he also described multiple forms of limb apraxia that were inherently tied to dysfunction in the various components of the proposed underlying mechanism. He suggested that the clinician could discover the underlying mechanism by providing theoretically motivated action testing methods in combination with critical assessment of the nature of the error responses.

ACKNOWLEDGEMENTS

This work was supported by the Medical Research Service of the Department of Veterans Affairs, U.S.A., and National Institutes of Health.

DEDICATION

Hugo Liepmann was born in 1863 in Berlin to Jewish parents and lived in Germany until his death in 1925. His daughter Kate wrote (*Epilogue to H. Liepmann*, 1977; see Liepmann, 1900) that her father's professional aspirations were continually thwarted in the context of the anti-semitism of his day and that this "... continual disappointment threw a shadow over Hugo Liepmann's life." And so, this chapter is dedicated to Hugo Liepmann in recognition of the significance of his contributions. In spite of the antisemitism, his ideas have lived on and continue to influence us.

REFERENCES

Brown, J.W. (Ed.). (1988). *Agnosia and apraxia: Selected papers of Liepmann, Lange, and Pötzl* (pp. 3–39). Hillsdale, NJ: Lawrence Erlbaum Associates Inc.
Haaland, K.Y., & Flaherty, D. (1984). The different types of limb apraxia errors made by patients with left versus right hemisphere damage. *Brain and Cognition, 3*, 370–384.

Heilman, K.M., Rothi, L.J.G., & Valenstein, E. (1982). Two forms of ideomotor apraxia. *Neurology, 32,* 342–346.

Kimura, D. (1980). *Translations from Liepmann's Essays on Apraxia* (Research Bulletin No. 506). Department of Psychology, The University of Western Ontario, London, Canada.

Liepmann, H. (1900). Das Krankheitsbild der Apraxie (Motorische Asymbolie). *Monatschrift für Psychiatrie und Neurologie, 8,* 15–44. Translated in 1977 as The syndrome of apraxia (motor asymboly) based on a case of unilateral apraxia. In D.A. Rottenberg and F.H. Hochberg (Eds.), *Neurological classics in modern translation* (pp. 155–183). New York: Macmillan.

Liepmann, H. (1905). *The left hemisphere and action.* Republished in 1908 in *Drei Aufsatze aus dem Apraxiegebiet.* Berlin: Karger. Translated in 1980 by D. Kimura, *Translations from Liepmann's essays on apraxia* (Research Bulletin No. 506). Department of Psychology, University of Western Ontario, London, Canada.

Liepmann, H., & Maas, O. (1907). Fall con linksseitiger Agraphie und Apraxie bei rechsseitiger Lahmung. *Z. Psychol. Neurol., 10,* 214–227.

Ochipa, C., Rothi, L.J.G., & Heilman, K.M. (1992). Conceptual apraxia in Alzheimer's disease. *Brain, 115,* 1061–1071.

Rothi, L.J.G., Ochipa, C., & Heilman, K.M. (1991). A cognitive neuropsychological model of limb praxis. *Cognitive Neuropsychology, 8,* 443–458.

Steinthal, P. (1871). *Abriss der Sprachwissenschaft.* Berlin.

Watson, R.T., & Heilman, K.M. (1983). Callosal apraxia. *Brain, 106,* 391–403.

10 Balint–Holmes' Syndrome

Ennio De Renzi
Clinica Neurologica, Universita' di Modena, Italy.

The eponym of Balint syndrome was first introduced in neurological parlance by Hécaen and Ajuriaguerra (1954) to acknowledge the outstanding contribution that the Hungarian physician Reszö Balint made in 1909 to the identification of some of the spatial behaviour disorders that ensue bilateral damage to the posterior parietal lobe. Although the spectrum of these deficits is larger than that reported in this paper and Balint (1909) was not the first to draw attention to them, he must receive full credit for having carefully analysed the symptoms of attentional disorders and misreaching and established their association with parietal damage.

Ten years later, the English neurologist Gordon Holmes (1918) added a third symptom, which had not been reported by Balint and is now considered a constitutive component of the syndrome, oculomotor disorders. They are often erroneously identified with the term "psychic paralysis of gaze" ("Seelenlähmung des Schauens") that Balint used to designate the attentional impairment of his patient, but this is a misunderstanding, since the two disorders are basically different in nature. For this reason I propose to identify the full-blown syndrome of bilateral posterior parietal damage with the eponym of Balint–Holmes' syndrome.

It is a recurrent feature of the history of science that for every discovery attributed to an author a forerunner will sooner or later be found. This rule also holds for Balint. Twenty years before the publication of his case, a French ophthalmologist, Jules Badal (1888), reported in detail a patient who, following an episode of eclampsia, presented with a striking impairment of all performances requiring the appreciation of spatial information, among which there were those on which Balint (1909) and Holmes (1918) subsequently focused. Both authors were apparently unaware of this contribution, probably because it had been published in an ophthalmalogical journal which neurologists in the pre-Medline era had little opportunity to access. It would have remained buried therein, had Benton and Meyers (1956) not discovered it and brought it to the attention of the scientific community. We will start with Badal's report because it highlights both the impressive ability of a 19th-century ophthalmologist to find his way out of the forest of neuropsychological disorders consequent to brain damage, and with the decisive contribution of Balint (1909) to the identification of the anatomical underpinnings of the syndrome.

BADAL'S CASE

Badal's (1888) patient was a 31-year-old woman, who became eclamptic a week before a twin birth. She regained consciousness, but remained in a delirious state for some days after the delivery. When two months later Badal saw her, she was co-operative and did not appear mentally deteriorated, though being slow and hesitant in answering questions. The only elementary neurological deficit she presented was a bilateral lower quadrantopsia and a restriction of the upper fields, without, however, any deficit of acuity and chromatic discrimination in central vision. Her impairment became apparent as soon as she was asked to perform tasks that required the processing of spatial information. The spectrum of deranged performances can be subsumed under the following headings:

1. Errors in appreciating the spatial features of an object, namely its size, distance, and relative position with respect to other objects.
2. Errors in reaching for an object under visual guidance. The limb was misdirected and reached outside the target.
3. Though ocular movements were full, she was unable to direct voluntarily her gaze to a target and to maintain fixation on it, once it had by chance been found.
4. She was unable to find her way in familiar surroundings. The impairment was not a mere consequence of her oculomotor and perceptual disorders, because she also failed to describe from memory an itinerary or the layout of the buildings of a well-known place. The profound disorder in guiding ocular and manual movements in space and in estimating spatial relationships was reflected in a series of defective performances, spanning over the whole spectrum of symptoms that were to become popular in the subsequent literature as elements of the parietal syndrome: alexia, agraphia, right–left (and

also top–bottom) disorientation, finger agnosia, acalculia, dressing apraxia, constructional apraxia. The only disorder missing from the list was neglect.

Badal was a keen and painstaking observer of the patient's behaviour and correctly attributed her manifold disorders to the disruption of a basic ability, identified as the sense of space and kept quite distinct from either dementia or primary visual disorders. He was shy, however, of speculating about the biological correlates of the syndrome and, in spite of signs (the bilateral lower quadrantopsia) strongly suggestive of parieto-occipital damage, refrained from venturing into anatomical considerations. Rather, he advanced an interpretation couched in psychiatric terms, speaking of a "neuropsychosis due to physical and moral shock" that he linked to the picture of traumatic hysteria described by Charcot.

BALINT'S PATIENT

Balint had some advantages over Badal that enabled him to put on a firm basis the interpretation of the clinical picture shown by his patient. First, he had a training in neurology, as shown by his previous contributions to the study of hemiplegia, tabe dorsalis, and epilepsy (Husain & Stein, 1988), and was familiar with the literature on brain anatomy and its damage. Second, he had the opportunity to examine the patient over a period of two years, during which he remained substantially stable. Third, and most important, the patient died and autopsy could be carried out. It was also probably an asset to him that his patient presented with a more limited spectrum of disorders than Badal's patient, which allowed him to focus on their specific mechanisms. Symptoms were categorised under two headings: visual and motor disorders.

Visual disorders were in fact disorders of visual attention. They manifested themselves in two ways: (1) Orientation of attention in the extrapersonal space to the right of the body midline and neglect for stimuli lying to the left of the point he was fixating: e.g. when shown a row of letters, he only read that located 35° to the right, stating that nothing else was present. Verbal promptings succeeded in shifting attention to letters lying to the right of that initially perceived, but were less effective for those lying to its left. If the examiner approached the patient, who was sitting on a bench, from the left and reached out his own hand, no reaction was apparent, while his presence was immediately noticed if he repeated the same performance from the right. It is easy to recognise in this behaviour the manifestation of a disorder we are now familiar with and know to be frequently associated with right parietal damage, left neglect; (2) Extreme restriction of visual attention to the point that if, while the patient was focusing on a stimulus, another object was placed close to it, he did not perceive its presence. For instance, if he looked at a pin, he did not notice a candle light, located 5cm away. Visual fields were full and neither the size of the target, nor that of the neighbouring stimuli affected the performance, which could only be improved if the examiner warned the patient to search around more carefully, i.e. by a verbal and not a visual stimulation.

Motor disorders consisted of the directional errors made when the patient tried to reach for an object. For instance, he tried to light a cigar in the middle and not at the end; could not cut a piece of meat, because the knife was directed outside of the plate; made errors in pointing to the middle of a line and, if he lifted the pen from the sheet while drawing or writing, he was unable to bring it back to the right place. That misreaching was not attributable to motor, sensory, or co-ordination deficit of the right limb could be confidently maintained, because elementary motor actions were carried out flawlessly, and because his right-hand movements were correct when they were steered by proprioceptive information: e.g. he was able to point to his own body parts, or to draw a line between two points, provided his right hand was guided by the examiner to one point and the forefinger of the left hand was put on the other.

Last, but not least, the hypothesis that misreaching was secondary to a visuo-spatial deficit could be ruled out by the finding that it was confined to the right limb and did not show up when the patient used his left hand. Such a dissociation between hand performance (a rare event, incidentally, in patients with bilateral damage) was a fortunate feature of this case, because it obviated the inadequate assessment that Balint made of space perception, which was too hastily considered normal in spite of contrary evidence. For instance, the patient was at times uncertain in deciding which of two objects was closer or higher, or in estimating the distance of an approaching vehicle. Since, however, a perceptual disorder would be expected to affect reaching with either hand and not only movements carried out with the right hand, its bearing on the motor performance appeared highly unlikely.

The patient died after six years of disease, during which the clinical pictures remained unmodified. In the last month of life he deteriorated, developing first right hemiparesis, then motor aphasia and dementia.

Autopsy revealed the presence of two nearly symmetrical softenings centred on the posterior parietal areas of the two hemispheres and encroaching upon the surrounding postero-temporal and anterior occipital lobe (Fig. 10.1). The lesion was cortico-subcortical and encroached deep upon the centrum semiovale. On the left, the infarct destroyed the angular and the posterior parietal gyrus entirely, impinging only partially on the superior parietal lobe, the first occipital gyrus, and the second temporary gyrus. On the right, the cortical lesion was somewhat larger extending forwards to the supramarginal gyrus and backwards to the superior parietal

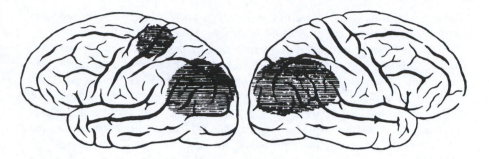

FIG. 10.1   Balint's drawing of the extent of lesion in his case.

lobe and the occipital lobe. White matter damage was more marked on the left. There was also a smaller infarct encroaching upon the left precentral and postcentral gyrus.

The interpretation Balint (1909) proposed for the symptoms of restriction of attention and misreaching was couched in disconnectionistic terms. The integrity of the optic radiations and the primary visual cortex, found at autopsy, confirmed the clinical evidence that the visual fields of both eyes were full and that stimuli appearing in any of their sectors could be transmitted to the visual centres and adequately processed. Yet objects at the periphery of the fixation point did not attain conscious awareness and failed to trigger the automatic eye movements needed to bring them into macular vision. Balint argued that the reason why visual stimuli went unnoticed was that the lesion in the parietal white matter interrupted the fibre bundles connecting the occipital lobe with the remainder of the cerebral mantle and isolated the information in the visual cortex. Consequently, it could not reach other cortical regions and access the associations that mediate attentional processes.

Balint emphasised that the disorder of attention was specific for visual information and not general, since the patient promptly reacted to auditory and tactile stimuli and improved his performance when urged to look more carefully for the missing target. Admittedly, this interpretation of restriction of attention is formulated in vague terms and betrays, as Husain and Stein (1988) have pointed out, the absence of a model of attention in which to frame empirical data. Also, the anatomical account is unsatisfactory, for it leaves unspecified where the pathways transmitting visual information end and does not explain why the interruption of the outflow from the visual cortex did not affect awareness of macular stimuli.

The hypothesis of a disconnection between visual and motor centres looks more plausible for a symptom, such as optic ataxia, which implies that the guidance of hand movements by visual information is hampered. The deeper extension of the lesion in the white matter of the left hemisphere was held responsible for the restriction of misreaching to the right hand.

The only symptom that Balint attributed to the breakdown of a centre, and not to the interruption of fibre bundles, was the shift of attention to the right side of space that the patient manifested when confronted with an array of stimuli spanning over the whole visual field. It was thought to reflect the imbalance between the eye and the head movement apparatuses located in each hemisphere, which govern gaze movements to the contralateral side. Balint tentatively located the gaze centre in the supramarginal gyrus and argued that, since this area was damaged in the right brain only, the intact left-hemisphere apparatus prevailed and led to rightwards displacement of attention. Left neglect was traced back to the disruption of an oculomotor mechanism and interpreted as a minor manifestation of the phenomenon of ipsilateral gaze deviation, which had been described by Prevost (1868) and attributed to the inferior parietal lobe damage by Landouzy (1876).

HOLMES' PATIENTS

Balint's (1909) case report did not attract much attention from the subsequent literature and when, nine years later, Holmes (1918) reported a syndrome that overlapped to a considerable extent with that described by the Hungarian neurologist, he barely mentioned Balint. Holmes' study concerned six patients with penetrating missile wounds of the brain, to whom a seventh patient was added a year later (Holmes & Horrax, 1919). They presented with an array of symptoms, summarised in Table 10.1, that pointed to a profound disorder of visual orientation.

The main difference between this picture and that reported by Balint (1909) was the presence of oculomotor disorders, for which Cogan and Adams (1953) subsequently proposed the appropriate label of oculomotor apraxia. Although Balint (1909) had used the term "psychic paralysis of gaze" to define his patient's inability to explore space, it is clear from his description that he attributed the gaze impairment to "restriction of visual attention" and not to a defective oculomotor control. He was adamant in stating that eye movements were "correct" (p. 52) and "completely free' (p. 70). Admittedly, his description of how the different types of eye movements were assessed was not as fastidious as would have been desired and it is possible that minor deficits went unnoticed, but it seems unlikely that he missed oculomotor disorders as severe as those shown by Holmes' patients. They could move their eyes in any direction spontaneously, in response to a sudden sound, or towards a part of their own body that had been named or touched by the examiner (with the exception of patient 5), but failed when requested to search for a visual target or to direct their gaze to a stimulus

TABLE 10.1
Symptoms Displayed by Holmes' Patients

Patient no.	Oculomotor apraxia	Misreaching	Disorders of attention	Space perception disorders	Run into things	Topographical disorientation
1	+	+	+	+	+	+
2	+	+	Right neglect	+	+	
3	+	+		+	+	
4	+	+	Left neglect	+	+	
5	+	+		+	+	+
6	+	+		+	+	+
7	+	+	+	+		+

+ = presence of symptoms. Patient 7 was reported by Holmes and Horrax (1919).

129

suddenly appearing in the peripheral field. In such a case eye movements often initiated with the patient staring in the wrong direction and then rolling his eyes about until he found, as if by chance, the target. For instance, asked to look at the ceiling, Holmes' (1918) patient 1 "pointed correctly to it with his hand, but moved the eyes first to the right, then to the left and finally downwards." In less severe cases the search was slow and awkward and when the patient's eyes eventually fell on the target, they easily lost it and could hardly find it again. Not only visually elicited saccades and fixation, but also following movements, convergence upon a near object, and the blinking reflex in reaction to a threatening stimulus were poorly controlled.

Another symptom, which Holmes emphasised and investigated much more carefully than Balint, was the inability to appreciate the relative position of objects in space, namely, to say which of them was the nearer or the higher, at what distance did it lie and to discriminate between two lines of different length or two objects of different size. The impairment shown in space perception was held responsible for the patients' difficulty in reading (they frequently lost the place, skipping some lines, and settling on another column), in counting scattered points (some were neglected and some counted twice or more), in walking (they easily bumped into objects) and in reaching for a target. Optic ataxia was as striking in Holmes' patients as it had been in Balint's (1909) patient; it affected equally both hands and was more marked when the patient kept central fixation and the target appeared at the periphery of the visual . field. Holmes, however, interpreted misreaching in a radically different way from Balint (1909), since he viewed it as a direct consequence of defective space perception and not as an autonomous symptom, produced by the disconnection of motor from visual centres.

Disorders of visual attention, which represented a key symptom of Balint's patient, were not to the forefront in Holmes' patients. A consistent shift of attention to the right with consequent neglect for the left space was mentioned in just one patient (No. 4), while another (No. 2) showed poor attention for stimuli lying to the right. Restriction of attention with consequent inability to see more than one object at a time was more common and particularly evident in the patient reported by Holmes and Horrax (1919) who, though able to recognise a large object and even a complex geometrical figure presented at a near distance, missed a second stimulus placed close to it. For instance, he immediately recognised a square, but, when a cross was drawn in its centre, at first he only saw that, and identified the surrounding figure only after considerable hesitation.

Autopsy was available in two patients, while in the remainder the locus of damage was reconstructed from the entrance and exist wounds produced by the missile. From these strands of evidence Holmes (1918) argued that the lesion was bilateral and roughly symmetrical. On the lateral surface of the hemispheres it involved an area centred on the angular and supramarginal gyrus and extending into the adjoining occipital, temporal, and parietal convolutions. The missile trajectory was thought to have likely injured the fibre bundles running in the white matter of the parietal lobe and the splenial region.

The relative role played by cortical and subcortical damage in causing the symptoms was not altogether clear to Holmes, but he was inclined to attribute oculomotor disorders to the damage of the angular gyrus and space perception deficit to the severing of "the association fibres between those portions of the occipital cortex concerned in visual perception and the rest of the brain."

FURTHER DEVELOPMENTS OF BALINT–HOLMES' SYNDROME

The bilateral involvement of the posterior parietal lobe that characterises Balint–Holmes' syndrome was instrumental in magnifying the role this region plays in mediating space-directed behaviour and provided impetus for investigating other manifestations of spatial disorders, occurring after unilateral damage, such as constructional apraxia (Kleist, 1934), finger agnosia, and right–left disorientation (Gerstmann, 1930). Following the Second World War, new case reports of Balint–Holmes' syndrome were published, some showing its full-blown picture and some its elements in isolation, associated with bilateral and even with unilateral parietal damage. A major contribution to the comprehension of these data came from monkey studies, which recorded single neuron activity contingent on the animal's behaviour and replicated aspects of the clinical syndrome by making well-circumscribed parietal lesions. These advances in the understanding of the syndrome will be reviewed separately for each symptom.

Oculomotor Apraxia

The uncommitted term "oculomotor disorders", used by Holmes (1918), was substituted by Cogan and Adams (1953) with that of "oculomotor apraxia", which underscores the dissociation, shown by these patients, between the integrity of random eye movements and the disruption of intentional ocular movements, whether elicited verbally or by the presentation of visual or auditory stimuli. Tracking movements also are impaired, and Cogan and Adams' patient 1 showed spasm of fixation, i.e. the inability to divert her gaze from the object she was fixating. Other elements of Balint–Holmes' syndrome can be absent in patients with oculomotor apraxia (Brekelmans & Tijssen, 1990; Cogan & Adams, 1953; Monaco, Piresi, Sechi, & Cossu, 1980; Pierrot-Deseilligny, Gautier, &

Loron, 1988; Waltz, 1961), attesting to the independence of the oculomotor impairment from attentional and reaching disorders. For instance, Pierrot-Deseilligny et al. (1988) reported a patient who, though unable to initiate saccades and keep his eyes permanently immobile, could easily name objects placed in any part of the visual field.

There is an ongoing debate as to whether the lack of control on eye movements is entirely ascribable to bilateral parietal damage or whether it also requires the involvement of the frontal eye field (FEF, area 8), a region that has been traditionally associated with saccade generation.

In 1938 Holmes published an influential paper in which he claimed that control of saccades was the province of the FEF, while that of tracking movements and fixation was contingent on parieto-occipital cortex activity. This conceptualisation received wide acceptance in the literature and led Daroff and Hoyt (1971) to posit that bilateral damage to area 8 produces "global saccadic paralysis" or "acquired apraxia of saccades". Animal and human evidence supporting this contention is meagre. In monkeys, unilateral FEF ablation causes at most a fleeting reduction of contralateral saccades (Latto & Cowey, 1971; Schiller, True, & Conway, 1980). In humans, Guitton, Buchtel, and Douglas (1985) found the performance of patients with removal of the dorso-lateral frontal cortex indistinguishable from that of temporal lobectomised patients and normal controls, when they were required to move their eyes towards a cue appearing in either visual field. It was only when the task requested to inhibit the response to the cue and to move the eyes in the opposite direction that a deficit in suppressing disallowed glances at the cue appeared. Even this defective inhibition of reflexive glances could not be replicated by Paus, Kalina, Patockova, Angerova, Cerny, Mecir, Bauer, and Krabec (1991), who pointed out that in Guitton et al.'s (1985) patients the lesion extended into the mesial side of the frontal cortex and almost certainly encroached upon the supplementary motor area. Since damage confined to this region was sufficient to impair the suppression of reflexive saccades to a peripheral cue, Paus et al. (1991) challenged the specific role of FEF. That the frontal cortex (not only the FEF, but also the supplementary motor area, see Schall, 1991) participates in the generation of goal directed saccades is not questioned, and has been confirmed by intracellular recording (Bruce & Goldberg, 1985). The relevance of its lesion to the disruption of voluntary eye movements remains, however, to be proven, and there is no evidence that it has consequences comparable to those of parietal damage. Most of the patients with isolated oculomotor apraxia have lesions involving the upper fronto-parietal region, but there are patients with Balint–Holmes' syndrome and damage confined to the parietal lobe (Guard, Perenian, Vighetto, Giroud, Tommasi, & Dumas, 1984; Holmes, 1918), whose eye movement disorder is no less severe than that of patients with damage to both lobes.

Neurons discharging before and during the execution of optically elicited and memory-guided saccades have been recorded in the lateral intraparietal area (Anderson, Asanuma, & Cowan, 1985; Lynch, Graybiel, & Lobeck, 1985) and have been implicated in the transformation of visual information for the planning of saccades (Barash, Bracewell, Fogassi, Gnadt, & Anderson, 1991). They project to the deep layers of the superior colliculus, which is connected with the paramedian pontine reticular formation, where also ends the pathway coming directly from the FEF (Leichnetz, 1981). Thus, we have two cortical areas, the FEF and the parietal lobe, involved in the generation of saccades but, as far as can be judged from human pathology, the role of the latter is overwhelmingly superior.

Attentional Disorders

Two disorders of visual attention were pointed out by Balint (1909) in his patient. The former was the shift of attention to a stimulus lying to the right of the midline and the extreme reluctance to reorient attention towards stimuli located to its left. This is the well-known phenomenon of left neglect, occurring after right parietal damage, which Balint (1909) tentatively attributed to the more extensive involvement of the parietal region in the right than in the left hemisphere. The unique feature of Balint's patient was, however, his inability to see more than one object at a time, a deficit pointing to the disrupted distribution of attentional resources between focal vision and panoramic vision. The behavioural consequence of the attentional disorder spans over a gamut of performances from reading to counting, pointing to objects, writing, etc. However, the manifestation that has been given more emphasis is the inability to grasp the meaning of a scene, in spite of the correct identification of its elements. Following Luria (1959), this impairment is referred to in the literature under the name of "simultanagnosia", a term first introduced by Wolpert (1924) to define a particular form of recognition deficit, in which the patient, though not agnosic in the classical sense, fails to establish meaningful relations among the figures of a complex picture and to organise them in a coherent whole. No other element of Balint–Holmes' syndrome was present in Wolpert's patient, nor could his recognition deficit be attributed to elementary perceptual or motor deficits.

Simultanagnosia was conceived of by Wolpert (1924) as a disorder intermediate between intelligence and recognition, a rather vague formulation that did not help in defining the boundaries of the symptom and favoured its use in the subsequent literature to cover phenomena having different features and mechanisms and just linked by the defective understanding of the meaning of a scene. Thus, in addition to simultanagnosia observed in the context of Balint–Holmes' syndrome, such as in Luria's (1959) patient, and associated with parietal damage, the same label has been given to a second form, associated with left inferior temporo-occipital damage (Kinsbourne & Warrington, 1962, 1963; Levine & Calvanio, 1978). Farah (1990) has called them dorsal and ventral simultanagnosia, respectively. Ventral simultanagnosia is characterised by the defective interpretation of a scene and by letter-by-letter reading, but not by the failure to see more than one object at a time, typical of dorsal simultanagnosia. On tachistoscopic presentation these patients can easily identify single letters or shapes, but have an abnormally elevated threshold with two items and need longer intervals to identify stimuli presented in succession. Consequently, the basic deficit of this form was thought to reside in a slowed rate of visual information processing, which would increase the "refractory period" between the successive perceptual acts that occur in the scanning of a picture or a word (Kinsbourne & Warrington, 1962). The term simultanagnosia has also been used by Rizzo and Hurtig (1987) to label a clinical syndrome featured by fragmentary perception of the environment or of complex pictures and dependent on the sudden disappearance of the stimulus the patient is actively fixating. In a sense this phenomenon is the opposite of that seen in dorsal simultanagnosia: Here the patient is aware of objects outside of fixation, while the central stimulus intermittently fades; in dorsal simultanagnosia the opposite occurs.

Dorsal simultanagnosia appears not only in the context of Balint–Holmes' syndrome, but also in an attenuated and isolated form, as in the case of Coslett and Saffran (1991), in whom ocular movements were normal and there was only a mild misreaching of the left hand. To grasp the meaning of a complex picture—the authors argued—the patient has to carry out successive fixations, each of which provides data on both the content and the location of an item. Content is identified through the activation of a structured representation but, to identify the meaning of the whole picture, the output of this system must be kept in registration with the sites of a spatial buffer, where the location of single items is temporarily stored. The patient's performance on a series of tests led Coslett and Saffran (1991) to argue that his simultanagnosia was contingent on the weakness of the attentional process linking the structured descriptions with their corresponding sites in the visual buffer. The abnormally quick fading of the linkage between content and spatial information would make it impossible to associate object identity with is location and would render the patient unable to integrate in a whole the products of the single acts of fixation.

In the extreme forms of simultanagnosia manifested by patients who cannot see but a single object at a time, more than a mere weakening of the linkage between content and spatial information is likely to be implicated. Luria (1959) invoked a very broad pathophysiological mechanism, by which in a lesioned brain the focus of excitation would induce the abnormal inhibition of the surrounding tissue, making unresponsive the visual cortex receiving input from the peripheral retina when the macular cortex is activated. Such a general account leaves unexplained many features of the disorder, e.g. the inability shown by these patients (Luria, 1959; Sorgato, 1976) to see two points drawn 5mm from each other, while they can perceive a large Star of David. It would appear that a single stimulus absorbs all attentional capacity, independently of the size of the cortex by which it is processed, leaving no resource available for surveying the periphery of the visual field.

Based on the fractionation of the attentional process into computation subcomponents (shifting, engaging, disengaging), Posner, Walker, Friedrich, and Rafel (1984) have proposed that the basic difficulty met by right parietal patients to orient their attention to the side contralateral to the lesion resides in their inability to disengage attention from its previous right location. If the same mechanism is extended to cases with bilateral parietal lesion (Farah, 1990), we are faced with a patient who becomes a prey of a sort of spasm of focal attention. This is reminiscent of the phenomenon of spasm of fixation, pointed out by Holmes (1930, 1938) and sometimes reported in patients with Balint–Holmes' syndrome (Hausser, Robert, & Giard, 1980; Hécaen & Ajuriaguerra, 1954; Michel, Jeannerod, & Devic, 1965):They stare open-eyed, as if their gaze were locked to the spot they are fixating and can only dissociate their eyes from the target by rapidly turning their head, or closing their lids. Spasm of attention can be conceived of as an attenuated form of spasm of fixation.

The anatomo-physiological foundation of restriction of attention has been clarified by animal studies, which have shown that the posterior parietal cortex contains neurons that increase their discharge rate when, and only when a stimulus that is relevant to the animal, because it has been associated with a reward, appears in a specified sector of visual space, while the animal is maintaining central fixation (Bushnell, Goldberg, & Robinson, 1981; Yin & Mountcastle, 1977). Following a unilateral lesion of the same area, contralateral neglect has been reported following double simultaneous stimulus presentation and even following single stimulus presentation (Denny-Brown & Chambers, 1958; Deuel, 1987). With bilateral removal, the monkey would not notice an object approaching to him from the periphery, if his visual attention was intently fixed on the examiner (Denny-Brown & Chambers, 1958). Rizzolatti and Gallese (1988) argue that the crucial area is located in the lateral bank of the intraparietal sulcus (are POa). The pattern of connectivity characterising this sector of the posterior parietal cortex makes it a suitable candidate for serving visual attentional mechanisms: it receives information from the lunate gyrus and sends afferents to the frontal eye field and the superior colliculus (Anderson et al., 1985). The posterior parietal lobe is not the only region equipped with neuronal networks mediating attentional performances, but its role is prevalent, as shown by the finding that it represents the most frequent anatomical correlate of unilateral neglect in man (Vallar & Perani, 1986). It is, therefore, understandable that bilateral damage to this area results in the inability to take cognisance of stimuli lying outside the point of fixation.

Disorders of Reaching

Reaching movements involve two components, the displacement of the whole limb near the target, which in the normal adult is executed with a single ballistic movement, and the preshaping of fingers to prepare them for grasping, which consists of small, corrective movements, guided by the spatial orientation of the target (Gheorgopoulos, 1986). The two components can be differentiated both in terms of the information they receive and of the motor system they use to steer the cervical spine neurons. The input for arm movements comes from visual centres concerned with the spatial location of the target, that for hand movements must also involve information from centres processing the shape of the target. The efferent pathways for proximal movements are bilateral, those for distal movements originate from the contralateral cortex only (Brinkman & Kuypers, 1973).

Haaxma and Kuypers (1975) have tested Balint's (1909) hypothesis that misreaching is due to the disconnection of motor from visual centres, produced by the transection of occipito-frontal pathways running in the parietal white matter. They submitted monkeys to unilateral parieto-occipital leucotomy and then to callosal section, in order to isolate the motor cortex from both ipsilateral and contralateral visual information. The animal was trained to pick up small pellets from a circular well, by inserting two fingers into the opposite grooves that gave access to the well and that were differently oriented from trial to trial. When the monkey was tested two months following the leucotomy, the hand ipsilateral to the lesion retrieved the pellets carefully, while the contralateral one came near the target but adapted its fingers poorly to the groove orientation. The subsequent section of the commissures further deteriorated finger shaping, but not arm movements.

It is worth comparing this behaviour with that of patients who show misreaching after a unilateral lesion localised in the posterior parietal region (Castaigne, Pertuiset, Rondot, & de Recondo, 1971; Castaigne, Rondot, Ribadeau Dumas, & Tempier, 1975; Ferro, 1984; Levine, Kaufman, & Mohr, 1978; Riddoch, 1935; Rondot, de Recondo, & Ribadeau Dumas, 1977, case 5; Tzavaras & Masure, 1976, case 2). The most substantial series has been reported by Perenin and Vighetto (1988). The main differences between monkeys and man can be summarised as follows:

(1) Monkeys fail while looking at the target, while most patients only fail in peripheral vision. The deficit increases if the patient is not allowed to see the moving limb.

(2) In the monkey the disorder affects finger shaping and is more akin to apraxia than to optic ataxia. In man it mainly concerns the direction and amplitude of the limb movement and results in the hand reaching beside or beyond the target. However, also a deficit in the orientation of the hand movement with respect to the spatial features of the target was detected in patients with misreaching, when a test modelled on that of Haaxma and Kuypers (1975) was used (Perenin & Vighetto, 1988). It was present in both hands and its severity did not correlate with that of apraxia.

(3) While in the monkey errors are confined to the contralateral hand (but movements in peripheral vision were not tested by Haaxma & Kuypers, 1975), the most common pattern of impairment found in man is misreaching of both hands in the contralateral field. Other patterns have also been occasionally reported, e.g. misreaching of the contralateral hand alone in the contralateral field (Castaigne et al., 1971), or of the contralateral hand in both fields and of the ipsilateral hand in the contralateral field (Ferro, 1984; Levine et al., 1978). The detailed analysis of three right brain-damaged patients and seven left brain-damaged patients with optic ataxia convinced Perenin and Vighetto (1988) that the hand–field pattern they exhibited in misreaching differs according to the involved hemisphere. While both groups showed a field effect—both hands failed in the contralateral field— left brain-damaged patients also exhibited a hand effect, manifest through the errors made by the contralateral (right) hand in the ipsilateral (left) field. The various combinations of hand and field effects have been attributed by Rondot et al. (1977) to the interruption at different levels of the connections linking the visual cortex of one side with the ipsilateral and contralateral motor cortex (for a detailed account, see De Renzi, 1982), but this interpretation, which has been recently endorsed by Pierrot-Deseilligny, Gray, and Brunet (1986), remains largely speculative, because of the incomplete knowledge we have of the course of the pathways relevant to the task and the difficulty we meet in identifying the locus and extent of lesion in clinical cases.

By and large, the conclusion seems warranted that the lesion assumed by Balint (1909) to be responsible for optic ataxia in his patient, i.e. fibre transection in the parietal white matter, does not produce a comparable form of misreaching in animals. Optic ataxia does occur in monkeys, but only when damage involves the parietal cortex. Unilateral removal of a region including the intraparietal sulcus and the bordering areas 5 and 7 caused gross errors in direction and amplitude of contralateral hand movements in both visual fields (Hartje & Ettlinger, 1973; Mountcastle,

1975). A subsequent study (Faugier-Grimaud, Frenois, & Stein, 1978) pointed to area 7 as the crucial region, although misreaching was transient if the ablation did not extend to area 5. Single cell recordings have shown neurons in areas 5 and 7 discharging before and during reaching to an object (Hyvarinen & Poranen, 1974). Most cells of area 5 fired in association with movements of the contralateral hand, while those of area 7 were related to the activity of either hands (Mountcastle, Lynch, Gheorgopoulos, Sakata, & Acuna, 1975). The discharge of these neurons begins before the onset of the movement, reaches a peak as the arm moves to the target and declines to zero before the target is reached. Their activity is, consequently, correlated with the ballistic, transport phase of reaching and not with the grasping phase. There is, therefore, evidence that the programming of reaching movements is mediated by the posterior parietal region, where the visuo-spatial co-ordinates of the target are coded and transformed in appropriate commands guiding the motor displacement of the limb.

How does the visual information processed by the posterior parietal cortex reach the motor cortex? Direct connections do not exist, and it is, therefore, generally assumed that the parietal outflow travels through intermediate relays: first area 8, then area 6, and finally area 4. On this account, one would, however, predict that following area 8 ablation the same impairment obtains as following damage to the posterior parietal lobe, but Glickstein and May (1982) maintain that in monkeys the effect of area 8 removal on hand performance is surprisingly meagre. They suggest that the transfer of visual information is accomplished trough a cortico-subcortical loop, involving the parieto-ponto-cerebellar pathway and the cerebellar-thalamic (nucleus ventralis-lateralis) area 4 connections.

It remains to spend a few words on the view, advanced by Holmes (1918), that optic ataxia is not an autonomous disorder, but the mere consequence of the errors parietal patients make in appreciating the spatial location of objects (De Renzi, 1982). This reductionist approach was justified in some of his patients by the severe distortion of the spatial co-ordinates of objects they showed. Although a perceptual contribution to misreaching cannot be excluded in a few bilateral cases, its role is minimal in unilateral cases, who make correct estimates of the distance and orientation of the target (Levine et al., 1978) and who do not show a correlation between space perception errors and reaching errors (Perenin & Vighetto, 1988). Also, the perceptual deficit is clearly inadequate to account for reaching errors confined to one hand.

CONCLUDING REMARKS

Several strands of evidence concur to support the position that a disconnection between visual and motor centres is an oversimplified interpretation of the symptoms of Balint–Holmes' syndrome. Such an oversimplification does not do justice to the paramount role played by the posterior parietal cortex in processing space information and guiding eye and limb movements towards extrapersonal targets. The parietal cortex extends widely behind the postcentral gyrus and it would be interesting to identify the areas that are responsible for the disruption of oculomotor, reaching and attentional mechanisms. Unfortunately, the available evidence is scanty and conflicting and its interpretation meets with the difficulty common to any attempt to draw anatomo-clinical correlations from large lesions. Holmes (1918) focused on the angular gyrus, but his speculation rested on autopsy data (available in two cases only), which were confined to macroscopic anatomy and lacked histological documentation. In the subsequent literature the involvement of the inferior parietal lobe has not been consistently confirmed: vis-à-vis cases (Pierrot-Deseilligny et al., 1986; Rapcsak, Cimino, & Heilman, 1988; Rousseaux, Delafosse, Devos, Quint, & Lesoin, 1986) where this location has been proved, there are others (Kase, Troncoso, Court, Tapia, & Mohr, 1977; Michel et al., 1965) in which it was the superior parietal lobe which bore the brunt of the lesion. These conflicting sets of data might be reconciled, if we assume that the critical locus of damage resides in a region that is intermediate between the superior and the inferior subdivision of the posterior parietal cortex, i.e. the intraparietal sulcus, which separates the two zones. Its two banks, particularly the lateral one (called area PO in the monkey), receive a strong visual input from the lunate gyrus and send important projections to the FEF and the superior colliculus. Its neurons have been implicated in visual attention and in the control of saccades. Perenin and Vighetto (1988) emphasised the role that damage to the intraparietal sulcus and the adjacent cortex plays in optic ataxia and contrasted this locus of lesion with that implicated in attentional disorders, which would be centred around the inferior parietal lobe.

However, this parcellation of the anatomical substrate of Balint–Holmes' syndrome is at variance with the findings of Michel et al. (1965) and Kase et al. (1977), whose patients, though suffering from severe restriction of attention, had superior parietal damage that left the inferior parietal lobe unaffected. It is worth stressing that the figures displaying the extent of lesion in Balint's (1909) patient did show the involvement of the intraparietal sulcus. The emphasis given to the intraparietal sulcus does not exclude the participation of other parietal areas. For instance, the precuneus has been found involved on the right side in Guard et al.'s (1984) patient, who had a full-blown Balint–Holmes' syndrome, and in the patient of Levine et al. (1978) who showed misreaching alone.

So far we have focused on disorders of visually guided behaviour and discussed them as consequent to the impairment of the neural apparatus involved in the computation and transmission of visuo-spatial data to motor centres. In fact, this is the prevailing pattern of disturbance of Balint–Holmes' syndrome and most case reports explicitly mention that the patients' responses were appropriate when the information on the target location was given tactually (touching the patient's body) or by the sound emitted by the object. There are, however, patients who also fail to orient their gaze or their hands towards the source of a sound (Guard et al., 1984; Holmes, 1918, patient 5; Kase et al., 1977) and De Renzi (1988) has reported a patient who, when blindfolded, made gross errors in looking and pointing to the direction of a sound and to his own thumb, passively moved by the examiner. Little is known from cell recording and ablation studies on the distribution of neurons that process the spatial co-ordinates of auditory or somatosensory stimuli and it is, therefore, open to question whether they are intermingled with visually elicited neurons or are packed in separate cortical areas.

A few patients with Balint–Holmes' syndrome show an inability to orient to a target, which is not limited to eye and hand movements but also involves whole body movements. When Holmes' (1918, p. 225) patient 5 was told to sit on a chair, "he either walked abruptly into it, or mistaking its direction passed it". On trying to get in her bed, Kase et al.'s (1977, p. 269) patient laid down perpendicular to the long axis of the bed and "after many unsuccessful attempts to correct her position ... including a completely upside-down one, she should react catastrophically". Requested to sit down on a chair, De Renzi's (1988) patient failed to orient his body with respect to its plane, sat down on the arm of the chair instead of the seat and fell down painfully. All of these patients made errors in estimating the position of objects relative to each other, but it is dubious that the perceptual deficit can on its own account for the inability to take the correct body position and it is more likely that the motor centres were completely bereft of any detailed information on how to adapt body orientation to the target.

REFERENCES

Anderson, R.A., Asanuma, C., & Cowan, W.M. (1985). Callosal and prefrontal associational projecting cell populations in area 7a of the macaque monkey: A study using retrogradely transported fluoroescent dyes. *Journal of Comparative Neurology, 232*, 443–465.

Badal, J. (1888). Contribution a l'étude des cécités psychiques: Alexie, agraphie, hémianopsie inferieure, trouble du sens de l'espace. *Archives d'Ophthalmologie, 140*, 97–117.

Balint, R. (1909). Seelenlähmung des "Schauens", optische Ataxie, räumliche Störung der Aufmerksamkeit. *Monatshrift für Psychiatrie und Neurologie, 25*, 51–81.

Barash, S., Bracewell, R.M., Fogassi, L., Gnadt, J.W., & Anderson, R.A. (1991). Saccade-related activity in the lateral intraparietal area: No. 1. Temporal properties: Comparison with area 7a. *Journal of Neurophysiology, 60*, 1095–1108.

Benton, A.L., & Meyers, R. (1956). An early description of the Gerstmann syndrome. *Neurology, 6*, 838–842.

Brekelmans, G.J.F., & Tijssen, C.C. (1990). Acquired ocular motor apraxia in an AIDS patient with bilateral fronto-parietal lesions. *Neuro-ophthalmology, 10,* 53–56.

Brinkman, J., & Kuypers, H.G.J.M. (1973). Cerebral contralateral and ipsilateral arm and finger movements in the split-brain rhesus monkey. *Brain, 96,* 653–674.

Bruce, C.J., & Goldberg, M.E. (1985). Primate frontal eye fields: No. 1. Single neurons discharging before saccades. *Journal of Neurophysiology, 53,* 603–635.

Bushnell, M.C., Goldberg, M.E., & Robinson, D.L. (1981). Behavioural enhancement of visual responses in monkey cerebral cortex: No. 1. Modulation in posterior parietal cortex related to selective visual attention. *Journal of Neurophysiology, 46,* 755–772.

Castaigne, P., Pertuiset, B., Rondot, P., & de Recondo, J. (1971). Ataxie optique dans les deux hémichamps visuels homonymes gauches après exérèse chirurgicale d'un anéurysm artériel de la paroi du ventricule latéral. *Revue Neurologique, 124,* 261–268.

Castaigne, P., Rondot, P., Ribadeau Dumas, J.L., & Tempier, P. (1975). Ataxie optique localisé au coté gauche dans les deux hémichamps visuels homonymes gauches. *Revue Neurologique, 131,* 23–28.

Cogan, D.G., & Adams, R.D. (1953). A type of paralysis of coniugate gaze (ocular motor apraxia). *Archives of Ophthalmology, 50,* 434–442.

Coslett, H.B., & Saffran, E. (1991). Simultanagnosia. To see but not two see. *Brain, 114,* 1523–1545.

Daroff, R.B., & Hoyt, W.F. (1971). Supranuclear disorders of ocular control system in man: Clinical, anatomical and physiological correlations. In P. Bach-y-Rita, C.C. Collins, & J.E. Hide (Eds.), *The control of eye movements.* New York: Academic Press.

Denny-Brown, D., & Chambers, R.A. (1958). The parietal lobe and behaviour. *Proceedings of the Association for Research in Nervous and Mental Disease, 36,* 35–117.

De Renzi, E. (1982). *Disorders of space exploration and cognition.* Chichester: J. Wiley.

De Renzi, E. (1988). Oculomotor disturbances in hemispheric disease. In C.W. Johnston & F. Pirozzolo (Eds.), *Neuropsychology of eye movements.* Hillsdale, NJ: Lawrence Erlbaum Associates Inc.

Deuel, R.K. (1987). Neural dysfunction during hemineglect after cortical damage in two monkey models. In M. Jeannerod (Ed.), *Neurophysiological and neuropsychological aspects of spatial neglect.* Amsterdam: Elsevier.

Farah, M.J. (1990). *Visual agnosia.* Cambridge, MA: MIT Press.

Faugier-Grimaud, S., Frenois, C., & Stein, D.G. (1978). Effects of posterior parietal lesions on visually guided behavior in monkeys. *Neuropsychologia, 16,* 151–169.

Ferro, J.M. (1984). Transient inaccuracy in reaching caused by a posterior parietal lobe lesion. *Journal of Neurology, Neurosurgery and Psychiatry, 47,* 1016–1019.

Gerstmann, J. (1930). Zur Symptomatologie der Hirnlasionen in Übergangsgebiet der unteren Parietal und mittleren Occipitalwindung. *Nervenartz, 3,* 691–695.

Gheorgopoulos, A. (1986). On reaching. *Annual Review of Neuroscience, 9,* 147–170.

Glickstein, M., & May, J.G. (1982). Visual control of movement. In W.D. Neff (Ed.), *Contributions to sensory physiology (Vol. 7).* New York: Academic Press.

Guard, O., Perenin, M.T., Vighetto, A., Giroud, M., Tommasi, M., & Dumas, R. (1984). Syndrome pariétal bilatéral proche d'un syndrome de Balint. *Revue Neurologique, 140,* 358–367.

Guitton, D., Buchtel, H.A., & Douglas, R.M. (1985). Frontal lobe lesions in man cause difficulties in suppressing reflexive glances and in generating goal-directed saccades. *Experimental Brain Research, 58,* 435–472.

Haaxma, R., & Kuypers, H.G.J.M. (1975). Intrahemispheric cortical connexions and visual guidance of hand and finger movements in the rhesus monkey. *Brain, 98,* 239–260.

Hartje, W., & Ettlinger, G. (1973). Reaching in light and dark after unilateral posterior parietal ablations in the monkey. *Cortex, 9,* 346–354.

Hausser, C.D., Robert, F., & Giard, N. (1980). Balint's syndrome. *Canadian Journal of Neurological Sciences, 7,* 157–161.

Hécaen, H., & Ajuriaguerra, J. (1954). Balint syndrome (psychic paralysis of gaze) and its minor forms. *Brain, 77,* 373–400.

Holmes, G. (1918). Disturbances of visual orientation. *British Journal of Ophthalmology, 2,* 449–468, 506–518.

Holmes, G. (1930). Spasm of fixation. *Transactions of the Opthalomological Society, U.K., 50,* 253–262.

Holmes, G. (1938). The cerebral integration of the ocular movements. *British Medical Journal, 2,* 107–112.

Holmes, G., & Horrax, G. (1919). Disturbances of spatial orientation and visual attention with loss of stereoscopic vision. *Archives of Neurology and Psychiatry, 1,* 385–407.

Husain,M., & Stein, J. (1988). Rezsö Balint and his most celebrated case. *Archives of Neurology, 45,* 89–93.

Hyvarinen, J., & Poranen, A. (1974). Function of the parietal associative area 7 as revealed from cellular discharges in alert monkey. *Brain, 97,* 673–692.

Kase, C.S., Troncoso, J.F., Court, J.E., Tapia, J.F., & Mohr, J.P. (1977). Global spatial disorientation. *Journal of the Neurological Sciences, 34,* 267–278.

Kinsbourne, M., & Warrington, E.K. (1962). A disorder of simultaneous form perception. *Brain, 85,* 461–486.

Kinsbourne, M., & Warrington, E.K. (1963). The localizing significance of limited simultaneous form perception. *Brain, 86,* 697–202.

Kleist, K. (1934). *Gehirnpathologie.* Leipzig: Barth.

Landouzy, L. (1876). Contribution à l'étude des convulsions et paralyses liés aux méningo-éncephalites fronto-pariétal. Unpublished thesis, Paris.

Latto, R., & Cowey, A. (1971). Fixation changes after frontal eye-field lesions in monkeys. *Brain Research, 30,* 25–36.

Leichnetz, G.R. (1981). The prefrontal cortico-oculomotor trajectories in the monkey. *Journal of Neurological Sciences, 49,* 387–396.

Levine, D., & Calvanio, R. (1978). A study of the visual defect in verbal alexia-simultanagnosia. *Brain, 101,* 65–81.

Levine, D.N., Kaufman, K.J., & Mohr, J.P. (1978). Inaccurate reaching associated with a superior parietal lobe tumor. *Neurology, 28,* 556–561.

Luria, A.R. (1959). Disorders of "simultaneous" perception in a case of bilateral occipito-parietal brain injury. *Brain, 82,* 437–449.

Lynch, J.C., Graybiel, A.M., & Lobeck, L.J. (1985). The differential projection of two cytoarchitectonic subregions of the inferior parietal lobule of macaque upon the deep superior colliculus. *Journal of Comparative Neurology, 235,* 241–254.

Michel, F., Jeannerod, M., & Devic, M. (1965). Trouble de l'orientation visuelle dans les trois dimension de l'espace. *Cortex, 1,* 441–446.

Monaco, F., Pirisi, A., Sechi, G.P., & Cossu, G. (1980). Acquired oculo-motor apraxia and right-sided cortical angioma. *Cortex, 16,* 159–167.

Mountcastle, V.B. (1975). The view from within: Pathways to the study of perception. *John Hopkins Medical Journal, 136,* 109–131.

Mountcastle, V.B., Lynch, J.C., Gheorgopoulos, A.P., Sakata, H., & Acuna, C. (1975). Posterior parietal association cortex of the monkey: Command functions for operations within extrapersonal space. *Journal of Neurophysiology, 38,* 871–908.

Paus, T., Kalina, M., Patockova, L., Angerova, Y., Cerny, R., Mecir, P., Bauer, J., & Krabec, P. (1991). Medial versus lateral frontal lobe lesions and differential impairment of central gaze fixation maintenance in man. *Brain, 114,* 2051–2067.

Perenin, M.T., & Vighetto, A. (1988). Optic ataxia: A specific disruption in visuomotor mechanisms: I. Different aspects of the deficit in reaching for objects. *Brain, 111*, 643–674.

Pierrot-Deseilligny, C., Gautier, J.C., & Loron, P. (1988). Acquired ocular motor apraxia due to bilateral frontoparietal infarcts. *Annals of Neurology, 23*, 199–202.

Pierrot-Deseilligny, C., Gray, F., & Brunet, P. (1986). Infarcts of both parietal lobules with impairment of visually guided eye movements, peripheral visual inattention and optic ataxia. *Brain, 109*, 1–17.

Posner, M.I., Walker, J.A., Friedrich, F.J., & Rafal, R.D. (1984). Effects of parietal injury on covert orienting of attention. *Journal of Neuroscience, 4*, 1863–1874.

Prevost, J.L. (1868). De la déviation conjuguée des yeux et de la rotation de la tête dans certains cas d'hémiplégie. Thèse de Paris.

Rapcsak, S.Z., Cimino, C.R., & Heilman, K.M. (1988). Altitudinal neglect. *Neurology, 38*, 277–281.

Riddoch, G. (1935). Visual disorientation in homonymous half-fields. *Brain, 58*, 376–382.

Rizzo, M., & Hurtig, R. (1987). Looking, but not seeing: Attention, perception and eye movements in simultanagnosia. *Neurology, 37*, 1642–1648.

Rizzolatti, G., & Gallese, V. (1988). Mechanisms and theories of spatial neglect. In F. Boller & J. Grafmen (Eds.), *Handbook of neuropsychology (Vol. 1)*. Amsterdam: Elsevier.

Rondot, P., de Recondo, J., & Ribadeau Dumas, J.L.T. (1977). Visuomotor ataxia. *Brain, 100*, 355–376.

Rousseaux, M., Delafosse, A., Devos, P., Quint, S., & Lesoin, F. (1986). Syndrome de Balint par infarctus bipariétal: Analyse neuropsychologique. *Cortex, 22*, 267–277.

Schall, J.D. (1991). Neuronal activity related to visually guided saccades in the frontal eye fields of rhesus monkeys: Comparison with supplementary eye fields. *Journal of Neurophysiology, 66*, 559–579.

Schiller, P.H., True, S.D., & Conway, J.L. (1980). Deficits in eye movements following frontal eye-field and superior colliculus ablations. *Journal of Neurophysiology, 44*, 1175–1189.

Sorgato, P. (1976). Analisi neuropsicologica delle complicanze cerebrali a lungo termine dell'eclampsia. *Rivista di Patologia Nervosa e Mentale, 97*, 371–384.

Tzavaras, A., & Masure, M.C. (1976). Aspects différents de l'ataxie optique selon la latéralization hémisphérique de la lésion. *Lyon Medical, 236*, 673–683.

Vallar, G., & Perani, D. (1986). The anatomy of unilateral neglect after right-hemisphere stroke lesions: A clinical/CT scan correlation study in man. *Neuropsychologia, 24*, 609–622.

Waltz, A.G. (1961). Dyspraxia of gaze. *Archives of Neurology, 5*, 638–647.

Wolpert, I. (1924). Die Simultanagnosie: Störung der Gesamtauffassung. *Zeitschrift der Gesamte Neurologie und Psychiatrie, 93*, 397–415.

Yin, T.C.T., & Mountcastle, V.B. (1977). Visual input to the visuomotor mechanisms of the monkey's parietal lobe. *Science, 197*, 1381–1383.

11

Lewandowsky's Case of Object–Colour Agnosia

Jules Davidoff
Department of Psychology, University of Essex, U.K.

In 1967, Ennio De Renzi and Hans Spinnler, two Italian neurologists, published a paper on colour tasks pioneered by Lewandowsky (1908). They examined the effects of cortical damage in a large sample of aphasic and non-aphasic patients (100 left brain damaged and 73 right brain damaged). De Renzi and Spinnler (1967) employed what now would be unfashionably large samples but they felt the need to determine the frequency with which impairments for colour tasks occurred in brain-damaged patients.

De Renzi and Spinnler (1967) first assessed their patients on verbal colour tasks. For naming colours, as to be expected, the 57 aphasic patients of their sample performed very poorly compared to nonaphasic groups. However, they were not particularly impaired on colour naming as opposed to other sorts of naming. In fact, Goodlgass, Klein, Carey, and James (1966) had shown the previous year that a specific impairment for colour naming was rare (see also Chapter 16). De Renzi and Spinnler confirmed the rarity. Only four of their group had a specific impairment for colour naming and, indeed, only one of these was considered to be aphasic.

The next verbal colour task assessed by De Renzi and Spinnler was the patients' verbal memory for the colours of objects. Again, most of the aphasics were poor at recalling the colour of, say, a poppy or a sailor's uniform; very few of the other patients had difficulty with the task. However, it is the results of another task that still cause some surprise. De Renzi and Spinnler asked the patients to colour in line drawings of common objects (e.g. artichoke, cherry, cigar, the Italian flag) in the colour they thought to be the most appropriate. Once again, it was only the aphasic group that had difficulty with the task. Despite a belief that it was a visual task, approximately half of the aphasic patients fell below the criterion of normal performance. Perhaps, it was the apparent paradox of an impairment of visual imagery being more common in language-disturbed patients that has submerged these findings after they were made for the first time by Lewandowsky (1908).

The translation of Lewandowsky's work by Davidoff and Fodor became available in 1989. It only then became apparent that Lewandowsky not only produced all the paradigms used in subsequent research but also initiated most of the theoretical arguments from just one case. So revealing is the case that it is worth giving Lewandowsky's report in more detail. Rather in the modern fashion, Lewandowsky presented the paper at a conference in Amsterdam in 1907 prior to the publication of the longer journal article in 1908 (Davidoff & Fodor, 1989, pp. 167–169):

Now, my case concerns a fifty year old man—a book-keeper—who suddenly became ill on the 2nd of April of this year. While he was sitting at his desk he suddenly noticed that he could no longer read or write. He quickly left his shop. In the street he noticed that the name plates attached to buildings all looked the same; he was unable to read the words. It was only after a long time that he was able to find the house where he lived. He also noticed that he could no longer communicate with people. As, indeed, communication with him was entirely impossible he was admitted to the Friederichsheim Hospital in Berlin the next day. At first, he showed the picture of a typical Wernicke's sensory aphasia; he did not understand what was said to him and he spoke an incomprehensible paraphasic gibberish. The case did not seem to offer anything special. The peculiarities only showed themselves after 3–4 weeks when the sensory aphasia had faded away and disappeared to the extent that one could communicate very well with the patient. In this case, I can therefore entirely disregard the speech disturbance which can be taken as a remote symptom of the original focal lesion. With respect to disturbances of language in the widest sense, the subcortical alexia lasted longest. The patient could not read but could write fluently, although he could not decipher what he himself had written. The relative persistence of this symptom is of value to us in so far as it tells us that the focal lesion obviously present in our patient lies quite far back about in the interior areas of the left occipital lobe somewhat behind the angular gyrus. There were also pure motor disturbances. In association with the alexia were further disturbances in the visual domain. First, the patient had a right hemianopsia which resolved into a hemiamblyopia. However, this hemianopsia did not prevent the patient recognising forms or objects. There was no mind blindness. He was, at all times, completely capable of comprehending the pictures and images shown to him. Furthermore, he was also able to draw even if a little clumsily. He drew in a quite recognisable manner a bottle, a glass, even a house and a face, and even trying to show perspective. Thus nothing by way of mind blindness was found which could have possibly related to the disturbances of the colour sense to be discussed.

Now concerning the colour sense, the first test we carried out required the patient to name wool probes shown to him or to point at those that were named. He failed completely either stating that he was not capable of doing it, or after being urged to respond giving any wrong colour without any recognisable regularity to his mistakes.

Furthermore, the patient was not able to give the colour of objects familiar to him, e.g. the colour of a lemon, a leaf etc. He gave colour names at random, some of them being of a quite peculiar sort as, for example, bluish-red or such like. (Footnote here: The interpretation of his symptom—that the patient was not capable of giving the colours of objects orally—will be dealt with in the detailed communication. It seems possible, that, at least for a number of people, in order to have "knowledge" of the colour of an object, the respective colour representation needs to be evoked.) And now it was possible to show by a very simple test that this was not due to a speech disturbance for when one placed a selection of colours, e.g. wool probes before the patient and asked him to indicate and pick out the colour of blood, grass and a lemon, he failed in exactly the same way. He selected, if at all, entirely wrong colours and again without any regularity.

It should be noted in passing that in all respects our patient regarded black and white as colours, but despite that he was fully oriented to dark and light. He could not give the colour of snow or coal but answered the question whether the night was dark or light with "DARK", when the moon shines with "LIGHT". When seeking out the colour of a certain object he always took account of lightness but never the colour itself. This should be of considerable significance for the psychology of colour perception and its separation from brightness perception.

Of course we confirmed that on all trials the patient understood the meaning of all named objects for which he had to indicate the colours. For example, he answered the question whether he knew what blood is with, "naturally, that which flows everywhere in the body" and what leaves are with "that which grows on trees". Actually, it should be emphasised that his intelligence, as the word is commonly used, was quite unusually good. To entirely exclude the verbal expression of the examiner, we extended the test by giving the patient uncoloured pictures of objects, for example a lemon, cigar or leaf which he recognised straight away.

We even made the patient draw a leaf himself and then asked him to find the matching colour and again he failed completely. It is thus out of the question that any form of language disorder could have a causal significance for this symptom complex.

We even went so far as to show the patient wrongly coloured pictures and even here he was very uncertain; nonetheless, this condition provided the limit (of his poor performance). He frequently chose correctly when he saw the wrongly coloured next to the correctly coloured object, for example a green ox next to a brown ox. However, when he saw the pictures individually he was uncertain and sometimes declared that quite correctly coloured objects, for example a green meadow, were wrong.

Lewandowsky then went to great lengths to show that the patient's colour vision was normal. Indeed, even his memory for colour patches shown half an hour before was very good. Lewandowsky continues (Davidoff & Fodor, 1989, p. 170):

> He was given a colour and told "to pick out the one which seemed to him to be similar." At first he usually refused saying: "I don't know what I'm supposed to do. I can't grasp it." Being pressed, he proceeded in a correct fashion but he repeatedly said "That is too dark" or "Too light". One then had to make him understand that it was not the darkness or the lightness that was the point but that it was actually something else to which he was to pay attention. Even though the matches were correct, they were subjectively unsatisfactory to him; mostly he said "They are all different." For complete subjective satisfaction he needed both colour and brightness to be the same. If one cut, say, a number of wool probes in two halves and told him to find the two that matched he did so with great speed and with subjective certainty. Here, of course, colour and brightness were the same.

Lewandowsky's patient had a cluster of impairments that led him to talk of a "disconnection of the colour sense" from the rest of cognitive functions. Subsequent work has had two somewhat opposing directions. The first is to try to discover artifacts in his work and, in particular, with the finding of a selective impairment for the retrieval of the colours of objects (object–colours). The second is to place Lewandowsky's findings within a framework of object representations and object naming. The aim of that work has been to decide whether dissociations can be found within the cluster of deficits present in his patient.

Lewandowsky's patient had a profound colour anomia and it is this that has presented subsequent sceptics with the most obvious weapon to oppose his claim for a disconnection of object–colour knowledge. Colour anomia is a common concomitant impairment in patients who have poor retrieval of object–colour knowledge.

There have been only a few cases of colour anomia that could demonstrate intact retrieval of object–colour knowledge from visually presented achromatic drawings of objects (Beauvois & Saillant, 1985; Coslett & Saffran, 1989; Fukuzawa, Itoh, Sasanuma, Suzuki, & Fukusako, 1988; Geschwind & Fusillo, 1966; Gil, Pluchon, Toullat, Michenau, Rogez, & Levevre, 1985; Larrabee, Levin, Huff, Kay, & Guinto, 1985). The reverse dissociation of good colour naming and poor object–colour retrieval is even rarer; it is limited to two (or three) cases (Farah, Levine, & Calvanio, 1988; Schnider, Landis, Regard, & Benson, 1992; these last authors also report a case in German by Engerth in 1934). Indeed, close inspection of the data from both cases reveals that neither had perfect colour naming. Therefore, it is not surprising that impaired object–colour retrieval from line drawings has been attributed to interference from erroneous colour names used "out of habit" even when not required for the task (Damasio, McKee, & Damasio, 1979; Kinsbourne & Warrington, 1964). As proof of verbal interference, Beauvois and Saillant (1985) demonstrated that performance could be improved by placing plaster over the mouth of their patient M.P.

The interpretation of faulty retrieval of object–colour as due to colour name interference may not be correct. Group studies have shown that colour naming ability did not predict object–colour retrieval (Basso, Faglioni, & Spinnler, 1976; De Renzi & Spinnler, 1967). Furthermore, case studies that have normal colour naming have now been found (Luzzatti & Davidoff, 1994). So, while we will never know whether colour name interference was the cause of the poor performance of Lewandowsky's patient, it becomes less likely as an explanation of all faulty retrieval of object–colour knowledge.

Difficulty with object–colour retrieval was found by De Renzi and Spinnler (1967) in a variety of aphasic conditions. Impairments were not confined to patients with comprehension problems (Wernicke's aphasia) (Basso et al., 1976; De Renzi, Faglioni, Scotti, & Spinnler, 1972) since patients with nonfluent speech, but without comprehension difficulties (Broca's aphasia), are similarly impaired (Basso, Capitani, Luzzatti, Spinnler, & Zanobio, 1985). The group studies, therefore, suggest more general deficits than that proposed by Lewandowsky who said of his patient: "Colour vision was isolated; it led in this brain a life of its own and could not be connected or associated with the sense of brightness or form." (Davidoff & Fodor, 1989, p. 170).

The nature of these supposed general deficits has not been easy to isolate. A simple relationship of object–colour retrieval to language disturbance can be eliminated from case studies of object recognition disorders. Such patients, perhaps not surprisingly, fail at Lewandowsky's visual tasks but some do so without any general aphasic disturbance (Beauvois & Saillant, 1985, case R.V.; Ferro & Santos, 1984; Larrabee et al., 1985, case 1). Aural comprehension has also been ruled out from the results of a group study of aphasic patients (Varney, 1982). Cohen and Kelter (1979) suggested, following Goldstein (1948), a loss of abstract attitude. The difficulties exhibited by left brain-damaged patients, according to Goldstein, was not so much that knowledge was lost but that new categories cannot be formed. The study of Cohen and Kelter was in the Goldstein tradition and was a reaction to the remarks of Lewandowsky concerning the difference between brightness and colour.

Cohen and Kelter (1979) compared the ability of aphasic patients to retrieve hue, brightness and saturation of colour patches. They found that their patients were impaired on memory for all three aspects of the colour and concluded, reiterating Lange's opinion (1936/1989) of the problem for Lewandowsky's patient, that the inability to retrieve object–colour was due to a loss of abstract attitude. There is some justification for Lange's conclusion because the patient was unable to sort colours into groups. Lewandowsky did not produce any counter-evidence for his patient's ability to think abstractly except to remark on his intelligence (mentioned previously) and to declare him free of his initial Wernicke's aphasia.

According to Lewandowsky, the difficulty for the patient was not in any general conceptual loss but rather in the integration of stored object–colour with object–shape. There are two reasons for supporting his interpretation against that put forward by Cohen and Kelter. First, the three aspects of a colour are integral (Shepp, 1991) and difficult to separate when the colour is in view let alone from memory. It is, therefore, not surprising that memory for lightness, saturation and hue were all impaired. Second, and more direct, it has been shown that failure to recognise object–colours need not be associated with a loss of abstract attitude (Beauvois & Saillant, 1985, case R.V.; Kinsbourne & Warrington, 1964). These case studies show, contra the group results (De Renzi et al., 1972), that failure on Lewandowsky's tasks can be combined with the preserved conceptual ability required to categorise colours.

The second line of subsequent work has been to flesh out models of visual cognition. Lewandowsky's patient demonstrated a cluster of deficits. If these could be shown to dissociate, then we would understand more clearly how objects are remembered and named. Lewandowsky's patient could not categorise and name colours, nor could he recall or recognise object–colours. Also, he could not read. However, his recognition and imagery of object–shape appeared to be good. The essence of Lewandowsky's interpretation of his patient's performance is that object–colour memories are stored with colour memories and these are "split off" from other object memories. Recent research does not completely agree. To illustrate current ideas on the representation of colour in memory, it will help to follow the flow diagram in Fig. 11.1. The model was proposed by Davidoff and De Bleser (1993) to account for the selective loss of naming from visual input (optic aphasia) but it is, in fact, based on a more general account of visual cognition (Davidoff, 1991).

Visual information is first held at a temporary register before making contact with specialised recognition systems. In the model, there are three such systems. They are, those for objects (entry level stored structural descriptions), those for words (orthographic input lexicon) and those for colours (internal colour space). Lewandowsky's patient had no problems with object recognition and imagery, so we might conclude that the structural descriptions were intact. Thus, his patient gives evidence for the dissociability of the object recognition system from other recognition systems (see Chapters 7 and 8) and also for the separation of the memories for object–shape from those concerned with object–colour. For the latter dissociation, object–colour knowledge is placed within the sensory knowl-

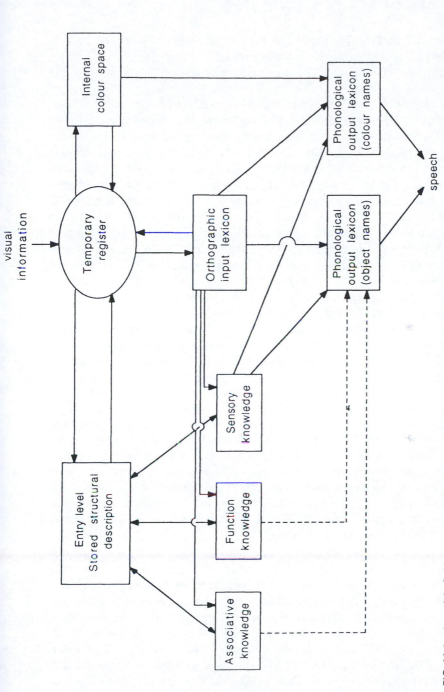

FIG. 11.1 A model of object naming and colour naming. Object-knowledge is divided into three types. Dotted lines represent weaker connections but are not critical for the discussion of Lewandowsky's paper. Object–colour knowledge is within the box labelled sensory knowledge. (Taken from Davidoff & De Bleser, 1993.)

151

edge box in Fig. 11.1. The section of the recognition system concerned with faces (see Chapter 6) was also probably intact as otherwise one feels that a perspicacious investigator like Lewandowsky might have noticed the deficit.

The neurological site for object–colour storage is of considerable interest to models of knowledge storage. If anatomical distinctions can be found between areas associated with the imagery for object–colour and those for structural descriptions, it adds support to the functional dissociation made in Fig. 11.1. Such evidence is available. The retrieval of object–colour must be based on distinct neural networks since impaired imagery for object–colour can accompany preserved imagery for object–shape (Riddoch & Humphreys, 1987; Stengel, 1948). Thus, it ought to be possible to distinguish object–shape and object–colour neurologically and add support to the difference between entry level and sensory knowledge representations. Visual imagery impairments, in general, are associated with damage to the posterior left hemisphere (see Farah, 1984). The site has been confirmed in normals from regional cerebral blood flow patterns while judging the correctness of a sentence requiring visual imagery (Goldenberg, Podreka, Steiner, Willmes, Suess, & Deecke, 1989). The neurological site for the impairment of object–colour retrieval is also associated with the left hemisphere but Goldenberg and Artner (1991) have recently connected it to a different locus. They have shown, in a group study, that imagery for colour is more reliably associated with damage to a different branch of the left posterior cerebral artery than impoverished imagery for shape. It is damage to the temporo-occipital branch rather than the occipital branch of the posterior artery that is associated with reduced colour imagery.

The findings of Goldenberg and Artner suggest a left temporal-occipital site as a separate store for object–colours. One might have supposed that, if the retrieval of pictorial storage was a lateralised function, it would be to the other hemisphere. It is the right hemisphere which, if damaged, causes most problems in recognising poor quality drawings (Milner, 1958; Warrington & James, 1967), overlapping drawings (De Renzi & Spinnler, 1966), and objects seen from unusual views or only partially illuminated (Warrington & Taylor, 1973). However, the function of the right hemisphere with respect to object recognition does not seem to be one that involves mental rotation (Mehta, Newcombe, & Ratcliff, 1988) or other processes requiring imagery but a failure to form an object-centred mental representation (for theoretical alternatives see Humphreys & Riddoch, 1984; Warrington & James, 1986). So, why is imagery a left hemisphere function? According to Farah et al. (1988), it is not because loss of visual image generation arises from a disconnection from language (Basso, Bisiach, & Luzzatti, 1980). Lewandowsky believed the same but was concerned that his patient had a unilateral left hemisphere lesion; it was the one serious difficulty he saw for his explanation of the patient's impairment in retrieving object–colour. With that lesion, it would be quite reasonable to explain the patient's performance by some disorder of language. Lewandowsky wondered why the intact right hemisphere could not be capable of integrating object–colour with object–form. The question is still unanswered.

Beauvois (1982) argued that all object–knowledge, including object–colour memories, are represented in both a verbal and a visual form. She, therefore, would want to divide the sensory knowledge box in Fig. 11.1 into two. Beauvois would, in fact, not separate the types of associated object–knowledge as shown in Fig. 11.1; her verbal–visual distinction is for all object–knowledge. On Beauvois' account (see Fig. 11.2), the output to the phonological output lexicon proceeds only from verbal semantics. Davidoff & De Bleser (1993) provide some evidence, from a review of case studies, that supports her division between visual and verbal object–colour knowledge.

On Beauvois' account (see Beauvois & Saillant, 1985), impairments in object–colour retrieval arise from a disconnection between the two memory stores. We have already noted that Beauvois and Saillant removed the erroneous object–colour retrieval of their patient by placing plaster across the mouth to prevent verbalisation. We also noted that it did not seem likely that this method would remove all such erroneous retrieval (Luzzatti & Davidoff, 1994).

The separation of memories for object-colours from the second recognition system in Fig. 11.1 (orthographic input lexicon) does not seem problematic (see Chapters 14 and 15) yet, in Lewandowsky's case, an alexia was present; this may not be surprising. His case fits, in some ways, the description of an optic aphasia (see Davidoff & De Bleser, 1993). Optic aphasics, even where recognition impairments have been ruled out, invariably have a reading impairment. That is not to doubt the existence of a separate reading route. Indeed, it may be possible to show "hidden" reading in optic aphasia (Shallice & Saffran, 1986) and alexia may be accompanied by good retrieval of object–colours (Assal & Regli, 1980; Coslett & Saffran, 1989; Gil et al., 1985). Unfortunately, it is not clear from Lewandowsky's report whether or not his patient could name visually presented objects.

It is most interesting with respect to assigning the functional locus of object–colour memories to note that it is more common for patients with object recognition impairments than optic aphasics to exhibit intact reading (Albert, Reches, & Silverberg, 1975; Levine, 1978; Newcombe & Ratcliff, 1974); this also suggests that object–colour memories are "split off" from other object memories. It indicates that object–colours are more closely linked to the phonological output lexicon than are the stored descriptions used for recognition.

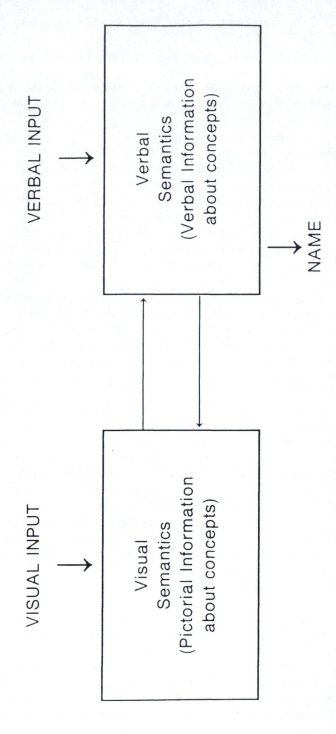

FIG. 11.2 A model of object naming from visual input according to Beauvois (1982). It includes both visual and verbal semantics. Object–colour knowledge would be contained in both boxes. (Taken from Davidoff & De Bleser, 1993.)

The third recognition system of Fig. 11.1 is between the pictorial register and the lexicon for colour names; this is the stage (the internal colour space) at which colours are categorised. Some part of this space may derive from the categorial output of chromatically opponent mechanisms (Mullen & Kulikowski, 1990) at the temporary register; other parts of the space must be the result of experience (see Davidoff, 1991). Selective damage within the route to the colour lexicon could spare the internal colour space; that is to say, there ought to be patients who cannot name colours but who can nevertheless categorise them (e.g. into reds, blues, and browns). Other patients will have damage to the internal colour space; Lewandowsky gives in his case report a perfect description of how such patients sort colours.

Sittig (1921) clarified the theoretical distinctions between the multiple colour impairments shown by Lewandowsky's patient. He drew a distinction between Farbenagnosie and Farbennamenamnesie. Sittig's use of the term colour agnosia (Farbenagnosie) is more precise than many who have used the term since his day. In his terminology, an agnosia for colour meant an inability to categorise colours and need not necessarily be accompanied by an impairment in the memory of object–colour nor a loss of colour names (Farbennamenamnesie). Other similar cases have been reported (Beauvois & Saillant, 1985, case M.P.; Stengel, 1948). The dissociation is also supported by cases of visual agnosia in which there is preserved ability to categorise colours with (Beauvois & Saillant, 1985, case R.V.; Kertesz, 1979) and without (Levine, 1978) the ability to name colours.

The further dissociation between colour agnosia and the memory for object–colour is predictable because the extraction of colour information from the pictorial register does not rely on an input from the stored knowledge of objects; the dissociation has been confirmed in only a few cases (Beauvois & Saillant, 1985; Kinsbourne & Warrington, 1964) because colour categorisation is so infrequently examined.

Lewandowsky wanted to link the retrieval of object–colours to the retrieval of our memories for colours. A similar notion was proposed by Werner (1940) to explain why children find it so hard to acquire colour names (see Davidoff, 1991). Werner (1940) assumed that we learn colour names from object–colour names; recent research has shown this to be false (Davidoff & Mitchell, 1993). It appears that young children make mistakes in the retrieval of object–colours, especially from visually presented stimuli, after they have acquired a good colour name vocabulary. So, while we may have here an example of a false conclusion reached by Lewandowsky, it stands out only because of the clarity of the rest of his examination. His study rightly stands as a classic case in neuropsychology.

REFERENCES

Albert, M.L., Reches, A., & Silverberg, R. (1975). Associative visual agnosia without alexia. *Neurology, 25,* 322–326.

Assal, G., & Regli, F. (1980). Syndrome de disconnexion visuo-verbale et visuo-gestuelle. *Revue Neurologique, 136,* 365–376.

Basso, A., Bisiach, E., & Luzzatti, C. (1980). Loss of mental imagery: A case study. *Neuropsychologia, 18,* 435–442.

Basso, A., Capitani, E., Luzzatti, C., Spinnler, H., & Zanobio, M.E. (1985). Different basic components in the performance of Broca's and Wernicke's aphasics on the colour–figure matching test. *Neuropsychologia, 23,* 51–59.

Basso, A., Faglioni, P., & Spinnler, H. (1976). Non verbal color impairment in aphasics. *Neuropsychologia, 14,* 183–192.

Beauvois, M.-F. (1982). Optic aphasia: A process of interaction between vision and language. *Philosophical Transactions of the Royal Society of London, B298,* 35–47.

Beauvois, M.-F., & Saillant, B. (1985). Optic aphasia for colours and colour agnosia: A distinction between visual and visuo-verbal impairments in the processing of colours. *Cognitive Neuropsychology, 2,* 1–48.

Cohen, R., & Kelter, S. (1979). Cognitive impairment of aphasics in a colour-to-picture matching task. *Cortex, 15,* 235–245.

Coslett, H.B., & Saffran, E.M. (1989). Preserved object recognition and reading comprehension in optic aphasia. *Brain, 112,* 1091–1110.

Damasio, A.R., McKee, J., & Damasio, H. (1979). Determinants of performance on color anomia. *Brain and Language, 7,* 74–85.

Davidoff, J. (1991). *Cognition through color.* Cambridge, MA: MIT Press.

Davidoff, J., & De Bleser, R. (1993). Optic aphasia: A review of past studies and reappraisal. *Aphasiology, 7,* 135–154.

Davidoff, J., & Fodor, G. (1989). An annotated translation of Lewandowsky (1908). *Cognitive Neuropsychology, 6,* 165–177.

Davidoff, J., & Mitchell, P. (1993). The colour cognition of children. *Cognition, 48,* 121–137.

De Renzi, E., Faglioni, P., Scotti, G., & Spinnler, H. (1972). Impairment in associating colour to form concomitant with aphasia. *Brain, 95,* 293–304.

De Renzi, E., & Spinnler, H. (1966). Visual recognition in patients with unilateral cerebral disease. *Journal of Mental and Nervous Disease, 142,* 515–525.

De Renzi, E., & Spinnler, H. (1967). Impaired performance on color tasks in patients with hemispheric damage. *Cortex, 3,* 194–217.

Farah, M.J. (1984). The neurological basis of mental imagery: A componential analysis. *Cognition, 18,* 245–272.

Farah, M.J., Levine, D.N., & Calvanio, R. (1988). A case study of mental imagery deficit. *Brain and Cognition, 8,* 147–164.

Ferro, J.M., & Santos, M.E. (1984). Associative visual agnosia: A case study, *Cortex, 20,* 121–134.

Fukuzawa, K., Itoh, M., Sasanuma, S., Suzuki, T., & Fukusako, Z. (1988). Internal representations and the conceptual operation of color in pure alexia with color naming defects. *Brain and Language, 34,* 98–126.

Geschwind, N., & Fusillo, M. (1966). Color-naming defects in association with alexia. *Archives of Neurology, 15,* 137–146.

Gil, R., Pluchon, C., Toullat, G., Michenau, D., Rogez, R., & Levevre, J.P. (1985). Disconnexion visuo-verbale (aphasie optique) pour les objets, les images, les couleurs et les visages avec alexie "abstractif". *Neuropsychologia, 23,* 333–349.

Goldenberg, G., & Artner, C. (1991). Visual imagery and knowledge about the visual appearance of objects in patients with posterior cerebral artery lesions. *Brain and Cognition, 15,* 160–186.

Goldenberg, G., Podreka, I., Steiner, M., Willmes, K., Suess, E., & Deecke, L. (1989) Regional cerebral blood flow patterns in visual imagery. *Neuropsychologia, 27,* 641–664.

Goldstein, K. (1948). *Language and language disturbances: aphasic symptom complexes and their significance for medicine and theory of language.* New York: Grune & Stratton.

Goodglass, H., Klein, B., Carey, P., & James, K.J. (1966). Specific semantic word categories in aphasia. *Cortex, 2,* 74–89.

Humphreys, G.W., & Riddoch, M.J. (1984). Routes to object constancy: Implications from neurological impairments of object constancy. *Quarterly Journal of Experimental Psychology, 36A,* 385–415.

Kertesz, A. (1979). Visual agnosia: The dual deficit of perception and recognition. *Cortex, 15,* 403–419.

Kinsbourne, M., & Warrington, E.K. (1964). Observations on colour agnosia. *Journal of Neurology, Neurosurgery and Psychiatry, 27,* 296–299.

Lange, J. (1936/1989). Agnosia and apraxia. In J.W. Brown (Ed.), *Agnosia and apraxia: Selected papers of Liepmann, Lange and Pötzl.* New York: Institute for Research in Behavioral Neuroscience.

Larrabee, G.J., Levin, H.S., Huff, F.J., Kay, M.C., & Guinto, F.C. (1985). Visual agnosia contrasted with visual disconnection. *Neuropsychologia, 23,* 1–12.

Levine, D.N. (1978). Prosopagnosia and visual object agnosia: A behavioral study. *Brain and Language, 5,* 341–365.

Lewandowsky, M. (1908). Über Abspaltung des Farbensinnes. *Monatsschrift für Psychiatrie und Neurologie, 23,* 488–510.

Luzzatti, C., & Davidoff, J. (1994). Impaired retrieval of object–colour knowledge with preserved colour and object naming. *Neuropsychologia, 32,* 933–950.

Mehta, Z., Newcombe, F., & Ratcliff, G. (1988). Patterns of hemispheric asymmetry set against clinical evidence. In J. Crawford & D. Parker (Eds.), *Developments in clinical and experimental neuropsychology.* New York: Plenum Press.

Milner, B. (1958). Psychological defects produced by temporal lobe excisions. *Proceedings of Association for Research in Nervous and Mental Disease, 36,* 244–257.

Mullen, K.T., & Kulikowski, J.J. (1990). Wavelength discrimination at detection threshold. *Journal of the Optical Society of America, A7,* 733–742.

Newcombe, F., & Ratcliff, G. (1974). Agnosia: A disorder of object recognition. In F. Michel & B. Schott (Eds.), *Les syndromes de disconnexion calleuse chez l'homme.* Lyon: Colloque International de Lyon.

Riddoch, M.J., & Humphreys, G.W. (1987). Visual object processing in optic aphasia: A case of semantic access agnosia. *Cognitive Neuropsychology, 4,* 131–185.

Schnider, A., Landis, T., Regard, M., & Benson, F. (1992). Dissociation of color from object in amnesia. *Archives of Neurology, 49,* 982–985.

Shallice, T., & Saffran, E. (1986). Lexical processing in the absence of explicit word identification: Evidence from a letter-by-letter reader. *Cognitive Neuropsychology, 3,* 429–458.

Shepp, B.E. (1991). Perception of color. In G.R. Lockhead & J.R. Pomerantz (Eds.), *The perception of structure.* Washington D.C.: American Psychological Association.

Sittig, O. (1921). Störungen im Verhalten gegenüber Farben bei Aphasischen. *Monatsschrift für Psychiatrie und Neurologie, 49,* 63–68, 169–187.

Stengel, E. (1948). The syndrome of visual alexia with color anomia. *Journal of Mental Sciences, 94,* 46–58.

Varney, N.R. (1982). Colour association and "colour amnesia" in aphasia. *Journal of Neurology, Neurosurgery and Psychiatry, 45*, 248–252.

Warrington, E.K., & James, M. (1967). Disorders of visual perception in patients with localised cerebral lesions. *Neuropsychologia, 5*, 253–266.

Warrington, E.K., & James, M. (1986). Visual object recognition in patients with right hemisphere lesions: Axes or features. *Perception, 15*, 355–366.

Warrington, E.K., & Taylor, A.M. (1973). The contribution of the right parietal lobe to object recognition. *Cortex, 9*, 152–164.

Werner, H. (1940). *The comparative psychology of mental development*. New York: Harper.

12 Monrad-Krohn's Foreign-accent Syndrome Case

Inger Moen
Department of Linguistics, University of Oslo, Norway.

INTRODUCTION

Occasionally, brain damage may result in what appears to be a foreign accent. The most widely known case of this type is a study by the neurologist Monrad-Krohn (1947) of a woman, Astrid L., who developed what sounded like a German accent in her Norwegian, as a result of a shrapnel wound to the head. "What above all characterized her speech was her broken foreign accent, her completely changed 'melody of language'" (Monrad-Krohn, 1947, p. 411). However, to Monrad-Krohn's surprise, her musical abilities did not seem to be affected. She could sing and hum in tune, although (p. 411) "she never had the natural Norwegian accent when she had to link several words together into a sentence." Why, asked Monrad-Krohn, was there a prosodic disturbance in a patient who could sing? He failed to find a satisfactory answer.

In the following I shall present Astrid L., a case of "the foreign-accent syndrome", as she was described and discussed by Monrad-Krohn. Furthermore, I shall show that in terms of recent phonological models her aberrant speech patterns can be accounted for in a principled way. Her "foreign accent", though still an interesting phenomenon, is no longer inexplicable.

THE FOREIGN-ACCENT SYNDROME

Brain damage which results in aphasia or apraxia of speech often causes deviant articulation, but the deviations are not normally of a type to alter the apparent identity of the patient's dialectal or linguistic background.

There is in the literature a handful of descriptions of aphasic patients who do not fit into this general pattern. Their speech takes on characteristics normally associated with a dialect that is not their own, or it resembles the performance of a non-native speaker of the language. The earliest description of this kind of disturbance (Whitaker, 1982, p. 195) was made by Marie in 1907; the patient, a Parisian, had developed an "Alsatian" accent. In 1919, Pick published a description of a 26-year-old Czech butcher who sounded Polish after having suffered a stroke. Pick's patient is the only previous description of a "foreign accent" mentioned by Monrad-Krohn. Since Pick's study, a number of cases have been reported in the literature (see for instance Aronson, 1980).

Whitaker has proposed calling this type of deviation "the foreign-accent syndrome", and he attributed four characteristics to it (Whitaker, 1982, pp. 196 & 198):

1. The accent is considered by the patient, by acquaintances and by the investigator, to sound foreign.
2. It is unlike the patient's native dialect before insult.
3. It is clearly related to central nervous system damage (as opposed to an hysteric reaction, if such exist).
4. And there is no evidence in the patient's background of being a speaker of a foreign language (i.e., this is not like cases of polyglot aphasia).

The foreign-accent syndrome is usually the result of a cerebro-vascular accident, and the patients tend to have symptoms associated with Broca's aphasia. Abnormal prosodic features are mentioned in all the reported cases—deviant stress, rhythm, and intonation. A tendency towards the use of long vowels in unstressed syllables, syllables where a short vowel would be expected, has also been noted. Since long vowels are associated with stressed syllables, this feature contributes to the impression of deviant stress and rhythm (see Ingram, McCormack, & Kennedy, 1992).

ASTRID L.

We now turn to Monrad-Krohn's study of Astrid L., a 30-year-old Norwegian woman from Oslo who developed a "German" accent after a shrapnel wound to the fronto-temporo-parietal region of the left hemisphere.

The insult also resulted in a marked agrammatism, though as time went by this became less pronounced. Monrad-Krohn examined the patient in 1943, two years after her lesion (1947, p. 410):

> She walked into hospital without any noticeable limp and she spoke quite fluently but with such a decided foreign accent that I took her for German or French. She complained bitterly of constantly being taken for a German in the shops, where consequently the assistants would sell her nothing. One must bear in mind the hatred of everything and everybody German that had developed after the German assault and occupation without any declaration of war, further accentuated by the atrocious behaviour of the "Gestapo" ... She had never been outside Norway and never had anything to do with foreigners.

One of the features which presumably contributed to the impression of a foreign accent in her speech was a failure to produce a proper distinction between the Norwegian pitch accents. In Norwegian, accented syllables are associated with one of two possible pitch patterns—the so-called pitch accents, normally referred to as Accent1 and Accent2. Typical pitch contours of Accent1 and Accent2 words spoken in isolation are shown in Fig. 12.1.

The accent distinction is phonemic and can be used to distinguish between pairs of words which consist of the same segmental phonological

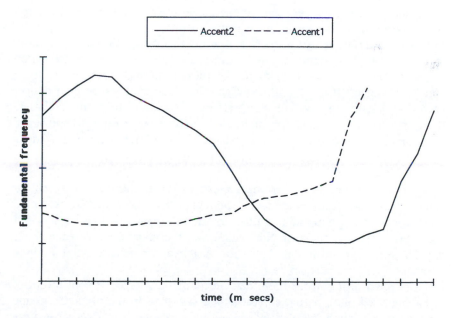

FIG. 12.1   Typical pitch contours of Accent1 and Accent2 words.

string. Three years after the accident the patient was tested on her ability to distinguish between the pair *bønder*/[1]bøner (farmers) and *bønner*/[2]bøner/ (beans). She failed to do this, a failure which annoyed her (accent type is indicated by a [1] or a [2] in front of the accented syllable). Monrad-Krohn assumed that she then practised the distinction at home, because she was able to produce it on her next examination, a little over a month later (1947, p. 411):

> What particularly struck me in my first interviews with the patient was that in short sentences like "Jeg sa det" ("I said it") she pronounced the final pronoun slightly overemphasized and with a raised pitch of voice instead of with a lowered one. In other short sentences as "Jeg tok den" ("I took it") she did the same thing (slightly over-emphasizing and raising the pitch on the last word) and failed to amalgamate it with the previous word (tok[d]n) as is the natural habit of the natives of Oslo and surroundings to do.
>
> Very often she inappropriately raised the pitch at the end of the sentence instead of lowering it.
>
> These were some of her principal and most common offences against the intrinsic prosody of the language, as spoken in the district of Norway, where she was born and had always lived.
>
> The variations of pitch had by no means disappeared. On the contrary they were rather greater than usual in Norwegian, but they were neither adequate nor quite constant in their inadequacy.

A pertinent question is why the patient's speech was perceived as a foreign accent rather than as a mixed dialect, the accent of someone who originally came from a different part of Norway. In most Norwegian dialects, not only in East Norwegian, accented syllables are associated with one of two pitch patterns. The shape and distribution of these patterns, though, vary from dialect to dialect. It is a well-known characteristic of the speech of dialect switchers that the prosody of their first dialect is more resistant to change than are the vowels and consonants. Therefore, a prosodic disturbance alone would not necessarily identify the patient as a foreigner, rather than as a mixed dialect user. Her mild agrammatism could perhaps have been a contributing factor.

Why was her accent perceived as German rather than as the accent of some other European language? Norwegian is a so-called stress-timed language, as is German and the other Germanic languages. This implies that the rhythmical structures of Norwegian and German resemble each other and that they are different from, for instance, French, a syllable-timed language.

Norwegian differs from the other Germanic languages, except Swedish, in having fixed pitch patterns on accented syllables. In the other Germanic languages the pitch pattern of individual accented syllables will vary depending on the intonation pattern of the utterance in which they occur. A loss of the distinction between the two Norwegian pitch accents, coupled with retained stress-timed rhythm, could lead to utterance prosodic patterns which resemble those found in other Germanic languages. In addition, there is a phonetic similarity between many of the vowels and consonants in East Norwegian and the vowels and consonants in German.

To sum up, a speaker of Norwegian who makes occasional grammatical mistakes and fails to exhibit a distinction between the two pitch accents, but does have an acceptable segmental pronunciation and correct rhythmical patterns, could—from a contrastive point of view—be a person whose mother tongue was German.

ALTERED "MELODY OF LANGUAGE"— DYSPROSODY, APROSODY

In the light of Astrid L.'s symptoms, Monrad-Krohn raised the question of whether the "melody of language" is a musical faculty (1947, p. 411):

> In respect of the musical faculties nothing abnormal could be found. Her sense of rhythm, as tested by drumming on the table, seemed to be excellent. When the examiner hummed the beginning of any well-known tune, she joined in at once and continued by herself correctly as to time and tune. She was never heard to sing a false note or out of tune. She could give the names of several well-known tunes. Some of them, but not all, she could sing with correct words. Those that she could not name correctly or sing with correct words, she could hum. At request she could sing a fair number of songs quite correctly with a musical voice and correct rhythm. Her sense of melody as evidenced by humming thus did not seem to be impaired in the slightest degree.

Since Astrid L.'s musical abilities were preserved, Monrad-Krohn concluded that the "melody of language" could not be regarded as a specifically musical expression (p. 414): "It seems to be more closely related to the propositional factors in speech than to musical faculties. It is also evident that many unmusical persons, utterly devoid of any musical faculties, both appreciative and expressive, may yet have well-developed 'melody of language' in their speech." Monrad-Krohn further suggested the term "dysprosody" as a name for Astrid L.'s speech disturbance, rather than "altered melody of language" (p. 414), "in order to avoid confusion with disturbances of the musical faculties."

Monrad-Krohn was at a loss when it came to explaining Astrid L.'s dysprosody. He pointed out that altered melody is not the same as loss of melody. Loss of melody of speech, "aprosody", is frequently observed in connection with extra-pyramidal lesions, paralysis agitans, and allied disorders, but (p. 414) "as regards the peculiar alteration of language here described no obvious explanation presents itself."

THE RELATIONSHIP BETWEEN PROSODIC AND GRAMMATICAL FEATURES

In many respects modern linguistic theories share Monrad-Krohn's views on what constitutes a sentence or an utterance, which elements they are made up of, and how these elements are organised relative to each other. Speech, according to Monrad-Krohn (1947, p. 405), does not only involve finding the appropriate words and pronouncing them correctly:

> An analysis of spoken language reveals the following elements, all necessary— if not of equal importance—to normal speech: choice of the correct words and their precise articulation; correct inflection of the words; correct placing of the words in the sentences; correct placing of stress upon syllables *and words* within the sentence (including prolongations); natural rhythm, pauses and rate of speaking (rhythm and speed should perhaps be listed as two different elements); natural shifting of pitch from syllable to syllable and from word to word, some being pronounced on a higher, some on a lower note, varying from sentence to sentence (the pitch rising and falling, gradually or abruptly); accompanying mimicry and gesture.
>
> The last four elements, except mimicry and gesture, constitute, what I propose to call the prosodic quality of speech.
>
> They are of great importance in conveying the meaning of the speaker, particularly the more subtle shades of meaning, and are therefore to be considered as psychosomatic functions, showing considerable individual and racial variations. They are less tangible and therefore more difficult to analyse than words and the grammatical construction of language.

Where Monrad-Krohn is out of tune with recent theories is in considering prosodic variations in speech to be to a large extent idiosyncratic and to convey (p. 405) "subtle shades of meaning", a different type of meaning than that conveyed by grammar and syntax. In recent phonological models, variations in stress, rhythm, and pitch are considered to be integrated elements of the grammar, on a par with elements like vowels and consonants, words, and phrases (see, for instance, van der Hulst & Smith, 1982). However, there is no disagreement that stress, rhythm, and pitch can also signal extralinguistic features—such as the speaker's emotional state.

LINGUISTIC FUNCTIONS OF VARIATIONS IN PITCH

Pitch variation is a property of all natural languages. No language is spoken on a monotone. But pitch differences function differently in different languages. It is possible to divide languages into groups based on criteria related to different linguistic functions of pitch. One taxonomy of this type has three categories (Cruttenden, 1986): (1) tone languages; (2) pitch accent languages; (3) intonation languages. Type 1, tone languages, includes languages which use differences in pitch for lexical purposes, like Thai, Chinese, and Vietnamese. The distinction between tone languages on the one hand and pitch accent languages on the other is a problematic one (see, for instance, van der Hulst & Smith, 1988). Tone languages are commonly defined as languages where there are potential tonal oppositions on every syllable in a word. A pitch accent language, like Norwegian, is a language where the pitch contrast is restricted to one syllable in a word. Most languages where tonal distinctions are used will be found somewhere between these two extreme types. Type 3, intonation languages, encompasses languages, like English, where differences in pitch are not tied to the lexicon, but are associated with phrases or sentences.

Tone languages and pitch accent languages also exhibit sentence intonation, but generally with fewer possibilities of variation than intonation languages.

NEUROLINGUISTIC ANALYSIS OF ASTRID L.'S ACCENT

One of the aims of neurolinguistics is to explain the patterns of impaired and intact language performance seen in the brain-injured population, in terms of damage to one or more of the components of a model of normal language processing.

One of the language models used in neurolinguistic investigations—a model which has proved successful in accounting for different types of deviant language—assumes the existence of relatively independent cognitive components, modules. One of these modules is the language system—a system with rules and representations not shared by other cognitive components. The language system itself is also considered to be made up of modules, to consist of a set of independent, but interacting, subcomponents. Among these subcomponents are a phonological component, a lexicon, a syntax, and a semantic component.

In a cognitive model of this type, language and speech on the one hand, and music and song on the other, are assumed to be supported by different cognitive components. This will account for the dissociation of musical abilities and speech prosody in Astrid L.'s symptomatology: Damage to one cognitive component does not necessarily affect the functions of a different component.

Astrid L.'s deviant speech can be assumed primarily to be the result of damage to the linguistic subcomponent which supports sound production, the phonological component. According to Monrad-Krohn's description, the syntactic and semantic aspects of her language production—after a time—were relatively normal.

Our task then is to specify where, in the phonological component, disruption would lead to the types of deviation found in Astrid L.'s speech.

Description of Astrid L.'s Deviant Pitch Accents in Terms of a Nonlinear Phonological Model

The model has the following structure. The phonological elements are organised on separate tiers: the tonal tier, the syllable tier, the skeletal tier (the skeleton), the segmental tier, and a set of articulatory tiers which specify the phonetic content of the segment (Clements, 1985; Goldsmith, 1990).

The Tonal Tier.   The units on the tonal tier are the Norwegian pitch accents, Accent1 and Accent2. For East Norwegian, Accent1 can be marked as L (low) and Accent2 as H (high).

The Syllable Tier.   The units on this tier are the constituents which make up the syllable structure: onset (O), nucleus (N), and rhyme (R).

The Skeletal Tier.   The units on the skeletal tier (the skeleton) are only specified with regard to the features vocalic (V) and consonantal (C). The skeleton is the centre of the phonological structure. The units on the other tiers are linked, directly or indirectly, to one or more of the points on the skeleton.

The Segmental Tier.   The units on this tier are vowels and consonants (represented by phonetic symbols).

The Articulatory Feature Tiers.   This is a set of tiers with units that are of an articulatory nature: the laryngeal tier, the supralaryngeal tier, the manner tier, and the place tier.

In Fig. 12.2 we compare the phonological representations of the words /¹løve/ (the leaves) and /²lø:ve/ (lion). (In the representations in Fig. 12.2, the articulatory feature tiers are not included.)

We see that the units on the syllable tier, the skeleton, and the segmental tier are the same in both representations. The difference between the two

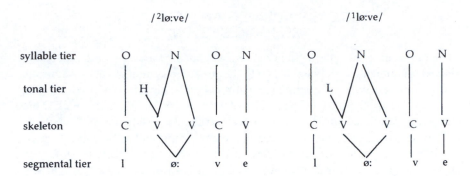

FIG. 12.2   Phonological representations of the words /²lø:ve/ (lion) and /¹ø:ve/ (leaves).

representations can be located to the elements on the tonal tier, the pitch accents.

In East Norwegian both pitch accents are associated with a low pitch level. Accent2 involves a fall in pitch from the beginning of the syllable to the end of the syllable, or extending into the following unstressed syllable. Accent1 has its lowest pitch level earlier in the syllable than Accent2. There are two possible pitch patterns before the lowest pitch level in Accent1. The entire pitch pattern may be low level, or the low level may be preceded by a fall (see, for instance, Fintoft, 1970).

A disruption of the element(s) on the tonal tier will lead to deviant pitch patterns on the words in question. We know that Astrid L. failed to distinguish properly between the two pitch accents, but we do not know from Monrad-Krohn's description in what way the failure manifested itself. There are two ways in which a tonal disruption could occur. Either one of the words could be produced with the accent of the other word, a tonal substitution mistake, in which case the two words would become phonologically identical, or the tonal pattern(s) could be changed in such a way that the resultant pitch does not match either accent. Both types of deviation have been found to occur as the result of brain damage. In an investigation of the accent production of East Norwegian brain-damaged patients, Broca aphasics were found occasionally to produce Accent1 instead of the appropriate Accent2 (Moen & Sundet, submitted); and in an investigation of another East Norwegian case of the foreign accent syndrome (Moen, 1990)—a woman with an "English" accent—it was found that the patient sometimes produced a high pitch instead of the low pitch associated with both pitch accents in East Norwegian.

The pitch pattern of the syllable(s) following the accented syllable varies. This variation is not part of the tonal distinction, but belongs to the domain of sentence intonation and signals differences in the information structure of the utterance (Fretheim, 1988).

THE EAST NORWEGIAN UTTERANCE
PROSODIC SYSTEM

The model used to describe the East Norwegian utterance prosodic system is based on a theory which assumes: (1) the prosodic system is an autonomous part of the grammar of a language, (2) it is hierarchically organised, and (3) it maps on to the surface structure of the syntax by a set of rules. This mapping produces an intonated surface structure (Fretheim, 1988; Nilsen, 1989; Selkirk, 1984). The prosodic hierarchy proposed for East Norwegian includes the following categories: the syllable, the (tonal) foot, the intonational phrase, and the intonational utterance. The syllable is at the bottom and the intonational utterance at the top of the hierarchy.

The basic prosodic unit at utterance level in East Norwegian is the foot (Fretheim, 1988). The foot starts with an accented syllable, either Accent1 or Accent2, and includes all syllables up to the next accented syllable. The foot may be focal or nonfocal, that is, it may either be assigned the value [+focal] or the value [-focal]. A focal foot is distinguished from a nonfocal one by its pitch contour. In a focal foot there is a sharp rise in pitch following the lowest pitch level of the accented syllable. In a nonfocal foot there is either no rise, or a more moderate rise, following the lowest pitch level of the accented syllable. The end of a focal foot also signals the end of an intonational phrase.

The prosodic structure can be illustrated by the two hierarchies in Fig. 12.3, two of many possible hierarchies (IU stands for intonational utterance,

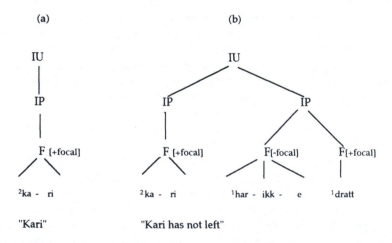

FIG. 12.3   The prosodic structure of ^{2}kari (Kari) and ^{2}kari ^{1}har ikke ^{1}dratt (Kari has not left). IU = intonational utterance; IP = intonational phrase; F = foot.

IP for intonational phrase, and F for foot). The first IU, (a), consists of one IP and one foot. The first syllable has the pitch pattern of Accent2; and since the foot is [+focal], the second syllable ends in a sharp rise. The second IU, (b), consists of two IPs and three feet, two focal and one nonfocal. The first foot in (b) has the same pitch pattern as the intonated surface structure of (a). The first syllables in the two other feet in (b) have the pitch pattern of Accent1. The first and final foot are focal and end in a sharp rise. The middle foot is nonfocal and ends in a moderate rise, or no rise.

The two prosodic hierarchies in Fig. 12.3 illustrate the interaction between pitch accents and utterance prosodic structures. In an utterance, the domain of the Norwegian pitch accents is not the word but the foot. In a syntactic string of words, a word may be accented or not accented. If it is accented, it will be assigned the pitch accent which is appropriate for that particular word, and the pitch contour between one accented syllable and the next will cover the entire foot—also when the foot consists of more than one word. The pitch contour of a Norwegian utterance is a function of the pitch contours of the individual feet which make up the utterance, the type of pitch accent (Accent1 or Accent2), and the degree of prominence—whether the foot is assigned the value [+focal] or [–focal] (Nilsen, 1989).

DESCRIPTION OF ASTRID L.'S DEVIANT SENTENCE PROSODY IN TERMS OF DISRUPTION OF THE COMPONENTS OF THE PROSODIC SYSTEM

There were two particularly striking prosodic deviations in Astrid L.'s speech: (1) At the end of utterances, when Monrad-Krohn expected a final low pitch level, she raised the pitch instead of lowering it; (2) She tended to overemphasise final pronouns in object position in sentences like "Jeg sa det" ("I said it"—Monrad-Krohn's translation, 1947, p. 411).

Since a final rise in pitch is the normal pitch pattern when there is an utterance final focal foot, Astrid L.'s deviant intonation in sentence final position can be accounted for by assuming that she assigned the feature [+focal] to utterance final feet, also when the feature [–focal] would have been the appropriate one.

Her inappropriate use of full vowel qualities in the pronunciation of final pronouns in sentences with the structure SVO, where O is a pronoun, may be accounted for in terms of the distribution of feet. The sentence "Jeg sa det" ("I said it") may be divided into feet in different ways: Either the pronoun, "det", belongs to the same foot as the preceding verb, or it forms a foot of its own. In the first case the meaning of the sentence is "I said it"— the meaning expected by Monrad-Krohn. If the pronoun forms a foot of its own, the meaning of the sentence is "I said that". When the pronoun belongs to the same foot as the preceding verb, it will generally be pronounced with a reduced vowel, the pronunciation expected by Monrad-Krohn, whereas when it forms a separate foot, it will have a full vowel (Moen, 1991). If Astrid L. pronounced the final pronoun as a separate foot, the pronoun would, in consequence, be pronounced with a full vowel quality.

IN SUMMARY

The aim has been to account for Astrid L.'s deviant prosody in terms of damage to specific components of a model of normal language processing.

Monrad-Krohn was particularly intrigued by two aspects of Astrid L.'s symptomatology: (1) Her language prosody was changed, not lost, that is, her speech was not monotonous; (2) Her musical abilities were not affected—she could sing and hum in tune.

The dissociation of her language abilities and her musical abilities can be accounted for in terms of a modular cognitive model, a model which assumes that the different cognitive components, among them the language component, are relatively independent. Damage to one component—in this case the language component—will not necessarily affect other cognitive components.

The deviant prosodic features mentioned by Monrad-Krohn were: (1) inability to distinguish properly between the two Norwegian pitch accents; (2) inappropriate rise in pitch in utterance final position; (3) a tendency to pronounce utterance final pronouns with full vowels in contexts where a reduced vowel was expected.

The patient's deviant pitch accents can be accounted for in terms of a nonlinear phonological model, a model which assumes that the phonological elements are organised on separate, but interacting, tiers, one of which is the tonal tier. The elements on the tonal tier are the two pitch accents. Damage to this tier will lead to deviant pitch accent contours, but will not necessarily affect any of the other tiers—precisely the type of deviation found in Astrid L.'s speech. The segmental phonological structure of her words was apparently normal.

Astrid L.'s tendency to raise the pitch in utterance final position when a low pitch level was expected can be accounted for in terms of faulty assignment of the feature [+/–focal] on utterance final feet. The basic utterance prosodic unit in the model of the East Norwegian prosodic system is the foot. If a foot is assigned the feature [+focal], the syllables following the accented syllable will exhibit a sharp rise. A foot which is assigned the feature [–focal] will exhibit a more moderate rise, or no rise. Thus, the assignment of [+focal] on a foot in an inappropriate context, will lead to an inappropriate rise in pitch on the syllables following the accented syllable.

Faulty assignment of full vowel quality in utterance final pronouns could be the secondary result of an inappropriate division of the utterance into feet. If the final pronoun is made into a separate foot, it will be pronounced with a full vowel. If this happens in contexts where the pronoun should have formed the unstressed part of the same foot as the preceding verb, a concomitant feature will be an inappropriate full vowel.

Since the pitch pattern of a Norwegian utterance is a function of the pitch patterns of the individual feet that make up the utterance, disruption of the pitch at the level of the foot will directly affect the pitch pattern of the utterance as a whole. Astrid L.'s failure to produce (1947, p. 411) "the natural Norwegian accent when she had to link several words together into a sentence" can be ascribed to the combined effect of her deviant pitch accents, inappropriate division of utterances into feet, and faulty assignment of the values of the feature [+/–focal].

REFERENCES

Aronson, A.E. (1980). *Clinical voice disorders: An interdisciplinary approach.* New York: Thieme-Stratton.

Clements, G.N. (1985). The geometry of phonological features. *Phonology Yearbook, 2,* 225–252.

Cruttenden, A. (1986). *Intonation.* Cambridge: Cambridge University Press.

Fintoft, K. (1970). *Acoustical analysis and perception of tonemes in some Norwegian dialects.* Oslo: Universitetsforlaget.

Fretheim, T. (1988). *Intonational phrases and syntactic focus domains* (Working Papers in Linguistics No. 6). University of Trondheim.

Goldsmith, J.A. (1990). *Autosegmental and metrical phonology.* Oxford: Basil Blackwell.

Ingram, J.C.L., McCormack, P.F., & Kennedy, M. (1992). Phonetic analysis of a case of foreign accent syndrome. *Journal of Phonetics, 20,* 457–474.

Moen, I. (1990). A case of the "foreign-accent syndrome". *Clinical Linguistics and Phonetics, 4*(4), 295–302.

Moen, I. (1991). Functional lateralisation of pitch accents and intonation in Norwegian: Monrad-Krohn's study of an aphasic patient with altered "melody of speech". *Brain and Language, 41,* 538–554.

Moen, I., & Sundet, K. (submitted). *Production and perception of word tones (pitch accents) in patients with left and right hemisphere damage.*

Monrad-Krohn, G.H. (1947). Dysprosody or altered "melody of language". *Brain, 70,* 405–415.

Nilsen, R. (1989). *On prosodically marked information structure in spoken Norwegian* (Working Papers in Linguistics No. 7). University of Trondheim.

Pick, A. (1919). Über Änderungen des Sprachcharacters als Begleiterscheinung aphasischer Störungen. *Zeitschrift für die gesamte Neurologie und Psychiatrie, 45,* 230–241.

Selkirk, E.O. (1984). *Phonology and syntax.* Cambridge, MA & London: MIT Press.

van der Hulst, H., & Smith, N. (Eds.). (1982). *The structure of phonological representations, Parts 1 and 2.* Dordrecht: Foris Publication.

van der Hulst, H., & Smith, N. (Eds.). (1988). *Autosegmental studies on pitch accents.* Dordrecht: Foris Publication.

Whitaker, H. (1982). Levels of impairment in disorders of speech. In R.N. Malatesha & L.C. Hartlage (Eds.), *Neuropsychology and cognition (Vol. 1).* The Hague: Nijhoff.

13 Paterson and Zangwill's (1944) Case of Unilateral Neglect:[1] Insights from 50 Years of Experimental Inquiry

Jason B. Mattingley
Department of Experimental Psychology, University of Cambridge, U.K. and M.R.C. Applied Psychology Unit, Cambridge, U.K.

INTRODUCTION

In 1944, Andrew Paterson and Oliver Zangwill published a report describing a patient who had suffered a penetrating wound of the right cerebral hemisphere. In the months following his injury, the patient exhibited behaviours which today would be characterised as reflecting a lateralised disorder of spatial cognition known as *unilateral neglect*. Unlike many classic cases in neuropsychology, the patient studied by Paterson and Zangwill (1944) was not the first to exhibit a disorder hitherto undescribed in the scientific literature. Indeed, workers such as Hughlings Jackson (1876/1932), Poppelreuter (1917/1990), Holmes (1918), and Brain (1941) had all described patients with disorders of spatial orientation and attention following either unilateral or bilateral damage. Unfortunately, these early reports were typically of patients with extensive lesions who suffered from a conglomeration of distinct functional impairments. Of potentially greater concern, however, is that these early reports were often based upon relatively brief neurological tests and anecdotal observations, the results of which were rarely quantified or subjected to objective analysis. The case reported by Paterson and Zangwill represents a paradigm shift towards objectivity, both in the approach to assessment of patients with unilateral neglect and in the interpretation of their preserved and impaired capacities.

In contrast to the traditional clinical methodology adopted in earlier studies, Paterson and Zangwill used a battery of experimental tasks to tease apart what was apparently a set of distinct underlying impairments. For the first time, they were able to quantify in an objective manner the heterogeneous nature of their patient's deficits, and to consider the cognitive basis for their occurrence. Indeed, many of the tests used by Paterson and Zangwill continue to be used in clinical and experimental investigations of unilateral neglect: These include line bisection, figure copying and drawing, completion of fragmented figures, visual half-field tachistoscopic presentations, and tests involving mental imagery. Moreover, because Paterson and Zangwill's patient suffered a relatively circumscribed and well-localised lesion, it is possible to interpret his pattern of deficits in light of current knowledge about the neuroanatomical correlates of impaired spatial cognition.

CLINICAL DETAILS OF THE CASE

The case to be considered in this chapter was the first of two reported in Paterson and Zangwill's 1944 paper. The patient was a previously healthy 39-year-old man who suffered a penetrating wound of the right parieto-occipital region following an explosion on 20th September, 1943. He lost consciousness for two or three minutes only, and showed minimal post-traumatic and retrograde amnesia. He complained of headache and "mistiness of vision", but exhibited no difficulty in hearing. He was ambulant within two days of his accident. His most salient deficit was a strong neglect of the left side of space: he collided with objects on his left, knocked over dishes on the left while sitting at the table, and missed food on the left side of his plate. These deficits were investigated over an extended period until his discharge approximately four months later. I shall return to consider the findings of these investigations after presenting the results of his neurological examination.

Unlike many early investigators, Paterson and Zangwill were able to obtain images of the locus and extent of their patient's damage (pp. 335–336):

> Stereoscopic X-rays of skull (28.9.43) showed metallic foreign body consisting of a hexagonal nut about 1 in. in diameter with a short length of screw-headed bolt projecting from its upper lateral surface. No fissures extended from the skull fracture. Beneath the foreign body and lying around it were a large number of small bony fragments.

Two weeks post-injury a limited craniectomy was performed, in which the steel nut and a "considerable quantity" of pus and necrotic brain tissue were removed. The traumatic aetiology, though common to many other classic neurological cases from the early- and mid-20th century (e.g. Poppelreuter's case of Merk; see Humphreys, Riddoch, & Wallesch, this volume), is atypical of unilateral neglect. Today, virtually all cases are encountered after acute ischaemic or haemorrhagic stroke affecting one (usually the right) cerebral hemisphere. The fact that unilateral neglect occurs only rarely in cases of slow growing tumours, and that its most salient clinical manifestations frequently resolve over time, implies that the disorder reflects an abrupt, circumscribed disruption of neural functions involved in spatial cognition.

A neurological examination performed one week post-injury revealed a complete left homonymous hemianopia. During his recovery, repeated perimetric testing of the patient's visual fields revealed progressive (though incomplete) expansion of the left upper quadrants. In contrast, the defect remained "virtually complete" in the left lower quadrants. These findings confirm that the primary focus of damage included part of the superior optic radiation which courses through the parietal region. These fibres carry visual information representing the lower visual fields. More inferiorly located fibres in the temporal region, though perhaps dysfunctional in the acute stage post-injury, are likely to have been spared, thereby permitting some widening of the visual field into the left upper quadrant.

Although visual field defects frequently co-occur with unilateral neglect, it is now known that the various manifestations of the latter cannot be attributed to field cuts alone. Indeed, the two deficits are clearly dissociable. Moreover, unilateral neglect and the related disorder of *extinction* are also manifest in the auditory (De Renzi, Gentilini, & Barbieri, 1989), tactile (Mattingley & Bradshaw, 1994), and olfactory (Bellas, Novelly, Eskenazi, & Wasserstein, 1988) modalities, and may even appear on tasks of visual imagery (Bisiach & Luzzatti, 1978).

All of the patient's other cranial nerve functions were assessed as being normal. It is noteworthy that his eyes reacted normally to light and accommodation, and that there was no apparent deficit in oculomotor functioning. As we shall see, these observations are particularly important in view of the profound perceptual anomalies exhibited by the patient on experimental tests. It is also noteworthy that limb power was equal (and presumably normal) on both sides, and that there was no impairment of sensation or reflexes. Once again, these findings are atypical of patients with unilateral neglect, and probably reflect the unusual aetiology. Because most reported cases of unilateral neglect have had relatively large lesions of cerebrovascular origin, the occurrence of profound sensory and/or motor disturbances has tended to be the rule.

Locus of Lesion

In contrast to the reports of unilateral neglect by many authors in the late 19th and early 20th centuries, Paterson and Zangwill were able to document with some precision the locus of their patient's lesion. Using information obtained from X-rays and from surgical notes, they described (p. 337) their patient's lesion thus: "The upper borders of the supramarginal and angular gyri on the right side were damaged on the surface and their deeper connections interrupted by the in-driven bone fragments to a depth of just over 1 in. The lesion was circumscribed and there was minimal contusional damage."

Prior to 1944, several workers had suggested that the critical lesion for producing unilateral neglect involved posterior regions of the right hemisphere. Indeed, both Lange (1936) and Brain (1941) had emphasised the importance of the right parietal lobe in mediating spatial orientation and attention. These authors based their conclusions upon converging lines of evidence from several patients with massive posterior lesions. Paterson and Zangwill were able to confirm in a single patient the importance of damage to the right parietal lobe for producing impairments of spatial cognition. More importantly they obtained the first clear evidence that damage to a specific subregion, the inferior parietal lobule (IPL), may underlie the emergence of unilateral neglect in humans. Interestingly, the precise location of their patient's lesion occasioned little comment from Paterson and Zangwill, and appears to have been largely overlooked by many subsequent workers. More recent neuroanatomical studies have shown that clinical manifestations of unilateral neglect occur more frequently (and are more severe) after IPL damage than after damage to other brain regions (Vallar & Perani, 1986).

We now know that the IPL, at least in nonhuman primates, is part of the so-called dorsal visual processing stream (Mishkin, Ungerleider, & Macko, 1983; Ungerleider & Haxby, 1994), whose anatomy includes a hierarchy of interconnected regions between the occipital and parietal lobes. The dorsal stream is critical for processing the locations of objects in space, and for co-ordinating goal-directed actions towards discrete objects (Goodale & Milner, 1992); for this reason, it is often referred to as the "where" system (Mishkin et al., 1983). In humans, parietal lesions affecting the dorsal stream result in disorders such as optic ataxia, constructional apraxia, and unilateral neglect (Newcombe & Ratcliff, 1989; Newcombe, Ratcliff, & Damasio, 1987).

In contrast the ventral visual processing stream, which comprises the occipital and inferior temporal regions, mediates the visual identification of objects and is referred to as the "what" system. Humans with damage involving the ventral stream may exhibit such disorders as visual object agnosia and prosopagnosia. In order to become aware of a specific object in a particular spatial location, information from both processing streams must be combined (Coslett & Saffran, 1991). Many of the deficits exhibited by Paterson and Zangwill's patient can be understood in terms of a selective impairment of the "where" system, with relative preservation of the "what" system.

EXPERIMENTAL TESTING

A unique feature of the Paterson and Zangwill case is that a thorough analysis of both impaired and preserved cognitive functions was undertaken. It is therefore possible to obtain a relatively unambiguous picture of the patient's general cognitive status. Speech and language functions were unimpaired: recognition of letters, words, and phrases was normal, and oral comprehension was intact. In writing, both spelling and grammar were normal and calculation was unaffected. Despite his very obvious problems with visuo-spatial cognition, the patient nevertheless retained a number of important visual capacities. He could estimate, for example, absolute and relative distance in central vision. He also showed normal shape and size constancy. Bisection of vertical and oblique lines was relatively accurate, though paradoxically he bisected horizontal lines too far to the left of their midpoint, instead of the usual rightward bisection error characteristic of most left unilateral neglect patients. It is now known that factors such as line length (Halligan & Marshall, 1988), spatial location (Heilman & Valenstein, 1979), and the presence or absence of lateralised cues (Riddoch & Humphreys, 1983) can affect the direction and extent of bisection errors made by patients with unilateral neglect. Unfortunately, Paterson and Zangwill did not provide any such information for their patient.

Appreciation of depth also remained intact. There was no evidence of left–right disorientation or apraxia (though as we shall see later, the patient did exhibit constructional difficulties in tasks requiring visually guided manual activity). Most importantly, there was no evidence of visual object agnosia or colour agnosia. These findings suggest that the patient's "what" system was functioning within normal limits, a conclusion that is consistent with sparing of the ventral visual processing stream within temporal cortex. Paterson and Zangwill's patient also appeared to have some knowledge of his disorder: He spontaneously reported (p. 336) "a tendency to neglect objects on his left-hand side," but was unable to use this knowledge to overcome his impairment.

Set against this background of preserved functioning, the patient exhibited severe deficits in perceiving and attending to the contralesional side of space. Paterson and Zangwill distinguished three broad categories of spatial disorder: (1) unilateral visual symptoms, which comprised visual disorientation, left-sided inattention, and agnosia for the left hemispace; (2) oculomotor symptoms, which involved an impairment in controlling voluntary eye movements during reading; (3) visual-constructive disabilities, which involved a failure to perceive and to reproduce spatial relationships in the central field of vision. In the following sections, I will consider the findings relevant to each of these categories in turn.

Unilateral Visual Symptoms

Spatial localisation in the horizontal and vertical planes was impaired with a standard object presented in the upper left quadrant of the binocular field, relative to judgements in the upper right quadrant. In addition, the patient showed a tendency to mislocalise the distance of a standard object in the affected quadrant: The distance of objects presented within the patient's reach (250mm) was overestimated, whereas that of objects presented beyond his reach (1000mm) was underestimated. In interpreting this latter finding, Paterson and Zangwill referred to the work of Brain (1941), who suggested that separate mechanisms might exist for controlling visual perception within and beyond reaching space. Curiously, this hypothesis has been largely ignored by contemporary theorists, despite the fact that recent animal studies have shown that distinct, parallel circuits involving inferior parietal and prefrontal regions do indeed provide separate representations of near and far space (Rizzolatti, Matelli, & Pavesi, 1983).

Such a distinction makes sense from an evolutionary perspective: Within reaching space, perceptual and attentional processes must extract information necessary for the coherent control of reaching and grasping movements, whereas the representation of more distant regions is likely to be based on the coding of eye movements. In patients with left unilateral neglect, dissociations have been observed between performances within and beyond reaching space (Cowey, Small, & Ellis, 1994; Halligan & Marshall, 1991). Moreover, there is evidence that self-generated movements of the contralesional upper limb can improve visual attention towards the affected side (Robertson & North, 1992).

Paterson and Zangwill also examined their patient's ability to shift selective attention in the azimuthal (left–right) axis. They presented visual stimuli to the (intact) upper quadrants using a tachistoscope, which permitted fine control of the content, positioning, and exposure duration of different items. Stimuli were exposed for durations which varied between 200 and 500msec. These could appear in either visual field alone (unilateral presentations), or simultaneously in both visual fields (bilateral presentations). The patient's perception of stimuli with left unilateral presentations was retarded. Moreover, with bilateral presentations only the stimulus appearing in the ipsilesional (right) visual field was detected. This latter phenomenon, commonly known as extinction, was evident even when the exposure duration was adjusted so that left unilateral stimuli were readily perceived.

These findings clearly demonstrate an impairment in processing isolated visual stimuli presented briefly in the contralesional hemifield, despite apparently normal perception in the same field with extended viewing time. More importantly, the contralesional stimulus was extinguished by the simultaneous presence of a competing stimulus in the ipsilesional (right) visual field. Paterson and Zangwill attributed their patient's lateralised impairment (p. 339) to "a unilateral restriction of the perceptual process itself." They rejected the possibility of an attentional defect because, they argued, the patient was not attending to either visual field, but to a central fixation point.

Central fixation of the eyes, however, does not preclude attention shifts. It is now well known that selective attention can be moved covertly while the eyes remain stationary (Posner, 1980). Patients with parietal lesions tend to orient their covert attention spontaneously towards stimuli in extreme ipsilesional locations (De Renzi, Gentilini, Faglioni, & Barbieri, 1989; Làdavas, 1990), even when their eyes remain directed straight ahead. Such patients also experience difficulties in disengaging covert attention when preparing for a shift toward more contralesionally located stimuli (Posner, Walker, Friedrich, & Rafal, 1984). Interestingly, the possibility of shifting attention without eye movements was not unfamiliar to Paterson and Zangwill; in their paper (p. 334), they cite a study by Scheller and Seidemann (1932) in which the suggestion was made that voluntarily controlled eye movements "follow rather than precede shifts of attention."

Whereas the methods used by Paterson and Zangwill to detect and quantify visual extinction were ground breaking, the context in which they interpreted their data was limited by prevailing views of the processes involved in representing visual information. In contrast to the "perceptual" interpretation offered by Paterson and Zangwill, contemporary workers (e.g. Desimone & Duncan, 1995; Kinsbourne, 1993; Ward, Goodrich, & Driver, 1994) have viewed such extinction effects (as well as many other impairments associated with unilateral neglect) in terms of an attentional imbalance between laterally competing visual inputs. At any given moment the brain receives much more visual information than can be used to guide behaviour effectively. It is, therefore, necessary to have an attentional system which selects just a subset of this information for further processing. Although the precise mechanisms by which the selection of relevant information is achieved by the intact brain remain controversial (Driver & Mattingley, 1995), studies of patients with unilateral neglect and extinction have provided several clues as to the nature of this selective process.

The spatial location of visual information is one important determinant of selection. Following unilateral damage of the kind shown by Paterson and Zangwill's patient, stimuli occupying an ipsilesional position are more likely to be selected than those in a more contralesional position, regardless of the absolute location of these stimuli in the environment (Làdavas, Petronio, & Umiltà, 1990). One explanation for this bias is that the two hemispheres normally control opposing contralateral orienting tendencies, such that damage to one hemisphere releases the other from inhibitory control (Kinsbourne, 1993). In such cases, attentional selection is likely to favour more ipsilesionally located stimuli. Thus in extinction paradigms such as that used by Paterson and Zangwill, the more ipsilesional of two simultaneously presented stimuli has a competitive advantage over the contralesional stimulus, and is therefore more likely to be selected for further processing. In contrast, contralesional stimuli presented in isolation (i.e. without simultaneously presented ipsilesional stimuli) no longer suffer such a competitive disadvantage, and may now be selected, albeit with somewhat reduced efficiency (Desimone & Duncan, 1995).

A second important determinant of normal attentional processing involves selection of distinct objects from visual representations. In normals, attention may bind together properties belonging to distinct objects according to Gestalt grouping principles such as good continuation and common motion (Kanwisher & Driver, 1992). Processes involved in visually recognising and identifying objects are assumed to be subserved by the ventral processing stream, which is preserved in patients with unilateral neglect and extinction following parietal (dorsal stream) lesions. Consistent with this assumption, Paterson and Zangwill's patient, who had circumscribed parietal damage, was able to recognise and identify objects and pictures normally when these were presented in free vision and without time restrictions. When such stimuli were flashed briefly in the contralesional visual field with competing ipsilesional stimuli, however, the patient failed to report the contralesional item.

Paterson and Zangwill assumed that because contralesional stimuli were not reported by their patient they were not perceived. There is now evidence, however, that processing of neglected or extinguished stimuli may proceed to a relatively high level (see Driver, in press, for review). Thus, despite their apparent inability to detect or identify contralesional stimuli, such patients nevertheless may demonstrate implicit knowledge about the colour, shape, and even semantic content of such stimuli (Baylis, Driver, & Rafal, 1993; Berti, Frassinetti, & Umiltà, 1994; Mattingley, Bradshaw, & Bradshaw, 1995; McGlinchey-Berroth, Milberg, Verfaellie, Alexander, & Kilduff, 1993). For instance, normal semantic priming effects have been found for responses to ipsilesional targets from undetected picture and word primes presented in the contralesional visual field (Berti & Rizzolatti, 1992; McGlinchey-Berroth et al., 1993). Returning to the notion of parallel visual processing streams, patients with primarily dorsal (parietal) damage remain unaware of contralesionally located stimuli, although they nevertheless may continue to process object properties of such stimuli, including relevant semantic information, via an intact ventral processing stream. Had Paterson and Zangwill conducted the appropriate tests, they may have found evidence for preserved implicit knowledge of extinguished stimuli in their patient.

Among the other unilateral visual symptoms reported by Paterson and Zangwill was their patient's "agnosia for the left half of space". As noted earlier, the patient was observed to collide with objects on his left, despite having apparently perceived them moments before. He also missed food on the left of his plate and omitted the initial (left-sided) items from lines of disconnected words. These particular problems resolved after several months, though not before Paterson and Zangwill were able to conduct a number of specific tests in order to quantify the disorder.

One of the most striking results was obtained from a test in which the patient was required to set the hands of a large clock-face to indicate prespecified times. Although the hour hand was consistently positioned correctly, on nearly half the trials the minute hand was incorrectly positioned on the right instead of the left side of the clock-face. Thus, for example, when asked to show "twenty to four" the patient set the hands to show twenty past four. He made only one error in the opposite direction (i.e. from right to left). Such transpositions from the impaired to the intact side (known as *visual allochiria*) had been observed in earlier reports of patients with right hemisphere lesions (e.g. Brain, 1941), but had not been properly quantified. More recent investigations have shown that visual allochiria is often a key feature of unilateral neglect. Patients may transpose details from the impaired to the intact side when copying pictures or drawing from memory (Halligan, Marshall, & Wade, 1992), and may misplace towns lying on the contralesional side of a familiar map toward the ipsilesional side (Bisiach, Capitani, Luzzatti, & Perani, 1981; Rode & Perenin, 1994). Paterson and Zangwill's patient was apparently able to perceive objects (or certain subcomponents thereof) lying toward his affected side, but incorrectly placed them on the ipsilesional side.

Similar errors were observed when the patient was asked to localise objects arranged in a semicircle in front of him. Despite his obvious difficulties in detecting contralesionally located objects in activities of daily living (e.g. eating and walking), the patient made no errors in pointing to all objects before him with eyes open. In contrast, with eyes closed objects on the left were mislocalised toward the ipsilesional side, so that even items on his extreme left were pointed to as if they lay straight ahead.

The ipsilesional bias in spatial localisation observed by Paterson and Zangwill has been noted in several more recent studies. Thus, individuals with left unilateral neglect may mislocalise free-field sounds ipsilesionally (Bisiach, Cornacchia, Sterzi, & Vallar, 1984). They also may deviate toward the ipsilesional side when attempting to align a distant visual target with their midsagittal axis (Karnath, 1994c). It has been suggested that such errors in pointing stem from misalignment of the egocentric spatial co-ordinate frame (Karnath, 1994a). The transformation of sensory input co-ordinates (e.g. from the retina, muscles, etc.) into an egocentric co-ordinate frame operates with a systematic ipsilesional distortion, such that stimuli lying opposite the body midline are now perceived as lying towards the ipsilesional side. Consistent with this view is the observation that vestibular and proprioceptive stimulation on the contralesional side help to re-establish accurate midline judgements in patients with left unilateral neglect (Karnath, 1994c), perhaps by providing additional afferent information regarding orientation of the head and body in space.

Oculomotor Symptoms

Although Paterson and Zangwill's patient showed no oculomotor deficits on routine neurological examination, he nevertheless had a marked impairment in controlling eye movements during reading. He often lost his place and experienced difficulty in shifting fixation from the end of one line of text to the beginning of the next. In addition, the eye movements themselves were noted (p. 339) to be "erratic and atypical." The use of modern infrared eye-movement recorders has confirmed that patients with left unilateral neglect may indeed show abnormal contralesional eye movements in the absence of any primary oculomotor abnormality. When attempting to shift fixation from the end of one line of text to the beginning of another, patients initially return fixation to the centre of each new line, followed occasionally by a series of short corrective saccades to find a more plausible continuation of the sentence (Karnath & Huber, 1992). In scanning pictures of objects or scenes, such patients also tend to restrict their eye movements to the ipsilesional side (Karnath, 1994b), though they may occasionally use contextual information present within the fixated region to guide shifts of attention (and possibly eye movements) contralesionally (Seron, Coyette, & Bruyer, 1989). When using eye movements to search for the presence of a light in an otherwise completely darkened room, left unilateral neglect patients leave their contralesional hemispace largely unexplored, whereas patients with contralesional visual field defects (but no neglect) search equally in both sides of space (Hornak, 1992).

Unfortunately, the interpretation of eye-movement deficits in patients with unilateral neglect remains unresolved, despite the fact that it has important theoretical implications for understanding the disorder. Paterson and Zangwill were probably correct in adducing that their patient was not suffering a primary oculomotor deficit, since more recent evidence has shown that such patients are capable of executing a full range of eye movements. They considered the possibility (p. 354) that the disorder may have reflected "a primary apraxic disorder of eye-movement co-ordination and control." This seems a plausible explanation in light of recent evidence from a patient with left unilateral neglect showing that contralesional eye movements were often hypometric and contained abnormal staircase saccades (Butter, Rapcsak, Watson, & Heilman, 1988). They also considered (p. 354) that their patient's eye-movement deficit may have stemmed from his lateralised "perceptual disorder." Such a notion is reminiscent of a more recent model which assumes that unilateral neglect patients are unable to construct a representation of the contralesional side of their environment; hence, there is no spatial map to represent the region into which voluntary eye movements are to be directed (Bisiach & Berti, 1987).

Visual-constructive Disabilities

Paterson and Zangwill performed a number of specific tasks in order to test their patient's perceptual and constructional abilities. Unfortunately, in view of the patient's previously discussed problems in directing selective attention and eye movements contralesionally, it is difficult to provide an unambiguous interpretation of many of his performances on these tasks. Indeed, Paterson and Zangwill were acutely aware of this potential problem, implying that some of the visuo-constructional difficulties they observed may have stemmed from purely perceptual and/or eye-movement deficits. When shown a solid cube constructed from 27 square blocks, for instance, the patient was unable to deduce how many blocks it contained because he neglected the left-most layer altogether, in addition to failing to count blocks occluded by those within his immediate view. In copying and spontaneous drawing, the patient failed to produce salient left-sided elements, in addition to showing displacement of parts and abnormal perspective and depth.

Despite the difficulties in interpretation outlined above, one consistent feature of the patient's performance *is* worthy of specific mention, since it provides a clear link with contemporary models of hemispheric specialisation. When faced with tasks involving analysis or construction of an integrated whole from smaller subcomponents, the patient consistently adopted what Paterson and Zangwill called a "piecemeal" approach. Thus, complex objects and scenes were reproduced in a slavish, detail by detail, manner without any apparent appreciation of the configuration of the whole. This impairment was elegantly illustrated by tests in which the patient was required to place local elements within a familiar global context. When presented with fragmented capital letters on a page, for example, he was unable to complete them, even when he knew the identity of the letters concerned and could readily print them from memory. Similarly, when reproducing from memory a plan view of his hospital ward, the patient drew a series of vaguely connected features which in no way conformed to the square and symmetrical layout of the real scene.

In explaining the piecemeal approach adopted by their patient, Paterson and Zangwill (1944, p. 356) again cited the earlier study of Scheller and

Siedemann (1932), who had suggested that such anomalies may be due to a pathological constriction of visual attention: "On such a view, it might be argued that the piecemeal effect arises from undue restriction of attention to one aspect of the drawing with consequent neglect of the rest. This implies neglect of what has already been drawn and of what still remains to be added."

Although the location of the patient's omissions in the letter-completion task was not reported by Paterson and Zangwill, the example performances included in their paper suggest a tendency to fill in right-sided fragments, leaving left-sided fragments of letters incomplete (see their Fig. 4, p. 343). Similarly, in the plan-drawing task, although the patient rotated the page by 90° during his performance, the elements of the scene were again restricted to one side of the location from which he started the drawing.

Recent work suggests that the impairment in integrating the local features of real or imagined displays with their global configurations is likely to reflect an underlying asymmetry in the perceptual scale at which the intact hemispheres operate. Normal healthy subjects show an advantage in responding to the local features of visual displays presented in the right visual field (left hemisphere), whereas they show a left visual field (right hemisphere) advantage in responding to their global features (Sergent, 1982). Unilateral damage to either hemisphere results in congruent deficits of local/global processing: individuals with left hemisphere lesions are impaired in responding to local compared with global features relative to controls, whereas those with right hemisphere damage are impaired in responding to global compared with local features (Robertson & Lamb, 1991).

Recently it has been suggested that many of the manifestations of left unilateral neglect can be explained in terms of an ipsilesional attentional bias, in combination with an overemphasis on processing local over global features of visual stimuli (Halligan & Marshall, 1994b). This explanation is consistent with the notion that the intact left hemisphere controls a strong orienting bias toward the right (Kinsbourne, 1993), in addition to exerting a local bias in visual perception (Robertson & Lamb, 1991). Occasionally, such patients may exhibit some knowledge of global form: thus, they may reproduce the full circumference of a clock-face but omit numbers (i.e. local elements) from the left (Bisiach et al., 1981). Similarly, their midpoint judgements of "global" shapes such as squares may be normal,[2] although they may show substantial ipsilesional errors when asked to bisect narrow lines of the same horizontal extent (Halligan & Marshall, 1994a). They also may be able to indicate the global dimensions of an array of discrete visual stimuli, but when asked to mark each of the local elements they neglect those toward the contralesional side (Halligan & Marshall, 1993). In each of these examples patients appear to perceive some aspects of global form, but cannot exploit this information to guide selective attention to local features on the contralesional side.

CONCLUDING REMARKS

Several of the observations made by Paterson and Zangwill foreshadowed the development of contemporary models of unilateral neglect. It is now apparent that damage to the dorsal visual stream after parietal lesions impairs spatially selective attention, leaving the ventral object-recognition system relatively intact. Unilateral neglect and extinction reflect a lateral bias in competitive interactions between representations of objects in different spatial locations, with ipsilesionally located items being selected over more contralesionally located ones. The outcome of these competitive processes seems to depend upon the region of space in which objects are located, so that the asymmetry may be more apparent for stimuli close to the body, compared with those beyond arms' reach, or vice versa. In addition, patients may retain some implicit knowledge of neglected or extinguished stimuli via preserved object-recognition processes. Relative specialisation of the left and right hemispheres for perception of local and global features, respectively, may explain the overemphasis upon local visual details shown by right parietal patients with left unilateral neglect.

In the half-century since Paterson and Zangwill published their case, our knowledge of the neural and cognitive mechanisms underlying human behaviour has advanced considerably. By adopting a modular view of brain functioning, in which discrete processing units are dedicated to specific cognitive operations, it is possible to make sense of dissociations and fractionations observed in clinically defined syndromes such as amnesia, agnosia, and aphasia. The study of patients with unilateral neglect has enabled us to identify the seams along which modules subserving spatial perception and attention may be divided, and to tease apart the relevant contributions of these functions to spatial cognition. Unlike several of their predecessors who sought overarching models of unilateral neglect, Paterson and Zangwill assumed that the heterogeneity of impairments shown by such patients reflects disruption of distinct underlying mechanisms. Half a century of experimental inquiry has largely supported their claim.

ACKNOWLEDGEMENTS

This work was supported by a National Health and Medical Research Council (Australia) Neil Hamilton Fairley Fellowship. Many thanks to Ada Kritikos for her helpful comments on an earlier draft of this chapter.

NOTES

1. Paterson and Zangwill published several reports during the 1940s and 1950s on patients with visuospatial disorders after right hemisphere damage. In this chapter, I have focused upon their Case 1, described in Paterson, A. and Zangwill, O.L. (1944). Disorders of visual space perception associated with lesions of the right cerebral hemisphere. *Brain*, *67*, 331–358.

2. It is noteworthy that Paterson and Zangwill's patient was accurate in judging the midpoint of a circle, despite his obvious difficulties in bisecting horizontal lines.

REFERENCES

Baylis, G.C., Driver, J., & Rafal, R.D. (1993). Visual extinction and stimulus repetition. *Journal of Cognitive Neuroscience*, *5*, 453–466.

Bellas, D.N., Novelly, R.A., Eskenazi, B., & Wasserstein, J. (1988). The nature of unilateral neglect in the olfactory sensory system. *Neuropsychologia*, *26*, 45–52.

Berti, A., Frassinetti, F., & Umiltà, C. (1994). Nonconscious reading? Evidence from neglect dyslexia. *Cortex*, *30*, 181–197.

Berti, A., & Rizzolatti, G.(1992). Visual processing without awareness: Evidence from unilateral neglect. *Journal of Cognitive Neuroscience*, *4*, 345–351.

Bisiach, E., & Berti, A. (1987). Dyschiria: An attempt at its systemic explanation. In M. Jeannerod (Ed.), *Neurophysiological and neuropsychological aspects of spatial neglect* (pp. 183–201). Amsterdam: North-Holland.

Bisiach, E., Capitani, E., Luzzatti, C., & Perani, D. (1981). Brain and conscious representation of outside reality. *Neuropsychologia*, *19*, 543–551.

Bisiach, E., Cornacchia, L., Sterzi, R., & Vallar, G. (1984). Disorders of perceived auditory lateralization after lesions of the right hemisphere. *Brain*, *107*, 37–52.

Bisiach, E., & Luzzatti, C. (1978). Unilateral neglect of representational space. *Cortex*, *14*, 129–133.

Brain, W.R. (1941). Visual disorientation with special reference to lesions of the right cerebral hemisphere. *Brain*, *64*, 244–272.

Butter, C.M., Rapcsak, S., Watson, R.T., & Heilman, K.M. (1988). Changes in sensory inattention, directional motor neglect and "release" of the fixation reflex following a unilateral frontal lesion: A case report. *Neuropsychologia*, *26*, 533–545.

Coslett, H.B., & Saffran, E. (1991). Simultanagnosia: To see but not two see. *Brain*, *114*, 1523–1525.

Cowey, A., Small, M., & Ellis, S. (1994). Left visuo-spatial neglect can be worse in far than in near space. *Neuropsychologia*, *32*, 1059–1066.

De Renzi, E., Gentilini, M., & Barbieri, C. (1989). Auditory neglect. *Journal of Neurology, Neurosurgery and Psychiatry*, *52*, 613–617.

De Renzi, E., Gentilini, M., Faglioni, P., & Barbieri, C. (1989). Attentional shift towards the rightmost stimuli in patients with left visual neglect. *Cortex*, *25*, 231–237.

Desimone, R., & Duncan, J. (1995). Neural mechanisms of selective visual attention. *Annual Review of Neuroscience*, *18*, 193–222.

Driver, J. (in press). What can visual neglect and extinction reveal about the extent of "preattentive" processing? In A. Kramer & M. Coles (Eds.), *Convergent methods in the study of attention*. APA Press.

Driver, J., & Mattingley, J.B. (1995). Selective attention in humans: Normality and pathology. *Current Opinion in Neurobiology*, *5*, 191–197.

Goodale, M.A., & Milner, A.D. (1992). Separate visual pathways for perception and action. *Trends in Neurosciences*, *15*, 20–25.

Halligan, P.W., & Marshall, J.C. (1988). How long is a piece of string? A study of line bisection in a case of visual neglect. *Cortex, 24*, 321–328.

Halligan, P.W., & Marshall, J.C. (1991). Left neglect for near but not far space in man. *Nature, 350*, 498–500.

Halligan, P.W., & Marshall, J.C. (1993). Homing in on neglect: A case study of visual search. *Cortex, 29*, 167–174.

Halligan, P.W., & Marshall, J.C. (1994a). Focal and global attention modulate the expression of visuo-spatial neglect: A case study. *Neuropsychologia, 32*, 13–21.

Halligan, P.W., & Marshall, J.C. (1994b). Towards a principled explanation of unilateral neglect. *Cognitive Neuropsychology, 11*, 167–206.

Halligan, P.W., Marshall, J.C., & Wade, D.T. (1992). Contrapositioning in a case of visual neglect. *Neuropsychological Rehabilitation, 2*, 125–135.

Heilman, K.M., & Valenstein, E. (1979). Mechanisms underlying hemispatial neglect. *Annals of Neurology, 5*, 166–170.

Holmes, G. (1918). Disturbances of vision by cerebral lesions. *British Journal of Ophthalmology, 2*, 353–384.

Hornak, J. (1992). Ocular exploration in the dark by patients with visual neglect. *Neuropsychologia, 30*, 547–552.

Hughlings Jackson, J. (1876/1932). Case of large cerebral tumour without optic neuritis and with left hemiplegia and impercepton. *Royal Ophthalmological Hospital Reports, 8*, 434–444. Reprinted in I. Taylor (Ed.), *Selected writings of John Hughlings Jackson (Vol.2)*. London: Hodder & Stoughton.

Kanwisher, N., & Driver, J. (1992). Objects, attributes and visual attention: Which, what and where. *Current Directions in Psychological Science, 1*, 26–31.

Karnath, H.-O. (1994a). Disturbed coordinate transformation in the neural representation of space as the crucial mechanism leading to neglect. *Neuropsychological Rehabilitation, 4*, 147–150.

Karnath, H.-O. (1994b). Spatial limitation of eye movements during ocular exploration of simple line drawings in neglect syndrome. *Cortex, 30*, 319–330.

Karnath, H.-O. (1994c). Subjective body orientation in neglect and the interactive contribution of neck muscle proprioception and vestibular stimulation. *Brain, 117*, 1001–1012.

Karnath, H.-O., & Huber, W. (1992). Abnormal eye movement behaviour during text reading in neglect syndrome: A case study. *Neuropsychologia, 30*, 593–598.

Kinsbourne, M. (1993). Orientational bias model of unilateral neglect: Evidence from attentional gradients within hemispace. In I.H. Robertson & J.C. Marshall (Eds.), *Unilateral neglect: Clinical and experimental studies* (pp. 63–86). Hove, U.K.: Lawrence Erlbaum Associates Ltd.

Làdavas, E. (1990). Selective spatial attention in patients with visual extinction. *Brain, 113*, 1527–1538.

Làdavas, E., Petronio, A., & Umiltà, C. (1990). The deployment of visual attention in the intact field of hemineglect patients. *Cortex, 26*, 307–317.

Lange, J. (1936). Agnosien und Apraxien. In O. Bumke & O. Foester (Eds.), *Handbuch der Neurologie* (Vol. 6, pp. 807–960).

Mattingley, J.B., & Bradshaw, J.L. (1994). Can tactile neglect occur at an intra-limb level? Vibrotactile reaction times in patients with right hemisphere damage. *Behavioral Neurology, 7*, 67–77.

Mattingley, J.B., Bradshaw, J.L., & Bradshaw, J.A. (1995). The effects of unilateral visuospatial neglect on perception of Müller–Lyer illusory figures. *Perception, 24*, 415–433.

McGlinchey-Berroth, R., Milberg, W.P., Verfaellie, M., Alexander, M., & Kilduff, P.T. (1993). Semantic processing in the neglected visual field: Evidence from a lexical decision task. *Cognitive Neuropsychology, 10*, 79–108.

Mishkin, M., Ungerleider, L., & Macko, K.A. (1983). Object vision and spatial vision: Two cortical pathways. *Trends in Neurosciences, 6,* 414–417.

Newcombe, F., & Ratcliff, G. (1989). Disorders of visuospatial analysis. In F. Boller & J. Grafman (Eds.), *Handbook of neuropsychology (Vol. 2)* (pp. 333–356). Amsterdam: Elsevier.

Newcombe, F., Ratcliff, G., & Damasio, H. (1987). Dissociable visual and spatial impairments following right posterior cerebral lesions: Clinical, neuropsychological and anatomical evidence. *Neuropsychologia, 25,* 149–161.

Paterson, A., & Zangwill, O.L. (1944). Disorders of visual space perception associated with lesions of the right cerebral hemisphere. *Brain, 67,* 331–358.

Poppelreuter, W. (1917/1990). *Disturbances of lower and higher visual capacities caused by occipital damage.* (J. Zihl with L. Weiskrantz Trans.). Oxford: Clarendon Press.

Posner, M.I. (1980). Orienting of attention. *Quarterly Journal of Experimental Psychology, 32,* 3–26.

Posner, M.I., Walker, J.A., Friedrich, F.J., & Rafal, R.D. (1984). Effects of parietal injury on covert orienting of attention. *Journal of Neuroscience, 4,* 1863–1874.

Riddoch, M.J., & Humphreys, G.W. (1983). The effect of cueing on unilateral neglect. *Neuropsychologia, 21,* 589–599.

Rizzolatti, G., Matelli, M., & Pavesi, G. (1983). Deficits in attention and movement following removal of postarcuate (area 6) and prearcuate (area 8) cortex in macaque monkeys. *Brain, 106,* 655–673.

Robertson, I.H., & North, N. (1992). Spatio-motor cueing in unilateral left neglect: The role of hemispace, hand and motor activation. *Neuropsychologia, 30,* 553–563.

Robertson, L.C., & Lamb, M.R. (1991). Neuropsychological contributions to theories of part–whole organisation. *Cognitive Psychology, 23,* 299–332.

Rode, G., & Perenin, M.T. (1994). Temporary remission of representational hemineglect through vestibular stimulation. *NeuroReport, 5,* 869–872.

Scheller, H., & Seidemann, H. (1932). Zur Frage der optischräumlichen Agnosie (zugleich ein Beitrag zur Dyslexie). *Monatschrift der Psychiatrie und Neurologie, 81,* 97–188.

Sergent, J. (1982). The cerebral balance of power: Confrontation or co-operation? *Journal of Experimental Psychology: Human Perception and Performance, 8,* 253–272.

Seron, X., Coyette, F., & Bruyer, R. (1989). Ipsilateral influences on contralateral processing in neglect patients. *Cognitive Neuropsychology, 6,* 475–498.

Ungerleider, L.G., & Haxby, J.V. (1994). "What" and "where" in the human brain. *Current Opinion in Neurobiology, 4,* 157–165.

Vallar, G., & Perani, D. (1986). The anatomy of unilateral neglect after right hemisphere stroke lesions: A clinical/CT-scan correlation study in man. *Neuropsychologia, 24,* 609–622.

Ward, R., Goodrich, S., & Driver, J. (1994). Grouping reduces visual extinction: Neuropsychological evidence for weight-linkage in visual selection. *Visual Cognition, 1,* 101–129.

14 G.R., The *Prime* "Deep Dyslexic": A Commentary on Marshall and Newcombe (1966)

Christopher Barry
School of Psychology, University of Wales College of Cardiff, U.K.

G.R.—or G. to those who knew him well—and it is certain that John Marshall and Freda Newcombe came to know him very well indeed—was a big, strong man. It is easy, if perhaps a little sad, to imagine him, in 1944 during the first days of the allied landings in Normandy, as a very young man in the uniform and attitude of combat. At over six-feet tall, and as strong as an ox, he must have cut an impressive and somewhat daunting figure. He was an experienced and battle-hardened soldier of demonstrable bravery, who had already spent two years in active service, and yet he was younger than most of the students I now teach. Indeed, he lied about his age to enter the army. In 1942 it must have been easy to convince eager army authorities that one wanted to enlist, as Britain was darkly at war, and G.R.'s physical stature would have been powerfully convincing. Although G.R. told me a story of joining the army to escape being persuaded into a looming marriage, I prefer to think of him as an idealistic young man wishing to liberate Europe of fascism. Either way, his terrible injury cut him down in his prime: Not yet 20 years' old, he suffered a massive assault to his brain when a bullet was shot through his head. The injury was, in fact, a dreadful accident. He fell from the back of a lorry and a bullet, discharged from his own sten gun, penetrated his head at the front of the left ear, travelled upwards through his left cerebral hemisphere and made a large exit wound at the top left-hand side of his head (in the superior parietal region). G.R. offers a different story of the incident: He claims to have been hit by a German sniper bullet, but the upward trajectory of the bullet through his brain makes this most unlikely. It is quite reasonable that a Royal Marine might not wish it to be known that his war injury was an accident, but I believe we should see G.R. as a hero nevertheless.

Marshall and Newcombe tested G.R. in the mid-1960s as part of Newcombe's important studies of a series of patients with penetrating missile injuries to the brain (Newcombe, 1969). Their 1966 paper, published in *Neuropsychologia*, was not the first report of a patient who makes semantic errors in reading aloud—there were previous reports, particularly in the early (and rich) German literature (see references in Marshall & Newcombe, 1980)—but it was an extremely important paper for two main reasons. First, although it was not uncommon to observe semantic substitution errors in other aspects of aphasic production (such as spontaneous speech and picture naming), Marshall and Newcombe's paper showed that the presence of semantic errors in reading aloud single words was not an isolated phenomenon but a part of a constellation of problems. They showed that these included the production of other paralexic errors (including visual and what we would now call "derivational" errors) and also claimed that there was a grammatical class effect on reading accuracy (as they observed that nouns were read more accurately than adjectives which were, in turn, read more accurately than verbs). Although they did not mention an effect of concreteness upon reading accuracy (which we now know to be very powerful) or the patient's inability to read nonwords (taken as a measure of the ability to read via assembled phonological recording), we can see that their paper laid the foundation for characterising this acquired dyslexia as a fairly cohesive *association* of co-occurring reading impairments. This variety of acquired dyslexia is now widely known as "deep dyslexia", the resonant term coined by Marshall and Newcombe (1973).

Second, it could also be said that the paper re-established a more general interest in semantic errors for their potential to illuminate notions of the nature of semantic representations (and how these are used to drive reading responses). Marshall and Newcombe offered an explanation of G.R.'s semantic errors in terms of how normal semantic representations (conceived in terms of Katz and Fodor's 1963 theory of "dictionary entries") are used to specify the phonological forms of words. Both by its neuropsychological description of G.R.'s "syntactic and semantic errors in paralexia"—the title of their paper—and its use of conceptions of normal processing to interpret these errors, Marshall and Newcombe's paper has had a deep and major influence on the development of what we now know as *cognitive neuropsychology*. The cognitive neuropsychological enterprise involves a reciprocal relationship between (1) the detailed case studies of neurological patients with acquired disorders of cognitive functions (by using focused tasks designed to assess specific aspects of processing in which there are experimental comparisons between carefully constructed sets of stimulus material), and (2) how such patterns of intact and impaired processing may be interpreted within, and may also inform, models of normal functioning. A patient's pattern of performance, particularly in terms of the dissociations shown between functions which are impaired and those which are reasonably preserved, may be explained by appeal to functional fractionations within a model of the component processes of normal processing. However, dissociations shown by patients may also be used to motivate new hypotheses concerning the organisation of the subcomponents of normal functioning.

Cognitive neuropsychology has emerged from a distinguished, if empirically diverse, collection of studies of patients with acquired disorders of cognitive functions, particularly the well-established literature on aphasic disturbances of language functioning, going back to Broca and Wernicke. However, it is my opinion that cognitive neuropsychology in its modern guise has blossomed from two key papers. The first was Warrington and Shallice's (1969) report of the patient K.F. who showed severely impaired short-term memory performance—he had a digit span of only one item—despite appearing to have essentially intact long-term memory performance, as indicated by his normal ability to learn paired associates. The importance of this paper for the development of cognitive neuropsychology was not so much the clinical report of this rather clear dissociation but the theoretical interpretation drawn from it: the dissociation suggested that the then prevailing "modal" model of memory organisation, in which information could enter long-term memory only via processes operating in short-term memory (S.T.M.), was wrong. The fact that K.F. could learn new information in the absence of S.T.M. suggested that he had a means of entry to long-term memory which effectively bypassed S.T.M.—and that such a "route" would also be available to everyone. This study provides an example of how a dissociation shown by an individual neurological patient acts as the stimulus to derive new hypotheses concerning the organisation of the components of normal functioning. This illustrates the theoretically radical contribution that cognitive neuropsychology can make, as it represents the inductive use of finding a dissociation in a single patient to motivate a theoretical generality.

I believe that the second major paper for the development of cognitive neuropsychology (and possibly the one which established its identity within British psychology) was Marshall and Newcombe's (1973) seminal attempt to offer a theoretical framework for understanding different kinds of neuropsychological patient in terms of a common model of normal processing. They presented three varieties of acquired dyslexia: visual dyslexia, in which reading errors could be described as "visual confusions" (e.g. *beg* → "leg" and *pod* → "pad"); surface dyslexia, in which oral reading could be characterised by an over-reliance on assembled phonological recoding, which resulted in greater accuracy for "regular" than for "irregular" words and the production of regularisation errors (e.g. *island* → "izland" and *omit* → "ommit"); and deep dyslexia, to which I shall turn shortly. The importance of this paper lay in its provision of a common theoretical framework which permitted the synthesis of results from normal and impaired reading.

It is noteworthy that deep dyslexia had a presence in both papers. Although not made prominent in Warrington and Shallice's paper (1969), their patient K.F. was deep dyslexic in addition to his impaired short-term memory (see Shallice & Warrington, 1975). Marshall and Newcombe (1973) described two deep dyslexics, G.R. and K.U., whose semantically mediated reading, particularly when contrasted with the phonologically mediated reading of surface dyslexics, provided important support for their model of reading. In my estimation, the subsequent development of cognitive neuropsychology owes a great deal to studies of and reflections upon deep dyslexia. The important book, *Deep Dyslexia*, edited by Coltheart, Patterson, and Marshall (and published in 1980) has been widely cited and has provoked considerable interest. Semantic errors have certainly aroused the attention of a wide audience and continue to do so, as can be seen in the importance deep dyslexia has for the recent developments in connectionist accounts of impaired reading (Plaut & Shallice, 1993).

The remainder of this chapter will focus on G.R. as a classic case of deep dyslexia. I submit that G.R. is a "prime" deep dyslexic, in the sense that he is a major and salient case of the pattern of impairments, as we now understand and appreciate them. As already mentioned, G.R. was not the first deep dyslexic to be reported and it might be argued that he cannot be considered to be a "pure" case. He certainly has other impairments arising from his extensive left hemisphere brain damage and has, in particular, poor spontaneous speech and imperfect picture naming. It is not clear to what extent any such general word production problems constrain his reading attempts (or whether the proposal that he has a possible "output block" may impinge upon any theoretical accounts of his reading), but it cannot be claimed that his impairments are necessarily specific to the domain of reading. Neither can it be argued that G.R. is in any sense a "prototypical" deep dyslexic, a term which implies that we can accept that there is a unified "syndrome" of deep dyslexia. Both Shallice and Warrington (1980) and Friedman and Perlman (1982) have argued convincingly that there are subvarieties of deep dyslexia. A patient may be included in the general "category" of deep dyslexics if they produce semantic reading errors, but the members of the group are not at all homogeneous in all other respects. Nevertheless, G.R. is a fascinating deep dyslexic patient and certainly one worthy of discussion. I shall now review the data presented in Marshall and

Newcombe (1966) and also say something more about G.R.'s reading from the privileged position of having been able to test him in the early 1980s under the benevolent supervision of John Richardson (Barry, 1984; Barry & Richardson, 1988).

Marshall and Newcombe's (1966) paper contained an extremely short introduction (of only 13 lines) which was concerned, quite rightly, to announce the interest of semantic errors. Their case report of G.R. provides a good deal of clinical (and anatomical) information and it may be of some interest to compare both the content and the style of this with what one would expect in a contemporary paper reporting a single case study. Perhaps we are now either more sensitive or simply more squeamish, but Marshall and Newcombe's clinical report of G.R.'s injury seems somewhat gory: They say that the bullet "ploughed up" the left temporal and parietal cortex and they quote from the report of the surgeon who notes (as if he could fail to miss it) that G.R.'s brain was "bulging out" from the exit wound, which was a "tear about 6 cm" in diameter. The general background of G.R.'s post-injury life is provided in a tone which would probably not be heard commonly today, e.g. "His post-war interests seem to have been limited to football pools, television, two pints of beer in the local public house in the evening and fruitless attempts to read paperback books of the Cowboy and Indian genre." (I now find the expression "public house" to be charmingly nostalgic.) Their case report also contains the results of quite a lot of informative background tests, such as non-verbal I.Q. and memory tests, although some of the tests used, such as the Graham and Kendall Memory-for-Designs Test, might perhaps only be found now where one could also obtain G.R.'s Cowboy and Indian "paperback books".

Marshall and Newcombe's paper then gives a very useful description of G.R.'s "selective language impairment". His spontaneous speech was "telegrammatic" and they inferred a "slight loss" of the ability to understand speech from the fact that instructions for the Token Test had to be paraphrased occasionally. However, there was no formal testing of G.R.'s comprehension, especially of words he was unable to read aloud, an omission that is, regrettably, not uncommon today. G.R.'s oral repetition was perfect, even for "foreign words". This finding has important implications; it tells us that it cannot be the case that G.R.'s reading impairments result from a global inability to produce items in speech. His object naming was described as being "fairly good". When I tested him some 15 years later he produced some semantic errors in naming pictures but a lower rate than the production of such errors in reading the same object names. Marshall and Newcombe also found this: He produced 6 errors naming 53 line drawings, and spontaneously corrected all but one, whereas he produced 17 errors reading 60 words (which included the names of the pictures) and spontaneously corrected only 4. Marshall and

Newcombe reported that G.R.'s short-term memory span was reduced—it was only three items—and that his spelling was also impaired (despite good copying and cross-case transcription). Coltheart (1980a) noted that reduced memory span and dysgraphia are common features in deep dyslexia.

The fulcrum of all characterisations of deep dyslexia is the presence of the semantic error. Indeed, semantic paralexias in reading (such as G.R.'s *canary* → "parrot") could be said to be the signature of deep dyslexia. Marshall and Newcombe tested G.R. on the same set of items in a variety of different tasks and found many semantic errors in reading and some in writing (even if some responses were also mis-spelled, e.g. "cousin" written as NEPHIL). However, there were no semantic errors made in the visual copying of words or in the immediate written recall of printed words. He also made no semantic errors in the oral repetition of spoken words (and so was not "deep dysphasic"). They note (p. 173) that his semantic reading errors "ranged from almost pure synonymity to cases where the stimulus word and the response error had only one or two semantic markers in common", with examples from their paper being: *ill* → "sick", *city* → "town", *bush* → "tree", and *cheer* → "laugh". Some of my own favourites from those he produced in the 1980s include: *little* → "small", *foot* → "shoe", *lion* → "tiger", *poetry* → "Shakespeare", and the wonderful *bitter* → "pints".

The substance of Marshall and Newcombe's paper is the report of G.R.'s reading of "approximately" 2000 individual words, a substantial empirical exercise (and one which excuses the lack of precision of the number of words presented). Like all deep dyslexics, G.R. was able to read some words correctly but he omitted others (either by saying "no" or "don't know"). He also made a variety of errors. Marshall and Newcombe classified his paralexic errors using only five categories: semantic (e.g. *liberty* → "freedom"); visual (e.g. *next* → "exit"); visual completion (e.g. *gentle* → "gentleman"); visual + semantic (e.g. *sympathy* → "orchestra"); and indeterminate (which accounted for only 6% of the sample).

The classification of deep dyslexic reading errors has been elaborated since their original study. What they called "visual completion" errors are now known as derivational errors (although they would be more appropriately called morphemic errors), in which the response word shares the same root morpheme as the stimulus (e.g. *painting* → "painter"). What they called "visual + semantic" errors are better described as visual–then–semantic errors, where the response word is semantically related to a putative intermediary word which is itself visually similar to the stimulus word (e.g. *foster* → "cold", via *frost*), the detection of which engages the imagination most pleasingly. There can also be true semantic and/or visual errors (e.g. *home* → "house") which share both visual and semantic similarity. There are also function word substitution errors (e.g. *his* → "she"). As with many natural taxonomies, there are always some unclassified errors (such as *carpet* → "letters"). Some authors separate errors that involve the production of a single word as an error response and various kinds of "circumlocution" errors (e.g. *bride* → "getting married, wedding").

Deep dyslexic patients differ in terms of the relative frequency of the production of errors in these categories, as well as in their overall levels of reading accuracy. It is difficult, however, to make straightforward comparisons between patients if they have been tested on different samples of words that vary along dimensions which may affect reading accuracy. Barry and Richardson (1988) were able to compare G.R.'s reading of the set of Brown and Ure (1969) words (which he attempted to read in 1980) with K.F.'s reading of the same words (using the data supplied by Shallice and Warrington and presented in Coltheart et al., 1980). The percentages of the main response categories for each patient are shown in Table 14.1. G.R. is a prolific producer of semantic errors: Not only does he make very many semantic errors in absolute terms—and indeed he produces almost as many as correct responses—he is unlike a number of other deep dyslexics, including K.F., in that he produces more semantic than visual errors. Marshall and Newcombe found that G.R. tended to make more semantic errors to nouns than to verbs (and that his error responses to both nouns and verbs tended to be nouns) but, as we will now see, they may have overestimated the effects of grammatical class in deep dyslexic reading.

Marshall and Newcombe (1966, p. 171) claimed that the "grammatical category of the stimulus word was a major variable" in determining G.R.'s reading success. They reported that he was able to read 45% of unambiguous nouns, 16% of adjectives, and only 6% of verbs. They went on to note that G.R. was able to read virtually no grammatical function words (i.e. words from the closed-class vocabulary): he read no prepositions, adverbs, determiners, or question markers (such as "where" and "when"),

TABLE 14.1

The Percentage of Reading Responses (to Words from Brown & Ure, 1969) Produced by G.R. (Barry & Richardson, 1988) and K.F. (Shallice & Warrington, 1980, pp. 429–433, in Coltheart et al., 1980)

	G.R.	K.F.
Correct	20.7	32.6
Omitted	35.5	45.7
Semantic errors	20.2	2.5
Visual errors	9.0	9.6
Derivational errors	4.0	3.1

and he was able to read only one personal pronoun ("I") and one conjunction ("and"). It is common to see modern descriptions of the characteristics of deep dyslexia include this claimed part-of-speech effect on reading accuracy (e.g. Hinton, Plaut, & Shallice, 1993). However, it now appears that much of the difference between nouns, adjectives, and verbs is due to confounded effects of stimulus word concreteness. Concreteness (and/or imageability, with which it is very highly correlated) exerts an extremely powerful effect on the reading accuracy of deep dyslexics—and it is quite surprising that Marshall and Newcombe (1966) did not remark upon it! (Indeed, I see Marshall and Newcombe's failure to report a difference between concrete and abstract nouns as being the only serious shortcoming of their paper. However, it was one which was soon corrected: Marshall, Newcombe, and Marshall (1970) found that G.R. could read nine of 10 concrete mass nouns but only one of 10 abstract nouns.) Barry and Richardson (1988) found that there was a substantial difference between the concreteness values of the Brown and Ure words G.R. read correctly (mean = 5.52) and those he omitted (mean = 4.16). G.R. is a man who was able to read the word "chrysanthemum" but not the word "good". Concreteness is a very potent variable indeed—and it is also involved in G.R.'s visual errors, which tend to be made to words that are less concrete than those read correctly. Barry and Richardson found that visual errors involve the production of a more concrete word (e.g. *deep* → "deer" and *anger* → "angel"): independent judges rated 64% of G.R.'s visual errors as being more concrete, 27% as being equal in concreteness, and only 9% as being less concrete. These results assist in the provision of an explanation of visual errors as reflecting a "central" rather than a perceptual impairment of reading (discussed later).

In order to see whether there exists an affect of part of speech over and above that of concreteness, Barry and Richardson (1988) compared G.R.'s correct responses with his omissions in an analysis of covariance in which syntactic class was the single independent variable and concreteness, word frequency and the other of the Brown and Ure ratings were included as covariates. Syntactic class had no effect at all upon reading accuracy when other variables were statistically controlled. Allport and Funnell (1981) matched thirty nouns and thirty verbs on both concreteness and word frequency and found that five deep dyslexic patients showed no differences in their reading accuracy of the two sets. Thus, both the multivariate analysis of G.R.'s reading and Allport and Funnell's factorial study have shown that syntactic class—at least among content words—has no independent effect upon reading accuracy. The reason Marshall and Newcombe "found" an apparent syntactic class effect was due to the fact that nouns tend to be more concrete than adjectives or verbs. However, there remains the distinct but quite open possibility that deep dyslexics have a special difficulty with function words, which are frequent but among the most abstract in the language.

The final empirical section of Marshall and Newcombe's paper reports a preliminary examination of the consistency of G.R.'s reading. Following an interval of one week, G.R. was re-presented with 100 words he had previously read correctly and 100 words to which he had produced a semantic error. G.R. showed moderate reliability: For those words initially read correctly, he was correct on 61 and made semantic errors to a further 21; for those initially eliciting a semantic error, he was correct on 18, produced the identical semantic error to 37, and produced a different semantic error to 27. These data show that a simplistic "output" explanation of G.R.'s semantic errors cannot easily be maintained: It seems unlikely that there were certain words that G.R. could not access or produce and so produced semantic errors as "the next closest" word. (This is further supported by Barry and Richardson's observation that G.R. produced words as errors that he could not read correctly, e.g. *sick* → "bandage", *bad* → "sick".) Barry (1984) reports a more detailed analysis of G.R.'s reading consistency, stimulated by Marshall and Newcombe's report. He presented the Brown and Ure set of words twice and found a similar pattern of reliability, which is summarised in Table 14.2. Although, as Marshall and Newcombe say (1966, p. 174), "the same response patterns do not rigidly persist", there is a fair degree of consistency for all major response categories. For G.R.'s correct reading responses and semantic errors (i.e. his meaning preserving responses), this consistency is also linked to the concreteness of the stimulus words. Thus, words G.R. read correctly on both occasions are significantly more concrete

TABLE 14.2

G.R.'s Reading Consistency (Barry, 1984) of 643 of the 650 Brown and Ure (1969) Words

	Percentage of reading response on second presentation					
First presentation	*Correct*	*Omissions*	*Semantic errors*	*Visual errors*	*Derivational errors*	*All other errors*
Correct	66	4	20	2	5	3
Omissions	2	58	10	14	1	15
Semantic errors	13	6	65	5	5	6
Visual errors	3	21	15	59	0	2
Derivational errors	8	0	27	4	54	8
All other errors	4	27	11	20	4	33

For each major response category on the first presentation, the rows show the percentage of the words in each response category on the second presentation.

(mean = 5.65) than those to which he produced the identical semantic error (mean = 5.05), which were, in turn, more concrete than those to which he produced different semantic errors (mean = 4.20).

Patients with deep dyslexia—and G.R. in particular—present an empirically rich (and intuitively interesting) set of observations. Most contemporary theoretical interpretations of deep dyslexic reading have suggested that it results from a complex (but necessarily co-occurring) set of impairments to the cognitive processes that underlie normal reading, a simplified modular model of which (based on Morton & Patterson, 1980) is presented in Fig. 14.1. There is not space here to evaluate the alternative account of deep dyslexia, which is that it reflects the operation of a right hemisphere reading system (Coltheart, 1980b) not necessarily involved in normal reading. However, it could be argued that the interpretation to be advanced here (in terms of a restricted set of normal reading processes) will provide a functional description of deep dyslexic reading which will be useful wherever the neural mechanisms subserving the reading process turn out to be localised.

Figure 14.1 proposes that normal readers are able to call upon three routes to power oral reading: (1) assembled phonological recoding (which is the route used to pronounce nonwords); (2) direct lexical reading, using word-specific connections between visual word recognition units and spoken word production units; and (3) semantically mediated reading, in which recognised words activate their corresponding semantic representations which then drive word production. To cut a long story short, deep dyslexics are able to use only one of these procedures, the semantically mediated route—and even this is flawed as a means of supporting error-free reading.

Assembled phonological recording is inoperative in deep dyslexia. Marshall and Newcombe (1966) did not have the theoretical motivation to test G.R. for "nonlexical" phonological recoding (and it is difficult to chastise psycholinguistic researchers for not inventing "nonsense words" to present to a patient who was producing a torrent of intriguing and linguistically "deep" semantic errors). Phonological recording is totally abolished in G.R. When presented with nonwords to read aloud in the 1980s, he omitted 87%, although he occasionally (and insightfully) said "don't mean a thing"! To the remaining 13% he either produced a visually similar word (e.g. *laks* → "lake") or made a visual–then–semantic error (e.g. *tob* → "pipe", via *tobacco*?). It is probably true to say that G.R. has not read a nonword since 1944. He was also hopelessly unable to perform any task requiring "phonics"; for example, he could not match a simple printed nonword (*nis*) to one of two spoken nonwords ("pog–nis"). However normal subjects perform phonological recoding (either by a set of nonlexical rules or by a process of analogy), deep dyslexics are unable to use it to assist their oral reading.

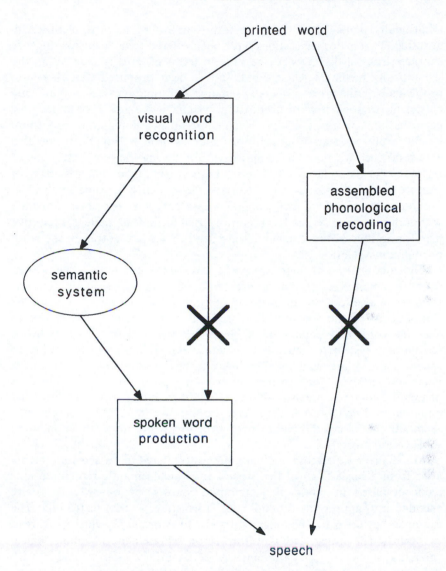

FIG. 14.1 A simplified modular model of the component processes involved in oral reading. The crosses indicate the routes not available to deep dyslexic patients.

Reading in deep dyslexia cannot proceed via the "direct" route either: If lexically specific recognition-to-production connections were available, then patients would make no reading errors at all. The arresting fact that deep dyslexics make semantic errors demands the conclusion that their reading is semantically mediated but it also persuades us that this route is either additionally damaged or that, operating in isolation, it is intrinsically unstable. Two major suggestions have been offered to account for the core characteristics of deep dyslexic reading in terms of impairments within the semantically mediated route. First, it has been proposed that there are problems with the process whereby semantic information is used to activate entries in the spoken word production system. It is fairly easy to see how perturbations or instability in this meaning-to-word mapping procedure would result in semantic substitutions such as *little* → "small". If one also entertains the idea that spreading activation among the representations of related items takes place within the semantic system, then semantic errors of a more associative kind (e.g. *kissing* → "love") also become explicable. Second, a deficiency of the semantic representations for abstract words within the semantic system has been proposed (or at least there is a selective problem in how abstract semantics are used to activate entries in the word production system).

The combination of these two proposals enables accounts to be offered for both semantic errors and the effect of concreteness on reading accuracy. If one were also to allow the possibility of interactive processing between the components of the semantically mediated route, then visual errors to abstract words may be accounted for as a "second attempt" by the word recognition system to activate a semantic representation that is able to generate a response, which will be likely to be a concrete word (Morton & Patterson, 1980). If one further allowed the possibility that a syntactic processing component exists within the reading route, which is additionally impaired in deep dyslexics, then derivational errors too become explicable, as might the severe difficulties with function words (and function word substitution errors).

Marshall and Newcombe (1966) suggested that G.R.'s semantic errors arise from a breakdown of the process by which semantic representations (conceptualised in terms of Katz and Fodor's dictionary entries) are encoded into appropriate phonological forms (i.e. words) in reading. The example they use is the dictionary entry for the word *bush*, which G.R. read as "tree". They suggested that this error represented the phonological encoding of the key semantic markers of BUSH (< plant > and < with branches >) but not its distinguisher (< arising from or near the ground >). It is noteworthy that this example is for an error to a concrete word. It may be less easy to imagine how the "normal" dictionary entry for an abstract word, such as *idea*, can uniquely specify a word. (The representation < plan or thought formed in the mind > might apply to very many words, such as *idea, plan, notion, thought, concept, hypothesis*, etc., which might cause the lexical selection process to become overburdened and effectively to collapse.) It is therefore highly likely that any general problems of meaning-to-word mapping will affect abstract words severely.

Deep dyslexia still holds consideration and substantial theoretical interest (see, for example, Plaut & Shallice, 1993). G.R. is most certainly a classic deep dyslexic but is also a classic neuropsychological case in general. Marshall and Newcombe's (1966) paper (despite its silence on the effects of concreteness) revealed simulating and important features of a major variety of acquired dyslexia and has had a profound influence. Marshall and Newcombe must be applauded—by which I mean justly acknowledged and warmly thanked—for introducing us to G.R. and for their attempt to provide the foundation of an account of impaired reading in terms of conceptions of normal processes.

REFERENCES

Allport, D.A. & Funnell, E. (1981). Components of the mental lexicon. *Philosophical Transactions of the Royal Society London, B295*, 397–410.

Barry, C. (1984). Consistency and types of semantic errors in a deep dyslexic patient. In R.N. Malatesha & H.A. Whitaker (Eds.), *Dyslexia: A global issue*. The Hague: Martinus Nijhoff.

Barry, C., & Richardson, J.T.E. (1988). Accounts of oral reading in deep dyslexia. In H.A. Whitaker (Ed.), *Phonological processes and brain mechanisms*. Berlin: Springer-Verlag.

Brown, W.P., & Ure, D.M.J. (1969). Five rated characteristics of 650 word association stimuli. *British Journal of Psychology, 21*, 233–249.

Coltheart, M. (1980a). Deep dyslexia: A review of the syndrome. In M. Coltheart, K. Patterson, & J.C. Marshall (Eds.), *Deep dyslexia*. London: Routledge & Kegan Paul.

Coltheart, M. (1980b). Deep dyslexia: A right-hemisphere hypothesis. In M. Coltheart, K. Patterson, & J.C. Marshall (Eds.), *Deep dyslexia*. London: Routledge & Kegan Paul.

Coltheart, M., Patterson, K., & Marshall, J.C. (Eds.). (1980). *Deep dyslexia*. London: Routledge & Kegan Paul.

Friedman, R.B., & Perlman, M.B. (1982). On the underlying causes of semantic paralexias in a patient with deep dyslexia. *Neuropsychologia, 20*, 559–568.

Hinton, G.E., Plaut, D.C., & Shallice, T. (1993). Simulating brain damage. *Scientific American, 269*(4), 58–65.

Katz, J.J., & Fodor, J.A. (1963). The structure of a semantic theory. *Language, 39*, 170–210.

Marshall, J.C., & Newcombe, F. (1966). Syntactic and semantic errors in paralexia. *Neuropsychologia, 4*, 169–176.

Marshall, J.C., & Newcombe, F. (1973). Patterns of paralexia: A psycholinguistic approach. *Journal of Psycholinguistic Research, 2*, 175–199.

Marshall, J.C., & Newcombe, F. (1980). The conceptual status of deep dyslexia: An historical perspective. In M. Coltheart, K. Patterson, & J.C. Marshall (Eds.), *Deep dyslexia*. London: Routledge & Kegan Paul.

Marshall, M., Newcombe, F., & Marshall, J.C. (1970). The microstructure of word-finding difficulties in a dysphasic subject. In G.B. Flores d'Arcais, & W.J.M. Levelt (Eds.), *Advances in psycholinguistics*. Amsterdam: North-Holland.

Morton, J., & Patterson, K. (1980). A new attempt at an interpretation, or, an attempt at a new interpretation. In M. Coltheart, K. Patterson, & J.C. Marshall (Eds.), *Deep dyslexia*. London: Routledge & Kegan Paul.

Newcombe, F. (1969). *Missile wounds of the brain: A study of psychological deficits*. Oxford: Oxford University Press.

Plaut, D.C., & Shallice, T. (1993). Deep dyslexia: A case study of connectionist neuropsychology. *Cognitive Neuropsychology, 10*, 377–500.

Shallice, T., & Warrington, E.K. (1975). Word recognition in a phonemic dyslexic patient. *Quarterly Journal of Experimental Psychology*, *27*, 187–199.

Shallice, T., & Warrington, E.K. (1980). Single and multiple component central dyslexic syndromes. In M. Coltheart, K. Patterson, & J.C. Marshall (Eds.), *Deep dyslexia*. London: Routledge & Kegan Paul.

Warrington, E.K., & Shallice, T. (1969). The selective impairment of auditory verbal short-term memory. *Brain*, *92*, 885–896.

15 W.L.P.: A Case for the Modularity of Language Function *and* Dementia

Elaine Funnell
Department of Psychology, Royal Holloway University of London, U.K.

Two classic papers describe the cognitive breakdown of W.L.P., a patient with a diagnosis of primary degenerative dementia. Appearing in successive years, these papers detail her breakdown of semantic memory and the remarkable retention of syntactic knowledge (Schwartz, Marin, & Saffran, 1979) and preserved oral reading of irregular words that she could not understand (Schwartz, Saffran, & Marin, 1980).

Although these were not the first papers to describe the characteristics of cognitive breakdown in single case studies of dementia, they have several notable features which, to my mind, set W.L.P. apart. The most important of these is the application of an information-processing framework, allowing the dissociation in performance observed in dementia to be explained in terms of a modular theory of normal language processing. In particular, the study of W.L.P. provided the first evidence requiring a direct lexical route in reading.

The study followed the course of W.L.P.'s cognitive decline over 30 months, from the time when she reported, with her daughter, to the out-patients' clinic of a Baltimore city hospital, complaining of memory loss and declining ability to communicate. At this time she was able to keep house, cook simple meals, and care for herself. The study ends two and a half years later, at a time when she was no longer able to care for herself, or her home, and her sole occupation was to walk to the local shopping centre and back. Her spoken language reflected this deterioration: Already severely anomic at the start of the study, at its close she retained only one lexical item in her spoken language—the word shopping centre—which she used indiscriminately as both noun and verb.

W.L.P. was not the first patient to be described whose knowledge of word meaning was particularly impaired: Whitaker (1976) had previously reported a remarkable patient (H.C.E.M.) who, while generally mute, would repeat back words spoken to her, so long as eye contact was established. Notably, H.C.E.M. would correct errors of syntax, phonology and stress in her repetitions, restoring such erroneous sentences as "He ask a question", "This is a dolly-pop", and "The President lives in the White house" to their correct form. In contrast, she repeated, unaltered, such nonsensical sentences as "The book is very happy" and "I ate a car for dinner". Whitaker argues convincingly that H.C.E.M. has lost the higher mental and intellectual functions required for the creative aspects of language (which include spontaneous speech), while retaining a syntactic filter that responds automatically to auditory input in a conversational situation. In this patient, the brain areas which process these automatic aspects of language—Wernickes' area, Brocas's area, and the cortex of the inferior parietal lobe—have apparently been preserved in isolation, in a brain otherwise ravaged by generalised atrophy.

W.L.P. also demonstrated preserved knowledge of syntax, accompanied by severe loss of comprehension for the lexical content of words (Schwartz et al., 1979). She could translate sentences on command into other forms, including the negative, "I like fish" → "I don't like fish"; the plural "I have one tooth" → "I have lots of teeth"; the past tense "Today I am cooking dinner" → "Yesterday I cooked dinner"; and into question form "Mary looks ill" → "Does Mary look ill?". On most occasions, she could also match correctly a sentence such as "The car pulls the truck" to one of two pictures depicting either the correct arrangement, or the reverse (i.e. a picture of a truck pulling a car). All her errors were attributable to lexical rather than syntactic confusions. W.L.P. could even use the surface structure of a sentence to identify referents she could not identify by name. Thus, given pictures of a dog chasing a cat or of a cat chasing a dog and told "The dog is chasing the cat. Show me the cat", W.L.P. would point to the animal running behind, regardless of its real identity. As Schwartz et al. observe, in order to apply a knowledge of semantic roles, W.L.P. must have understood the meaning of the verbs in the sentence.

Another consequence of W.L.P.'s preserved knowledge of syntax deserves comment: This is the marked effect of context upon the spelling of homophones. When homophones were spoken to her in a semantic context such as "ocean, lake, /sI/ (see/sea)" and two, six, /eit/ (ate/eight)", the spelling of only four out of thirty homophone pairs were correctly disambiguated in comparison with her score of eighteen out of thirty pairs when these were presented in a syntactic context such as "The /sI/" and "He

/eit/". However, as yet, no models of the mental lexicon incorporate a role for syntactic procedures in the selection of lexical items for spelling to account for the evidence for such a role obtained from W.L.P.

LEXICAL COMPREHENSION

The papers by Schwartz et al., while demonstrating preserved knowledge of syntax, also investigated the nature of the cognitive loss. Over a series of repeated tests, they measured the breakdown of specific lexical knowledge, as the ability of W.L.P. to select a specific name for an object declined. Again, these investigators were not the first to examine the nature of semantic loss. Warrington, in a seminal paper published in 1975, described a series of experiments investigating the semantic knowledge of three patients with a diagnosis of progressive dementia. While these patients had, in many instances, retained the broad category knowledge pertaining to an item and thus were able to sort pictures and words into categories, they appeared to have lost the defining feature knowledge necessary to answer correctly such questions as "Is it foreign or English?", "Is it larger or smaller than a cat?"

Where Schwartz et al. contribute to the investigation is by capturing the breakdown of semantic concepts through repeated tests. Their study used 70 pictures of common objects presented to W.L.P. first for naming. Only one item, the cup, was named, indicating a profound anomia. The 70 pictures were then presented with a set of five written words composed of the correct name, the name of a close semantic co-ordinate, a word that looked and sounded like the correct name, and two totally unrelated words. As her condition worsened, W.L.P. selected fewer correct names, usually selecting instead the name of the close semantic co-ordinate. Only in the latest stages of the study did W.L.P. select a significant number of unrelated names. The matching data provided by Table 3 of Schwartz et al., 1979 are reconstructed in Table 15.1.

Interestingly, even while correct responses declined in number from 61% to 43%, the majority of names selected belonged to the correct semantic

TABLE 15.1

W.L.P.'s Choice of Written Names to Match Pictures of Seventy Common Objects Reported Across Four Presentations of the Test

Month	Target name		Semantic co-ordinate (N = 1)		Unrelated names (N = 3)	
3	43	(61%)	23	(33%)	4	(6%)
15	39	(56%)	28	(40%)	3	(4%)
24	31	(44%)	28	(40%)	11	(16%)
27	24	(34%)	28	(40%)	18	(26%)

field: at three months this amounted to 94% choices; at 15 months, to 96% choices; at 24 months, to 84% choices; and at 27 months, still a relatively high 74% choices. Schwartz et al. (1979) concluded that, increasingly, W.L.P.'s ability to specify a unique item was breaking down, such that "a picture specified a population of names bound together in a semantic field."

Schwartz et al. did not investigate W.L.P.'s knowledge of category membership and defining features, but assumed (in line with Warrington, 1975) that the breakdown within semantic fields arose from the loss of the critical defining features essential for distinguishing one member of a semantic field from another. Subsequently, a specific loss of defining feature knowledge has been reported by Chertkow, Bub, and Seidenberg (1989) in a study of a group of patients with a diagnosis of dementia, supporting the notion of a critical role for feature knowledge in distinguishing items within a semantic field.

However, recent studies which have controlled for the level of difficulty across category and feature questions have failed to find the expected difference (Bayles, Tomeoeda, Kasniak, & Trosset, 1990; Funnell, 1992), and it is important to note that an inherent problem plagues the use of language in investigations into the status of word concepts: If the words used to investigate the concepts are themselves not understood, the patient may well understand the concept under investigation, but yet answer the question wrongly. In a recent study of a patient, not dissimilar to W.L.P., the patient was able to establish knowledge of the concepts fish and bird, through appropriate definitions of the words, yet could not locate the critical, defining features, such as beak, wings, scales, and fins, on prototypical pictures of these basic level items that she recognised (Funnell, 1993).

Schwartz et al. also analysed the consistency of name choices across repeated tests of the picture–word matching task carried out during the third month of the study. The breakdown appeared to be gradual, affecting some items before others. Some items produced a correct response on both occasions tested, suggesting that the semantic codes for these items remained intact. Further items were responded to correctly on one occasion but on another occasion the semantic co-ordinate was selected instead, indicating a breakdown in the ability to distinguish between items belonging to the same semantic field. As semantic memory became increasingly degraded, the likelihood of W.L.P. selecting an unrelated distracter increased, suggesting that the breakdown broadened to affect the ability to discriminate between semantic fields.

To date, longitudinal studies of cognitive breakdown have been scarce, but a recent study has confirmed the course of semantic breakdown observed in W.L.P. in a further patient with a progressive dementia (Funnell, 1992). Although this patient's decline in semantic memory was much more rapid, changing from excellent comprehension to total breakdown within the space of eighteen months, the nature of the course mirrored that of the relatively benign decline of W.L.P.: that is, the contrasts within semantic fields broke down first, followed by an inability to distinguish between items belonging to different semantic fields.

With hindsight, what questions might we wish to ask now of W.L.P.'s semantic memory deficit? On the question of category-specific disorders of semantic memory (e.g. Warrington & McCarthy, 1983; Warrington & Shallice, 1984) W.L.P. has nothing to say since no mention is made in this study of any differences observed in comprehension across different categories. So, too, is W.L.P. silent on the possibility that the items most affected were those of low concept familiarity (Funnell & Sheridan, 1992; Stewart, Parkin, & Hunkin, 1992), for familiarity was not a construct of significance to semantic memory at the time of this study. As for the question of material/modality specific semantic systems (Beauvois, 1982; Warrington, 1975), the evidence inclines towards a unitary theory of semantic memory (Caramazza, Hillis, Rapp, & Romani, 1990; Riddoch, Humphreys, Coltheart, & Funnell, 1988), since investigations revealed equivalent degrees of semantic deficit, irrespective of the type of stimulus material or the modality of input.

SYNTAX, SEMANTICS, AND THE BRAIN

The study of W.L.P. and before her the transcortical patients, such as H.C.E.M., who evidence echolalia (Whitaker, 1976), and patients with a language pathology associated with primary degenerative dementia, all suggest that in dementia, the more automatic, rule-governed aspects of phonology and syntax have become functionally isolated from cognition (Schwartz et al., 1979). Schwartz et al. speculated that since the processes subserving syntax and phonology are known to be strongly lateralised in the brain, they may be "tightly wired" and less susceptible to the effects of a diffuse cerebral pathology associated with dementia, than to focal lesions to the left side of the brain, which occur commonly in cases of stroke, and frequently result in severe disruption to syntactic processes. In contrast, representations of semantic memory may be more widely represented in the brain, and thus more susceptible to diffuse cerebral pathology. Schwartz et al. (1979) speculated further that "One implication of this view is that we should not see cases of focal left hemisphere pathology which display the systematic dedifferentiation of semantic fields documented in W.L.P.".

However, two recent studies of patients with semantic dementia contradict this prediction. In these studies, the breakdown in semantic memory is, in most cases, associated with temporal neocortical damage, which is sometimes restricted to the dominant hemisphere (Hodges, Patterson, Oxbury, & Funnell, 1992; Snowden, Goulding, & Neary, 1989).

ORAL READING

W.L.P.'s preserved knowledge of the syntactic structure for sentences containing words she did not understand is not the only striking dissociation observed in her use of language. A further dissociation, and perhaps the one for which she is most often quoted, was observed between her comprehension for words and her ability to read these same words aloud; W.L.P. could correctly pronounce written words she could not, apparently, comprehend.

Investigations showed that W.L.P. could read nonsense words (e.g. *fud* and *spig*) and real words that conform to regular spelling patterns (e.g. *road* and *bone*), and she could also pronounce irregular words that do not conform to regular English spelling patterns (Schwartz et al., 1979; Schwartz et al., 1980). Given 26 pairs of high frequency words, each with similar spellings, but dissimilar pronunciations (e.g. *home—come*; *cost—post*), W.L.P. pronounced only one word incorrectly (reading *bury* as "biury"). However, in marked contrast to her excellent oral reading, W.L.P. failed to comprehend many of the written words she pronounced correctly. While she read correctly 18 out of 20 low frequency animal names, she matched only 2 out of 20 to the correct category label and only 2 out of 20 to the correct picture within sets of 4 animals. It should be noted, however, that while some of these low frequency words do not conform to the regular spelling patterns of English (e.g. *leopard*, *hyena*) many do (e.g. *baboon*, *hippo*, *panther*, *raccoon*, *kangaroo*), and it is possible that some oral reading was accomplished by the use of grapheme–phoneme correspondences.

At the time this study was carried out, the predominate theory of reading proposed two procedures for reading aloud: a phonic grapheme–phoneme procedure, available for translating novel letter strings and words that conformed to the regular mappings of English; and a lexical procedure, available for processing familiar written word forms, based on a lexical look-up procedure in which familiar written words are recognised and mapped first onto their meaning (in semantic memory) and, from there, onto the spoken word form in the speech vocabulary (e.g. Coltheart, 1980).

The two-route theory of reading was proposed initially in an innovative and highly influential paper by Marshall and Newcombe (1973). They reported the cases of patients with acquired dyslexia, and distinguished three different forms, two appearing to be mirror images of each other, which required different explanations within a theory of reading (but see Marcel, 1980). Patients with deep dyslexia, correctly read aloud meaningful words, such as *book*, *hospital*, and *soldier*, but frequently made errors in which they produced words related in meaning, but not in form. For example, Marshall and Newcombe's patient, G.R., read *little* as "small", *city* as "town", and *daughter* as "sister". Words with little lexical meaning, such as the function words *and*, *but*, and *so*, were read incorrectly. Subsequently, it has been shown that deep dyslexic patients are generally unable to pronounce novel letter strings, such as *wid* and *fol*, while able to pronounce written words, such as *widow* and *follow*, which contain these letter strings as syllables (Saffran & Marin, 1977). Deep dyslexic readers, Marshall and Newcombe argued, rely for reading on a procedure which maps familiar word forms onto meaning, and thence onto word forms in the spoken vocabulary.

Patients with the mirror-image reading pattern appeared to read by the surface form of the words, as if the words themselves were no longer familiar. These surface dyslexic patients mispronounced many words, often, though not invariably, in line with the regular grapheme-phoneme correspondences of English. Notably, S.T., one of two patients studied, failed to understand the written word form, and instead based his comprehension on his spoken production, making some memorable errors which included reading the word *begin* as "beggin", which he defined as "collecting money", and *listen* as "Listen ... that's the boxer" (i.e. Sonny Liston). Marshall and Newcombe proposed that patients with surface dyslexia read many words on the basis of sublexical grapheme–phoneme procedures, and fail to comprehend from print many previously familiar words.

A model of reading was proposed which captured the reading processes revealed by these contrasting forms of dyslexia: This model comprised a lexical semantic process for reading familiar, meaningful words, and a distinct grapheme–phoneme correspondence system, available for processing novel stimuli and words conforming to the regular spelling patterns of English.

W.L.P.'s reading performance posed problems for this model. She read correctly many words she failed to comprehend, and some at least of these words (e.g. *leopard*, *hyena*) were irregular in form, failing to conform to the regular spelling patterns of English coded in the grapheme—phoneme conversion procedures. The evidence suggested a third reading route, specialised for mapping directly between familiar written words and their equivalent spoken word forms, without reference to word meaning. The two-route model evolved into a three-route model, comprising two lexical routes and a functionally independent sublexical grapheme–phoneme conversion route. Subsequently, further patients were described, with non-dementing disorders, whose patterns of reading are also best explained within a three-route model of reading (Coslett, 1991; Funnell, 1983).

However, models of reading which specify independent lexical and sublexical processing routes have not gone unchallenged. Even as W.L.P.'s pattern of reading was reported, there appeared, within the same volume, two papers which questioned the independence of lexical and sublexical reading processes. The first of these, and the less radical of the two, proposed that two routes were required for reading: a lexical–semantic route, and a multilevel, phonological route that operated not only upon graphemes but also upon syllables and short words (Shallice & Warrington, 1980). Within this theory, it was assumed (Shallice, 1988) that a progressive neurological disease which affected the lexical semantic route, "would also increasingly restrict the range of correspondences available, and that correspondences based upon larger units would be particularly susceptible to damage." The second paper proposed a lexical processing route which processed novel letter strings by analogy with familiar lexical items (Marcel, 1980). More recently, Seidenberg and McClelland (1989) have proposed a two-route model of reading in which sublexical and lexical knowledge is mapped between print and sound over the identical hardware.

It is not the purpose of this chapter to evaluate the power of these models to explain W.L.P.'s pattern of reading, but to underline the fact that the contribution of W.L.P. to theories of reading was to suggest, for the first time, that words might be read by lexical processes that mapped directly between letter strings and spoken word forms. As Shallice (1988, p. 91) states: "Before W.L.P. had been described, it was not standard in either neuropsychology or cognitive psychology to assume that morphemic correspondences existed independently of the semantic system... It is now a standard assumption."

But not quite. Hillis and Caramazza (1991) have recently proposed that the original two-route model of reading can adequately account for good word reading when semantic memory is impaired, by summating phonological evidence from the lexical–semantic route and the sublexical grapheme–phoneme route, even when both routes are severely impaired.

W.L.P. AND SURFACE DYSLEXIA

In the time since the study of W.L.P., further patients with a diagnosis of a dementing disorder have been described whose reading performance also well exceeds word comprehension (Bub, Cancelliere, & Kertesz, 1985; Shallice & Warrington, 1983). As Shallice (1988) and Patterson and Hodges (1992) have observed, in every case the pattern of reading has developed into surface dyslexia: That is, words are pronounced on the basis of phonological rules, replacing the lexical reading of words, so that patients increasingly mispronounce irregular words in accordance with the regular spelling patterns of English. Thus the patient will pronounce *yacht* to rhyme with *hatched*, and *pint* to rhyme with *mint*, but will read correctly regular words such as *boost* and *planet*, so that a marked difference emerges between oral reading scores, given regular and irregular words. Thus H.T.R. (Shallice & Warrington, 1983) correctly read 87% regular words and 33% irregular words, and M.P. (Bub et al., 1985) read 98% low frequency regular words and 73% low frequency irregular words. In addition, Japanese readers, whose comprehension is compromised in Gogi aphasia, are reported to fail to understand the meaning of the logographic Kanji characters of the written language that they, nevertheless, accurately read aloud (Sasanuma, Sakuma, & Kitano, 1992).

Did W.L.P. too become surface dyslexic? Schwartz et al. (1980) claimed that W.L.P. made more errors to irregular words, and was thus influenced by the spelling patterns within words: the pattern characteristic of surface dyslexia. But the evidence for this is weak. W.L.P. was asked to read aloud a list of 52 high frequency words consisting of 26 pairs sharing similar spelling patterns (e.g. *cost—post*; *mother—bother*; *floor—flood*), but varying in regularity. W.L.P. did indeed read correctly more regular than irregular words, but the difference, even at the final test, was small, and certainly fails to reach statistical significance (Table 15.2). A further set of words taken from Baron (1977) also showed only a marginal difference between scores on regular words (33 out of 39 correct) and irregular words (18 out of 39 correct). In addition, of the total errors made to irregular words in the paired word set, only 6 out of 11 gave rise to errors in which the pronunciation of irregular words conformed to the regular reading of the word (*come* → "kome" (comb); *blow* → "blough" (to rhyme with plough); *bury* → "biury"; *both* → "bawth"; *deny* → "denny" (made twice). One of these (*come* → "comb") could also be classified as a lexical error based on visual similarity, for she made further errors of this sort: *own* → "owen"; *foot* → "food". Thus, on re-examination of the data, there is little evidence that W.L.P.'s oral reading of exception words was influenced by regular spelling patterns. Moreover, unlike other patients with impaired semantic memory, over the course of the reported study, her reading did not appear to develop the pattern of surface dyslexia.

TABLE 15.2
W.L.P.'s Oral Reading: Number of Correctly Read Regular and Irregular Words Presented on Three Occasions

	Regular words (N = 22)	Irregular words (N = 22)
January 1976	22	21
September 1976	20	17
January 1977	17	16

How can W.L.P.'s retention of lexical reading be explained? Or, alternatively, why is it that other patients suffering damage to semantic memory have developed surface dyslexia? One such patient, M.P., was found to be unable to judge whether written word forms were familiar, suggesting to Bub et al. (1985) that her lexical memory was compromised for written word forms of low frequency, and that since written words no longer looked familiar they were read by sublexical, rather than lexical, mechanisms. A further patient, P.P., tested by Patterson and Hodges (1992), failed to repeat lists of words she no longer produced in language tests, but repeated well lists of words within her vocabulary, leading Patterson and Hodges to argue that the lexical phonological codes, normally "held together" by semantic memory, but now falling apart, could no longer be addressed in tasks of naming and lexical reading. In order to read aloud, this patient had to assemble a pronunciation using sublexical processes instead.

However, a breakdown in lexical orthography and phonology is not an inevitable consequence of a severe loss of comprehension, for if it were, Japanese readers should fail to read those Kanji characters which they cannot comprehend, for these characters, unlike the alphabetic script of English, carry no clues to pronunciation and therefore cannot be read by sublexical procedures. Yet Japanese patients with semantic impairments have been reported to read Kanji characters successfully (Sasanuma et al., 1992). Moreover, an English-speaking patient studied recently, who showed a developing pattern of surface dyslexia together with a severe disorder of comprehension, had well-preserved recognition of written word forms she read sublexically and repeated these words in lists as successfully as words she read correctly (Funnell, 1993). Thus, while the surface dyslexic reading pattern of some patients with disorders of comprehension may result from further lexical disorders, such disorders cannot be found in all such patients.

A possible solution to W.L.P.'s preserved lexical reading of exception words, is that her comprehension, though compromised, remained sufficiently intact to bias her oral reading of exception words towards the lexical form. Although unable to specify the unique referent of many objects, she was nevertheless able to specify the appropriate semantic field, selecting as an error in picture–word matching tasks, the name of the close semantic co-ordinate in preference to any of three semantically unrelated names. It was noted above, that even towards the end of the study, almost 75% of her choices reflected preserved knowledge of the semantic domain to which the written word belonged. It has been argued recently that such lexical–semantic knowledge may be sufficient to prevent the sublexical processes from "capturing" the pronunciation of the written word. In an analysis of a patient with a progressive semantic memory disorder and developing surface dyslexia, it was shown that for those irregular words read correctly, knowledge of the broad semantic field was present, while for those words read incorrectly, such knowledge was lost (Funnell, in press).

MODULARITY

The detailed study of individual cases of language disorders in dementia, which include W.L.P., has revealed a range of deficits which selectively affect some aspects of language processing, while sparing others. There is a reciprocity about the modularity of function revealed by these studies; on the one hand, neurological disease can expose to view functionally distinct parts of the language processing system (and other cognitive systems too); on the other, the modularity of function exposed indicates a reciprocal modularity of the disease process itself. As Schwartz (1987, p. 34) notes, the modularity of function revealed in certain cases of dementia suggests:

> that we are dealing with a single disease entity with multiple dimensions of variation. Conceivably, these multiple dimensions of variation reflect distinct underlying processes, as, for example, different neurotransmitter abnormalities. Alternatively, or in addition, it reflects the differential involvement of particular brain regions or cytoarchitectonic layers. At this point, we can do no more than speculate.

The evidence from dementia for a modular organisation of the language system, reported in the mid- to late 1970s, accorded with the modular view of language emerging at that time from the study of individual cases of aphasia (e.g. Marshall & Newcombe, 1973; Morton & Patterson, 1980). What was not generally accepted at that time, and perhaps not even yet, is that, in some cases, dementia can affect specific areas of cognitive processing, while sparing others.

The prevailing view of the patterns and course of cognitive decline in dementia, at the time of the study of W.L.P., held that breakdown followed a fixed order of stages. Even a few years later, Schwartz (1987) pointed out that still "It is widely accepted that the natural history of Alzheimer-type dementia is accurately described by a relatively fixed, invariable sequence of stages of behavioural, cognitive, and neurological symptoms." The case of W.L.P., and others like her, have shown this view to be incorrect: a variety of focal symptoms, including the breakdown of semantic memory, progressive visual agnosia (de Renzi, 1986), and visual attention (Saffran, Fitzpatrick-DeSalme, & Coslett, 1990) have contributed to the evidence for modular deficits in Alzheimer-type dementia. As Schwartz notes, "An examination of the evidence shows that there is no generalization about the inevitable ordering of symptoms that has not been contradicted by reports in the literature." The significance of this variation in clinical symptoms of dementia for the understanding of the disease process itself has yet to be determined.

UNFINISHED BUSINESS

A backwards look at famous cases in neuropsychology, which dwells upon only those established features of the case which have most influenced the development of theory, could fix the relevance, and interest of the study, firmly in the past. Classic papers should, if possible, raise questions for the future too. Here then, to tease the mind, are some puzzling features of the study that remain unanswered.

Schwartz et al. (1979) argued that W.L.P.'s failure to name items, either spontaneously or in a picture–word matching task, arose from a breakdown in her knowledge of referential meaning. How was it then that W.L.P., while able to name only 1 out of 70 common objects and, at best, match only 61% to the correct written name, nevertheless could gesture the use of these objects with such precision that the examiner was left in no doubt that W.L.P. had specified a particular item, rather than a semantic co-ordinate within the semantic field? Further, was it really the case that W.L.P. comprehended the lexical meaning of verbs, while losing her comprehension for nouns (as her comprehension for the surface form of reversible sentences might suggest)? And if so, could her ability to gesture precisely the use of objects she could not apparently otherwise precisely comprehend, be related to her preserved comprehension for verbs—the action words of sentences? In the addressing these questions may lie a classic paper for the future.

REFERENCES

Baron, J. (1977). Mechanisms for pronouncing printed words: Use and acquisition. In D. LaBerge and S.J. Samuels (Eds.), *Basic processes in reading: Perception and comprehension.* Hillsdale, NJ: Lawrence Erlbaum Associates Inc.

Bayles, K.A., Tomoeda, C.K., Kasniak, A.W., & Trosset, M.W. (1990). Alzheimer's disease effects on semantic memory: Loss of structure or impaired processing? *Journal of Cognitive Neuroscience, 3,* 166–182.

Bub, D., Cancelliere, A., & Kertesz, A. (1985). Whole-word and analytic translation of spelling to sound in a non-semantic reader. In K. Patterson, J.C. Marshall, & M. Coltheart (Eds.), *Surface dyslexia.* Hove, UK: Lawrence Erlbaum Associates Ltd.

Caramazza, A., Hillis, A.E., Rapp, B., & Romani, C. (1990). The multiple semantics hypothesis: Multiple confusions? *Cognitive Neuropsychology, 7,* 161–190.

Chertkow, H., Bub, D., & Seidenberg, M. (1989). Priming and semantic memory in Alzheimer's disease. *Brain and Language, 36,* 420–446.

Coltheart, M. (1980). Reading, phonological recoding and deep dyslexia. In M. Coltheart, K. Patterson, & J.C. Marshall (Eds.), *Deep dyslexia.* London: Routledge & Kegan Paul.

Coslett, B. (1991). Read but not write "idea": Evidence for a third reading mechanism. *Brain and Language, 40,* 425–443.

De Renzi, E. (1986). Slowly progressive visual agnosia or apraxia without dementia. *Cortex, 22,* 171–180.

Funnell, E. (1983). Phonological processes in reading: New evidence from acquired dyslexia. *British Journal of Psychology*, *74*, 159–180.

Funnell, E. (1992). The progressive loss of semantic memory in a case of Alzheimer's disease. *Proceedings of the Royal Society of London*, *B249*, 287–291.

Funnell, E. (1993). Breakdown of object concepts and the organisation of semantic memory. In *Neuropsychology of semantic memory*. Symposium of the Experimental Psychology Society, Cambridge, U.K.

Funnell, E. (in press). Responses biases in oral reading: An account of the co-occurrence of surface dyslexia and semantic dementia. *Quarterly Journal of Experimental Psychology*.

Funnell, E., & Sheridan, J. (1992). Categories of knowledge? Unfamiliar aspects of living and nonliving things. *Cognitive Neuropsychology*, *9*, 135–154.

Hillis, A., & Caramazza, A. (1991). Mechanisms for accessing lexical representations for output: Evidence from a category-specific semantic deficit. *Brain and Language*, *40*, 106–144.

Hodges, J.R., Patterson, K., Oxbury, S., & Funnell, E. (1992). Semantic dementia. *Brain*, *115*, 1782–1806.

Marcel, A. (1980). Surface dyslexia and beginning reading. In M. Coltheart, K. Patterson, & J.C. Marshall (Eds.), *Deep dyslexia*. London: Routledge & Kegan Paul.

Marshall, J.C., & Newcombe, F. (1973). Patterns of paralexia. *Journal of Psycholinguistic Research*, *2*, 169–176.

Morton, J., & Patterson, K.E. (1980). A new attempt at an interpretation, or an attempt at a new interpretation. In M. Coltheart, K. Patterson, & J.C. Marshall (Eds.), *Deep dyslexia*. London: Routledge & Kegan Paul.

Patterson, K.E., & Hodges, J.R. (1992). Deterioration of word-meaning: Implications for reading. *Neuropsychologia*, *30*, 1025–1040.

Riddoch, M.J., Humphreys, G.W., Coltheart, M., & Funnell, E. (1988). Semantic system or systems? Neuropsychological evidence re-examined. *Cognitive Neuropsychology*, *5*, 2–26.

Saffran, E.M., Fitzpatrick-DeSalme, E.J., & Coslett, H.B. (1990). In M.F. Schwartz (Ed.), *Modular deficits in Alzheimer-type dementia*. Cambridge, MA: MIT Press.\

Saffran, E.M., & Marin, O.S.M. (1977). Reading without phonology; Evidence from aphasia. *Quarterly Journal of Experimental Psychology*, *29*, 515–525.

Sasanuma, S., Sakuma, N., & Kitano, K. (1992). Reading Kanji without semantics: Evidence from a longitudinal study of dementia. *Cognitive Neuropsychology*, *9*, 465–586.

Schwartz, M.F. (1987). Focal cognitive deficits in dementia of the Alzheimer type. *Neuropsychology*, *1*, 27–35.

Schwartz, M.F., Marin, O.S.M., & Saffran, E.M. (1979). Dissociations of language function in dementia: A case study. *Brain & Language*, *7*, 277–306.

Schwartz, M.F., Saffran, E.M., & Marin, O.S.M. (1980). Fractionating the reading process in dementia. In M. Coltheart, K.E. Patterson, & J.C. Marshall (Eds.), *Deep dyslexia*. London: Routledge & Kegan Paul.

Shallice, T. (1988). *From neuropsychology to mental structure*. Cambridge: Cambridge University Press.

Shallice, T., & Warrington, E.K. (1980). Single and multiple component central dyslexic syndromes. In M. Coltheart, K. Patterson, & J.C. Marshall (Eds.), *Deep dyslexia*. London: Routledge & Kegan Paul.

Shallice, T., & Warrington, E.K. (1983). Reading without semantics. *Quarterly Journal of Experimental Psychology*, *35A*, 111–138.

Siedenberg, M., & McClelland, J. (1989). A distributed, developmental model of visual word recognition and naming. *Psychological Review*, *96*, 523–568.

Snowden, J.S., Goulding, P.J., & Neary, D. (1989). Semantic dementia: A form of circumscribed cerebral atrophy. *Behavioural Neurology*, *2*, 167–182.

Stewart, F., Parkin, A., & Hunkin, N.M. (1992). Naming impairments following recovery from herpes simplex encephalitis. *Quarterly Journal of Psychology*, *44A*, 261–284.

Warrington, E.K. (1975). The selective impairment of semantic memory. *Quarterly Journal of Psychology*, *27*, 635–657.

Warrington, E.K., & McCarthy, R. (1983). Category-specific access dysphasia. *Brain*, *107*, 829–859.

Warrington, E.K., & Shallice, T. (1984). Category-specific semantic impairmants. *Brain*, *107*, 829–859.

Whitaker, H. (1976). A case of the isolation of the language function. In H. Whitaker & H.A. Whitaker (Eds.), *Studies in neurolinguistics (Vol. 2)*. New York: Academic Press.

16 Warrington and Shallice's (1984) Category-specific Aphasic J.B.R.

Carlo Semenza and Patrizia S. Bisiacchi
Dipartimento di Psicologia Generale, University of Padova, Italy.

In the late 1970s a question was discussed in cognitive psychology whether the information contained in the semantic system might be organised in independent compartments in which information acquired through a sensory modality would remain independent of information acquired through a different sensory modality. Popular examples of this view are models encompassing two distinct types of semantic representation: a visual and a verbal one, the latter mainly built on the basis of acoustic/linguistic information (see Potter & Faulconer, 1975; Seymour, 1979; Snodgrass, 1984). At about the same time, neuropsychological cases featuring dissociations seemingly supporting such distinctions were beginning to be described (e.g. Beauvois, 1982; Warrington, 1975). Within a few years the debate massively invaded neuropsychology, since an impressive variety of dissociations concerning lexical/semantic abilities were reported. Distinctions in the semantic system apparently implemented in a different neuroanatomy were not limited to information coming from different modalities. The semantic category of the lexical item also appeared to determine a different neural organisation. Already in the 1960s, Goodglass et al. (1966) had convincingly shown that some semantic categories could be either selectively spared or impaired in aphasia. These somewhat specific disturbances in some cases seemed to concern only the input or the output processes, while in other cases all the information in a single semantic realm was apparently lost or disrupted. Semantic category and modality of input were thought to be related to each other and the study of this relation brought to light some very interesting generalisations.

A paradigmatic example of a category-specific semantic impairment is the case of J.B.R., described by Warrington and Shallice in 1984. A description of this case will be followed by a thorough discussion of all its theoretical and methodological implications; this will lead the reader to the actual conception of category- and modality-specific aphasias.

CASE DESCRIPTION

J.B.R. was recovering from herpes simplex encephalitis, which caused extensive damage to both temporal lobes. In contrast to his normal intelligence he was disoriented in time and place with a severe anterograde and retrograde amnesia. On recognition memory tests for words and faces he scored at chance level. His perceptual skills were considered to be intact with regard to his ability to match conventional and unusual views correctly. His spontaneous speech was fluent with normal articulation, syntax, and phrase length; occasionally he showed some word-finding difficulty and tended to use circumlocutory expressions. He scored at ceiling on a shortened version of the Token Test. He failed in naming tests and performed poorly on object recognition. His impairment, however, was disproportionately severe for living things and foods compared to inanimate objects. This effect was found irrespective of whether the patient was tested on a verbal description, naming, mimed responses, or picture–word matching (see Table 16.1).

TABLE 16.1
J.B.R.'s Percentage of Correct Responses Across Tasks

(a)

Modality	Visual		Auditory	
	Living	*Not-living*	*Living*	*Not-living*
Naming or description	6	90	NT	NT
Naming	6	67	NT	NT
Defining	10	75	8	79

(b)

	Living	*Food*	*Not-living*
Word/picture matching	67	60	98
Miming	NT	20	65

NT = not tested

Few exceptions to this general trend were found. A failure in defining most musical instruments, fabrics, and precious stones was observed in contrast to the success in defining body parts. Superordinate information was preserved for a high proportion of items on which subordinate information could not be retrieved.

On separate occasions, a somewhat different pattern of responses was obtained for the presentation of stimulus items within a modality and between modalities. In general there was a non-significant degree of consistency for comparison of responses between modalities. Thus, if, for example, the picture of a dog was not identified (i.e. named or described), the auditory presented word "dog" could be correctly described. However, there was a significant degree of response consistency for all comparisons within a modality. Hence the pictures identified or failed on a second presentation tended to be the same (identified or failed) at the first.

Warrington and Shallice suggested that J.B.R. (and three other patients that they described in less detail in the same article) suffered from a degradation of the semantic representations of certain categories of things, notably living objects. They argued in favour of a storage rather than an access deficit because of the consistency of responses, the vulnerability of subordinate information, and marked frequency effects, all signs of a storage deficit according to their own, previously presented, theory (Warrington, 1975; Warrington & Shallice, 1979). The non-significant degree of consistency between modalities (a single concept is spared in one modality and not in the other) was believed to support the existence of two separate semantic systems—visual and verbal.

The relative impairment for the living categories as opposed to inanimate objects was contrasted with a previously observed case showing the opposite pattern (Warrington & McCarthy, 1983). This provided a double dissociation eliminating any explanation concerning general task difficulty or vulnerability of particular categories: Living and non-living things would therefore occupy a different space in the semantic system. Warrington and Shallice ultimately attributed this separation to two different yet basic qualities of living and non-living things. Living things would be best described by their sensory features while inanimate objects would better lend themselves to a description in terms of functional attributes. The selective loss of one of these two categories of attribution would then be at the basis of the living/non-living effect. Thus, J.B.R. would not be able to identify living things because of a deficit in dealing with sensory features. Also the exceptions found in J.B.R.'s performance to the living/non-living trend could be better dealt with according to this new perspective. The difficulty with musical instruments (a non-living category) would be explained because, to non-musicians like J.B.R., musical instruments are known primarily by their appearance. Body parts, on the other hand, are used frequently and, therefore, are best known on the basis of their function rather than their appearance.

THE IMPORTANCE OF THE CASE

J.B.R. is not the first nor the clearest or most intriguing known case of category-specific aphasia. Its importance (and the impact it actually had) is not derived from the fact that the observation of the relative living things impairment has now been replicated several times without any significant advancement in theory with respect to the original. (Indeed in several cases the only theoretical efforts were just concerned with ruling out the possibility of artefacts; see Table 16.2 for a summary of the cases present in the literature.)

Rather, Warrington and Shallice's study is important for its synthesis of a constellation of methodological, heuristic, and theoretical issues; their study is rarely paralleled and is central to an ongoing debate. This debate does not only involve the meaning of category-specific neuropsychological problems with respect to the organisation of the semantic system, but extends to aspects relevant to the wider realm of cognitive (neuro)psychology. These issues, that recur not only in the description of J.B.R. but also elsewhere in Warrington and Shallice's work, are far from uncontroversial as the following comments, expanded upon later, will show.

The first question raised in J.B.R.'s case is, quite naturally, the possibility that the observed category effect is an artefact due to uncontrolled variables. However, once this possibility is ruled out, the task remains, as with all category-specific deficits, to identify the crucial quality (indicated by Warrington and Shallice in the sensory/functional distinction) that makes a category sufficiently different to require separate processing or space in the cognitive system. A second related question concerns the possible existence, suggested by Warrington and Shallice, of two (or more) semantic systems. The storage versus access distinction also deserves a separate comment. Finally, implicit in the discussion of the case, is the use of the dissociation and association method and the relative importance the neuropsychologist attributes to each of these type of findings.

The Question of Possible Artefacts: What Determines Category Effects?

When approaching the study of a patient with a suspected category-specific semantic impairment it is important to control stimulus parameters, task requirements, and modality of presentation since each of these aspects may lead to artefacts.

As far as the experimental material is concerned, semantic categories should be comparable in terms of word frequency, visual familiarity, and

TABLE 16.2

Summary of Cases Reported in the Literature with a Category-specific Deficit for Some Living Things

Authors	Patient	Aetiology	Category affected	Word definition	Word categorisation	Naming to definition	Picture identification	Drawing from memory	Object decision
Warrington and Shallice (1984)	J.B.R.	Herpes encephalitis	Animals and food	+	nt	nt	+	nt	nt
Warrington and Shallice (1984)	S.B.Y.	Herpes encephalitis	Animals and food	+	nt	nt	+	nt	nt
Hart, Berndt and Caramazza (1985)	M.D.	Cerebrovascular accident	Fruits and vegetables	nt	no specific impairment	+	+	nt	nt
Levine, Warach, and Farah (1985); Farah et al. (1989)	L.H.	Head injury	Animals and food	nt	nt	+	+	+	+
Riddoch and Humphreys (1987)	J.B.	Head injury	Animals and food	nt	nt	not impaired	+	nt	not impaired
Pietrini, Nertempi, Vaglia, Revello, Pinna, and Ferro-Milone (1988)	J.V.	Herpes encephalitis	Plants	+	nt	+	nt	nt	nt
	R.M.	Herpes encephalitis	Animals and plants	no specific impairment	nt	+	+	nt	nt
McCarthy and Warrington (1988)	T.O.B.	Cerebrovascular accident	Animals	nt	nt	nt	+	nt	nt
Sartori and Job (1988)	Michelangelo	Herpes encephalitis	Animals, fruits, and vegetables	+	no specific impairment	+ (mild)	+	nt	+
Basso, Capitani, and Laiacona (1988)	N.V.	Degenerative	Animals, fruits, vegetables, and food	nt	nt	+	+	nt	nt
Silveri and Gainotti (1988)	L.A.	Herpes encephalitis	Animals and food	+	nt	not impaired	+	nt	not impaired
Sartori Job, and Coltheart (1990)	Dante	Meningo encephalitis	Animals and food	nt	nt	nt	+	nt	not impaired
Hillis and Caramazza (1991)	P.S.	Head injury	Animals and vegetables	nt	nt	nt	+	nt	nt
Sheridan and Humphreys (1993)	S.B.	Herpes encephalitis	Animals and food	+	+	+	+	+	not impaired

+ = significant effect of category; nt = not tested

221

complexity of their elements. Most of the studies on this topic used Snodgrass and Vanderwart's (1980) pictures for which the word frequency, familiarity, and complexity of each item is available. Unfortunately, however, when the material is divided into the broad categories of animate and inanimate categories the animate (living) category turns out to be less frequent, less familiar, and more complex. Indeed two recent studies (Funnell & Sheridan, 1992; Stewart, Parkin & Hunkin, 1992) report two cases of apparent relative impairment of the animate category in which the effect disappears after an accurate control of stimulus parameters. In their work Funnell and Sheridan also suggest that a familiarity account could be compatible with the effect found in J.B.R. (they base this suggestion on a re-analysis of Snodgrass and Vanderwart's material used by Warrington and Shallice in one part of their investigation).

However, Shallice and Cinan (personal communication) recently obtained ratings in terms of word frequency, familiarity, and structural complexity of the Ladybird pictures used in the word–picture matching experiments with J.B.R. The Ladybird pictures are clear, large coloured pictures from books for under-fives. The objects represented in the set were not favoured in the ratings on any of these dimensions by comparisons with either the living things or food. When the ratings were taken into account the category effect—the inanimate object superiority over the other two categories—was still significant. This is a similar result to that of the analysis of covariance carried out on the Snodgrass and Vanderwart pictures reported in the original paper describing J.B.R. Moreover, the analyses of other cases examining the relative impairment of living things where word frequency, imaginability, familiarity, and visual complexity were specially controlled (e.g. Bastiaanse, 1993; Hillis & Caramazza, 1991; Sartori, Miozzo, & Job, 1993) also show the authenticity of the effect.

The possibility that the living/non-living effect may turn out to be an artefact in J.B.R. and similar patients is not likely because the complementary side of the dissociation has been observed, with living things spared and inanimate objects impaired (Warrington & McCarthy, 1983, 1987).

More generally it is very unlikely that reported category-specific effects could all arise from artefacts. A double dissociation has been indeed reported in several cases. They must then reflect some organisation in the neural implementation of the semantic system. What is important, but mostly neglected, in the discussion about category-specific aphasias, is the identification of the characteristics of a category which increases the chances of it being selectively impaired or spared after brain damage. Warrington and Shallice set the example by working on an explanation on the basis of the functional/structural distinction. It is, however, clear that such a distinction cannot explain other categorical effects. Yet the idea that the disturbance of some organising dimensions in the semantic system would underlie category effects may be generally accepted. Other categories may be prone to selective effects because they are more accurately defined by other dimensions: for instance, linguistic dimensions like pure reference for proper names (see the cases described by Semenza & Zettin, 1988, 1989) or pure physical dimensions such as colours (one cannot forget that for many years the only known cases of category-specific anomias were those concerning colours).

Categorical effects may also follow, as Farah and McClelland (1991) have shown, damage to a network with distributed representation whose input has different sources.

How Many Semantic Systems? Towards an Ecumenically Accepted Proposal

Whatever change or reshaping Warrington and Shallice's first ideas underwent in the studies that followed J.B.R., (see particularly Shallice, 1988b, in press; Warrington & McCarthy, 1987; but see also Shallice, 1987, 1988a, for an account closer to the original) the initial argument for the existence of separate visual and verbal semantic systems cannot be accepted in the form in which it was originally presented. Criticism has been offered by Caplan (1987), Caramazza, Hillis, Rapp, and Romani (1990), Hillis, Rapp, Romani, and Caramazza (1990), and Semenza (1990), on the general grounds that the line of reasoning leading to the postulation of multiple semantic systems seemed to be theoretically unmotivated and uneconomical. Indeed, this criticism may not even be proper regarding what Warrington and Shallice might have truly meant by "multiple semantic systems" (the term is, however, theirs) but, alas, people reacted to what they understood. In Caplan's words (1987, p. 184), following Warrington and Shallice's lead, "there could be as many semantic systems as there are sense modalities (vision, hearing, touch etc.), modes of linguistic representation (speech, writing, sign, Braille etc.) and many different forms of some of these modes (different forms of orthographies...)." Semenza (1988) also observed that the non-verbal output modality used in localising body parts in space is subject to categorical effects. Non-verbal output modalities should then be included in the list, thus multiplying the number of systems. To make things worse, the functional/structural and similar distinctions should be considered (cf. Shallice, 1987) in each single modality. Even though alternative explanations of cases analogous to J.B.R. (Humphreys, Riddoch, & Quinlan, 1988; Riddoch, Humphreys, Coltheart, & Funnell, 1988) also have weaknesses (Shallice, 1988a), the general argument of multiple semantic systems now seems to fade in favour of a more unitary account. Authors with apparently contrasting ideas encompassing

Warrington and Shallice and their critics (Caramazza et al., 1990; Semenza, Bisiacchi, & Romani, 1992; Semenza & Zettin, 1989; Shallice, 1988a, 1988b, 1993; Warrington & McCarthy, 1987) would probably now subscribe to an account that may be sketched as follows. The conceptual/semantic system would be represented as a giant store (implemented, perhaps, in a distributed neural network) where procedures or rules would depend on dimensions of a different sort, determined by the nature and strength of the links relating to various component features that jointly define a concept and, ultimately, the meaning of a term. Examples of these dimensions, each orthogonal to the others, have been identified as those defined by the prevalence of structural and functional attributes, or of relations of class and property (Semenza et al., 1992), or by descriptive values (Semenza & Zettin, 1989), abstract/concrete (Warrington & Shallice, 1984, also in the J.B.R. study), etc. The modality of input and output of the system would interact with these procedures, determining areas of relative specialisation (Caramazza et al., 1990; Shallice, 1988a, 1988b, 1993). Damage to parts of this system would determine, perhaps more likely when close to the input or the output (including procedures or other stored parts of information), the effects manifesting as modality or category-specific aphasias. Taking for granted a few distinctions and provisos, it is difficult to imagine how this admittedly grossly underspecified account could be very different from the ones already provided by each of the previously mentioned authors as an alternative to the multiple systems theory. Also, the willingness to consider the system as implemented in a distributed network (Shallice, in press) does not, by any means, make a significant difference given the limited conceptual status of the field. The semantic system is characteristically represented as an empty cloud in current cognitive neuropsychological models; perhaps progress may be expected only when the problem of its internal organisation is addressed by a critical mass of neuropsychologists via observations and experiments not necessarily concerned with category and modality effects.

Access Versus Storage Deficits

Warrington and Shallice conclude that J.B.R.'s deficit is better explained as a permanent loss, rather than a difficulty in accessing stored information. To reach this conclusion they used five criteria they developed in other works (Warrington, 1975; Warrington & McCarthy, 1983; Warrington & Shallice, 1979). The five criteria, expressed as conditions that must coexist in order to allow the diagnosis of a permanent loss of stored information ("storage" deficit) rather than a diagnosis of difficulty in accessing the same information ("access" deficit) are as follows:

1. The patient must fail consistently on the same items along successive administrations of the same test. In the case of an access disorder the same overall score would be obtained but there would not be consistency of performance on the single items.

2. No effect of priming or semantic cueing would be obtained in storage deficits. In access deficits it would be easy to demonstrate a benefit.

3. Loss of information should be sensitive to a hierarchy in storage deficits: Superordinate information would be more easily spared. In a storage deficit, detailed attribute information is more vulnerable than superordinate information.

4. Storage deficits are expected to be more sensitive to the frequency effect than access deficits.

5. Increasing the inter-trial interval between testing sessions would not favour performance in storage deficits while it would make it easier in the case of access problems (this criterion was added by Warrington & McCarthy, 1983).

Specific criticism regarding these five points can be found in Howard (1985), Caplan (1987), Semenza (1990), Caramazza et al. (1990), Hillis et al. (1990), and more recently Rapp and Caramazza (1993). All these authors argue that the rigid, hierarchically organised model of semantic memory that inspires the criteria is not tenable and may lead to the wrong conclusions. Superordinate information may be or may not be the information most resistant to loss (cf. for different views and findings Brownell, 1978; Goodglass & Baker, 1976; Rapp & Caramazza, 1989). Even patients with storage deficit from Warrington (1975) or Warrington and Shallice (1979) commit errors of the subordinate type with respect to the target, a fact incompatible with the theory.

Another weak point of Warrington and Shallice's theory is that it does not consider the possibility that the permanent loss of information about an item might be only partial. For example, a patient may not remember how many legs a frog has and yet be aware of where it lives, eats and of the quality and colour of its skin. Residual information might indeed be sufficient to be helped by priming or cueing. Also one cannot assume that the efficiency of the access channels is independent of frequency. Humphreys, Riddoch, and Quinlan (1988) argue that a frequency effect and a consistency effect are not incompatible with an access deficit if the reference model is a "cascade" model. Caplan (1987) suggests that the same is true in the case of a connectionist model. The "consistency" criterion has other problems: Strictly speaking, the only acceptable consistency value would be 100% (which is not the case even in J.B.R. and similar patients). Also, how many times should the deficit on a given item be found? A couple of times may not be sufficient. What if the patient succeeds on a third administration?

All this being said, Warrington and Shallice's suggestions on the access/ storage dichotomy would have merited further research (virtually none has been done outside the original group, except Chertkow & Bub, 1990; Chertkow, Bub, & Caplan, 1992) and, most important, more detailed theories. Indeed, one must recognise with Rapp and Caramazza (1993) that, while the access/storage distinction is potentially an exciting and useful one, the phenomena that have been reported are far from compelling. Furthermore, and more importantly, as again Rapp and Caramazza (1993) pointed out, the evaluation and verification of the validity of this distinction rely crucially on the theoretical framework within which it is presented. However, no theoretical development has emerged as yet.

The Use of Dissociation/Association Procedure

The main methodological procedure in J.B.R.'s case study is the use of the set of dissociations and associations across tasks. The particular position of the authors regarding these two types of neuropsychological findings leads to important consequences in their interpretation of the results and in the building of their theory. As will be shown, a different view concerning the relative importance of dissociations and associations would have led to radically different conclusions. To better illustrate this point it is useful to refer to Shallice's discussion of dissociations and associations in his book *From Neuropsychology to Mental Structure* (1988b).

Shallice's impressive effort toward a coherent account of cognitive neuropsychology is indeed centred on the one type of neuropsychological finding he considers to have a special status: dissociations. One cannot but admire how Shallice exploits the virtues of the dissociation approach, but on a single point one cannot but disagree: the asserted inferential asymmetry between dissociations and associations. Shallice's argument (1988b, p. 35) for the superiority of the dissociation approach is the following:

> ... if one patient shows an association between two types of deficits and a second shows a dissociation with one of the abilities being preserved, then a simple explanation of the overall pattern exists. The observed dissociation can be presumed to arise from a lesion that has affected only one side of a functional line of cleavage in the modular system; the association, however, is presumed to result from a lesion that has crossed this line. On this account, if the association is actually observed later, it does not affect any interpretation that has been made of the dissociation, but if the dissociation is observed after the association, it undermines any interpretation made of the association symptom complex as a unitary entity.

At the very best this is only a partial truth. It is contended here (see also Semenza, in press) that there are associations that have the same inferential value as dissociations because interpretation made of these associations could not be undermined by a dissociation involving the components of the association.

Shallice's account is incomplete because it rests on examples of symptom complexes which are theoretically indefensible, such as the "Gerstman's syndrome". It is thus easy to see that if an observed patient shows one of the components of the syndrome (e.g. acalculia) and not the other components, the idea of Gerstman syndrome as arising from damage to a single processing system would collapse. Examples are not mentioned of theoretically valid associations, whose value would not be invalidated or even diminished but enriched or even stressed by the observation of a dissociation (it has no relevance if it happens before or after the observed association). Indeed, Shallice (1991), in the light of recent examples of productive quantitatively parallel association, agrees that association deficits can also be used to constrain theoretical inferences.

A few of these examples will be offered here. The danger of ignoring associations will then be illustrated with particular reference to J.B.R.'s case.

Patient K.E., reported by Hillis et al. (1990), makes semantic errors on various types of lexical processing tasks (reading, writing, naming, and comprehension) at virtually identical rates regardless of the modality of stimulus or response. K.E.'s homogenous pattern of semantic errors across modalities is interpreted as evidence of selective damage to a semantic system common to all lexical processes. The value of this finding, an association, is not hampered by the dissociation in the performance of the same tasks observed still by Caramazza and Hillis (1990) on patients R.G.B. and H.W. These patients show similar, high rates of semantic errors in oral naming and oral reading but not in comparable written tasks. Further, they demonstrate unimpaired comprehension of printed or spoken words, including those that are orally produced as semantic errors. Taken together, these findings, associations and a dissociation, allow Caramazza and colleagues to support a theoretical model which distinguishes a single, modality neutral, central semantic system (disturbed in K.E.) from a more peripheral level of lexical representation, the phonological output lexicon (disturbed in R.G.B. and H.W.).

The same model is shown to need further specification by other associations observed in patients P.C. and L.S. (Semenza & Zettin, 1988, 1989), suffering a selective anomia for proper names, and in patient H.Y. (Zingeser & Berndt, 1988), suffering an impairment in the verbal retrieval of nouns. In these patients the same pattern of performance is shown in oral and written naming. In all cases comprehension was unimpaired which, on Caramazza and colleagues' account, would exclude a deficit in the modality neutral semantic system. One should then locate the defect in the output lexicons. However, according to their model, phonological and orthographic lexicons are independent from each other, as is nicely shown by the dissociation observed in R.G.B. and H.W. But how can both lexicons be affected in precisely the same grammatical category (as in H.Y.) or even more dramatically in the same, rather peculiar, semantic category (as in P.C. and L.S.)? This association forces one to further specify that either (1) the phonological and orthographic output lexicons, while distinct, interact to a certain extent (see also Miceli, Giustolisi, & Caramazza, 1991), or (2) intermediate processes between the central semantic system and the peripheral lexicons are sensitive to categorical information (as has been proposed in Zingeser & Berndt, 1988).

Ignoring associations may indeed mean missing important facts and hampering a theory, as shown by the following example that directly refers to Warrington and Shallice's analysis of J.B.R.'s case. They argue in favour of modality-specific semantic representation systems because J.B.R. and the other patients with semantic memory disorders are consistent in their errors over test sessions in a single modality, and show considerable differences between modalities. What Warrington and Shallice fail to comment upon (see also Semenza & Denes, 1988) is the association they find in the same patients: They do not identify, in various modalities, the same category of names (i.e. living things). Even if they do not find a significant degree of consistency between modalities, this fact cannot be ignored. Especially if, like Warrington and Shallice, one wants to identify precisely the representation component that is disturbed (the structural specification of the semantic system necessary to identify living things). It would follow that, in these cases, distinct modality-specific semantic representation systems would each be disturbed in the same single component of semantic memory. A surprising coincidence if modality-specific representation systems were really distinct. With respect to this data, if modality-specific representation systems do exist, the amount of interaction between them is far from negligible.

These examples seem sufficient to illustrate how associations are as useful as dissociations; of course, this is true only if they are interpreted within the framework of a theoretically sound model. Conversely, both associations and dissociations become irrelevant if no theory endorses the observation.

CONCLUSIONS

These considerations converge, leading to the conclusion that Warrington and Shallice's study on J.B.R. represents a landmark in the history of neuropsychology. Its value clearly transcends the mere observation of a dissociation that has been replicated many times. As already stated, the methodological and theoretical richness must have pre-eminence in assigning this study its true value. The frequent criticisms reported in these pages are the result of a debate that would have never started without Warrington and Shallice's first effort. The positions they assume in later studies show that they are still ahead in the game, with an impressively stimulating effect on fellow neuropsychologists.

REFERENCES

Basso, A., Capitani, E., & Laiacona, M. (1988). Progressive language impairment without dementia: A case with isolated category-specific semantic deficit. *Journal of Neurology, Neurosurgery and Psychiatry, 51*, 1201–1207.

Bastiaanse, R. (1993). *Studies in aphasia.* Unpublished Ph.D. dissertation, Rijksuniversiteit, Groningen.

Beauvois, M.F. (1982). Optic aphasia: A process of interaction between vision and language. *Philosophical Transactions of the Royal Society of London, B298*, 35–47.

Brownell, H.H. (1978). *Picture perception and semantic memory.* Unpublished doctoral dissertation, Johns Hopkins University, Baltimore.

Caplan, D. (1987). *Neurolinguistics and linguistic aphasiology: An introduction.* Cambridge: Cambridge University Press.

Caramazza, A., & Hillis, A.E. (1990). Where do lexical errors come from? *Cortex, 1*, 95–122.

Caramazza, A., Hillis, A.E., Rapp, B.C., & Romani, C. (1990). The multiple semantic hypothesis: Multiple confusions? *Cognitive Neuropsychology, 7*, 161–189.

Chertkow, H., & Bub, D. (1990). Semantic memory loss in dementia of Alzheimer's type. *Brain, 113*, 397–417.

Chertkow, H., Bub, D., & Caplan, D. (1992). Constraining theories of semantic memory processing: Evidence from dementia. *Cognitive Neuropsychology, 9*(4), 327–365.

Farah, M.J., Hammond, K.M., Mehta, Z., & Ratcliff, G. (1989). Category-specificity and modality-specificity in semantic memory. *Neuropsychologia, 27*, 193–200.

Farah, M.J., & McClelland, J.L. (1991). A computational model of semantic memory impairment: Modality specificity and emergent category specificity, *Journal of Experimental Psychology: General, 120*(4), 339–357.

Funnell, E., & Sheridan, J. (1992). Categories of knowledge? Unfamiliar aspects of living and not living things. *Cognitive Neuropsychology, 91*(2), 135–153.

Goodglass, H., & Baker, E. (1976). Semantic fields, naming, and auditory comprehension in aphasia. *Brain and Language, 3*, 359–374.

Goodglass, H., Klein, B., Carey, P., & Jones, K.J. (1966). Specific semantic word categories in aphasia. *Cortex, 2*, 74–89.

Hart, J., Berndt, R., & Caramazza, A. (1985). Category specific naming deficit following cerebral infarction. *Nature, 316*, 439–440.

Hillis, A.E., & Caramazza, A. (1991). Category specific naming and comprehension impairment: A double dissociation. *Brain, 114*, 2081–2094.

Hillis, A.E., Rapp, B.C., Romani, C., & Caramazza, A. (1990). Selective impairment of semantics in lexical processing. *Cognitive Neuropsychology, 7*, 191–244.

Howard, D. (1985). *The semantic organisation of the lexicon: Evidence from aphasia.* Unpublished doctoral dissertation, University College, London.

Humphreys, G.W., Riddoch, M.J., & Quinlan, P.T. (1988). Cascade processes in picture identification. *Cognitive Neuropsychology, 5*, 67–103.

Levine, D.N., Warrach, J., & Farah, M. (1985). Two visual systems in mental imagery: Dissociation of "what" and "where" in imagery disorders due to bilateral posterior cerebral lesions. *Neurology, 35*, 1010–1018.

McCarthy, R.A., & Warrington, E. (1988). Evidence for modality-specific meaning systems in the brain. *Nature, 334*, 328–429.

Miceli, G., Giustolisi, L., & Caramazza, A. (1991). The interaction of lexical and non-lexical processing mechanisms: Evidence from anomia. *Cortex, 27,* 57–80.

Pietrini, V., Nertempi, P., Vaglia, A., Revello, M.G., Pinna, V., & Ferro-Milone, F. (1988). Recovery from herpes-simplex encephalitis: Selective impairment of specific semantic categories with neurological correlation. *Journal of Neurology, Neurosurgery and Psychiatry, 51,* 1284–1293.

Potter, M., & Faulconer, B.A. (1975). Time to understand picture and words. *Nature, 253,* 437–438.

Rapp, B.C., & Caramazza, A. (1989). General to specific access to word meaning, a claim re-examined. *Cognitive Neuropsychology, 6*(2), 251–272.

Rapp, B.C., & Caramazza, A. (1993). On the distinction between deficits of access and deficits of storage: A question of theory. *Cognitive Neuropsychology, 10,* 143–184.

Riddoch, M.J., & Humphreys, G.W. (1987). Visual object processing in optic aphasia: A case of semantic access agnosia. *Cognitive Neuropsychology, 4,* 131–185.

Riddoch, M.J., Humphreys, G.W., Coltheart, M., & Funnell, E. (1988). Semantic systems of system? Neuropsychological evidence re-examined. *Cognitive Neuropsychology, 5,* 3–25.

Sartori, G., & Job, R. (1988). The oyster with four legs: A neuropsychological study on the interaction of visual and semantic information. *Cognitive Neuropsychology, 5,* 105–132.

Sartori, G., Job, R., & Coltheart, M. (1990). *The neuropsychology of visual semantics.* (Attention and performance XIV). Hillsdale, NJ: Lawrence Erlbaum Associations Inc.

Sartori, G., Miozzo, M., & Job, R. (1993). Category specific semantic impairment? Yes. *The Quarterly Journal of Experimental Psychology, 46A,* 489–504.

Semenza, C. (1988). Impairment in localisation of body parts following brain damage. *Cortex, 24,* 443–449.

Semenza, C. (1990). Disturbi semantico-lessicali nell'afasia. In G. Denes & L. Pizzamiglio (Eds.), *Manuale di neuropsicologia.* Bologna: Zanichelli.

Semenza, C. (in press). Methodological issues. In G. Beaumont, P. Kernealy, & M. Rogers (Eds.), *Dictionary of neuropsychology.* Oxford: Basil Blackwell.

Semenza, C., Bisiacchi, P.S., & Romani, L. (1992). Naming disorders and semantic representations. *Journal of Psycholinguistic Research, 5,* 349–364.

Semenza, C., & Denes, G. (1988). Modality and category specific aphasias. *Aphasiology, 2,* 405–410.

Semenza, C., & Zettin, M. (1988). Generating proper names: A case of selective inability. *Cognitive Neuropsychology, 5*(6), 711–721.

Semenza, C., & Zettin, M. (1989). Evidence from aphasia for the role of proper names as pure referring expression. *Nature, 342,* 670.

Seymour, P.H.K. (1979). *Human visual cognition.* Collier McMillan: London.

Shallice, T. (1987). Impairments of semantic processing: Multiple dissociations. In R. Job, G. Sartori, & M. Coltheart (Eds.), *The cognitive neuropsychology of language.* Hove, UK: Lawrence Erlbaum Associates Ltd.

Shallice, T. (1988a). Specialisation within the semantic system. *Cognitive Neuropsychology, 5,* 133–142.

Shallice. T. (1988b). *From neuropsychology to mental structure.* Cambridge: Cambridge University Press.

Shallice, T. (1991). Précis of "From neuropsychology to mental structure". *Behavioural and Brain Sciences, 14,* 429–469.

Shallice, T. (1993). Multiple semantics: Whose confusions? *Cognitive Neuropsychology, 10,* 251–261.

Sheridan, J., & Humphreys, G.W. (1993). A verbal–semantic category-specific recognition impairment. *Cognitive Neuropsychology, 10*(2), 143–184.

Silveri, M.C., & Gainotti, G. (1988). Interaction between vision and language in category specific impairment. *Cognitive Neuropsychology*, *5*, 677–709.

Snodgrass, J.G. (1984). Concepts and their surface representations. *Journal of Verbal Learning and Verbal Behaviour*, *23*, 3–22.

Snodgrass, J.G., & Vanderwart, M. (1980). A standardised set of 260 pictures: Norms for name agreement, image agreement, familiarity and visual complexity. *Journal of Experimental Psychology: Human Learning and Memory*, *6*, 174–215.

Stewart, F., Parkin, A.J., & Hunkin, N.M. (1992). Naming impairments following recovery from herpes simplex encephalitis: Category-specific? *Quarterly Journal of Experimental Psychology*, *44A*(2), 261–284.

Warrington, E.K. (1975). The selective impairment of semantic memory. *Quarterly Journal of Experimental Psychology*, *27*, 635–657.

Warrington, E.K., & McCarthy, R. (1983). Category specific access dysphasia. *Brain*, *106*, 859–878.

Warrington, E.K., & McCarthy, R. (1987). Categories of knowledge: Further fractionations and an attempted integration. *Brain*, *110*, 1273–1296.

Warrington, E.K., & Shallice, T. (1979). Semantic access dyslexia. *Brain*, *102*, 42–63.

Warrington, E.K., & Shallice, T. (1984). Category specific semantic impairments. *Brain*, *107*, 829–854.

Zingeser, L.B., & Berndt, R. (1988). Grammatical class and context effects in a case of pure anomia: Implications for models of language production. *Cognitive Neuropsychology*, *5*(4), 473–475.

II

STRUCTURE AND FUNCTION

17 Broca's First Two Cases: From Bumps on the Head to Cortical Convolutions

John Ryalls
Department of Communicative Disorders, University of Central Florida, Orlando, U.S.A.

André Roch Lecours
Centre de Recherche, Centre Hospitalier Côtes-des-Neiges, Montréal, Canada and Faculté de Médecine, Université de Montréal, Canada.

> *...j'avais pensé que s'il y avait jamais une science phrénologique, ce serait la phrénologie des circonvolutions, et non la phrénologie des bosses.*
>
> *... I had thought that if there were ever a phrenological science, it would be the phrenology of convolutions [in the cortex], and not the phrenology of bumps [on the head].*
> —Paul Broca (1861a, p. 406)

Modern neuropsychology has a long and rich tradition which is often presented in a rather truncated version. Even though our main interest in this chapter is the first clinical cases of Broca, the contribution of other founding fathers must also be alluded to, at least in passing. Thus, we must acknowledge the work of Gall, an excellent anatomist who is now usually only remembered as a somewhat misguided phrenologist. But if Gall had not been looking for the location of faculties on the outside of the skull in the first place then, arguably, Broca would never have attempted to localise them inside the brain at a later time.

The founding work of the "other" French neurologist Lordat (Lecours, Nespoulous, & Pioger, 1987) should also be pointed out, as well as the contributions of Bouillaud, Gratiolet, and Auburtin—even in a chapter that will serve to reconfirm Broca's predominance.

235

Broca's association with the aphasia that bears his name is now such a part of the basic knowledge of neuropsychology that history has somewhat blurred exactly what Broca said and when. Determining exactly when and what Broca said is complicated by the fact that his conceptualisation evolved considerably, and over a relatively short period of time, as new cases emerged. Part of the difficulty in interpreting Broca may also lie in the very reason why he is remembered in history. That is, he was somewhat of a "jack of all trades", not only a surgeon and anthropologist but also a founder of the discipline, that was later called neuropsychology, which Broca distinguished from its parent doctrine of phrenology.

Here we take another look at Broca's two original cases—those of Leborgne and Lelong—with the goal in mind of pointing out specifically what Broca said on the basis of these two cases. With the quotation from Broca given previously, we have already alluded to the most important innovation that can definitely be attributed to Broca—the notion that phrenology or the localisation of functions in the "mind" should take place on the basis of examining damage in the brain, rather than from the distribution of bumps on the outside of the head.

Thus we see the Broca's idea of looking directly at the brain distinguished neuropsychology from phrenology. While it must be conceded that other members of the Anthropological Society in Paris had already begun to shift to more brain-based notions (i.e. Bouillaud's notion of the frontal lobes being responsible for language), it was Broca who first brought a brain in for the members to examine. This leads us to Broca's first case, the patient whose brain Broca brought to the 18th April, 1861 meeting of the Anthropological Society.

There had already been a discussion at the Society on the representation for language in the brain for the past several meetings. On 4th April, at the meeting just before Broca presented his first case of aphasia, Auburtin had brought up medical disturbances of speech (Schiller, 1979). Thus, as with many great discoveries, there were some chance circumstances that led to a propitious moment. The other fortuitous circumstance was the otherwise unfortunate death of the patient Leborgne, the day before the next meeting of the Anthropological Society. The heuristic result was that Broca could examine Leborgne's brain post-mortem and give a short report on the patient at the meeting of the Anthropological Society the very next day (Broca, 1861b).

Broca pointed out that, when he examined the patient on 12th April, it was only speech that was affected and not the patient's intelligence—the patient "understood almost everything said to him" (p. 236). We can see that Broca was concerned about whether the syndrome he named aphemia was limited to a motor speech deficit or also involved more abstract aspects of language as well. This distinction has found its modern interpretation in the controversy between apraxia of speech and Broca's aphasia—an issue which is still not settled today. Blumstein (1991, p. 156) summarises the present state of affairs in regard to apraxia of speech in the following manner:

> There has been an active dialogue in the literature between those who see apraxia of speech as a nonaphasic and selective articulatory deficit (Aten, Darley, Deal & Johns, 1975; Johns & LaPointe, 1976) and those who consider apraxia of speech as a part of a larger language or aphasic disorder (Buckingham, 1979; Martin, 1974, 1975). Whether apraxia of speech is a linguistically based disorder (i.e. affecting the phonological and consequently the linguistic system) or simply an articulatory disorder is difficult to determine from the obtained data.

Upon autopsy of the patient, Broca found that most of the whole frontal lobe of the *left* (as Broca emphasised) hemisphere had degenerated. But (1861b, p. 237) the "primary site of the softening is the middle part of the frontal lobe of the left hemisphere." This is where the most extensive and oldest lesions were found. Broca (p. 238) ends his observation: "Thus, everything leads us to believe that in the present case, the lesion in the frontal lobe was the cause of the loss of speech."

But Broca's first case was far from ideal. The patient had first lost speech some 11 years earlier, and the brain had obviously undergone much further degeneration since. Clinical signs of Leborgne's further degeneration was the right hemiplegia which only became part of the clinical picture 10 years after the original loss of speech. Thus, the original case was hardly prototypical of the neurological disorder that was later to bear his name. Right hemiplegia usually accompanies Broca's aphasia from the very onset, and typically improves instead of worsening. The lesion was so large that Broca could only induce the original site of the lesion which he held responsible for the loss of speech.

The localisation is no more precise in the original report to the Anthropological Society. However, in the much more detailed article published in the August 1861 *Bulletins de la Société Anatomique de Paris* (1861c), Broca obviously had the time to make a more precise determination. (This is the report which is most often referred to. It has been translated into English in Von Bonin, 1960.) In this article, Broca has carefully examined the lesion in detail and reports a great deal of information about the lesion site. But he was most interested in determining the point where the lesion began, since it was degenerative in nature. He summarises the lesion site, noting (1861c, p. 353):

If one wished to make a more precise determination, one would remark that the third frontal convolution is the one which presented the most extensive loss of tissue ... that the second convolution or the middle convolution, although profoundly affected, still conserves its continuity in its more internal position, and that consequently, in all probability, it is in the third convolution that the disease began.

Broca summarises his position vis-à-vis the phrenologists in this second report (p. 341):

It is thus much less important to indicate the state of the disease as to say which are the diseased convolutions. This type of description is without a doubt less convenient than the other, since classical treatises of anatomy have not generally promoted the study of the cerebral convolutions which the phrenologists themselves made the greatest error in neglecting.

Broca's second case went a good deal further in localising the responsible area with greater precision, since this time the lesion responsible for the aphasia was, in Broca's words (Broca, 1861a, p. 404, original italics), "incomparably more circumscribed than that which existed for the patient Tan [i.e. Leborgne]; but comparing the two specimens, one observes that the center of the lesion is *identically the same* in the two cases." Upon post-mortem examination of this second case, in which the aphasia had suddenly appeared only a year and a half before the patient's death, Broca observed (p. 403) "a superficial lesion in the left frontal lobe, immediately below the anterior extremity of the Sylvian fissure." He further described (p. 405) the lesion for the second patient in the following manner: "Consequently, one can affirm that in our patient the aphemia had been the result of a deep lesion, but very neatly circumscribed, of the second and third frontal convolutions, in the portion of their posterior third." Then, he concluded (p. 406):

In the two cases, the second frontal convolution was less profoundly altered than the third; it is permitted to conclude that the latter had been, in all probability, the principal site of the primitive lesion. Two cases are few when it is a question of resolving one of the most obscure and controversial cases in cerebral physiology; I cannot however prevent myself from saying, until more amply informed, that the integrity of the third frontal convolution (and perhaps of the second) seems indispensable for the exercise of the faculty of articulated language.

Broca has quickly honed in on the third frontal convolution as the responsible target, even though he admits that there is only scanty evidence at this point. Here it can be seen that Broca was sticking his neck out somewhat in imputing the third frontal convolution, but it was a risk that paid off in the long term.

Although Broca can be seen to have changed the course of history with his contribution to the transformation of phrenology to neuropsychology, he still makes a minor concession to classical phrenology noting that "The original site of the disease, consequently, corresponded in the two cases to the same point on the side of the skull" (Broca, 1861a, p. 407). Thus, Broca can be seen as making a last tip of the hat to phrenology, as he also largely leaves it permanently behind.

Of course, like all good scientists, Broca went on to seek more evidence to support his theory. By 1863, two years later, he had already gathered together ten cases in support of the left frontal lobe (referred to in Broca, 1865, p. 378) which crystallised his position as the founding father of neuropsychology.

In 1984, Signoret, Castaigne, Lhermitte, Abelanet, and Lavorel under-took a C.T. scan of Leborgne's brain, then having recently been rediscovered. This article presents a number of photographs of the brain specimen. (There is also a photograph of the preserved specimen in Schiller, 1989.) The C.T. scan allowed them to confirm that, despite the extensiveness of the damage, there is no lesion involving Wernicke's area and that the lesion extends subcortically, involving insula and basal ganglia—especially the lenticular nucleus.

The fact that the lesion also extended subcortically is interesting to note in light of contemporary discussion on Broca's aphasia. Some researchers have insisted that subcortical damage is also necessary for the entire syndrome known as "Broca's aphasia" (Mohr, 1976; Mohr, Pessin, Finkelstein, Duncan, & Davis, 1978). Other researchers have shown that the syndrome known as Broca's aphasia can result from a lesion outside of Broca's area (Dronkers, Shapiro, Redfern, & Knight, 1992). There have been some recent attempts to characterise more precisely just what symptoms of Broca's aphasia are related to particular cortical and subcortical lesion sites using C.T. scans (Alexander, Naeser, & Palumbo, 1987; Baum, Blumstein, Naeser, & Palumbo, 1990).

Just because Broca promoted the role of the left hemisphere in articulated language does not mean that he ignored that of the right hemisphere. He pointed out (1865, p. 385) that in the early stages of the human embryo "the development of the left hemisphere is in advance of that of the right hemisphere." He even advanced the notion that the right hemisphere might be recruited to compensate (p. 389):

Similar to the way one sees with a single eye, one hears with a single ear, one ought to be able to speak with a single hemisphere... Why is it thus that the individual rendered aphemic by a partial or total destruction of the left third frontal convolution, does not learn to speak with the right hemisphere?

He answers himself to some degree pointing out (p. 390) that the weakened cognitive state of most aphemics "prevents them from learning to speak exclusively with the right hemisphere, which up till then played only an accessory role in the function of expression by articulated language." None the less, Broca (p. 390) questions:

> Then, how does one know that the aphemic is not capable of learning with the right hemisphere that he retains? Has one attempted to undertake his education? Given his lessons everyday, every hour, every occasion for help which in the long run one ends up giving in order to make the child speak? As for myself, I am convinced that, without returning to aphemics the part of their intelligence that perished with the part of their brain, one could, with enough perseverance, treating them with the infatigable consistency of the mother that teaches her infant to speak, one could, I say, obtain considerable results.

Not only has Broca been the first to point out the potential compensatory role of the right hemisphere here but, arguably, he was the first to point out the potential role for aphasia rehabilitation. He continues the discussion (p. 390) by indicating his own efforts with a patient in his service (who appears to be Lelong): "When I was at Bicêtre, I kept an aphemic for several months in my rooms; often, during a visit, I devoted a few minutes to him and finished by notably extending his vocabulary." So, not being content simply to indicate the potential role for re-education, he also seems to have been the first to undertake an effort in this direction, albeit limited.

Broca can also be seen as having originally observed the relationship between handedness and hemispheric specialisation (Henderson, 1986). He was the first to have alluded to the innate nature of handedness and its neurological antecedent.

Even though Paul Broca was a pioneer, he was still not without critics. For example, in 1863 Dax junior claimed that his father had been the first to proclaim the role of the left hemisphere in speech in 1836 (Lecours et al., 1987). Broca defended himself on this point in 1865 (p. 379): "I do not wish to leave the impression any longer that I sinned by ignorance or voluntary omission. The existence of the paper of Dax the father, before the mention of it made by his son, was as unknown in Montpellier as it was in Paris." He points out that not only was there no written trace of Dax senior's oral presentation, but 20 doctors who were then in Montpellier had no knowledge of it either being read or published somewhere.

Trousseau began his assault of Broca's term "aphemia" in 1864. The result was that today, almost ironically, it is Trousseau's term that is associated with Broca's name (Ryalls, 1984). While Trousseau may have won the battle over terminology, history has shown us that it is Broca who won the war. For while early neuropsychology actually has several founding fathers, it is still Broca's name at the forefront—a prominent position which he secured largely on the basis of his first two clinical cases reviewed here.

One can question why it is that after over 130 years, even though there are several founding fathers of modern neuropsychology, Broca is remembered above all of them. The main reason is that all of the essential features of the syndrome were present in these first two clinical cases: the sudden loss of speech resulting from a lesion in the anterior portion of the left hemisphere, despite preserved intelligence. Certainly the fact that Broca left behind such well-argued published traces of his discoveries, as well as his unique ability to bring together very different disciplines such as medicine, anthropology, and neurology in new and different ways, ensured his place in history.

REFERENCES

Alexander, M., Naeser, M., & Palumbo, C. (1987). Correlations of subcortical CT lesion sites and aphasia profiles. *Brain, 110*, 961–991.

Baum, S., Blumstein, S., Naeser, M., & Palumbo, C. (1990). Temporal dimensions of consonant and vowel production: An acoustic and CT scan analysis of aphasic speech. *Brain and Language, 39*, 33–56.

Blumstein, S. (1991). Phonological aspects of aphasia. In M.T. Sarno (Ed.), *Acquired aphasia* (2nd Ed.). New York: Academic Press.

Broca, P. (1861a). Nouvelle observation d'aphémie produite par une lésion de la moité postérieur des deuxième et troisième circonvolutions frontales. *Bulletins de la Société Anatomique de Paris, 36*, 398–407.

Broca, P. (1861b). Perte de la parole, ramollissment chronique et destruction partielle du lobe antérieur gauche du cerveau. *Bulletins de la Société Anthropologique de Paris, 2*, 235–238.

Broca, P. (1861c). Rémarques sur le siège de la faculté du langage articulé suivies d'une observation de'aphémie (perte de la parole). *Bulletins de la Société Anatomique de Paris, 36*, 330–357.

Broca, P. (1865). Sur le siège de la faculté du language articulé. *Bulletins de la Société Anthropologique de Paries, 6*, 377–393.

Dronkers, N., Shapiro, J., Redfern, B., & Knight, R. (1992). The role of Broca's area in Broca's aphasia. *Journal of Clinical Neuropsychology, 14*, 52–53.

Henderson, W. (1986). Paul Broca's less heralded contributions to aphasia research. *Archives of Neurology, 43*, 609–612.

Lecours, A.R., Nespoulous, J.-L., & Pioger, D. (1987). Jacques Lordat or the birth of cognitive neuropsychology. In E. Keller & M. Gopnik (Eds.), *Motor and sensory processes of language*. Hillsdale, NJ: Lawrence Erlbaum Associates Inc.

Mohr, J. (1976). Broca's area and Broca's aphasia. In H. Whitaker & H. Whitaker (Eds.), *Studies in neurolinguistics (Vol. 1)*. New York: Academic Press.

Mohr, J., Pessin, M., Finkelstein, S., Funkenstein, H., Duncan, G., & Davis, K. (1978). Broca aphasia: Pathologic and clinical. *Neurology, 28*, 311–324.

Ryalls, J. (1984). Where does the term "aphasia" come from? *Brain and Language, 21*, 358–363.

Schiller, F. (1979). *Paul Broca: Founder of French anthropology, explorer of the brain*. Berkeley, CA: University of California Press.

Signoret, J.-L., Castaigne, P., Lhermitte, F., Abelanet, R., & Lavorel, P. (1984). Rediscovery of Leborgne's brain: Anatomical description with CT scan. *Brain and Language, 22*, 303–319.

Trousseau, A. (1864, 12th January). De l'aphasie, maladie décrite récemment sous le nom impropre d'aphémie. *Gazette des Hôpitaux, 30.*

Von Bonin, G. (1960). *Some papers on the cerebral cortex.* Springfield, IL: Charles C. Thomas. (Chapter 3: Paul Broca: Remarks on the seat of the faculty of articulate language, followed by an observation of aphemia).

18 Phineas Gage: A Case for All Reasons

Malcolm Macmillan[1]
School of Psychology, Deakin University, Burwood, Australia.

> *In investigating the reports on diseases and injuries of the brain I am constantly being amazed at the inexactitude and distortion to which they are subjected by men who have some pet theory to support.*
> —David Ferrier (writing to Henry Pickering Bowditch about Gage on 12th October, 1877)

Phineas Gage is both a medical curiosity and a famous victim of brain injury, possibly the most famous. Over the years his symptoms have been interpreted in strikingly different ways: for and against Gall's doctrine of localisation, as negative evidence in the aphasia controversy, as resembling the changes produced in monkeys by ablation of the frontal lobes, as indications for frontal brain surgery, and as contributing to the development of psychosurgery. It is the paucity of data about Gage which so allows his case to be used to support these various "pet theories". Here I present as full an account of his case as possible and outline the main uses to which it has been put before concluding that it supports very few neuropsychological generalisations.

PHINEAS GAGE

Gage's Accident

When he was 25 years' old, Phineas P. Gage was employed by the Rutland and Burlington Railroad as foreman of a gang of workers constructing part of the line between Bellow's Falls and Burlington. Gage's duties included setting and firing the explosive charges. For packing the charges he used a specially forged crowbar-like implement called a tamping iron, 3 feet 7 inches long, weighing $13\frac{1}{4}$ pounds, and varying in diameter from $\frac{1}{4}$ inch at the thinner end to $1\frac{1}{4}$ inches at the wider. On the 13th September, 1848 his gang seems to have been blasting a cutting through a large rocky outcrop or ledge about 1 kilometre south-east of Duttonsville (now Cavendish) in Vermont. At 4.30pm, an accidental explosion blew the tamping iron through his skull. It entered, pointed end first, under the left zygomatic arch and made its exit near the median line, close to the junction of the coronal and sagittal sutures.

The tamping iron passed through Gage's head, landing some 30 metres behind him. During its passage, Gage was knocked over. He may have lost consciousness momentarily and there may have been convulsive leg movements. He then walked to an ox-cart in which, while sitting up, chatting, and making an entry in his time book, he was driven to the hotel where he resided. There Gage alighted and sat on the verandah for about half an hour until Edward Higginson Williams, M.D. arrived from nearby Proctorsville. Gage greeted Williams with one of the great understatements of medical history, "Doctor, here is business enough for you."

Williams confirmed Gage's claim that his injury had been caused by the iron and gave what help he could until John Martyn (or Martin) Harlow, M.D., the Duttonsville physician, arrived about an hour later. Haemorrhaging was initially profuse but had ceased by the morning of the 15th and over about the next 12 weeks Harlow and Gage fought a stormy battle against the other effects of the injury and later infection. By 18th November, Harlow recorded "[Gage] is walking about the house again; says he feels no pain in the head, and appears to be in a way of recovering if he can be controlled" (Harlow, 1848). He was well enough to return home to Lebanon, New Hampshire seven days later. On 3rd January, 1849, Harlow described him as "walking about the house, and riding out, improving both mentally and physically, fully recovered and out and about" (Harlow, 1849). His surviving such a terrible and freakish accident established him as a medical curiosity (Macmillan, 1986).

Gage Pre-accident

Harlow's first report of 1848 contains very little about Gage's behaviour and mental qualities before the accident: he was "of middle stature, vigorous physical organization, temperate habits, and possessed of considerable energy of character" (Harlow, 1848). There was not much more in his second report of 1868. Gage was physically:

> a perfectly healthy, strong and active young man, twenty five years of age, five feet six inches in height, average weight one hundred and sixty pounds, possessing an iron will as well as an iron frame; muscular system unusually well developed—having had scarcely a day's illness from his childhood. (Harlow, 1848)

Educationally and psychologically:

> although untrained in the schools, he possessed a well-balanced mind, and was looked upon by those who knew him as a shrewd, smart businessman, very energetic and persistent in executing all his plans of operation.

His contractors "regarded him as the most efficient and capable foreman in their employ."

I have found it extraordinarily difficult to extend this meagre baseline. Phineas P. Gage was probably born on 9th July, 1823, most likely in Lebanon, New Hampshire, the first son of five children born to Jesse Eaton Gage and Hannah Trussell (or Trusel) Sweetland (or Sweatland or Swetland).[2] We have no contemporaneous data on his early life but Gage almost certainly grew up on a farm in, or close to, Lebanon itself. He probably attended primary school because, as an adult, he could write well enough to keep records. From the circumstances of the accident, Gage was almost certainly right-handed and probably left-hemisphere dominant. Of his behaviour, an 1851 report says he was "quiet and respectful" (Anonymous, 1851).

Gage in the Immediate Post-Accident Period

By combining the slightly different selections from Harlow's original case notes in his 1848 and 1868 reports, we can form some picture of the significant behavioural and mental changes in Gage during the immediate post-accident period. These were minimal. On the evening of the accident, Harlow noted that Gage's "sensorial powers" were unimpaired, his mind was "clear", that he did "not wish to see his friends as he shall be at work in a day or two," and could give details of relatives in Lebanon. He recognised his mother and uncle early the next morning and was "rational." Apart from the episodes of delirium and coma, the most striking feature that Harlow notes is Gage's rationality.

However, about three weeks after the accident, shortly after the effects of a frontal abscess had subsided, ominous signs emerged. On 6th October Harlow recorded:

> General appearance somewhat improved ... more wakeful ... calls for his pants and desires to be helped out of bed, though when lying on his back cannot raise his head from the pillow ... Appears demented, or in a state of mental hebetude. (Harlow, 1868)

Five days later, exactly twenty-eight days after the accident:

> Intellectual faculties brightening. When I asked him how long since he was injured, he replied, "four weeks this afternoon at $4\frac{1}{2}$ o'clock." Relates the

manner in which it occurred and how he came to the house. He keeps the day of the week and time of day in his mind. Says he knows more than half of those who enquire after him. (Harlow, 1848)

However:

Does not estimate size or money accurately, though he has memory as perfect as ever. He would not take $1,000 for a few pebbles which he took from an ancient river bed where he was at work. (Harlow, 1848)

Two days later, the ominous features began to overshadow the benign:

Remembers passing and past events correctly, as well as before the injury. Intellectual manifestations feeble, being exceedingly capricious and childish, but with a will as indomitable as ever; is particularly obstinate; will not yield to restraint when it conflicts with his desires. (Harlow, 1868)

These features must have taken some time to become permanent because, when Dr John Barnard Swet Jackson of Boston travelled to Lebanon, in early August, 1849 to see Gage, he learned of only one psychological oddity. Gage (Jackson, 1849, Case 1777) had been:

weak and childish on getting home but now appears well in mind, exc. that his memory seems somewhat impaired; a stranger wd notice nothing peculiar.

Jackson obtained this information from Phineas' mother and brother-in-law because Gage himself was in Montpelier attempting "to get work on the Rail Road."

Dr Henry Jacob Bigelow made no comment on any of the psychological features when he examined Gage over a period of some weeks, later that year, just before he became the Professor of Surgery at Harvard.[3] After pronouncing the case genuine, Bigelow merely added that Gage had "quite recovered in his faculties of body and mind, with the loss only of the sight of the injured eye" Bigelow (1850). Bigelow represented the case simply as one of "the co-existence of a lesion so grave with an inconsiderable disturbance of function."

Gage After "Recovery"

In April, 1849, about six months after the accident, Gage returned to Cavendish. Harlow then said, "His physical health is good, and I am inclined to say that he has fully recovered." While Harlow's opinion is consistent with what Gage himself told the pseudonymous author of a letter published in the *National Eagle* (Claremont, New Hampshire) of 29th March, 1849 (Macmillan, 1986), it may not be entirely correct. Jackson's entry on Gage seems to indicate a diminished physical capacity at about that time:

> abt. February he was able to do a little work abt. ye horses & barn, feedg. ye cattle &c.; that as ye time for ploughing came he was able to do half a days work after that & bore it well. (Jackson, 1849, Case 1777)

And, from a description of Gage in *The American Phrenological Journal*, we know the psychological and behavioural changes were known early: "after the man recovered, and while recovering, he was gross, profane, coarse, and vulgar, to such a degree that his society was intolerable to decent people" (Anonymous, 1851). He was, this report went on, wanting in "respect and kindness" and the brain damage had given "the animal propensities absolute control in the character." It is very probable that Harlow was the source of this description (Macmillan, 1986. cf. Sizer, 1882, p. 194).

Gage never regained his job as foreman. Twenty years later, Harlow explained that his contractors: "considered the change in his mind so marked that they could not give him his place again" (Harlow, 1868, 1869). In about 160 words, Harlow set out the basis for their decision:

> The equilibrium or balance, so to speak, between his intellectual faculties and his animal propensities, seems to have been destroyed. He is fitful, irreverent, indulging at times in the grossest profanity (which was not previously his custom), manifesting but little deference for his fellows, impatient of restraint or advice when it conflicts with his desires, at times pertinaciously obstinate, yet capricious and vacillating, devising many plans of future operation, which are no sooner arranged than they are abandoned in turn for others appearing more feasible. A child in his intellectual capacity and manifestations, he has the animal passions of a strong man. Previous to his injury, although untrained in the schools, he possessed a well-balanced mind, and was looked upon by those who knew him as a shrewd, smart businessman, very energetic and persistent in executing all his plans of operation. In this regard his mind was radically changed, so decidedly that his friends and acquaintances said he was "no longer Gage." (Harlow, 1868, 1869)

When summing up, Harlow added:

> Mentally the recovery was only partial, his intellectual faculties being decidedly impaired, but not totally lost; nothing like dementia, but they were enfeebled in their manifestations, his mental operations being perfect in kind, but not in degree or quantity. (Harlow, 1868, 1869)

It was these changes, most of which Harlow observed for himself, which established Gage's fame as a victim of brain injury.

From Phineas' mother Harlow also learned that Phineas had been employed for some seven years after 1852, in my view possibly continuously, "in caring for horses, and often driving a coach heavily laden and drawn by six horses." After his return from South America he was in permanent employment except for a four-month period between what was apparently his first seizure and his death.[4] He had also become accustomed "to entertain his little nephews and nieces with the most fabulous recitals of his wonderful feats and hair-breadth escapes, without any foundation except in his fancy" (Harlow, 1868, 1869). In this 1868 report, Harlow also mentioned that Gage had returned to Lebanon 20 years before "in a close carriage," that is, in the enclosed and sometimes padded vehicle used for transporting the insane.

GAGE'S INJURIES

The differences in the reports of the injuries to Gage's skull and brain are such as to make it impossible to establish which parts of his brain were damaged or destroyed.

The Skull

Harlow's first report gave a very detailed account of the supposed passage of the tamping iron through the skull. It was driven:

> against the left side of the face, immediately anterior to the angle of the inferior maxillary bone. Taking a direction upward and backward toward the median line, it penetrated the integuments, the masseter and temporal muscles, passed under the zygomatic arch, and (probably) fracturing the temporal portion of the sphenoid bone, and the floor of the orbit of the left eye, entered the cranium, passing through the anterior left lobe of the cerebrum, and made its exit in the median line, at the junction of the coronal and sagittal sutures, lacerating the longitudinal sinus, fracturing the parietal and frontal bones extensively, breaking up considerable portions of brain, and protruding the globe of the left eye from its socket by nearly one half of its diameter. (Harlow, 1848)

Harlow's account was based on very privileged observation: he explored the wound by placing one index finger in the opening in the skull until it "received the other finger in like manner" from the wound in the cheek and he retrieved various large and identifiable pieces of bone from within the cranium.

However, from the beginning there was significant disagreement over the passage of the tamping iron. Edward Elisha Phelps, M.D., Professor of Anatomy at Dartmouth Medical College (Hanover, New Hampshire), told Jackson he had examined Gage about six weeks after the accident. Jackson's record of Phelps' conclusion was:

He thinks ye centre of ye wound on ye top of ye head must have been abt. $\frac{1}{2}$ inch in front of coronal suture & 1 inch *to ye left of ye median line* (Dr. H. says at ye juncture of ye sutures). He thinks ye long. sinus was not wounded (as acc. to Dr. H.). (Jackson, 1849, Case 1777, my italics)

When Bigelow (1850) examined Gage about a year after the accident, he came to a slightly different conclusion. He drilled a hole in "a common skull, in which the zygomatic arches [were] barely visible from above," from the "left angle of the lower jaw" to "the median line of the cranium just in front of the junction of the sagittal and coronal sutures" (Bigelow, 1850). When he enlarged the apertures until the iron could be passed through them, the damaged bony structures corresponded to those Harlow had described. However, Bigelow's illustration shows the tamping iron seemingly emerging more anteriorly *and more to the right* than in Harlow's account.

The Brain

All that Harlow's 1848 report contained about damage to Gage's brain is included in his description of the tamping iron as passing "through the anterior left lobe of the cerebrum" and his mention of it "breaking up considerable portions of brain" before "lacerating" the longitudinal sinus and "fracturing the parietal and frontal bones." Twenty years later he was more specific and extensive:

> The iron ... entered the left cerebrum at the fissure of Sylvius, possibly puncturing the cornu of the left lateral ventricle, and in its passage and exit must have produced serious lesion of the brain substance—the anterior and middle left lobes of the cerebrum—disintegrating and pulpifying it, drawing out a considerable quantity of it at the opening in the top of the head, and lacerating unquestionably the upper aspect of the falx major and the superior longitudinal sinus. (Harlow, 1868)

Harlow may again have been in a privileged position. The quadrangular opening in the front and top of the skull was almost $3\frac{1}{2}$ by 2 inches in diameter and it is just possible his initial examination allowed him to sense which parts of the brain were intact. He may also have been able to observe the brain when he personally changed the dressings and when he removed the "fungi." In his 1868 report, Harlow adduced "*the fact*" that the right hemisphere "*was left intact*" as accounting for Gage's "mental operations being perfect in kind, but not in degree or quantity" (my italics).

Despite his not having seen Gage until well after the skull had "perfectly healed," Bigelow's conclusions were similar but more definite:

> It is obvious that a considerable portion of the brain must have been carried away; that while a portion of its lateral substance may have remained intact,

the whole central part of the left anterior lobe, and the front of the sphenoidal or middle lobe must have been lacerated and destroyed. (Bigelow, 1850)

There was one very important difference between him and Harlow: the iron in emerging *must have largely impinged upon the right cerebral lobe*, lacerating the falx and the longitudinal sinus (Bigelow, 1850, my italics). Later authors have also disagreed over the extent, if any, of damage to the right hemisphere.

It is not possible for us to know in any real detail which parts of Gage's brain were injured or destroyed. Gage died of epilepsy on 21st May, 1860, $11\frac{1}{2}$ years after the accident.[5] And, as Harlow said in 1868, it was to be "regretted that an autopsy could not have been had, so that the precise condition of the encephalon at the time of his death might have been known." Nor would anything have been revealed about the brain when the body was exhumed several years later.

I do not believe two recent attempts to reconstruct the damage to Gage's brain requires this opinion to be modified. From their April, 1982 CAT scan of the skull, the Tylers concluded the damage was to the left anterior frontal lobe, part of the tip of the left temporal lobe, part of the anterior horn of the lateral ventricle on the left, the head of the caudate nucleus and the putamen, the superior sagittal sinus, and the right hemisphere, including parts of the right superior frontal and cingulate gyri (Tyler, personal communication, 8th October, 1993; Tyler & Tyler, 1982).

More recently, Hanna Damasio and her colleagues also attempted to reconstruct the damage to Gage's brain (H. Damasio, Grabowski, Frank, Galaburda, & A.M. Damasio, 1994. See also A.M. Damasio, 1993). From measurements, X-rays, and photographs of Gage's skull, Damasio and her colleagues generated a three-dimensional computer image of the skull and then mapped the entry and exit points of the tamping iron on to it. Entry points consistent with the known anatomical damage were then determined and by connecting them to the exit points, seven "acceptable" trajectories were generated. Two of these were rejected because, by hitting the anterior horn of the left lateral ventricle, "they would not have been compatible with survival" given that the "resulting massive infection would not have been controllable in the pre-antibiotic era." A "most likely trajectory" was chosen from the remaining five and the passage of the tamping iron along it traced through a model of Gage's brain deduced from the dimensions of the skull. Damasio et al. (1994) concluded that the damage to Gage's left hemisphere involved "the anterior half of the orbital frontal cortex ... the polar and anterior mesial frontal cortices ... and the anterior-most sector of the anterior cingulate gyrus." Right hemisphere damage was similar but less marked in the orbital frontal region.

Despite the skill with which these studies were conducted, significant uncertainties remain about the effects of damage to the brain. First, there must always be some guesswork in estimating the passage of the tamping iron through the skull. Second, individual differences in the position of the brain inside the skull and in the location of functions within the brain necessarily result in uncertainty about the passage of the iron through the brain and the areas damaged. Until double-blind studies of real cases with injuries similar to Gage's have been conducted, the validity of these kinds of reconstructions remains to be established.

GAGE AND THE LOCALISATION DEBATE

After about 1840 the framework within which the localisation debate was conducted changed from that of Gall's cranioscopy to that of sensory-motor physiology. According to this conception, distinct functions were localised as sensory-motor reflexes at levels of the nervous system below the medulla oblongata. The extension of this conception to the brain was made primarily by the clinical observations of Broca and Hughlings Jackson and the experimental studies begun by Fritsch and Hitzig and extended by Ferrier (Macmillan, 1986; Young, 1970).

Gage Contra Gall?

Barker (1993) shows that Harlow's report of Gage's failures to estimate size or money accurately and to overvalue pebbles are probably his way of drawing attention to the destruction of the faculty which, according to Gall, allowed the comparison of number and size. Harlow's attributing Gage's recovery to one hemisphere feebly taking over the functions of the other may have a similar phrenological basis. Barker also notes that Bigelow's failure to report on the changes in Gage, which he must have noticed, was almost certainly due to his opposition to Gall's doctrine.

Dalton's early and influential mention of Gage in the medical literature on localisation may be similarly motivated. Dalton did not mention the alterations and sited his remarks between his discussion of the "insensibility" of the hemispheres and Flourens' ablation experiments and before attacking Gall (Dalton, 1859, pp. 359–363; Macmillan, 1986). While Dalton may simply not have known of the changes, he could have known of them, either from an 1850 medical report (Barker, 1993) or the 1851 phrenological discussion (Anonymous, 1851). Others certainly neglected the changes in order to attack phrenology (Barker, 1993).

Gage Contra Broca?

The second arena in which Gage figured is that of aphasia. There his case was counted as evidence, usually as the main evidence, against Broca. To Sequin (1868), Hammond (1871), Dupuy (1873), and Bowditch (1874), Gage had no language disturbance despite what seemed to be a left-sided frontal lesion. David Ferrier probably caused this use of Gage's case to be abandoned (Macmillan, 1986).

Gage Contra Ferrier?

When Dupuy reviewed the localisation literature in 1877 he gave particular attention to Ferrier's *Functions of the Brain* (1876). He represented Ferrier's opinion as "that only the anterior part of [Gage's] frontal lobe was destroyed" (Dupuy, 1877). After examining Gage's skull, Dupuy concluded that the iron had not only destroyed:

> the left Sylvian artery, which sends a special branch to Broca's convolution, but it actually destroyed the greater part of the island of Reil.

He therefore claimed Gage as "the first and most striking case of destruction of the so-called speech centre without consequent aphasia" (Dupuy, 1877. cf. Dupuy, 1873, pp. 31–33).

Gage Pro Ferrier

When Ferrier ablated the "prefrontal region" in his monkeys he produced no sensory-motor symptoms. However, the monkeys lost their curiosity and interest:

> they remained apathetic, or dull, or dozed off to sleep, responding only to the sensations or impressions of the moment, or varying their listlessness with restless and purposeless wanderings to and fro. While not actually deprived of intelligence, they had lost, to all appearance, the faculty of attentive and intelligent observation. (Ferrier, 1876, pp. 231–232)

Ferrier then used his theory of a frontal lobe inhibitory function to explain the changes.

Ferrier based his theory of inhibition on that of Alexander Bain, with whom it seems to have been original (Macmillan, 1992a, 1992b, 1993). In Ferrier's version, all thought derived from sensory input and necessarily involved "throwing into action, but in an inhibited or suppressed manner" the motor response (1876, p. 285). Choice between ideas was only possible if the motor components were inhibited. The "power of fixing the attention and concentrating consciousness depends ... on inhibition of the movement" (p. 286). Consequently, the inhibitory centres formed "the chief factor in the control of consciousness and the control of ideation." Removal of the frontal lobes in the monkeys caused:

> a form of mental degradation which may be reduced in ultimate analysis to the loss of the faculty of attention. (Ferrier, 1876, p. 288)

Ferrier had cited Gage only as an example of brain destruction without symptoms. He made no comparison of his behaviour with that of the monkeys (1876, p. 232; cf. pp. 125–126), probably because he did not then know Gage had changed (Macmillan, 1986, forthcoming).

After Dupuy's attack, Ferrier sought out the facts. Ironically, it was Henry Pickering Bowditch, Professor of Physiology at Harvard, whom Ferrier asked if the exit point indicated whether the tamping iron had crossed the mid-line and if it had emerged more to the front than in Bigelow's reconstruction. If so "the left anterior lobe was alone injured" (Ferrier, 1877–1879, 28th December, 1877). It is likely Bowditch agreed and he seems to have sent Ferrier a copy of Harlow's second (1868) report, which described the changes. He certainly sent photographs of the skull and Harlow's woodcuts (Ferrier, 1877–1879, 15th January and 10th February, 1878; Ferrier, 1878a, and footnote p. 445). Ferrier was then able to make a devastating reply to Dupuy in the first of his 1878 Gulstonian Lectures. He told his audience they would clearly see on the slides of the woodcuts that:

> the whole lesion is situated anterior to the coronal suture. If you will now compare the track of the bar through the skull and brain with [Turner's diagram of the brain in situ] ... you will, I think, have no doubt in convincing yourselves that the whole track is included within that region ... I have described as prefrontal. (Ferrier, 1878a, 1878b, pp. 29–30)

Ferrier also presented Harlow's complete account of the changes in Gage and now used his 1876 theory of inhibition to explain them (Macmillan, 1992a). In so doing he gave Gage the most prominent place among his examples of the loss of inhibitory function because of frontal damage (Ferrier, 1878a; 1878b, p. 37).

Although Ferrier did not hold his inhibitory thesis for long, others took it up to explain "mental symptoms" and to guide brain surgeons into the frontal areas (Macmillan, in press).

GAGE AND FRONTAL LOBE SURGERY

Brain surgery is conventionally dated as beginning on the 25th November, 1884 with the operation by Bennett and Godlee (1882–1885, 1885). However, some four and a half years earlier, Macewen operated in the prefrontal area, very probably because of Ferrier's extension of his findings to the case of Phineas Gage. Macewen claims to have taken his patient's "mental" symptoms of "obstruction of intelligence, slowness of comprehension, [and] want of mental vigour" as alone pointing to "the probability of a lesion in the left frontal lobe" (Macewen, 1881). On operating, he found and removed a tumour of the dura mater which had spread "all over the anterior two-thirds of the frontal lobe." There was complete recovery.

There is some problem about Macewen's claim to have so used the "mental symptoms" (and to have planned an even earlier operation on the basis of Broca's language thesis. cf. Stone, 1991). Nevertheless, largely because Ferrier himself (1891–1892) gave Macewen "The honour of having actually led the way in human [cerebral] surgery," I have accepted Macewen's later reports as giving accurate accounts of how he had originally used the diagnostic indicators (Macewen, 1879, 1881, 1888. cf. Macmillan, in press).

Inhibition, Gage, and Frontal Surgery

While some doubt may be allowed about Macewen's knowledge of Phineas Gage, there can be no doubt that Gage's case was at the forefront of other and later operations in the frontal areas. His pre-eminence seems to have resulted from M. Allen Starr's comparative study of the effects of different kinds of lesions and tumours (Starr, 1884a, 1884b).

According to Starr, in half of the cases of frontal lesions there was a "decided mental instability" best described "as a loss of self-control, and a consequent change of character" (Starr, 1884a). Gage was Starr's standard and his explanation clearly drew on an inhibitory thesis very similar to Ferrier's although he did not mention Ferrier by name (Macmillan, in press). Inhibition enabled one "to fix attention upon a subject, and hold it there" (Starr, 1884a). Partial destruction of the frontal lobes led to:

a lack of that self-control ... shown by an inability to fix the attention, to follow a continuous train of thought, or to conduct intellectual processes. (Starr, 1884a)

Whenever frontal lobe lesions were suspected, Starr recommended seeing if the patient's reason, judgement, and character or behaviour had changed.

About eight years later, Starr used his recommendations in planning what he claimed was the first operation on the frontal lobes "directly dictated by the existence of mental symptoms" (McBurney & Starr, 1893). Starr summarised the patient's "mental symptoms" with phrases like "dullness of thought," "general hebetude," an uncharacteristic "aversion to work,", "slowness of mental activity," and "it took him longer to express his ideas." Starr also observed "it was not easy for him to hold his attention to any subject continuously for any length of time." On operating, McBurney found a very large sarcoma in "the posterior part of the second frontal convolution, just anterior to its junction with the anterior central convolution" (McBurney & Starr, 1893). Unfortunately the patient survived the operation by only eight hours.

Not every case so directly confirmed frontal localisation. As early as 1885, only four years after Starr's recommendation and in the very year of the original Bennett and Godlee operation, Gowers said that while "the mental change" was "rather more frequent" in frontal lesions, sometimes taking "the form of chronic insanity," the changes were "neither characteristic nor invariable" (1885, p. 146. cf. Gowers, 1879). Then, in two major addresses forming part of a symposium on Cerebral Localisation in its Practical Relations, held on 19th September, 1888, as part of the First Triennial Congress of American Physicians and Surgeons, Mills and Ferrier made similar points (Ferrier, 1889–1890; Mills, 1889–1890).

Inhibition and "Mental Symptoms"

There was another, and in my view, more serious problem: what was meant by a "mental symptom"? The point is seen especially clearly if we examine Ferrier's and Starr's descriptions of what they thought was caused by the loss of the inhibitory function.

Although Gage was impatient and showed, at least in some social circumstances, a lack of inhibition, can we attribute his obstinacy, capriciousness, and vacillation to that lack? May we not entertain similar doubts about the four other frontal cases Ferrier cited? Their behaviour ranged from that of Baraduc's patient, who was in a "state of complete dementia, marching about restlessly the whole day, picking up whatever came in his way, mute, and quite oblivious of all the wants of nature, and requiring to be tended like a child," to that of Davidson's who seemed to understand everything but "every action he performed left the impression ... that it was purely automatic" (Ferrier, 1878b, pp. 446–447).

Starr's cases were even more varied. Thus, he classed the "stupid and listless" behaviour of a post-suicidal depressive with what he called Gage's irritability, excitability, and emotionality, as showing "a deficiency of self-control" (Starr, 1884a). The symptoms of Starr's other cases are just as difficult to relate to the simple loss of an inhibitory or attentional function (Macmillan, in press).

GAGE AND PSYCHOSURGERY

In his 1888 address Mills (Mills, 1889–1890) also commented extensively on two then recent operations as opening "a possible new field for surgical interference in insanity." Bennett and Gould (1887) and Macewen (1888) attempted to cure or relieve visual psychiatric symptoms by modifications to the angular gyrus. The importance of the cases, Mills observed (1889–1890), was their raising "the question of the propriety of excising cortical areas in insanity."

Mills could not know, of course, that Burckhardt was already planning such excisions. However, as with the later operations by Moniz and Freeman, Gage probably played only an insignificant part in the one Burckhardt performed in the frontal area.

Burckhardt

On 29th December, 1888, Burckhardt operated on the first of six patients. All his operations were designed to modify purely psychiatric symptoms but only in one, a patient suffering from "dementia paralytica" with episodes of excitement, seemingly triggered by verbal auditory hallucinations, did he give consideration to the frontal lobes (Burckhardt, 1891). Dementia paralytica was, in his view, a disease with a large number of psychic symptoms due to a malfunction of the frontal lobe. He therefore decided to remove the lateral edge of the first and the foot of the second frontal convolutions, that is, excisions anterior to Broca's area. The operation on this patient was performed on 17th April, 1889 and, although he seemed less excited, he developed epilepsy and no further surgery was conducted (Burckhardt, 1891).

Why Burckhardt decided that dementical paralytica was particularly associated with "psychic symptoms" is not very clear. Nor is it clear, unless it was through an implicit consideration of Gage's "mental symptoms," why he thought "psychic symptoms" involved the frontal lobes. All we can be certain of is that Burckhardt did not mention Gage (Macmillan, in press), even though he knew the localisation literature very well (Whitaker, Stemmer, & Joanette, 1993).

Moniz

In the 1930s Moniz devised the operation he called prefrontal leucotomy. Gage was not explicitly mentioned among the "considerations" which led to the procedure (Macmillan, in press; cf. Moniz, 1936a, 1936b, 1948/1954) but he may have been implicit in two of them. First, Moniz argued that psychological activity was especially associated with the frontal lobes and, second, damage to the frontal lobes had only transitory effects, never deleterious psychological consequences. Moniz decided to cut the fibres responsible for maintaining the psychological symptoms primarily because "of the importance of the prefrontal lobes in mental activity" (Moniz, 1948/1954).

Freeman

Freeman and Watts did cite Harlow's description of Gage in the first edition of their *Psychosurgery* (1942, pp. 43–45). However, he was mentioned only as "the most famous" case of accidental frontal injury followed by "mental symptoms" and they did not expand on the reference to mental symptoms or make a connection between them and the new operation. As if to emphasise Gage's irrelevance, all references to him were dropped from the second edition (cf. Freeman & Watts, 1942, pp. 43–45, and 1950, Chapter 2).

It is possible that Freeman set out the connection of leucotomy with Gage in an undated manuscript from which the relevant chapters are now missing (Macmillan, in press) or when he told a press conference about "the results of the crowbar being driven through [Gage's] skull" (Freeman, undated). There is thus no positive evidence that Freeman, any more than Moniz, believed that the deliberate production of changes like those in Gage would benefit depressed or obsessional patients.

CONCLUSION

The main thrust of this chapter—that the paucity of data about Gage has allowed his case to be used to support many different theories—may be illustrated by considering Damasio et al.'s (1994) reconstruction. According to them, after the accident, Gage's "new learning was intact, and neither memory nor intelligence in the conventional sense were affected" but he had "become irreverent and capricious," "his respect for the social conventions by which he had once abided had vanished" and, most troubling, "he had taken leave of his sense of responsibility ... [and] could not be trusted to meet his commitments." The contrast they draw is with a pre-accident Gage who was "socially well-adapted," "a favourite with peers and elders," and who "had made progress and showed promise."

That Gage's memory and arithmetical reasoning (money and size) were not affected is at variance with Harlow's and Jackson's reports and, given Harlow's frequent references to Gage's "feeble" mental processes (and his later explication of them), it is doubtful there was no defect in "intelligence" (a term then having a different meaning from ours). Harlow says little about the specific ways in which Gage was socially "well-adapted" (i.e. in the societal and interpersonal spheres); nor does he mention Gage as being "a favourite" with any "elders," and does not say how Gage had shown "promise" or specify any starting point from which had he "made progress." Of course, Gage *was* profoundly changed by the accident and *was* irreverent and capricious, but there is nothing having the unequivocal implications that his respect for social convention "had vanished" (i.e. wholly), or his "sense of responsibility," was lost (i.e. completely), or that he "could not be trusted to meet his commitments." The translation of the source statements into these phrases is therefore questionable.

From their own cases Damasio et al. (1994) also concluded that bilateral frontal ventromedial lesions destroyed the ability to make moral decisions, but the picture they draw of Gage is much more readily related to that kind of deficiency than is Harlow's portrayal. They assert that the intellectual atmosphere of Harlow's time made it less acceptable to propose a biological basis for "moral reasoning" than for movement or language (see especially their footnote 3). The fact that they cite Ferrier's applying his concept of "mental degradation" to Gage suggests that they are speaking of *moral* degradation. Elsewhere, in a contemporaneous interview-report in the Science section of the *New York Times*, A. Damasio makes this claim quite explicit: the post-accident Gage began lying to his friends, not honouring his commitments, and behaving socially "like an idiot" (Blakeslee, 1994). Only one thing in the sources specifically resembles these characteristics: Gage entertaining his little nephews and nieces with fabulated stories. Is this lying? Or moral defect?[6]

Similarly, the estimation by Damasio et al. of the damage caused by the tamping iron seems to be more like that in their own cases than is warranted. Harlow believed there was ventricular damage and would have accepted the two trajectories they rejected; there are also many reports of survival of such damage in the pre-antibiotic era (e.g. by Theodoric, 1267/1955). The entry points for all five of the remaining "acceptable" trajectories are more lateral and the exit points more anterior and medial than those they describe as the a priori most likely points. Thus, the trajectories accepted by Damasio et al. were almost bound to damage the ventromedial areas of the left hemisphere and have some impact on the right but those they rejected may have spared both. Neither do they seem to have ruled out the possibility of individual differences in the position of the brain in the skull or the location of its functions resulting in a different outcome. They did test the effects of the selected trajectories on six other brains but the dimensions of those brains were on average within a few millimetres of those assumed for Gage's brain and probably also close to the position they assumed it occupied.

The assumptions made by Damasio et al. are best seen as another attempt to overcome the paucity of data about Gage, although neither their characterisation of his behaviour nor the pattern of damage in him seems to resemble that in their cases.

There are four points to be emphasised about the significance of the Gage case to neuropsychology.

1. It was essentially not until 1868 that the changes in Gage's behaviour were described in the medical literature and, even then, they did not become widely known until Ferrier's Gulstonian Lectures of 1878, 10 years later. Prior to 1878, the primary neuropsychological significance of the Gage case was that it counted against phrenological and other localisation doctrines.

2. Although the Gage case was important to early frontal lobe surgery, it played no essential part in the development of psychosurgery proper. At most it reinforced two beliefs relevant to psychosurgery: frontal operations

were not likely to prove fatal, and "mental symptoms," whatever may have been encompassed by that phrase, were, in some sense, localised frontally.

3. So little is known about Gage's behaviour before and after the accident, and even less about the location and extent of the injury to his brain, that no certain relations can be established between the two. The paucity of behavioural data would not require us to alter this conclusion even were we to find out today precisely what the damage was.

4. There will always be a difficulty in relating hypothesised damage to Gage's behaviour. The modern view is that frontal orbital, dorso-lateral, and mesial lesions have very different effects (e.g. Cummings, 1991; Damasio, 1985). Were Gage to have suffered more than one kind of damage, assessing the relative contribution of each would be difficult. The framework provided by 19th-century sensory-motor physiology was obviously inadequate to encompass the effects of frontal damage like those exhibited by Gage but it does not seem that we presently have a more adequate alternative.

NOTES

1. A veritable army of people has so far assisted me in my work on Gage and it is not possible to name them all here. However, this particular paper could not have been completed without the considerable help of Richard Wolfe, of the Countway Library, who directed India Tressalt (my research assistant) to the *Records of Meetings* of the Boston Society for Medical Improvement and the Ferrier–Bowditch correspondence, and me to J.B.S. Jackson's *Medical Cases*, and who gave me permission to quote from them. I am also much indebted to Drs Ken Tyler (University of Colorado Health Sciences Center, Denver) and Fred Barker (Neuro-Oncology Service, School of Medicine, University of California, San Francisco) for sharing their data with me.
   Most of the sources for the present work are listed in the references to my papers and unpublished manuscripts. Only the most essential, controversial, or novel points are fully documented here.

2. Because of my carelessness, the date of 9th September, 1823 in my 1986 paper is incorrect.

3. There are problems with the implication from Bigelow's paper that he presented Gage to the Boston Society for Medical Improvement in January, 1850. The *Records of Meetings* of the Society show that on 10th November, 1849 Gage, the medical curiosity, was sandwiched between Dr Strong's case of a child cured of an enlarged ankle by purgatives and Bigelow's display of a "Remarkable Stalagmite ... [having] a singular resemblance to a petrified penis" (Boston Society for Medical Improvement, 1849).

4. I have been unable to establish any details of the time Gage spent between 1850 and 1852 with Barnum's Museum (or Circus) and Currier's livery stables or, after 1852, with the coach line company in Chile and, after 1859, as a farm labourer in California. (Because the date Harlow gave for Gage's death was in error, I assume Gage returned in 1859 and not 1860).

5. Not $12\frac{1}{2}$ years after the accident, that is, in 1861, as Harlow reported in 1868 (Macmillan, 1986).

6. There is a number of exaggerations in the Damasio et al. (1994) account that add to their picture of moral deficit: they imply that Gage wandered during the whole of the post-accident period, and claim he never returned to a fully independent existence. There are

many other errors, some of which are also quite important (e.g. Gage survived for "a dozen years" instead of $11\frac{1}{2}$, some rather less so (e.g. the omission of the sand as the cause of the explosion), and others a mixture (e.g. Gage being buried alongside his skull and tamping iron; the former implies decapitation before burial and the latter is an undocumented claim). Although some of these minor errors appear to be careless summaries of the corresponding sections of Damasio's more recent book (1994), the picture of Gage as an acquired and lying psycho- or socio-path is even more explicit. However, no further evidence is adduced.

REFERENCES

Anonymous. (1851). A most remarkable case. *American Phrenological Journal and Repository of Science, Literature, and General Intelligence, 13,* 89.

Barker, F.G. (1993, May). *Phineas among the phrenologists: The American crowbar case and nineteenth century theories of cerebral localization.* Paper presented at the annual meeting of the American Association of Neurosurgeons, Boston, MA.

Bennett, A.H., & Godlee, R.J. (1882–1885). Case of cerebral tumour. *Proceedings of the Royal Medico-Chirugical Society, 1,* 438–444.

Bennett, A.H., & Godlee, R.J. (1885). Case of cerebral tumour. *Medico-Chirugical Transactions, 68,* 243–275.

Bennett, A.H., & Gould, A.P. (1887). Case of epilepsy of six years' duration: Complete recovery after surgical operation on the skull and brain. *British Medical Journal, i,* 12–13.

Bigelow, H.J. (1850). Dr. Harlow's case of recovery from the passage of an iron bar through the head. *American Journal of the Medical Sciences, 19,* 13–22.

Blakeslee, S. (1994, 24th May). Old accident points to brain's moral center. *New York Times* (Science Section), B5, B8.

Boston Society for Medical Improvement. (1849). *Records of meetings (Vol. VI)* (Countway Library manuscript, B Ms b 92.2).

Bowditch, H.P. (1874). Report on physiology. *Boston Medical and Surgical Journal, 89,* 79–84.

Burckhardt, A. (1891). Über Rinderexcisionen, als Heitrag zur operativen Therapie der Psychosen. *Allgemeine Zeitschrift für Psychiatrie, 47,* 463–548.

Cummings, J.L. (1991). Frontal sub-cortical circuits and human behavior. *Archives of Neurology, 50,* 873–880.

Dalton, J.G. (1859). *A treatise on human physiology.* Philadelphia: Blanchard and Lea.

Damasio, A.R. (1985). The frontal lobes. In K.H. Heilman & E. Valenstein (Eds.), *Clinical neuropsychology* (2nd. ed., pp. 339–375). New York: Oxford University Press.

Damasio, A. (1993, April). *Memory and language systems in humans.* Paper presented to the Decade of the Brain Plenary Session at the annual meeting of the American Academy of Neurology, New York. Published as Cassette Recording No. 11-47-93. Denver, CO: National Audio Video Inc.

Damasio, A.R. (1994). *Descartes' error: Emotion, reason and the human brain.* New York: Grosset/Putnam.

Damasio, H., Grabowski, T., Frank, R., Galaburda, A.M., & Damasio, A.M. (1994). The return of Phineas Gage: Clues about the brain from the skull of a famous patient. *Science, 264,* 1102–1105.

Dupuy, E. (1873), *Examen de quelques points de la physiologie du cerveau.* Paris: Delahaye.

Dupuy, E. (1877). A critical review of the prevailing theories concerning the physiology and pathology of the brain. *Medical Times and Gazette, 2,* 11–13, 32–34, 84–87, 356–358, 474–475, 488–490.

Ferrier, D. (1876). *The functions of the brain.* London: Smith, Elder.

Ferrier, D. (1877–1879). *Correspondence with Henry Pickering Bowditch* (Countway Library manuscript, H MS c 5.2).

Ferrier, D. (1878a). The Gulstonian lectures of the localisation of cerebral disease. *British Medical Journal, i,* 397–402, 443–447.

Ferrier, D. (1878b). *The localisation of cerebral disease: Being the Gulstonian Lectures of the Royal College of Physicians for 1878.* London: Smith, Elder.

Ferrier, D. (1889–1890). Cerebral localisation in its practical relations. *Brain, 12,* 36–58.

Ferrier, D. (1891–1892). Cerebral localisation in relation to therapeutics. *Edinburgh Medical Journal, 37,* 881–897.

Freeman, W., & Watts, J.W. (1942). *Psychosurgery in the treatment of mental disorders and intractable pain.* Springfield, IL: Thomas.

Freeman, W., & Watts, J.W. (1950). *Psychosurgery in the treatment of mental disorders and intractable pain* (2nd. ed.). Springfield, IL: Thomas.

Freeman, W. (undated). *Adventures in lobotomy.* Unpublished manuscript, Himmelfarb Health Sciences Library, George Washington University Medical Center, Washington, DC.

Gowers, W.R. (1879). Cases of cerebral tumour illustrating diagnosis and localisation. *Lancet, i,* 327–329, 363–365.

Gowers, W.R. (1885). *Diagnosis of diseases of the brain and of the spinal cord.* New York: Wood.

Hammond, W.A. (1871). *A treatise on the diseases of the nervous system.* London: Lewis.

Harlow, J.M. (1848). Passage of an iron rod through the head. *Boston Medical and Surgical Journal, 39,* 389–393.

Harlow, J.M. (1849). Letter in "Medical miscellany". *Boston Medical and Surgical Journal, 39,* 506–507.

Harlow, J.M. (1868). Recovery from the passage of an iron bar through the head. *Publications of the Massachusetts Medical Society, 2,* 327–347.

Harlow, J.M. (1869). *Recovery from the passage of an iron bar through the head.* Boston, MA: Clapp.

Jackson, J.B.S. (1849). *Medical cases (Vol. 4, Cases No. 1358–1929)* (pp. 720, 610) (Countway Library manuscript, H MS b 72.4).

McBurney, M.D., & Starr, M.A. (1893). A contribution to cerebral surgery. *American Journal of the Medical Sciences, 105,* 361–387.

Macewen, W. (1879). Tumour of the dura mater—convulsions—removal of tumour by trephining—recovery. *Glasgow Medical Journal, 11,* 210–213.

Macewen, W. (1881). Inter-cranial lesions illustrating some points in connexion with the localisation of cerebral affections and the advantages of antiseptic trephining. *Lancet, ii,* 541–543, 581–583.

Macewen, W. (1888). An address on the surgery of the brain and spinal cord. *British Medical Journal, ii,* 302–309.

Macmillan, M.B. (1986). A wonderful journey through skull and brains: The travels of Mr. Gage's tamping iron. *Brain and Cognition, 5,* 67–107.

Macmillan, M.B. (1992a). Inhibition and the control of behavior: From Gall to Freud via Phineas Gage and the frontal lobes. *Brain and Cognition, 19,* 72–104.

Macmillan, M.B. (1992b, May). *Phineas Gage and Freud's theory of thinking.* Paper presented at the seminars on the History of Psychiatry and the Behavioral Sciences, New York Hospital–Cornell University Medical Center, New York.

Macmillan, M.B. (1993, May). *Inhibition in some nineteenth century theories of thinking.* Paper presented to TENNET IV, Montreal.

Macmillan, M.B. (in press). Phineas Gage's contribution to brain surgery. *Journal of the History of the Neurosciences.*

Mills, C.K. (1889–1890). Cerebral localisation in its practical relations. *Brain, 12,* 233–288.

Moniz, E. (1936a). *Tentatives operatoires dans le traitement de certaines psychoses*. Paris: Masson et Cie.

Moniz, E. (1936b). Essai d'un traitment chirugical de certaines psychoses. *Academie de Medicine Bulletin (Paris)*, *115*, 385–392.

Moniz, E. (1948/1954). How I succeeded in performing the prefrontal leukotomy. *Journal of Clinical and Experimental Psychopathology*, *15*, 373–379. (Original work published 1948.)

Sequin, E.C. (1868). A statement of the aphasia question, together with a report of fifty cases. *Quarterly Journal of Psychological Medicine (New York)*, *2*, 74–119.

Sizer, N. (1882). *Forty years in phrenology; embracing recollections of history, anecdote, and experience*. New York: Fowler & Wells.

Starr, M.A. (1884a). Cortical lesions of the brain: A collection and analysis of the American cases of localized cerebral disease. *American Journal of the Medical Sciences*, *87*, 366–391.

Starr, M.A. (1884b). Cortical lesions of the brain: A collection and analysis of the American cases of localized cerebral disease. *American Journal of the Medical Sciences*, *88*, 114–141.

Stone, J.L. (1991). Paul Broca and the first craniotomy based on cerebral localization. *Journal of Neurosurgery*, *75*, 154–159.

Theodoric. (1267/1955). *The surgery of Theodoric, ca. A.D. 1267 (Vol. I)* (p. 109). (E. Campbell & J. Colton Trans.) New York: Appleton-Century-Crofts. (Original work published 1267.)

Tyler, K.L., & Tyler, H.R. (1982). A "Yankee Invention": The celebrated American crowbar case. *Neurology*, *32*, A191.

Whitaker, H.A., Stemmer, B., & Joanette, Y. (1993, April). *A psychosurgical chapter in the history of cerebral localization: G. Burckhardt (1891)*. Poster presentation to the annual meeting of the American Academy of Neurology, New York. Abstract No. 847P in *Neurology*, *43*, A377.

Young, R.M. (1970). *Mind, brain and adaptation in the nineteenth century*. Oxford: Clarendon Press.

19 Anomaly in Relations of Hand, Language, and Brain: Crossed Aphasia in History Cross-examined

Avraham Schweiger
Center for Cognition and Communication, New York, U.S.A.

INTRODUCTION AND BRIEF HISTORICAL BACKGROUND

This chapter is an essay on the scientific vicissitudes of a paper published in *The Lancet* at the end of the last century by Byrom Bramwell (1899), entitled "On 'Crossed' Aphasia." The paper, a case study of a left-handed patient with aphasia resulting from a left hemisphere lesion, presents neither ground-breaking research nor any novel theory. In fact, its central theme is based on an erroneous assumption about left handedness and cerebral lateralisation of language. Consequently, the inferences made by the author are also in error, hence the title of this chapter. Nevertheless, this case study is of interest because it marked the beginning of an ongoing series of case studies on crossed aphasia which still continues today (e.g. Sakuri, Kurisaki, Takeda, Iwata, Bandoh, Watanabe, & Momose, 1992). It is often cited as the source of the term "crossed aphasia," despite the fact that today the term is used with a different kind of patient—right-handed aphasics with a right hemisphere lesion—which Bramwell did not think could be found on theoretical grounds. Perhaps some authors who cite this paper do not even bother to read the original article, as is suggested by occasional misquotations. In addition, Bramwell offered some speculations on the cause of crossed aphasia which, unintentionally, offer a new perspective on the syndrome and perhaps on the whole issue of localisation of functions in the brain.

We know today that Bramwell's inference regarding the anomalous nature of his case, namely a left-hander aphasic with right hemiplegia (implying a left hemisphere lesion), was wrong. Nevertheless, the Physician to the Royal Infirmary in Edinburgh raised issues of central importance in neuropsychology regarding theories of handedness and hemispheric lateralisation, and the role of nature versus nurture in determining them. In his paper, Bramwell addressed the issue of (what he took to be) an anomalous case of hemispheric dominance in relation to handedness, namely a left-handed patient who presented with right hemiplegia and aphasia, a clinical presentation no longer referred to as crossed aphasia today. But what makes this paper relevant for today's reader interested in the brain, is the author's systematic attempt to draw inferences concerning normal cerebral organisation from a case of an anomalous cerebral organisation, and his cautious, even when misguided, explanations of the relations between handedness and the cerebral site for language functions. And, of course, Bramwell's approach of generalising to normal functioning from pathology remains a mainstream methodology in contemporary neuropsychology.

The significance of any "interesting" clinical case depends on the theoretical framework within which the case is studied. That is, the data offered by a patient are only relevant, or interesting, to the extent to which they inform, or speak to, a particular viewpoint. Patients always present with a large variety of symptoms, of which only a minor portion are usually described in case studies. To an aphasiologist, the pattern of error production in reading may be a focus of interest, whereas the patient's distorted time sense may be completely overlooked or ignored. This observation is hardly surprising, and has been known for quite some time. Similarly and more generally, the notion that even scientific discoveries in general, and what constitutes relevant scientific data in particular, are both determined by the current paradigm or zeitgeist, has been articulated eloquently by the philosopher Thomas S. Kuhn in his famous treatise *The Structure of Scientific Revolutions* (1970). There are also historical examples of selective attention to data reporting and interpretation in neuropsychology (for such instances see Efron, 1990). Almost every case study is a narrow presentation of only the "relevant" data, and group studies are even more restricted in their data consideration. Thus, Bramwell's case study can be understood as fitting into, or even emerging out of, a particular viewpoint and therefore reflecting belief in a particular brain/behaviour theory. As it turned out, some aspects of this theory regarding handedness and laterality of language functions happened to be wrong, and therefore Bramwell's inferences were also misguided. Nevertheless, a few issues raised by the author, through this case study, survived his erroneous inferences and still continue to occupy today's researchers (as clearly demonstrated by the plethora of case studies on crossed aphasia).

What is the fascination with cases of crossed aphasia? Why should a general physician, for whom neurology was a side interest, go to the trouble of investigating a case with this presentation, interview family members, and publish a protracted discussion of its causes? The answer, I believe, lies in the dogma of localisation of functions in the brain (of which manual control is but one manifestation) towards the end of the 19th century, and which continues well into the 20th century, and is still quite pervasive—if in a less rigid and perhaps more tentative form these days.

Towards the end of the 19th century, empiricism was widely entrenched in science (e.g. Russell, 1945). The works of such philosophers/scientists as Darwin and von Helmholtz were well known and accepted in the scientific community. Heredity was at the time an established concept, but the precise form it took was not decidedly Darwinian yet. Thus, Lamarck's view that certain traits were learned and then transmitted genetically was still pervasive. Moreover, whether or not the environment could shape the rate of certain advantageous mutations was still unresolved (and still is to some extent, as can be seen from a recent paper on this very topic, i.e. Lenski & Mittler, 1993). To think in Darwinian terms of random mutations and natural selection, where Homo sapiens do not represent the peak of an evolutionary progress, was probably very difficult for Victorian scientists, who equated increasing organic adaptation with "progress' (cf. Gould, 1977). Nevertheless, genetic transmission of some wort was assumed since the discoveries of the heredity of traits by Mendel in the first half of the 19th century, while learning was seen as adding its own marks. This whole evolutionary approach had its effect on views concerning handedness, which are abundantly reflected in Bramwell's discussion of the genetic transmission of handedness. For example, in attempting to explain the occurrence of left handedness, Bramwell arrived at a peculiar combination of causes for handedness, namely, heredity and acquisition: Where one falls short of explaining a fact, the other comes in to complement it. As will be discussed later, this combination, more than just an ad hoc explanation, may actually have implications for future theorising on brain functioning.

In psychology, experimental work in psychophysics was being carried out by scientists, such as Fechner, Weber, and G. Müller, attempting to quantify mental phenomena (Boring, 1957) and bring the rigor of physics to the study of the mind. In studies of the brain, the investigations and theory of Gall and Spurzheim sparked a whole new direction of research, namely, the localisation of functions in the cerebrum. Many case studies of aphasia appeared under a variety of terminology, but consistently associating the left hemisphere with language as evidenced by the clinical co-occurrence of left-sided lesions with speech impairment. It is interesting to note that although left-sided lesions were known to cause language disturbances far more often than right-sided lesions, it was not until around the 1860s that the theory of left hemisphere dominance (or "leading") for language took a strong position among neurologists, following the works of Broca, Dax, Bouillaud, Baillarger, and Hughlings Jackson (Riese, 1977). The assignment of language functions (which to many thinkers represented directly the thought process itself, and therefore the "mind") to a locus in the brain was central to 19th century science. It promised to resolve Cartesian dualism by "finding" the cause of language (and therefore thought). Thus the theory of lateralised language functioning promised to embody the mind in the "substance" of the brain.

Towards the end of the 19th century, many neurological case studies appeared, with possibly the most famous being those of Broca and Wernicke. In fact Broca himself stated not only that the left hemisphere of right-handers is dominant for language, but that the converse was true for left-handers, namely, right hemisphere dominance for language. Elaborate diagrams were proposed to account for the working of the brain. These diagrams reflected a rather naïve localisationist view of the brain–mind complex. This view was reinforced, for example, by the studies of Hitzig and Fritsch using direct electrical stimulation of the brain. The visualisation of neuronal processes and nuclei in the brain using the newly discovered staining techniques added fuel to the localisationists' view. There were some researchers who took exceptions to the localisationist view, most notably Hughlings Jackson with his hierarchical organisation of functions, and later Head and Marie. But, by and large, the localisationists dominated the field (and continue to do so to this day, at least in neurology).

The "fin de siècle" thus evidenced a rather mechanistic concept of the brain, accessible to the scientific methodology; mental phenomena were deemed reducible to mathematical quantification. The relations between the brain and mental phenomena were thought of as a causal one (with the former giving rise to the latter), in keeping with the materialistic influence inherent to 19th-century science. The concept of "specific nerve energies" of J. Müller in the early part of the 19th century (Boring, 1957) provided a firm basis for the materialistic realisation of mental phenomena in terms of physiological processes: Perceptual processes were now viewed as the straightforward transduction of physical stimuli in the environment. Motor activity was in accordance with these perceptions and constituted the organism's response to them. Mental activity finally had a firm basis in the workings of brain tissue. Consequently, the scientific community was ripe to deduce from the available observations (of aphasia with most left hemisphere lesions) the dogma of left hemisphere dominance for language. Once introduced, it apparently took on the power of a universally accepted fact (Riese, 1977). It is not that this fact was a solution to the riddle of brain functioning, but it seemed to be a step in that direction by confining functions to just a small part of the brain. This was especially promising for language, which was commonly thought to represent the mind.

It is not surprising, then, that Bramwell refers throughout his paper to the dominant hemisphere for language as having the "driving" or "leading" speech centres. Bramwell used quotation marks with these terms, suggesting he was perhaps aware of the problematic nature of these causal relations. This was a rather modular view of "mind", according to which neuronal centres operated as fairly independent units, analogous to the senses. This view is pervasive today as well, and is reflected in the concept, put in a somewhat simplified form, that specialised brain tissue is responsible for a particular behaviour. This view, despite its attending philosophical problems (e.g. who makes executive decisions regarding channelling of input prior to its processing—the homunculus problem, etc.), has the advantage of justifying readily the inference of specific functional/ anatomical loci in the brain from studies of patients with focal lesions.

As far as localisation of functions in the brain was concerned, specialisation of different anatomical areas for different functions was assumed. For example, it was an accepted fact that injury to the left hemisphere was very likely to produce aphasic symptoms, and therefore this hemisphere was somehow specialised for language. More importantly, it was already an accepted procedure to infer directly, and perhaps too readily, functioning of localised brain tissue from studies of patients with identified focal lesions, as did Broca in his own famous case studies. As left handedness was considered an exception, and its frequency underestimated significantly, it was also accepted that the right hemisphere of left handers is dominant for language. After all, this was stated by such authorities as Broca, and even J. Hughlings Jackson (1880). Cases with unusual clinical presentations are central to the localisationist approach popularised towards the end of the 19th century. Such anomalous cases may force a revision in existing theories or expand their boundaries. Moreover, being exceptional, their explanation within the existing framework can offer support for extant theories. I believe it is the latter reason which prompted Bramwell to present his case and attempt to explain it in terms of his present day concepts of lateral dominance for language.

By the time Bramwell (1847–1931) wrote his paper on crossed aphasia, he already had published three medical textbooks on the diseases of the heart, the spinal cord and intracranial tumours. He was actually a general physician who had an interest in neurology and who was later knighted (in 1924), most likely not in consequence of his paper on crossed aphasia. Nevertheless, this paper remains his only work still being cited today. Bramwell's paper is a series of cautious speculations on cerebral laterality and its causes. Some of these speculations are still unresolved almost a century later. It is worth noting that by presenting what appeared to

Bramwell as an "anomalous" clinical case, then speculating on the possible implications of the clinical case, he was very much in keeping with today's single case study approach in neuropsychology.

THE CASE STUDY

In his paper, Bramwell (1899) provided a detailed, if not entirely systematic, description of his patient. Lacking the modern tools of ascertaining localisation of lesions (C.T. or M.R.I. scans), he attempted to establish a firm pathological and anatomical diagnosis, the latter, of course, being crucial to his term "crossed" aphasia. He even raised, and quickly dismissed as unlikely, the possibility of no decussation of the pyramidial tract in his patient. Although the terminology of aphasic symptoms would seem arcane to contemporary readers, the author provided extended description of his patient's linguistic deficits for the reader to glean the essence of the patient's condition. As one example, Bramwell described in his patient the absence of "recurring utterances" (possibly referring to the absence of what today would be described as perseverations). It appears that the patient presented basically with Broca's aphasia (described as "motor–vocal aphasia" by Bramwell), but also presented with comprehension deficits, leading the writer to note the presence of "sensory aphasia" as well. The patient was noted to exhibit agraphia, although Bramwell qualified this inference as unsure due to the difficulty of assessing writing in the presence of right hemiplegia. Here, again, Bramwell proved to be very alert to issues of neuropsychological interpretations: He stated aptly that the agraphia was not simply due to motor—or kinesthetic—deficit, as the patient seemed to "... want of the knowledge of the manner in which the letters should be grouped to form words..." (p. 1474).

The patient was a left-handed individual, who used his left hand for all activities except writing. Bramwell noted that the patient used his right hand for writing only, observing astutely the importance of ascertaining the origin of this fact. Bramwell did not spare any effort in making his point and reported that he had obtained information in writing and from interviewing the patient's mother, the latter confirming that the patient had been always fully left handed. Moreover, she reported that it was under duress (namely, by strapping his left hand to his side) that the patient was forced to learn to use his right hand for writing. The author also noted that there were no known left-handed relatives or ancestors in the patient's family; his twin brother (Bramwell did not specify whether or not monozygotic) was also reported as being right handed. Arguably, there could be some mixed handedness present, judging by this lack of sinistrality in the patient's family. But from Bramwell's description the patient appeared to be (phenotypically) a left-handed individual.

In addition to presenting with marked aphasia, the patient was described as having right-sided hemiplegia and some sensory loss on the right side, without hemianopsia. Together with the clinical examination, the writer was satisfied that the lesion was cortical. He also noted that since the examination took place about four months following onset, the aphasic symptoms can be considered "persistent" and not due to any acute response of the brain. For Bramwell, who believed (most probably erroneously) the incidence of left handedness to be only about 2%, and that left handedness represents anatomically as a case of situs inversus (right hemisphere dominant for language and for control of the dominant left hand), such a presentation constituted a complete anomaly, deserving careful investigation. Moreover, the patient was forced to use his right hand for writing, a bona fide linguistic function, and had no known relatives who were also left handed. This latter fact suggested a possible cause for the anomaly presented by the patient.

DISCUSSION

Bramwell believed that cases of left-handed patients presenting with aphasia and right hemiplegia (and therefore implicating a left hemisphere lesion) are quite exceptional, but the case he had written about was not the first. Others noted it, and even Hughlings Jackson (1880) mentioned such patients. But Bramwell presented the case in detail, providing a detailed clinical picture, as well as quite good background information on familial sinistrality. He also obtained information on the purity of sinistrality in the patient. As far as cases of the "reverse" crossed aphasia, namely a right-handed patient with aphasia and left hemiplegia (i.e. right hemisphere lesion), Bramwell stated he knew of no such case. As will be discussed below, the absence of such cases was consonant with the author's view on hemispheric dominance for language, a fact which may explain this erroneous statement. For, as we now know, the incidence of this form of crossed aphasia is about 1–2% of right-handed aphasic patients (e.g. Gloning, Gloning, Haub, & Quatember, 1969). Not being a neurologist, Bramwell apparently had not encountered patients with such crossed aphasia, and nobody described such a case in the literature of his time. It is likely that such cases were not of great interest prior to the firm establishment of the left hemisphere as dominant for language in right handers.

For physicians in the 1890s the relations between handedness and hemispheric dominance was simple. In his paper Bramwell expresses these relations by stating as a given fact that right-handed persons have their "leading" centre in the left hemisphere, and the converse is the case for left-handed individuals. We know this not to be the case, certainly not for left-handed individuals. On the contrary, for the majority of left-handed patients, a left hemisphere lesion is more likely to be aphasiogenic (for review see Joanette, 1989). Despite this simplified concept, it is interesting to note that the author considered crossed aphasia only in cases of "persistent" aphasia, the reason being his report that many right-handed patients with right hemisphere lesions exhibit "transitory" aphasic symptoms. His explanation for this observation (p. 1476) was that the right hemispheres if right-handed people "are possessed of some sort of speech function, which is usually, I think, carried on in conjunction with, and in subordination to, the function of the speech centres in the 'leading' or 'driving' hemisphere..."

Here we have an unexpected surprise: Bramwell ascribed language functions to the right hemisphere more than 60 years before the research on the "split brain" patients actually demonstrated it in the isolated right hemisphere. However, it is quite certain that Bramwell, far from being a country doctor, and well versed in contemporary controversies (as can be gleaned from some of his footnotes), was aware of his famous contemporary brain theorist J.Hughlings Jackson. The latter had published a paper in *The Lancet* nine years earlier (Hughlings Jackson, 1880), in which he made a strong case for the idea that patients presenting with left hemiplegia and aphasia are all left handed. He presented briefly clinical cases to support this notion. Hughlings Jackson also discusses briefly his ideas of right hemisphere involvement in language processes. So Bramwell was not exactly a revolutionary in his thinking, either in ascribing some language to the right hemisphere (in right handers), or with the erroneous attribution of linguistic dominance always to the right hemisphere of left handers.

What causes the hand preference or its accompanying hemispheric specialisation is as mysterious and controversial today as it was at the time Bramwell wrote his paper. In attempting to explain lateralisation in any particular individual, the writer considered three factors as causing right handedness: (1) Heredity; (2) "Congenital organic aptitude" (he never clarified the distinction between these two points). This factor was added, most likely, to account for the observation that some left-handed individuals do not have relatives known to be left handed themselves. Bramwell also noted that some right handers have left-handed ancestry; (3) "Actual acquirement" i.e. learning. What kind of learning causes lateralisation is not specified, but later in the paper becomes clear.

Despite repeated (and occasionally tedious) qualifications and cautionary statements, the explanation of crossed aphasia favoured by Bramwell seems to be that sinistrals with right-handed ancestors may "revert" to having their hereditary "appropriate" left hemisphere dominant for language, especially if they learned to write with their right hand.

Moreover, Bramwell believed that learning to write with the non-preferred hand (most typically sinistrals who were forced to write with their right hand, but including also cases of injury to the preferred hand in dextrals) may in and of itself bring about a reversal in the hemispheric dominance for language. So this is the underlying reason for the clinical appearance of crossed aphasia: A left-handed individual, with the right hemisphere being dominant for language, is forced to use the right hand for writing. If this sinistral's family is right handed, the right hemisphere dominance for language is shaky to begin with, so when the right-hand writing is added, there is a reversal of the language dominance back to the "correct" left hemisphere. A left brain lesion will now cause aphasia in the sinistral patient. Bramwell was well aware that learning to write comes after language skills and hand preference are well established in children, and therefore writing cannot be the primal causal factor in the initial lateralisation of language functions.

This view of writing skill as influencing brain lateralisation is no longer held. More importantly, the evidence that a large number of sinistrals have their left hemisphere dominant for language explains better the clinical presentation of Bramwell's patient. And yet there is a sense in which Bramwell's explanation is surprisingly contemporary. That is, from a phylogenetic perspective this view is in keeping with some contemporary theories on lateralisation of language and other skills to one hemisphere, as originating in manual manipulations and postural tendencies (cf. MacNeilage, Studdert-Kennedy, & Lindblom, 1993). Nevertheless, his hypothesis concerning the cause of crossed aphasia provided Bramwell with the explanation for the "rarity" of the other form of crossed aphasia, namely right-handed patients with aphasia and a right hemisphere lesions (to which the term "crossed aphasia" is applied exclusively these days). Since right-handed individuals are never required to use their non-dominant hand for writing, cases of shifted hemispheric dominance for language as a result of switched handedness are extremely rare (in fact Bramwell considered such possibility in theory only, conceding that he had no knowledge of such cases).

Bramwell, apparently, was an imaginative physician who, despite his caution, did not shy away from speculations. Thus, for instance, he discussed in the paper the idea of "substitution" and compensation of functions following lesions in the brain. He suggested, for example, that a slowly developing lesion was more likely to produce compensation of one hemisphere for the functions of the damaged one, when compared with a rapid lesion (such as a stroke). Again, we can see how contemporary Bramwell was in his thinking.

A CONTEMPORARY VIEW OF
BRAMWELL'S PAPER

Several proposals to account for the phenomenon of crossed aphasia (aphasic dextral with exclusive right brain damage) have been advanced over the years since the publication of Bramwell's paper. They range from incomplete lateralisation (Brown & Hécaen, 1976), misdiagnosis of a second lesion (Castro-Caldas, Confraria, Paiva, & Trindaae, 1986), unusual organisation of cortical functions in crossed aphasics, such as situs inversus (Schweiger, Wechsler, & Mazziotta, 1987), or mixed lateralisation (Alexander, Fischette, & Fischer, 1989), to anatomical abnormalities and cross-callosal inhibition of the left hemisphere by the damaged right hemisphere (Schweiger et al., 1987). For other, less plausible theories see the recent review by Joanette (1989). But so far no single theory has accounted fully for the puzzling presentation of crossed aphasia. The reason may be, in part, the prominent position occupied by localisationist theory since the days of Broca, Wernicke, and Bramwell. That is, the strong belief that cognitive functions tend to be strongly localised in brain structure. It is only against the background of such a localisationist perspective that crossed aphasia seems an anatomical and (in some cases) functional anomaly. Similarly, cases of crossed aphasia have been regarded as "anomalous" from an aphasiological/symptomatic perspective (Alexander et al., 1989). Here, again, it is only against a background of rather fixed ideas concerning aphasic typology and syndromes that such a statement can be made.

Perhaps a hint at the solution to the puzzle of crossed aphasia harks back to Bramwell, and his suggestion that learning to write with the non-dominant right hand may lead to a reversal of hemispheric dominance for language. Even if this suggestion is far fetched and incorrect in its details, it regards actual experience in the world as having a direct effect on lateralisation. Perhaps in early childhood and prior to school years, experience does shape the evolution of brain tissue specialisation, so that every individual's brain presents with a unique "localisation" of functions, the latter conforming only in broad outlines to genetic predisposition. This hypothesis calls for a very close scrutiny and consideration of a crossed aphasic's personal history, and comparing it with histories of other patients with crossed aphasia. Of course, this is a complicated project, made all the more difficult by the fact that most published case studies include only a sketchy personal history, and even fewer neuro-developmental details.

Bramwell himself did not intend to embark on constructing a new theory of brain specialisation, but merely attempted to explain what he took to be an anomalous clinical presentation of a patient, with the conceptual tools available to him. His paper has been referenced often in reviews of crossed aphasia cases, probably more as an homage to his coining of the term, since his theoretical speculations regarding the cause of this condition are almost never mentioned. His erroneous inferences about the hemispheric dominance of left handers are a possible reason for this universal neglect of his theoretical discussion. But, as I have implied in this chapter, the significant and interesting contribution of Bramwell's paper is his theoretical speculations on the causal relation between handedness and hemispheric dominance for language. These speculations may reach, perhaps, further into brain/behaviour theorising than Bramwell himself ever intended.

REFERENCES

Alexander, M.P., Fischette, M.R., & Fischer, R.S. (1989). Crossed aphasia can be mirror image or anomalous. *Brain, 112*, 953–973.

Boring, E.G. (1957). *A history of experimental psychology*. New York: Appleton-Century-Croft.

Bramwell, B. (1899). On "crossed" aphasia and the factors which go to determine whether the "leading" or "driving" speech-centres shall be located in the left or in the right hemisphere of the brain. *Lancet, 1*, 1473–1479.

Brown, J.W., & Hécaen, H. (1976). Lateralization and language representation. *Neurology, 26*, 183–189.

Castro-Caldas, A., Confraria, A., Paiva, T., & Trindaae, A. (1986). Contrecoup injury in misdiagnosis of crossed aphasia. *Journal of Clinical and Experimental Neuropsychology, 8*, 697–701.

Efron, R. (1990). *The decline and fall of hemispheric specialization*. Hillsdale, NJ: Lawrence Erlbaum Associates Inc.

Gloning, I., Gloning, K., Haub, G., & Quatember, R. (1969). Comparison of verbal behavior in right-handed and non right-handed patients with anatomically verified lesion of one hemisphere. *Cortex, 5*, 43–52.

Gould, S.J. (1977). *Ever since Darwin, reflection in natural history*. New York: W.W. Norton.

Hughlings Jackson, J. (1880). On aphasia with left hemiplegia. *Lancet, 2*, 637–638.

Joanette, Y. (1989). Aphasia in left-handers and crossed aphasia. In F. Boller, & J. Grafman (Eds.), *Handbook of neuropsychology (Vol. 2)* (pp. 173–183). Amsterdam: Elsevier.

Khun, T.S. (1970). *The structure of scientific revolutions* (2nd ed.). Chicago, IL: University of Chicago Press.

Lenski, R.E., & Mittler, J.E. (1993). The directed mutation controversy and neo-Darwinism. *Science, 259*, 188–194.

MacNeilage, P.F., Studdert-Kennedy, M.G., & Lindblom, B. (1993). *The Sciences, January/February*, 32–37.

Riese, W. (1977). *Selected papers on the history of aphasia*. Amsterdam: Swets & Zeitlinger B.V.

Russell, B. (1945). *A history of western philosophy*. New York: Simon & Schuster.

Sakuri, Y., Kurisaki, H., Takeda, K., Iwata, M., Bandoh, M., Watanabe, T., & Momose, T. (1992). Japanese crossed Wernicke's aphasia. *Neurology, 42*(1), 144–148.

Schweiger, A., Wechsler, A.F., & Mazziotta, J.C. (1987). Metabolic correlates of linguistic functions in a patient with crossed aphasia: A case study. *Aphasiology, 1*(5), 415–421.

20 A Psychosurgical Chapter in the History of Cerebral Localisation: The Six Cases of Gottlieb Burckhardt (1891)[1]

Harry A. Whitaker
Département de Psychologie, Université du Québec à Montréal, Canada.

Brigitte Stemmer and Yves Joanette
Centre de Recherche, Centre Hospitalier Côtes-des-Neiges, Montréal, Canada.

> *A human brain after many years of life can be compared with a chess-board (of gigantic complexity) on which the layout of the pieces reflects the history and identity of one particular game. Normal interpersonal communication, as in education, can be likened to the making of moves that respect the rules of chess, and so preserve the continuity and identity of the game. By contrast, physical brain manipulation can be compared with the removal or addition or displacement of chessmen without regard to the rules. The end result might or might not be a legitimately playable game; but, in a sense that could be important, the play would not in general be a continuation of the same game.*
> —Donald Mackay (1987)

INTRODUCTION

It is generally agreed that modern neurosurgery began in the latter half of the 1880s: What distinguished brain surgery during this period from preceding ones, consisted in identifying the surgical target in the human brain by relying upon the newly acquired knowledge of centres and pathways derived from the neurological and neuroanatomical research in the 1860s through the 1880s. In England, Victor Horsley (1886) inaugurated epilepsy surgery, carrying out his first craniotomy to remove a scar believed to be causing epilepsy; the patient was one of John Hughlings Jackson's who attended the operation. Others who helped launch traditional modern

275

neurosurgery were E. von Bergman in Germany, W. Macewen in Scotland and C.K. Mills in the United States. In very short order, neurosurgeons described operations for brain tumour, brain abscess and traumatic epilepsy. Modern psychosurgery began during the same period.[2,3]

Gottlieb Burckhardt was born on 24th December, 1836 in Basel and died there on 6th February, 1907 (Bach, 1907). He studied medicine at the Universities of Basel, Goettingen, and Berlin, taking his doctorate in medicine in 1860 and his habilitation in internal medicine in 1862 at the University of Basel. He was in private practice for a period of time, but gave that up due to illness. He later turned to neurology with a particular emphasis on electrotherapy; the results of his research in this domain were published in a book *Die physiologische Diagnostik der Nervenkrankheiten* (Leipzig: Engelmann, 1875[33]). From 1876 to 1882 he was Privatdozent in psychiatry and neurology at the University of Bern, and from 1882 to 1896 he was medical director of the Préfargier, a psychiatric asylum in Marin, Canton of Neuchâtel, Switzerland. He returned to Basel in 1896 to work out the plans for a new sanatorium Sonnenhalde in Riehen, near Basel. At its opening in 1900 he became the clinical director of the new sanatorium until 1904; from 1904 to 1907 he was the consulting physician there. From 1875 to 1891 Burckhardt published over a dozen papers in psychiatry and neurology, including a study of sensory aphasia (1882), a didactic paper on functional centres of the brain and their relation to psychiatry and neurology, a study of an optic chiasm and temporal lobe tumour, and a study of traumatic hysteria. But the publication which earned him a place in history, and the publication with which we are concerned is: "Uber Rindenexcisionen, als Beitrag zur operativen Therapie der Psychosen"[4] *Allgemeine Zeitschrift für Psychiatrie und psychisch-gerichtliche Medicin, 47*, 463–548 (published in Berlin, 1891), which is a clinical study of the neurosurgical treatment of six patients with intractable psychiatric symptoms, and the subject of this chapter. Previous, and typically brief, discussions of Burckhardt's study can be found in: Freeman and Watts (1942), Fisher (1951), Fulton (1951), and Valenstein (1973). These sources agree that Burckhardt's study was the first published account of modern psychosurgery. Burckhardt began his series of cases at the end of 1888; it is clear that he was familiar with modern developments in neurosurgery, since he cites the work of Horsley, Macewen, and von Bergmann. It is even more certain that he was well acquainted with the new research in neurology and neuroanatomy that localised functions in various regions of the brain, as his 1891 text is liberally spiced with references to the work of Bechterew, Bernhardt, Bleuler, Broca, Exner, Ferrier, Friedlander, Fritsch and Hitzig, Goltz, Hofstetter, Jaeger, Jastrowitz, Lange, Luys, Mairet, Maudsley, Meynert, Monakow, Müller, Nothnagel, and Wernicke, among others. The dominant view of the brain in this period was a localisationist view, and it is reasonable to conclude that Burckhardt shared this opinion.

Both Freeman and Watts (1942) and Valenstein (1973, 1980[5]) suggest that Burckhardt was influenced by the ablation studies on dogs published by Friederick Goltz (1888).[6] Freeman and Watts also remark that Burckhardt studied very disturbed and deteriorated patients, in whom recovery could not reasonably be anticipated; this fact was noted by Burckhardt himself. Fisher's (1951) analysis is typical of these references to Burckhardt's paper:

> Goltz' description of placidity following resection of the brain stimulated Burckhardt, a supervisor of a small mental institution in Switzerland, to carry out cortical ablations for psychotic symptoms. The latter thought that specific symptoms might be eliminated by removal of the appropriate cortical center. For example, auditory hallucinations might be dissipated by a lesion of the auditory cortex in the temporal lobe. On a deteriorated, noisy destructive female schizophrenic patient, four operations were performed on the left side at several weeks' intervals;[7] five grams from the postcentral, five and a half grams from the temporal, five and one half grams from the parietal, and five grams from the third frontal convolution were removed.[8] Each operation was accompanied by progressive reduction in the patient's general restlessness and hallucinations. Her behavior was much better tolerated by the ward personnel. Burckhardt's object was not to cure the patient but to change a dangerous personality to a harmless one. He operated upon six patients, all of whom were somewhat improved. His work was ignored until Moniz started leucotomy. Although Puusepp sectioned the fibers between the parietal and frontal lobes in three psychiatric patients in 1910, he was not sufficiently impressed by the results to publish them until the advent of lobotomy.

It may be informative to look at Burckhardt's (1891, p. 463) opening remarks to his clinical study:

> The following communication might gain the interest of my distinguished colleagues in an area into which I stepped nearly 2 years ago with the intention of finding new remedies for the treatment of psychoses which are otherwise incurable. None of the cases operated on were of traumatic origin; the indication for surgery was thus a purely psychiatric one. These procedures were based partially on recognized experimental and clinical achievements of the last years, as well as partially, and this I am well aware of, on conclusions of my own, whose justification may not be evident at first.

The "recognized experimental and clinical achievements of the last years" to which Burckhardt refers to are, of course, the classical models of brain function developed during the 1860s, 1870s, and 1880s. On occasion the classical models were used to *explain* the recovery of language in aphasia;[9] however, these models were rarely if ever used as the rationale for the treatment of acquired language, cognitive or emotional disorders (Cot &

Joanette, 1991). The Burckhardt story is, to our knowledge, the first attempt at such a therapeutic application. The beginning of psychosurgery was inauspicious enough; Burckhardt's internal report for the year 1888 (de Meuron, 1949) noted:

> Le Comité m'ayant accordé les fonds, les installations et préparatifs nécessaires étant faits, et le consentement de la famille de la malade étant acquis, nous avons exécuté le 29 décembre la première opération. Ce n'est pas ici l'endroit de'entrer dans des détails. Je tiens seulement à constater que, à ma connaissance, Préfargier est le premier établissement où la trépanation du crâne et l'excision de parcelles de l'écorce cérébrale a été pratiquée non pas pour satisfaire à des indications chirurgicales, mais pour répondre à des indications psychiatriques. Le résultat obtenu m'a puissamment encouragé à continuer dans cette voie dorénavant ouverte.[10]

Thus, Gottlieb Burckhardt became, to our knowledge as well as to his own, the first modern psychosurgeon. Many of his heirs in psychosurgery, for example Moniz (1936) and Freeman and Watts (1942, 1950), cut into the brain to sever fibre tracts without actually removing cortical tissue (the so-called leucotomy or lobotomy procedure), while others, such as Mettler (1949), followed Burckhardt in using the topectomy procedure. As will become clear later, Burckhardt had convinced himself that he could help patients with severe behavioural disturbances either by diminishing the mass of some pathologically functioning centre or by diminishing the influence that such a centre could have on other parts of the brain. For one who accepted the dogma of the period, a centres-and-connections model of brain function,[11] the logic was impeccable.

In his 1891 paper, Burckhardt reported on six patients who suffered from various psychiatric diseases which appeared to be untreatable by the standard medical practices of the day. From the literature sources mentioned above and others who are less well known to us today, he deduced an anatomical model of pathological behaviour, from which he inferred that judiciously placed cortical extirpations might alleviate the symptoms from which his patients suffered. He was aware of the pioneering nature of his clinical experiments—one could interpret them in terms of a rudimentary version of the concept of clinical trials; he also anticipated that he might be criticised for his work. Near the end of his paper (p. 547), he makes the following comment: "Die Naturen der Aerzte sind verschieden. Der eine hält am Grundsatze fest: Primum non nocere. Der andere sagt: melius anceps remedium quam nullum. Ich gehöre allerdings eher der zweiten Categorie an."[12]

Burckhardt did not exaggerate. To illustrate this, we will present abbreviated versions of his six cases, followed by discussion and analysis.

CASE 1

35 y.o. married woman admitted to Préfargier on Feb. 3, 1872. This patient exhibited agitated dementia (chronic raving madness) over a period of 16 years, with violent, explosive episodes. Shortly after admission she had to be transferred to a locked ward because she had become dangerous: without reason and without warning, she kicked, punched, and spat at those passing by. She was considered to be the most dangerous patient in the institution. She made a lot of noise, yelled and cursed, and sang, hour after hour, day and night; occasionally she would produce an incoherent twaddle of partly self-invented words. Once in a while, like lightning, amongst all this jumble and confusion, she would make a remark that was to the point, showing that not all intelligence, observation and correct conclusions were lost. The first operation was done on Dec. 29, 1888, (age 51). There were 4 consecutive operations on the left hemisphere, with success: a permanent abatement of symptoms. After the fourth operation on Feb. 12, 1890 (the removal of pars triangularis of Broca's area) the patient exhibited no paralysis, did not use curse words, was not aphasic, but she did show phasic shifts of attention and inattention. The patient had changed from a dangerous and excited demented person to a calm demented one. The continuous flow of speech had been disrupted and she had become quiet. Although she has not regained her intelligence, she definitely has not lost anything of what she had before. She talks in a more natural voice than before and more frequently comments on what is happening around her.

Only a little information about the previous life of the patient and the development of her illness, up to 1882, was available as the patient's file had been lost. Mrs B. was born in 1837 and married in 1857. Her husband was alcoholic and the marriage was not a good one; they had three children. Earlier the patient seemed to have been healthy, but she was hereditarily predisposed (to mental illness?)[14] from her father's side. In summer 1871 it is said that she suffered gastric-nervous complaints, which were considered hysterical. In the fall of 1871 these re-occurred and were more severe; she complained of "great nervous excitement which caused her to cry without reason." At the beginning of November she was reported to be mentally ill by her family and was treated by a doctor for hysteria. It seems that already by this time she was predisposed to fits of rage and talked in a confusing manner. The certificate of admission describes her as melancholic with delusional ideas. At the time, hallucinations were not reported, however this is based on the uncertain testimony of the family. She exhibited suicidal tendencies. A certain weakness of intelligence was noted. Shortly after her admission the patient had to be transferred to the isolation ward because she became dangerous to everyone around her. Without provocation and without warning, she dealt out foot kicks and fist punches, and she spat at those passing by. At the same time, she was very confused and unclean. She also had better moments, such that her doctors hoped for improvement. But then she relapsed into excitement again. It was curious that she never became violent against the supervisor of the ward; on the contrary, Mrs B. often treated her with a certain degree of sympathy.

When Burckhardt became the director of Préfargier in 1882, Mrs B. was considered to be the most dangerous and in all respects the worst patient in the institution. As was the custom at that time, she was constantly kept in confinement. As soon as she was released, even for the shortest period of time, there were terrible scenarios. Like a fury she senselessly attacked the nearest person available, took her down to the floor and mistreated her with hands and feet. She made a lot of noise, yelled, cursed and sang hour after hour, day and night. There were times when she cried noisily; it was rare not to hear her, either it was fragments of persecution mania and the worst cursing, or an incoherent twaddle of partly self-invented words. Once in a while, like lightning, amongst all this confusion, she made a remark to the point, which showed that not all of her intelligence, observation and correct conclusions were lost. Her bodily hygiene left much to be desired. Her appetite was irregular, sometimes she ate too much, sometimes too little; her looks changed between an ash-grey paleness and a dark-red suffusion; her voice had a male tone. When she talked, she frequently grimaced and, through her own talking, often worked herself into a rage. The patient exhibited an obvious pre-menstrual aggravation of her state; after menstruation there was usually a certain abatement, and for some days a predominantly depressed mood during which she frequently cried. When such a depressive state occurred, she might say that she was afraid and asked not to be killed.

During the next few years her status remained unchanged. Since she continuously occupied a cell and monopolised the head of the department nearly exclusively, she prevented Préfargier from admitting acute curable cases; and because there was no hope of changing her status by medication or hygienic procedures, Burckhardt proposed to dismiss the patient. It was difficult for the family to find accommodation for her; finally, an institution for the poor in the neighbourhood which accommodated a number of incurable and restless mentally ill patients, admitted her. She was successfully moved on 30th July, 1988, with the help of two guards. Eight days later we were urgently asked to readmit the patient as the administration of the other institution refused to take further care of her and, furthermore, had declared the family to be responsible for all consequences. Mrs B. was obviously happy to be back—much more so than the staff were to see her. When asked where she had been, she answered smilingly: "J'ai été au Schallewerk du Canton de Berne."[15] But, she had not changed.

Summarizing what has been said so far, her condition was as follows (p. 467):

Patient is demented. Sensations are perceived but not used in a normal intelligent way but often activate pathologically degenerated moods and impulsive dangerous actions which lack any consideration. It is certain that there is also subjective activation of sensation, even though only indirectly deduced. For example, she slowly turns her head and eyes in one direction, as if following an object with her eyes, while appearing strongly agitated at the same time.

These are probably face (visual) hallucinations and one can also speculate that there were auditory hallucinations.

These two symptoms, the sudden change in mood with affective development and the fast transition to the respective action, made this patient very dangerous. According to Burckhardt, the question thus arose whether it would be possible to remove these emotive-impulsive elements from her brain mechanisms and thus transform her from an agitated to a calm demented patient. And the next question was, where does one have to look for these elements?

Burckhardt discussed two theories about the location of affective processes: (1) Regarding a subcortical location of affective processes, Bechterew[16] suggested that affect is located in the cortex but its mimic expression can be found in the optic thalamus. Lange (1887) agrees with Bechterew that the cortex is involved primarily by sensory or psychic stimulation provoking affect and secondarily by the vessel centre of Ludwig, located in the medulla oblongata; (2) A cortical location of affective processes is supported by authors such as Hofstetter (1880)[33], Bleuler (1885)[33], Nothnagel[33], Bernhardt (1881)[33] and others. Further, the dog experiments by Goltz (1881) suggested that there are different cortical areas which have different values for the expression of affect. However, Burckhardt did not find it permissible to transfer these results to humans because, amongst other reasons: (1) it is uncertain whether these were symptoms of stimulation, inhibition or loss; and (2) the frontal lobe remained undamaged in most dog cases.

Burckhardt proceeded to discuss the work of Broca[33], Flesch (1887)[33], and Meynert[33] which suggests that there is a difference between the anterior and posterior parts of the parietal lobe. He is particularly intrigued by Mairet's (1883) work which proposed that megalomanic disorder is located in the convex region of the frontal and temporal lobe whereas melancholic disorder is found in the first temporal gyrus, the anterior third of the sphenoid gyrus and the hippocampal gyrus. Burckhardt then refers to several authors who think it probable that affect is located only in the right hemisphere; e.g. Luys thinks that the cortex surrounding the right Sylvian fissure is particularly important in this respect. Burckhardt cites further evidence which comes from studies of the weight of brains. Tigges (1881) and Jensen[33] found that mania consumes more from the frontal lobes, melancholia more from the parietal and occipito-temporal lobes. Meynert suggested that the frontal and temporal lobes contribute to a decrease in brain weight in those patients who sustain softening of the brain. Burckhardt concludes (pp. 475–476) from these observations that the decrease in weight points to a decrease of inhibition in the cortex:

> If, as shown by the previous discussion, affect is a cortical event and is transformed into motion not in subcortical but in cortical regions, then the observed abnormally high emotionality in our patients, as well as the immediacy of their actions, can only be seen as a cessation of inhibition, i.e. of normal resistance. But it would not be the entire surface of the cortical area which, in my opinion, has been affected by this change. I think that it is precisely the motor region which should be excluded, because they have not shown any impairment in muscle coordination.

Burckhardt next refers to work by Nothnagel and Naunyn, Leyden, Jastrowitz, Hitzig, and others, who have shown that the motor cortical regions are responsible for the movement of the extremities. From this he concludes (pp. 477–478) that what is wrong with this patient:

> are the sources from which the motoric events are activated, i.e. the sensory areas, then the apperceptive processes which regulate and guide motor processes and finally the ideational[17] processes connected to speech function. To separate the apperceptive from the perceptive parts of the cortex with a knife could not be done; however, both parts could be separated from the motor area, and this even if the sensory areas themselves were not only recipient but also the origin of stimuli. That the latter was indeed true, to me seemed to follow from the patient's state.

Burckhardt referred to Weber's Law, which says that under normal conditions there are obstacles which prevent the spreading of stimuli. If these obstacles were diminished or totally omitted, then the sensory stimuli could more or less flow unweakened into the motor area, and there they could release a complex of movements.

Burckhardt applied these theoretical considerations as follows (p. 478):

> if one assumes that the agitation and impulsiveness of our patient is caused by stimuli in the sensory regions that are excessive in number, quality and strength and which penetrate the motor region, then an improvement can only be achieved by newly introducing inhibition between the two. However there would be an alternative. One could either remove the motor areas or sensory cortical areas.

Burckhardt refrained from such a procedure because of technical reasons and unpredictable functional consequences. Instead, he thought it sufficient to remove a small strip of cortical substance posterior (toward the occipital pole) to the motor zone on both sides and, at the same time, make a trench down to the temporal lobe (pp. 478–479):

> In so doing, I hoped for a sufficiently large interruption of the many association events, particularly those proceeding from the sensory areas of the eyes and the ears to the motor zones of the body muscles. I could not hope to have reached the language area with this removal. Not that the language area does not extend its roots to the occipito-temporal region. But its motor collection point is located more frontal from the central gyrus and the formation of the frontal lobe in the human brain indicates that not only the motor but also a large part of the ideational language area is located in the frontal brain. Thus, right from the beginning I had to tell myself that by making a trench behind the central gyrus, only half of the task would have been accomplished, at best, and that the other half, i.e. interrupting the continuous linguistic excitement with its stronger counter-current discharge, could only be solved by an analogous treatment of the frontal brain, i.e. by a trench in front of the central gyrus.

The first operation took place at 2pm, on 29th December, 1888, when a 2cm strip of the lateral part of the superior parietal lobe and medial part of the supramarginal gyrus, immediately posterior to the central gyrus, was removed. A total of a little over 5 grams of cortex was removed during a four-hour operation. Afterward, the patient developed a septic resorption fever. She was generally calm; her glance and looks were less wild and vehement. If one approaches her bed she murmurs something and, occasionally, talks in a very natural tone to her guard, e.g. "Donne-moi beaucoup d'eau, j'ai soif",[18] or "Prends une chaise et assoie toi à côté de moi."[19] On 6th January the patient got up for the first time; there were no signs of paralysis. Her behaviour was much quieter than before the operation, however, before going to bed, she again dealt out foot kicks. On 9th January, 1889, she developed a complete, flaccid paralysis of the left arm and shoulder and clear weakness in the left leg. Touch and pain sensation were also decreased. Two weeks later her sensibility reappeared and, after a few weeks, her hand was back to near normal. Two months after the operation she was still, albeit less, violent, and the changes in mood persisted; she still hallucinated.

Burckhardt decided upon a second operation which was done on 8th March, 1889, and lasted 2 hours, 30 minutes: The posterior part of the superior and medial temporal gyrus was extirpated—a total of 2.5 grams was removed. The operative report states that the surface of the brain looks like a pigmented lung, with black spots. After the operation a certain gaiety on the part of the patient was noticed; she laughed and talked. Her pre-operative depressive moods seem to have disappeared. The patient laughs, talks more, murmurs her confusions of words and sentences to herself, but otherwise, her condition has not been changed much by this operation: Her emotions were more or less the same, changes in mood still occur and again, no paralysis is observed. As no further changes were noted, Burckhardt decided to do a third operation on 29th May: This time the operative site is moved further back to account for the Exner–Jastrowitz' observation that the left motor area of the cortex has a larger extension. During this procedure, a strip of cortex from the left parietal lobe is removed, starting from the interparietal sulcus, through the lateral rim of the superior temporal lobe, to the lower temporal lobe, including parts of the supramarginal and angular gyri and the occipital end of the Sylvian fissure. The procedure lasted 4 hours 40 minutes and about 5.5 grams of cortex were removed. Post-operatively, Burckhardt observed some excitatory movements of the right fingers and right arm. Her hallucinations and mood-changes persisted, albeit less frequently and less pronounced. With respect to language, nothing had changed. Eight months post-operative, the impulsiveness and violence, spontaneous noisiness and singing, and also the visual and auditory hallucinations seemed to have disappeared. Despite her demented appearance, the patient frequently demonstrated the ability to make correct observations and to draw correct conclusions. However, according to Burckhardt, it was impossible to conduct a conversation with her; "she is word deaf. When one talks to her, her own verbigeration increases, culminating in threats. Only rarely does one get an answer to questions—Yet we notice favourably that the patient utters fewer indecencies" (p. 489).

More and more I convinced myself that a threat word did not follow a particular movement or change in mood but preceded it. The uttered word thus was not, as in a normal condition, the last act but, like in a hypnotic condition, the first act of the cerebral excitation event, the introductory one. I concluded that there was a pathological state of agitation in the motor centres for word formation—I thought I could conclude this because of the persistence of verbigeration, or, more correctly, logorrhea. I further concluded that, in pursuit of my original plan, the next location to attack had to be the region of the motor speech centers. The risk of making the patient aphasic was of not much concern to me, considering the advantages to be expected. Nevertheless, I did not intend to remove all of the lateral part of Broca's gyrus, but only a part thereof. The possibility that the lost language would be restituted by the homogeneous cortical field on the right side, could not be expected, considering the advanced age of the patient. (P. 490.)

The fourth operation (2 hours 30 minutes) was done on 12th February, 1890, during which 1.5 grams of the pars triangularis of Broca's area was removed. Post-operatively there was no paralysis, no curse words, no aphasia, no changes of phases of attention nor inattention.

> Mrs Borel has changed from a dangerous and excited demented person to a quiet demented one—The continuous overflowing speechflow has been disrupted. The patient has become quiet. She has not regained intelligence. But she definitely has not lost anything of what she had. ... She talks in a more natural voice than before and more often comments on what is happening around her. Finally I'd like to emphasize that my views, expressed above, on the cortical processes of our patient, are rather more supported by the success of the operation than refuted. I do not want to seem too positive about it. Things do not necessarily need to be the way we imagine them to be. But this cannot stop us from at least imagining them. (Pp. 493–494.)

CASE 2

> 31 y.o. man admitted to Préfargier on July 24, 1884. This patient exhibited primary dementia, beginning acutely 8 years ago, with explosively occurring defensive actions and verbal auditory hallucinations. The patient is totally absorbed, without interest in what is going on around him, won't listen to anybody without becoming mad and attacking right away, never looks anyone straight in the eyes, frequently looks up to the left, often makes a mocking (sarcastic) face, smiles and sometimes murmurs to himself. It is not clear whether he suffers from auditory hallucinations though he seems to be listening for voices. First and only operation: April 17, 1889, (age 36); Success: Definite abatement and better ease in verbal communication. Excision of cortex at the first and second left frontal gyrus, during which a strongly developed leptomeningitis was found. After the operation the patient developed several epileptic seizures which finally were controlled with 3g of potassium bromide. The patient is calmer, more talkative and more approachable than before. However, this success is not of much value if one cannot achieve more than making the patient easier to care for because he is less vehement and violent.

Patient is a 31½-year-old lithographer who had been admitted on 24th July, 1884; he was an only child who showed no hereditary predisposition to mental illness. As a pupil it was said he was talented, but he was said to have masturbated previously and debauched. One and a half years ago he was taken care of in a psychiatric clinic because of excitement and impulsive actions, first in a foreign country and then in Switzerland. The patient was indiscriminately chasing after prostitutes and caught gonorrhoea. On admission, the patient suffered from primary dementia, occurring acutely eight years ago, possibly on the basis of megalomania with a secondary impairment of ideas and explosively occurring defence actions. These were verbal auditory hallucinations. He barely gives any information, is totally absorbed and has no interest in what is going on around him; he is obviously affected with mega-ideas, will not listen to anybody without becoming mad and instantly attacking them. He never looks anyone straight in the eyes, but frequently looks up to the left, often making a mocking (sarcastic) face, smiling, and sometimes murmurs to himself. It is not clear whether he suffers from auditory hallucinations. He generally sleeps well, eats well, but looks pale and is thin.

In September, together with congestion in the head, he had a period of agitation, during which he became very arrogant and imperious, angry and impertinent, often laughing, or uttering single, discontinuous sentences. In November, 1884, he was calmer again, responds somewhat better but more briefly; if you want more he becomes angry. During the end of November and December, he again became more agitated, now obviously listening for voices. He does not occupy himself at all, but browses in ashtrays and spittoons. By February, 1885, he is somewhat calmer, once in a while picking up a book, most of the time walking back and forth in the hallway restlessly. He becomes aggressive and violent as soon as someone disturbs him. In April his goitre develops strongly. From August to October he showed increasing agitation. He deals out pushes if one approaches him too closely, and was consequently overthrown twice by fellow patients which he accepts, feeling the physical dominance of the others. Then there is a longer period of relative calmness during which he once in a while helps the coal carrier to carry coal. In August, 1887, again agitation and growth of goitre. Similarly, from January until March 1888, he sang, yelled and was unclean, especially at night. In May, again with a growing tendency towards uncleanliness, he looked pale and, despite his good appetite, thin. Up to November he was calmer, and smiling, after which he again became agitated and malicious, hurling things, such as stones, around him. Every attempt to keep him busy was to him an intrusion and he rejected it at once with erupting rage and violence. He did not talk except for short phrases, e.g. "pourqoi faire?"[20] or single words, though there was no paralytic speech impairment. It is impossible to get him to write. Visits by his parents usually do not interrupt this behaviour. We are dealing with a completely developed primary dementia, which has turned chronic. Due to the still existing stimulus conditions, this patient is troublesome and dangerous.

As before, the task was to interrupt or render more difficult, the connections between the parts of the brain, particularly the cortex, which are either stimulus generating or executing. I was looking for the next point of attack, not between the central gyri and the sensory brain, but between the central gyri and the frontal brain, because the entire condition shared with the dementia paralytica many psychic symptoms and therefore, as I assumed, also the localisation in the frontal brain. Furthermore, since it was suspected that the left frontal brain was more involved, because there were single motoric stimulus symptoms, the head and the eyes frequently moved to the left, and there were continuous hurling movements of the right foot. One must emphasize, again, that we cannot talk about a restitution of intelligence but only about a removal of impulses. I only want to try to shift the agitated dementia into a more quiet one. (Pp. 495–496.)

The first and only operation (3 hours) was done on 17th April, 1889; it was intended to enter the skull in such a way as to meet the lateral rim of the first and the foot of the second frontal gyrus, behind the parallel sulcus. "The pia mater appeared opaque, edematous, thickened, like fur, and streaked with strong veins. Also below the pia there was a jelly-like edematous mass from which a lot of liquid was released. ... The gyri were broad and massive, of solid consistency and of a cyanotic like colour (p. 496).[21] After the operation, the patient was still angry and agitated, but is now less vehement and less violent. He still suffers from mood changes. Since the operation, he talks more and the auditory hallucinations are more prominent. He developed several epileptic seizures that were controlled by 3 grams of potassium bromide. Burckhardt discussed several possible reasons for the development of seizures: predisposition, findings of the brain during the operation, or the operation itself. It seemed to him that the operative intervention itself was at least an incidental cause which allowed an existing predisposition to break out. Despite this, the operation did not seem to be without any gain at all. On the one hand, it has shown more clearly the relationship between auditory delusions and explosive actions and thus has given us a hint about future research. On the other hand, the patient is calmer, more talkative and more approachable than before. However, this success is not of much value if one can not achieve more than making the patient easier to care for, because he is less vehement and violent. However, Burckhardt did not believe that an additional operation could achieve any more, since, what was found in the dura, pia and cortex of the superior left frontal gyri, would most likely be found in many other places in the brain.[22]

This case is not complete and thus does not allow further conclusions. However, regarding questions of localization, it is not a total loss. The extirpated site is the one which has been viewed as the center for agraphia, by several authors. Our patient, however, is still able to write. What we weren't able to persuade him to do in earlier times, he now does. He wrote a card to his mother following the dictation of the guard. (Pp. 501–502.)

CASE 3

37 y.o. woman re-admitted to Préfargier on Feb. 2, 1886. Her condition was an acute primary insanity with predominantly verbal auditory hallucinations, with passive persecution mania. After 2 years there was a transition to an agitated dementia with persistence of hallucinations. Patient agreed to surgical

procedure and was operated on June 7, 1889, (age 40). Success: Significant improvement.

The patient is a 37-year-old widow with one child. Her mother had been convulsive-hysteric. As a child of eight years of age she already appeared to have been psychiatrically ill, probably with auditory hallucinations and hysteric complaints. Later on the patient started to hear voices, was restless, and suffered from insomnia. The patient went to Préfargier on 2nd February, 1886, and asked for admission in order to "calm down" and "to prevent a disaster" as voices had repetitively told her she would have to kill her sister or child. She suffered from hallucinations and periods of agitation. At times she had to be isolated because she attacked people.

In July, 1886 the patient was allowed to go home. However, she was readmitted three weeks later because the family could not endure her behaviour. In January, 1887, hypnotic treatment was started; sometimes it helped, sometimes it did not; the disease progressed and the patient became worse. There was decrease in intelligence as a consequence of a constant restlessness and a rapid progression of the main symptoms. The patient readily agreed to an operative treatment of her hallucinations. During the operation on 7th June, 1889, the posterior part of the first and the medial part of the second temporal gyri were removed, i.e. a part of the sensory word memory. The pia was totally transparent and could not be separated from the cortex without creating another lesion; the brain substance was extremely soft, which Burckhardt had never seen before. Three grams of cortex were removed, in a 2 hour 45 minute operation. On 13th–14th June, convulsions started in the right arm, then the right leg, and then spread over the entire body; the whole seizure incident lasted for 45 minutes. The next morning the left side of her face was swollen which was ascribed to a local, purulent inflammation in the temporal region resulting in the seizure.

After patient woke up from the anaesthesia, a certain degree of aphasia was noticed (p. 517):

Patient confused words, particularly the names of things, or she had problems naming them, e.g. scissors, clock. She spoke hesitantly, in short sentences, frequently interrupting herself. Sometimes the words were uttered unclear, more or less complete, or the words were well formed but incorrectly applied. The same was true for comprehension. Some things she understood correctly, but with other things it was dubious whether she understood. ... I noted particularly that, as soon as one spoke to her, she herself started to speak and continued until oneself stopped talking. After some weeks, however, these impairments mostly disappeared. What was left was a difficulty in forming and uttering longer sentences in a row, and evidently an endeavour to use paraphrases. With regard to the auditory hallucinations, I think I can observe a similar behavior. But they had definitely decreased in frequency and determination. The patient at times felt unhappy and tormented, but she does not accuse this or that person, having said this or that about her. I think I can interpret this with regard to a decrease in hallucinations.

In the late summer of 1889 the agitations seemed to increase but by the autumn of 1889 there was definitely more improvement. Burckhardt did not want to let her go home, in part because he had planned a second operation for spring 1890 and also he did not think the patient had sufficiently improved. However, it was decided on 21st November to dismiss her, partly because the patient had urged to be dismissed. On 24th December, 1889, a letter came from the family, that the patient's condition was satisfactory; on 28th December she disappeared and was found two days later, dead, in a river. Nobody knew whether it was an accident, suicide, or a crime. The relatives agreed to an autopsy and the brain was brought to Burckhardt who concluded that he had removed the desired target during the operation but now, seeing the brain, he thought that he could have safely removed more.

CASE 4

35 y.o. man admitted to Préfargier in February 1885; This patient exhibited chronic, inherent, craziness with hysteric symptoms predominating, and which threatened to lead to permanent agitation mainly through the increase of verbal auditory hallucinations. Patient was restless and suspicious of his wife whom he thought wanted to leave him or put him in prison. He became fearful and didn't want to be alone any more. Operated on April 24, 1889, (age 39). After an excision from the cortex of the acoustic word field, the patient's behavior was more calm, he no longer cursed, he replied very briefly but correctly, was less suspicious and not violent. Success: Significant improvement.

This patient was a 35-year-old gardener, married with two children; he was admitted at the end of February, 1885. No hereditary predisposition for mental illness was evident. Although he was not very intelligent he was a good worker. In the autumn of 1884 he began to behave strangely and was more agitated than usual. For the previous two weeks there had been a worsening of his symptoms. He was restless and suspicious of his wife, whom he thought wanted to leave him or put him into prison. He was fearful and afraid of being left alone. His wife had to accompany him everywhere and eat in front of him. During the day he closed the window shutters because he felt observed; he locked himself in the house and didn't work any more. He didn't sleep much and wandered about in the house. He expressed a mortal fear, predicted a major malfortune and threatened to defend himself with an axe against his pursuers.

According to Burckhardt (p. 505), this case is representative of a certain class of patient:

> After an introductory pre-stage, there follows an outbreak of an acute, hallucinatory insanity together with congestive appearances, which rapidly lead to dementia, despite all efforts. The delirium is characterized by impaired functioning, the mood is one of continuous fear, and the hallucinations provoke defensive reactions. After the acute stage, which in our case lasted $1\frac{1}{2}$ to 2 years, the patient moves on to the chronic stage in which dementia predominates, i.e. absolute incapability to do anything, loss of interest, dull brooding or a restless walking back and forth. Particularly because of the hallucinations, the patient remains dangerous, needs continuous supervision and frequently has to be isolated. As in other cases, in this case my intention couldn't be any other than to transform a dangerous patient to a non-dangerous one. The site of attack was more certain in this case. Since I regarded the auditory delusions as the ones which forced the patient to violence, I had to try and cut the ground under their feet. The question was, where to look for it.

In this case Burckhardt considered the auditory hallucinations as those which directed and dominated the patient and thus he decided to directly remove them. The only author who had mentioned anything concerning the relationship of auditory hallucinations to actions was Luys. Luys found a hypertrophic paracentral lobe on one side in active and lucid hallucinations, and hypertrophy on both sides in totally non-lucid hallucinations. Although, to Burckhardt, Luys does not express himself clearly, he interprets Luys such that this lobe is the bridge from which the hallucinatory excitations flow off to motor areas, i.e. the area of the leg (p. 505): "But what good would it have done to remove it? The hallucinations and megalomanic ideas most likely would stay the same. The patient only would need even more help because he would have been paralysed." Thus Burckhardt decided that he had to address the "logogen" cortical areas themselves.

> I have sometimes wondered why psychiatry has not seriously asked whether the cortical area of acoustic word memory is an integrating member in the chain of processes which create auditory hallucinations. If there is a cortical field in the brain which, when destroyed, robs the human being of acoustic word comprehension, then shouldn't a stimulation of the cortical area lead to an arousal of these functions in such a way that the patient thinks he perceives words and phrases which have not, as in the normal situation, been called by the periphery? This question would have been positively answered long ago if observation had taught us that involvement of the temporal lobe is invariably related to auditory hallucinations. But until now this has not been the case. (P. 505.)

Despite all efforts, Burckhardt could find nothing in the literature in this regard (by authors such as Ladame, Bernhardt, Wernicke, Friedlander, Nothnagel, Roger, Pierson, Schuele, Stenger, Reinhard, Wilbrand, Nauny[33]).

Burckhardt considered it possible that Wernicke's gyri are involved in the appearance of auditory hallucinations (as there was no counter example so far). He regarded it to be even more probable that, in addition to Wernicke's gyri, there are other cortical areas which serve speech functions and which are simultaneously activated. He mentions Broca's area and the possibility that only through the contribution of this motor area could hallucinations obtain the distinctness and strength of persuasion of the spoken word (cf. p. 507). It did not matter much to Burckhardt (p. 508) whether the first activation of a verbal hallucination had its origin in the cortical areas (as expressed by Tamburini and Wernicke) or if the origin was to be found in subcortical areas (as expressed by Hagen and Meynert): "Our question is not: where is the origin of verbal hallucinations? But: is it possible to weaken or remove verbal hallucinations by breaking out pieces of the auditory speech tract?"

Burckhardt thought that if Broca's area was extirpated then the patient would suffer from motor aphasia, and in the case of Wernicke's area, sensory aphasia. His criteria for choosing which area should be the first to be removed were: (1) the right or left handedness of the patient, and (2) the decision as to which type of aphasia to tolerate. He thought that motor aphasia was the more severe deficit and more difficult to restitute than sensory aphasia (pp. 508–509): "What I have observed from both, and especially from motor aphasias, has left the impression, that the one who cannot say what he wants is worse off and suffers more than the one who does not know that he does not understand." Therefore, Burckhardt decided to remove Wernicke's gyrus. The operation was done on 24th April, 1889: 2.8 grams of cortex were removed during a 2 hour 30 minute procedure. The colour of the cortex was described as slate. After the patient awoke from the anaesthesia, he uttered one of his habitual phrases and upon request protruded his tongue.

Burckhardt particularly noted that the patient did not suffer from word deafness. One could communicate as well or even better with the patient than before the operation. The patient's behaviour was more calm, he did not curse, replies briefly but correctly, was less suspicious and not violent. Additionally, an erotic characteristic has turned up; furthermore, not all of the hallucinations are gone.

The plainly visible result of the operation is that the patient has been altered from a disagreeable, occasionally violent patient, dangerous to his comrades and confined in a disturbed ward, into a harmless working patient inhabiting the quiet ward. Demented he remains. But, the dementia definitely has not increased and in many respects it has decreased. Furthermore, I am certain that the patient suffers less from hallucinations than he did before, although those that remain, seem to me, according to the patient's statement, as intense as before. (P. 511.)[23]

CASE 5

24 y.o. man admitted to Préfargier in July 1887; Primary insanity which has become chronic with strong predominance of verbal auditory hallucinations. Transition to fully developed dementia. The patient's mood changed from agitation to depression and several times he showed tendencies to commit suicide. First operated on the acoustic cortex on June 5, 1889, (age 26); the second operation on Broca's area, on February 19, 1890. Success: Significant improvement and restriction of hallucinations.

M.M., born 1863, is a painter. He has no direct hereditary predisposition to mental disease. At the age of 17 he went to Munich where his problem may have started; there, at times, he expressed very bizarre ideas. Four years later he went to Paris where restlessness and unsteadiness were noticed, as well as curious claims such as being the son of a prince. In February 1887 he was taken home where at first he seemed to recover. He was busy painting; however, to each painting he added a nose and a mosquito in one corner of the canvas. Auditory hallucinations were noticed. The patient's mood changed from agitation to depression and several times he showed tendencies to commit suicide. In July 1887 the patient was admitted to Préfargier. He looked very bad, frequently changing colour. His behaviour was restless and unsteady, his drawings were disorderly and he repeatedly painted a fat face. Besides auditory hallucinations there were also visual hallucinations and disturbance of sensation and smell. His memory for experiences in the past was good, but recent experiences were remembered only fragmentarily. Drive and motivation were decreased; confusion in thought, motivation, emotion and action were the characteristics of his state. As to physical symptoms, headache in the frontal and temporal area were noted, hot flashes as well as red-injected eyes, poor physical condition, irregular sleep, and masturbation. In a period of improvement his parents yielded to his urge to leave the hospital and the patient was sent home but had to be readmitted six months later as his condition had deteriorated. Burckhardt noticed a progression of the disease; the patient's gaze was restless and empty and the auditory and visual hallucinations had increased. He had nearly stopped painting but writes many letters to official institutions demanding that they stop the bad circumstances surrounding him. An attempt to involve him in gardening work was totally unsuccessful. Hypnotic treatment helped for a short time but then did not show any continuing effect. Electrical examination showed a negative result, i.e. there was vertigo and buzzing in the head followed by an acoustic reaction. Some sites on the skin of the head were strikingly sensitive.

As the condition deteriorated and one could not predict improvement, the parents decided to transfer the patient to a health resort. Three months later the patient had to be collected and was brought again to Préfargier. His condition had further deteriorated. During this short period of time his intelligence had markedly diminished. There was a childish aspect to this patient and his appearance and gaze resembled that of a fully developed dementia. His hallucinations were strongly erotic. Asymmetrical pupils, palish green appearance and weight loss were noted. Language articulation had not suffered; however, the patient invented words and used them repeatedly but did not furnish any information as to their meaning. The emotional element had increased, the patient was much more furious than earlier. He was less obedient. There were problems with nourishing him. This was the characteristic picture of hallucinatory insanity which eclipsed his intelligence and led to dementia. It was evident that auditory hallucinations played the major role.

Burckhardt thought that it was the motor parts of the language regions (Broca's area), which were more affected than Wernicke's area. He came to this conclusion because the disturbance of the visual sense influenced the patient's actions much less than the auditory hallucinations; the visual hallucinations could be interpreted as associated events. Consequently the operative therapy should have been directed towards Broca's gyrus, and the more so as word neologisms produced by the patient also pointed in this direction. However, following his reasoning in Case 2,[24] Burckhardt decided to operate on Wernicke's area first and only later on Broca's area. The family agreed to his suggestion of an operation, although Burckhardt could not promise a restitution of intelligence but, in the best case, an alleviation or removal of the auditory hallucinations. The way the patient presented now there was no thought of ever releasing him from the institution. Agitated idiocy would have been the continuation of the present condition and, possibly after many years, apathic idiocy. But the family appreciated the goal to be achieved, to enable them to take care of the patient at home, even if he sustained sensory or motor aphasia and feeble-mindedness.

The first operation was performed on 5th June, 1889; 4.6 grams of cortex were removed, during a 3 hour 15 minute procedure, from Wernicke's area—T1 and T2. During the first days after the operation the patient spoke very little and was very calm. He sometimes murmured something and it was deduced from these utterances that he still had auditory hallucinations. What he said was normally pronounced; he was not word deaf and could comprehend correctly. About a week after the operation traces of aphasic symptoms occurred (patient used wrong words and spoke non-fluently) which worsened over the next few days but then disappeared a week later. The patient remained much calmer than before the operation. One could exchange some words with him, sometimes he answered correctly before relapsing into his own talk and murmurs. Often he asked to be dismissed to go home. The vehemence and compulsion disappeared from his character. The patient remained like this all through the autumn and winter. In the mornings he remains in bed; in the afternoons he is in the company of other men, reading, drawing, or taking small walks. His hallucinations remain and he has not yet reached the state where he recognises these voices as something pathological.

Because no further improvement occurred, and (p. 529) "on the contrary the patient starts to talk more vividly," Burckhardt decided to perform a second operation, this time on Broca's area. On 19th February, 1890, during a 2 hour 30 minute procedure, 2.5 grams of cortex were removed from Broca's area. The pia presented itself as a dark reddish grey sack of solid consistency, upon which the vessels ascend from bottom to top in a fan-like fashion.

During the dressing of the operative site, the patient awoke and said "ecoutez"[25] in a normal voice, an utterance with which the patient usually preceded his discourse. No apraxic[26] speech impairment was observed after the second operation. His pronunciation was correct, he does not mix up words but utters more routine formulas (p. 531): "It is as if his vocabulary is decreased and at the same time his hallucinations [are decreased]." This was subsequently confirmed. The hallucinations referred more to trifles, much less to sexual things. Sometimes, when the patient talked to himself, there was some reflection or remark that his brain is not OK and that he can't go home. Since his second operation, the patient not only talks less but also with a lower voice; generally, he was much calmer, starts to draw again, play cards and billiards. He liked to look at magazines which show paintings by famous painters and to explain the paintings and the personalities of the painters. Burckhardt could talk to the patient for 15 minutes quite well; however, he sometimes had to remind him to answer questions. The patient was not quieter because he has become more demented but because he is "mentally freer and unrestrained." He was quieter because the hallucinations have decreased quantitatively and qualitatively. The impression that the patient was much quieter than before, better behaved, more manageable has been confirmed repeatedly by his mother.

Burckhardt then discussed why the patient did not become aphasic after the second operation. He refuted the possibility that he had not operated on the correct area, or that the motor speech area of the patient was not at the foot of the third left frontal gyrus. He discussed the patient's handedness: He painted and wrote with the right hand. He then suggested that it may also be possible that the speech area is more extended and that the part he cut out was too small of a part in order to lead to more pronounced speech impairment (pp. 532–533). As long as the patient continues to improve, Burckhardt did not want to operate again on this patient. But, in case it came to a relapse, he planned to remove a bigger part of this cortex and, possibly, of the underlying white matter. He regarded as very important in evaluating this disease, the appearance of the fronto-temporal pia matter. It proved that one is dealing with an inflammatory process or at least a process which was similar to an inflammation which had affected especially the lateral frontal parts of the brain, less so the temporal lobe. The operation had influenced this process positively, since an improvement of the inflammatory symptoms occurred. Since the operation, there have been no more elevated temperatures, and the frontal-temporal headaches have disappeared. Should all of this be a mere coincidence, Burckhardt asked himself? He did not think so.

CASE 6

33 y.o. man, a day-labourer, admitted to Préfargier on Nov. 18, 1889. This patient exhibited strong hereditary disposition to primary insanity with strong development of verbal auditory hallucinations. The progression became more and more acute, with dangerous defensive actions. He thought his fellow workers wanted to kill him. His mother had been in Préfargier twice and died there. Also some possible predisposition from his father's side. First operated on April 9, 1890; excision of cortex of the acoustic word field. Large area of softness in the brain and a huge development of the venae of the Sylvian fissure. Success: a complete word deafness with a complete cessation of hallucinations. On the fourth post-operative day there was a convulsive episode followed by progressively more frequent seizures; the patient died on April 14, 1890, 5 days after the operation.

The patient was a watch-maker by profession. He had moved to France, worked in various fields and moved around a lot for the last 10 years. When he came back he found a job in community administration. His strange behaviour—he thought his fellow workers wanted to kill him—was noticed. Working again as a watch-maker did not change anything and he still felt pursued. He suffered from insomnia. His family, in order to prevent a tragedy, asked for admission to Préfargier; the patient himself did not feel sick. Physically, aside from emphysema, he was healthy. At first the hallucinations were intermittent; later, they increased in frequency; he suffered from ideas of persecution and several times made a suicide attempt. On one occasion he attacked his neighbour. He became more and more restless and agitated and could not sleep anymore. The brother, as well as the patient himself during his "clear" moments, asked for an operation "to free him from his agony. He could not take this anymore." (P. 536.) After an especially strong attack of hallucinations and a suicide attempt, Burckhardt decided to operate.

This time, Burckhardt intended to extirpate more of the acoustic word field than in previous operations, i.e. to take the middle of the first and second temporal gyri. The operation was on 9th April. Due to the patient's restlessness, Burckhardt had difficulty making the appropriate measures for entering the skull. It turned out that the measures were not accurate and he ended up in the area of the lower part of the central gyrus and supramarginal gyrus. He tried to enlarge the craniotomy by hammering downwards with a chisel. As a consequence the dura became covered with fine, punctiform haemorrhagia and the surface of the brain began to look slate-like. Burckhardt then changed his approach and opened the lower part of the skull by drilling holes in the usual manner. The arteries in the dura released a lot of black coloured blood and the veins of the Sylvian tissue released a pencil-thick flow of blood. T1 and T2 were covered by a dense and strongly filled net of veins. The pia was barely visible and also very resistant. Burckhardt extirpated 3.4 grams of cortex, destroying the closely surrounding tissue. The operation lasted 3 hours 45 minutes. While the head was being dressed, the patient mumbled some words, and a sensory aphasic impairment was observed. The patient did not comprehend and could not answer any questions. Furthermore, there was a strong apraxic aphasia—the patient uttered many words in a mumbling fashion, slurring them and obviously using wrong words. Frequently he repeated "my mother, my mother"—and pointed with his hand away from himself—"she is gone" but he accompanied this by saying: "here, here." A day after the operation the sensory aphasia was complete and the apraxic aphasia had increased; there was also an apraxic agraphia.[27] Burckhardt wrote some questions for the patient which he answered in writing but with senseless words. On 11th April the word deafness was complete, and a relatively large decrease in vocabulary was seen. One cannot communicate with the patient in writing, perhaps because he cannot understand writing anymore, or he cannot concentrate his attention; it is as if he were in a foreign country. On 12th April the patient developed epileptic seizures, started at 10am and continuing to half past midnight, every 10 minutes. Burckhardt assumed that the status epilepticus was a consequence of the vibrations caused by the chiselling. The patient remained as if in a dream. In the afternoon of the next day, the seizures started again, albeit shorter but more regularly. The patient developed a fever and became weaker and on 14th April at 9.15am he died.

Burckhardt performed an autopsy,[28] from which he concluded that he had found a picture of generalised paralysis of the vessels. He thought it to be the consequence of the shocks (to the skull and brain) when he chiselled during the craniotomy.

BURCKHARDT'S CONCLUDING REMARKS

The reasons for surgical intervention certainly must first be scientific, and there is no doubt that in this regard, opinions will greatly diverge. Those who view psychosis merely as a diffuse disease of the cortex will not see any sense in extirpating parts of the cortex. One should take a different point of view, as I do. Our psychic life is constructed of single elements which are sitting in the brain, locally separated and which remain at their location all their lives. Nevertheless, they have and maintain many different connections with their close and their distant neighbours. (P. 544.)

Burckhardt emphasised that the study of language, its mechanisms and impairments, has contributed proof that there is a spatial separation of basic psychic mechanisms. He refers to Preyer's (observations from child development) and Dufour's (experiences with late operations on blind-born people) work as well as other anatomical-comparative studies[33].

... which show an increase of brain substance with increased psychic abilities and achievement,[29] but a transformation of the brain substance in the sense of a multiplication of room or space for new acquisitions at the cost of old stock.[30]

It was the study of language impairment which first led to the necessity to separate from the general psychic characteristic of memory ability, those different memories which store their material in locally separated storage bins in the cortex. Not only do script and language store their elements in a number of different memory compartments, but many other memory systems do so as well. Indeed the separation goes back to basic sensory events, and cases such as hemiachromatopsia as described by Verrey and by myself, support and extend the view given by Nothnagel three years ago [before 1891]. On the other hand, the unity of the will breaks apart if so-called actions of will can be individually detached from their apparently uniform cluster. We all know that our predispositions and capabilities are different, on the one hand, while our brains are different, on the other; but we do not look eagerly enough for the internal connections of these facts. We are used to viewing actions, at least the conscious ones, as the result of thinking and we forget that thinking also depends on the anatomical conditions of action; in other words, our psychic mechanism can also work in reverse, and thus have recourse to its individual elements more than we would like to admit. Therefore, I think that we have to distinguish (more sharply than we have done so far) in the psychic field between focal and general signs. For example, I will only refer to the rubric of consciousness and self-consciousness. As long as we view these as one "being", we consider them automatically as general, diffuse states; but as soon as we view them as emergent properties (what I think they really are), then we admit of a structure, and with this, an anatomical differentiation. Logically, we would not view psychoses as diffuse diseases of the cortex but as diseases which are a more or less large number of elements in a chain of psychic events, or of individual cortical foci, whereby the points of origin and spreading are different, and consequently also the symptoms. Only this view can explain that different types of deliria may exist at the same time, a fact which finds more and more agreement, and only this view can explain those cases where a psychosis with individual stable symptoms has been caused by a head injury and after many years is cured by cutting out the lesioned site, and only this view can explain that individual domains of psychic life can be changed whereas others remain free. Meynert has recently made an important step forward in this direction by separating association psychosis from projection psychosis. From this observation and other, previously discussed reasons, I believe one has the right to cut out those parts of the cortex which one views as the origin and center of psychic impairments, and further interrupt connections whose existence causes an important part of pathological events. (Pp. 545–546.)

COMMENTARY AND ANALYSIS

1. The intractability as well as the seriousness of the behavioural impairments of his patients was in large measure his justification for a surgical approach. His belief that he understood enough about the brain to be able to ameliorate severe psychiatric symptoms was an additional argument in his chain of logic.

2. Burckhardt developed a model of the affecting system of the human brain, by analysing both the positive and negative results of the experimental and clinical investigations of his contemporaries.

3. Like most localisationist models of the day, his implicitly accepted and phrenological principle of the relationship between the size of the cortical area and the "strength" of the behaviour.

4. And, like those of his contemporaries, his model employed associationist principles derived from Hartley and Bain. Accepting associationism led Burckhardt to believe that severing fibre connections prevented unwanted behaviours from being realised.

5. As well, several points of discussion remain, e.g. what did Burckhardt really learn from Friedrich Goltz? Goltz' paper of 1888 makes the following *clinical* points, among others, which can be subsequently directly traced in Burckhardt's paper: (a) Goltz emphasised that one can take out large portions of either hemisphere without endangering the life of the animal; Goltz did a left hemispherectomy and the dog survived; (b) Goltz claimed that functions are quite well restored after cortical extirpations, unless the lesions are very large; (c) Goltz sometimes did his cortical ablations in series, e.g. on one dog, Goltz operated on 11th December, 1885, on 11th February, 1886, and again on 17th March, 1886; (d) Goltz concluded that the anterior parts of the hemispheres are symmetrical apparatuses which can take each other's place; (e) Goltz said, "it is much easier to keep an animal alive after extirpation of the posterior part of the hemispheres than when the anterior

parts have been ablated."; (f) Goltz made a point of believing that the opposite hemisphere is able to assume some impaired functions; he argued that bilateral surgical lesions cause much more pronounced effects than unilateral ones; (g) Goltz described a dog who had had both occipital lobes removed but who remained nasty and bad tempered: "the experiment (whether the character of the dog could be changed by new defects placed more anteriorly) could not be performed because the animal died suddenly in an epileptic fit."; (h) Goltz argued for the "principle" that the larger the lesion the more long lasting the deficits. Burckhardt was probably influenced by these aspects of Goltz' work, in particular, the idea of serial brain operations and the idea of only removing small amounts of cerebral cortex, rather than the somewhat naïve and quite minority non-localisation theory to which Goltz subscribed.

6. In the opinion of Freeman and Watts (1942), Burckhardt lacked any good knowledge of emotional mechanisms and their localisation in the brain; the implication is that Freeman and Watts believed that Burckhardt was essentially operating blindly, mutilating more than curing. However, in Burckhardt's defence, a close analysis of his discussion reveals the rudimentary elements of a brain model for affective processes, perhaps the first derived from clinical and pathological research.

Burckhardt analysed two theories of emotions: (1) a subcortical location of the components of affective processes following Lange[31] (1887) which was also suggested by Bechterew, and (2) a cortical location of affective processes based upon his analysis of various authors such as Hofstetter (1880), Bleuler (1885), Nothnagel, Bernhardt (1881) and others.[33] Considering the work of Broca on the limbic lobe and Meynert on general brain anatomy, Burckhardt drew the conclusion that the anterior and posterior cortical regions (frontal versus parietal) played different roles in emotional expression. The dog experiments published by Goltz (1881, 1888) also supported a cortical localization of affect, however, Burckhardt did question the permissibility of transferring Goltz' results on dogs to humans. After reviewing the work of various other authors[33]: Jastowitz, Schloess, Jensen, Zacher, Oppenheim, Bernhardt, and L. Welt, Burckhardt was particularly intrigued with Mairet's ideas of melancholic dementia (1883) where he proposed that megalomanic dementia is located in the convex region of the frontal and temporal lobe whereas the melancholic form is found in the first temporal gyrus, the anterior third of the sphenoid gyrus and the hippocampal gyri.

Burckhardt noted that several authors thought it probable that affect is located only in the right hemisphere,[31] e.g. Luys who thought that the cortex surrounding the right Sylvian fissure was particularly important. Burckhardt believed that affect is a cortical event; it is transformed into motion in cortical regions not in subcortical ones. The observed abnormally high emotionality in his patients as well as the "immediacy" of their actions suggested to Burckhardt a cessation of inhibition. Finally, it is not the entire surface of the cortex which is affected, but specific, identifiable zones, i.e. he was a localisationist. His rationale for surgical intervention was explained thusly in one of his case studies: if the origin of the hallucinations which are the patient's primary problem is due to "stimuli in the sensory region which are excessive in number, quality and strength and which penetrate the motor region, then an improvement can only be achieved by creating a new inhibition between the two." This could be accomplished by causing "a sufficient interruption of ... the association events ... proceeding from the sensory areas ... to the motor zones." Evidently Buckhardt had learned enough from the literature to realise that no one had actually localised affective centres per se and therefore he defined his surgical goal as preventing the expression of disturbed behaviour rather than as curing it.

SUMMARY

De Meuron (1949) commented that Burckhardt's clinical research made his colleagues ill at ease, not unlike the reaction of David Ferrier on learning that Roberts Bartholow had inserted an electrode in the brain of a patient in order to determine the effects of electrical stimulation and, as well, not unlike the reaction that greeted later psychosurgeons. One readily infers that Burckhardt understood the implicit message from his colleagues, since he stopped this line of research after 1891, notwithstanding his claim that his patients were helped. Moutier (1908) found in Burckhardt support for his and Déjerine's view that Broca's area plays no special role in language, in view of the results of its extirpation; however, one must note that Moutier does not seriously discuss these results, since he offers no similar hypothesis to explain the lack of aphasic sequelae after left hemisphere temporal and parietal excisions which Burckhardt did in other cases.

The probable explanation for the lack of aphasic sequelae is that the amount of cortex Burckhardt removed was simply too small to generate permanent impairments, neither in speech and language nor in motor function. For example, it has been argued by Tomlinson and Henderson (1976) that the minimal amount of brain that has to be lesioned in multi-infarct dementia in order to cause an aphasia is in the 50cc range; others have proposed that infarctions or haemorrhages greater than 60cc cause permanent impairments. Although it is clear that Burckhardt's resections were smaller than these figures, one must hasten to add that the mental and cognitive status of his patients were such that some effects on language or cognition could easily have passed unnoticed. No one, to our knowledge, has offered any explanation for the behavioural improvements which

Burckhardt reported for his patients. In conclusion, the Burckhardt story has attributes which appear to belong to the world of the 19th century, and others that are quite contemporary. In some respects, what this young psychiatrist did can be perceived as offensive, despite the fact that his clinical observations remain of interest. Perhaps the most fitting evaluation is that Burckhardt went from theory to practice, in his mind for the benefit of a few unfortunate patients.

ACKNOWLEDGEMENTS

The senior author's research in history has been made possible by a grant from F.C.A.R. (Québec) and a grant from the Social Sciences and Humanities Research Council of Canada. B.S. is a Post-doctoral Fellow of the Conseil de la recherche médicale du Canada (C.R.M.C.) (Grant 9004FEN-1037-34749). Y.J. is supported by Program Grant PG-28 from the C.R.M.C. and by the F.R.S.Q.

NOTES

1. An earlier and abbreviated version of this chapter was presented at the annual meeting of the American Academy of Neurology, New York City (Whitaker, Stemmer, & Joanette, 1993) and a shorter, somewhat different analysis of two of Burckhardt's cases is given in Joanette, Stemmer, Assal, and Whitaker (1993).
2. It is often claimed that ancient Peruvian trepanned skulls, dating from around the 8th century A.D., represent early psychosurgical operations; surgery on the skull they surely were, but whether or not they were psycho-surgical procedures cannot in any way be determined, since we have no idea whether the ancient Peruvians had a theory of brain function that could have entailed a trepan procedure for the amelioration of a behavioural disorder.
3. There is some agreement on what the term "psychosurgery" means; its definition would likely include reference to the attempt to modify human cognitive and/or emotional behaviour by surgical means and would also include reference to the idea that the brain tissue targeted for removal or destruction is not known to be already damaged or diseased. F.A. Whitlock's (1987) definition is: "psychosurgery: . . . operative procedures on the brain specifically designed to relieve severe mental symptoms that have been unresponsive to other forms of treatment . . . the best results are obtained with patients suffering from severe, chronic anxiety, agitated depression carrying a high risk of suicide and those afflicted with incapacitating obsessive-compulsive disorder."
4. "Concerning the extirpation of cortex as a contribution to the operative treatment of psychoses."
5. Evidently it has been difficult to cite Burckhardt accurately. In his *Historical Perspective* (1980: Chapter 1, p. 19) Valenstein seems to believe that Burckhardt's source material was exclusively the animal literature when in fact human studies are extensively referred to; as noted later (Case 1) Burckhardt explicitly repudiated the idea that animal experiences can be simply translated to the human case. In addition, Valenstein says that Burckhardt believed that only one of his six patients improved after surgery, when in fact his claim is that three patients significantly improved, one slightly improved, one possibly showed improvement and one died too soon after surgery to evaluate. We hope that this chapter will finally set the record straight as to what is actually in the Burckhardt article.

6. It is interesting to note that everyone seems to accept the idea that Burckhardt was inspired by Goltz; however, Goltz was an avid non-localisationist. Burckhardt, on the other hand, knew that one had to accept localisation in order to believe that removing pieces of cortex could help one's patients; clearly, if his patients had suffered from diffuse cerebral disease, there would hardly have been justification for what he attempted to do. Goltz' contribution to Burckhardt's research is discussed later in the chapter.

7. In fact, the interval was over a year! The first operation was in December, 1888 and the fourth in February, 1890.

8. This, too, is inaccurate; see the case history discussed later.

9. Consider, for example, the one propounded by William Elder (Whitaker, 1988).

10. "The Committee, having funded me, and the installations and necessary preparations having been done, and the patient's family having consented, we performed the first operation on 29th December. This is not the place to provide all the details. Let me simply state that, to my knowledge, Préfargier is the first institution where cranial trepanation and the removal of small portions of the cerebral cortex have been performed, not just to satisfy surgical indications, but rather for psychiatric purposes. The results I have obtained have strongly encouraged me to continue in this now-opened avenue."

11. This was the neurological materialisation of associationist psychology on the one hand, traceable back through Alexander Bain to David Hartley, and of phrenology on the other hand, traceable back to F.J. Gall.

12. "Doctors are different by nature. One kind adheres to the old principle: first, do no harm; the other one says: it is better to do something than nothing. I certainly belong to the second category."

13. We have translated Burckhardt's article in two ways: where the translation is literal, as close to a phrase by phrase translation as possible, this text is set off in quotation marks or set out as an extract. Elsewhere, the translation is free; on occasion, in order to preserve coherence, we have changed the serial placement of certain phrases from the original text. Not all of the 70 pages of text have been translated.

14. Burckhardt does not actually specify what the patient was hereditarily predisposed for; we assume it is "mental illness" because that is the phrase he used for familial analysis in other cases.

15. "I have been to Schallewerk in the Canton of Bern."

16. Burckhardt frequently does not give the year or any other details of his citation.

17. The word Burckhardt uses is "ideogen."

18. "Give me a lot of water, I'm thirsty."

19. "Take a chair and sit beside me."

20. "Why bother?"

21. It is clear that this brain was not normal.

22. In other words, Burckhardt assumes that there is some widespread brain damage in this case.

23. Note that this is opposite to what Freeman and Watts (1942) say about the results of surgery for this patient.

24. Burckhardt actually cites Case 3 but it is clear from the context that he meant Case 2.

25. "listen!"

26. Burckhardt actually uses the word "ataxic" but it is evident that he means "apraxic" in the contemporary sense.

27. Burckhardt actually used the word "ataxic" in both places in this sentence but "apraxic", used in the modern sense, is more accurate.

28. The details of this autopsy encompass three pages of the original article.

29. The idea that the better the skill the more brain involved is one of the more common 19th-century neuropsychological ideas; it derives directly from phrenology, of course.

30. This could be called the "bucket theory" of brain function—there is only so much room, so if one more thing is added, something spills out.
31. Later recognised for his contribution to the James–Lange theory of emotion.
32. Although we have not mentioned it, Burckhardt did incorporate current ideas about the lateral organisation of the brain into his model as well as those of localisation; he operated on the left hemisphere specifically because of his belief that verbal auditory hallucinations played an important role in the pathophysiology of his patients' psychiatric disorders.
33. Cited in Burckhardt (1891).

REFERENCES

Bach (1907). *Nachruf G. Burckhardt.*

Burckhardt, G. (1891). Über Rindenexcisionen, als Beitrag zur operativen Therapie der Psychosen. *Allgemeine Zeitschrift für Psychiatrie und psychisch-gerichtliche Medicin, 47,* 463–548.

Cot, F., & Joanette, Y. (1991). La rééducation de l'aphasie en France, vers 1900. *Rééducation orthophonique, 29,* 165, 3–19.

de Meuron, A.-F. (1949). *La maison de santé de Préfargier 1849–1949.* Neuchâtel: P. Altinger.

Fisher, R. (1951). Psychosurgery. In A.E. Walker (Ed.), *A history of neurological surgery.* Baltimore: Williams & Wilkins.

Freeman, W.J., & Watts, J.W. (1942). *Psychosurgery: Intelligence, emotion and social behavior following prefrontal lobotomy for mental disorders* [with special psychometric and personality profile studies by Thelma Hunt] (2nd ed.). Springfield, IL: C.C. Thomas.

Freeman, W.J., & Watts, J.W. (1950). *Psychosurgery in the treatment of mental disorders and intractable pain.* Springfield, IL: Thomas.

Fulton, J.F. (1951). *Frontal lobotomy and affective behavior.* New York: Norton.

Goltz, F. (1881). Über die Verrichtungen des Grosshirns: Gesammelte Abhandlungen. Bonn: E. Strauss.

Goltz, F. (1888). Über die Verrichtungen des Grosshirns. *Pflügers Archiv für die gesamte Physiologie, 42,* 419–467.

Horsley, V. (1886). Brain surgery, *British Medical Journal, 2,* 670–674.

Joanette, Y., Stemmer, B., Assal, G., & Whitaker, H. (1993). From theory to practice: The unconventional contribution of Gottlieb Burckhardt to psychosurgery. *Brain and Language, 45,* 572–587.

Lange, K. (1887). *Über Gemütsbewegungen, eine psychophysiologische Studie:* Übersetzt von H. Kurella. Leipzig: Thomas.

Luys, J.-B. (1865). *Recherches sur le systeme nerveux cérébro-spinal: Sa structure, ses fonctions, et ses maladies.* Paris: Baillière.

Luys, J.-B. (1888). *Les émotions chez les hypnotiques: Étudiées à l'aide de substances médicamenteuses ou toxiques agissant à distance; étude de psychologie expérimentale.* (2nd ed.). Paris: Libraire Lefrancois.

Mackay, D. (1987). The ethics of brain manipulation. In Richard L. Gregory (Ed.), *The Oxford companion to the mind* (pp. 113–114). Oxford University Press.

Mairet, A. (1883). *De la démence mélancolique: Contribution à l'étude de la périencéphalite localisée, et à l'étude des localisations cérébrales d'ordre psychique.* Paris: Masson.

Mettler, F.A. (Ed.). (1949). *Selective partial ablation of the frontal cortex.* New York: Hoeber.

Moniz, E. (1936). *Tentatives opératoires dans le traitement de certaines psychoses.* Paris: Masson.

Moutier, F. (1908). *L'aphasie de Broca.* Paris: Steinheil.

Puusepp, L. (1937). Alcune considerazioni sugli interventi chirurgici nelle malattie mentali. *Gior. Accad. med. Torino, 100,* 3–16.

Tomlinson, B.E., & Henderson, G. (1976). Some quantitative findings in normal and demented old people. In R.D. Terry & S. Gershon (Eds.), *Neurobiology of aging* (pp. 183–204). New York: Raven.

Valenstein, E.S. (1973). *Brain control.* New York: Wiley.

Valenstein, E.S. (Ed.). (1980). *The psychosurgery debate: Scientific, legal and ethical perspectives.* San Francisco: W.H. Freeman.

Wernicke, C. (1874). *Der aphasische Symptomenkomplex.* Breslau.

Whitaker, H.A. (1988). William Elder (1864–1931): Diagram maker and experimentalist. In L.M. Hyman & C. Li (Eds.), *Language, speech and mind* (pp. 163–174). London: Routledge.

Whitaker, H.A., Stemmer, B., & Joanette, Y. (1993). *A psychosurgical chapter in the history of cerebral localization: G. Burckhardt (1891).* Paper presented at the annual meeting of the American Academy of Neurology, New York.

Whitlock, F.A. (1987). Psychosurgery. In Richard L. Gregory (Ed.), *The Oxford companion to the mind* (pp. 660–661). Oxford: Oxford University Press.

21
Akelaitis' Investigations of the First Split-brain Patients

Hannelore C. Sauerwein and Maryse Lassonde
Groupe de Recherche en Neuropsychologie Expérimentale,
Département de Psychologie, Université de Montréal, Canada.

INTRODUCTION

In 1940 Van Wagenen and Herren reported the first 10 of more than 30 cases in whom they divided the corpus callosum to prevent interhemispheric propagation of seizures. The surgery consisted of partial or complete division of the corpus callosum and fornix in a single operation or in several stages. One-third of the patients had a partial callosotomy involving predominantly the genu and the body of the callosum. In half of these patients the anterior two-thirds of the splenium were also divided. Two patients—one with partial, one with complete callosal section—underwent additional division of the anterior commissure.

The surgery was innovative in the treatment of epilepsy and the study of these patients allowed the exploration of the role of the corpus callosum, a structure whose functions were as yet unspecified. Although the work of Trescher and Ford (1937) had suggested a callosal involvement in interhemispheric communication, some authors still persisted in attributing a "psychic" role to the structure. In view of these different perspectives, the analysis of these first surgical cases proved to be important because it disconfirmed the callosal role in mental disturbances and, more importantly, because the careful examination of these cases allowed to the laying down of principles of callosal functioning.

The patients were extensively studied by Akelaitis between 1941 and 1945. Some of the studies were conducted in collaboration with colleagues but most of the research was carried out by Akelaitis alone. The author went about this task in a systematic, logical manner by gathering pre- and postoperative data of the patients and by studying the various aspects of behaviour that, according to available clinical and animal studies of callosal lesions, were thought to be dependent on the integrity of commissural pathways. In most cases, his analysis of the data took into account the extent of the callosal section as well as the presence of pre-existing or surgically introduced cortical damage. Although his predominantly negative results contributed to a loss of interest in the study of the role of the forebrain commissures over the subsequent two decades, it should not be overlooked that the author not only asked the correct questions but that most of his methods were appropriate to demonstrate disconnection deficits. Furthermore, several of his results have been directly confirmed by later researchers, using similar or new techniques (Goldstein & Joynt, 1969; Goldstein, Joynt, & Hartley, 1975), and many of his interpretations are in line with today's understanding of the callosal syndrome. In the following parts of this chapter we are reviewing and reconsidering some of his hypotheses, results, and interpretations in the light of contemporary knowledge about the role of the commissural system.

PERSONALITY AND COGNITIVE FUNCTIONING

In order to investigate the changes in mental state (personality changes, mental deterioration) that had previously been reported with lesions of the corpus callosum (Collier, 1930; Mingazzini, 1922), Akelaitis (1941a, 1941c) compiled the psychiatric histories and obtained pre- and postoperative scores of standardised intellectual tests from 10 patients. Two out of four patients (cases 1 and 2) with previous psychiatric problems (delusions, hysteric episodes; Akelaitis, 1941c) experienced an aggravation of the preoperative condition after complete callostomy, this effect being transient in one of the cases. The other two patients showed no appreciable changes in personality. In none of the cases was a new type of pathology introduced. These negative results led Akelaitis to conclude that no particular psychic syndrome was attributable to the section of the corpus callosum per se, a view that has been confirmed by subsequent studies in several series of commissurotomised and callosotomised patients (e.g. Bogen, 1985). It is now generally accepted that the mental syndrome that has been associated with callosal tumours in the clinical literature must be a consequence of intracranial pressure and/or infiltration of extra-callosal, often subcortical, regions of the brain (e.g. Lassonde, Lepore, & Ptito, 1987). These findings thus contributed to shift the attention from a long-standing historical preoccupation with a callosal role in mental disorders to a more anatomo-functional investigation of the corpus callosum.

In the same context and in contradiction to the prevailing view of mental deterioration as part of the callosal syndrome, Akelaitis found no differences between the pre- and postoperative I.Q. scores of most of the cases he studied (Akelaitis, 1941a). Only one case (case 3) out of the 10 he investigated showed a decline in attention span and immediate memory. However, this patient had a history of obsessive-compulsive behaviour and depression and showed postoperative dysarthria and diagnistic dyspraxia. Memory and attention deficits have since been reported in a minority of patients (Ferguson, Rayport, & Corrie, 1985; Zaidel & Sperry, 1974). In other cases improvement of these functions has been observed (Geoffroy, Lassonde, Delisle, & Décarie, 1983; Lassonde, Sauerwein, & Geoffroy, 1991; Ledoux, Risse, Springer, Wilson, & Gazzaniga, 1974). The most plausible explanation of these inconsistent postoperative impairments is that they represent an exacerbation of pre-existing deficits related to the epileptic lesion (Campbell, Bogen, & Smith, 1981). Taken together, the absence of changes in the patients' overall mental status and intellectual functioning reported by Akelaitis are congruent with the findings of subsequent split-brain studies (Bogen, 1985; Bogen & Vogel, 1975; Geoffroy et al., 1983; Lassonde et al., 1991; Sauerwein & Lassonde, 1994; Spencer, Gates, Reeves, Spencer, Maxwell, & Roberts, 1987; Sperry, 1968; Sperry, Gazzaniga, & Bogen, 1969).

LATERAL DOMINANCE AND MOTOR FUNCTIONS

The objective of this series of studies by Akelaitis and collaborators (Akelaitis, 1944; Akelaitis, Risten, Herren, & Van Wagenen, 1942; Smith & Akelaitis, 1942) was to investigate the notion of unilateral cerebral dominance for motor functions and to settle the controversy in the literature as to the callosal involvement in the performance of complex movements of the non-dominant hand. The authors hypothesised that motor control of the dominant hemisphere over the non-dominant hand and foot was achieved by transcallosal inhibition and that removal of the inhibitory influence following callosal section would result in various motor disturbances of the non-dominant limbs. The results were analysed firstly in terms of the general effect of callosal section on motor skills and secondly in terms of a laterality effect in order to substantiate Liepmann's (1905) view of a left hemisphere dominance over the motor output of the right, subordinate hemisphere. The tests included an extensive lateral dominance inventory, tasks of bilateral co-ordination, hand–eye co-ordination and graphic performance, as well as a battery of apraxia tests ranging from observation of spontaneous motor activity and object handling to the execution of imitative and verbally requested movements. Eighteen cases—eleven with partial and seven with complete callosotomy—were studied, most of them shortly after awakening and recuperating from the anaesthesia.

As may be expected, postoperative laterality tests showed no appreciable changes in manual, ocular, or pedestral dominance. However, contrary to contemporary observations, the results of the dyspraxia studies were also largely negative. That is to say, the majority of the patients showed, according to Akelaitis, none of the typical praxic and graphic disturbances of the non-dominant hand that are today thought to be among the most consistent symptoms of hemispheric disconnection in the immediate postoperative period (Bogen, 1969; Gazzaniga, Bogen, & Sperry, 1967; see also Lassonde et al., 1987; Spencer et al., 1987). As Brion and Jedynak (1975) have pointed out, the early onset of the epilepsy or the extent of the unilateral lesion may have entailed some reorganisation in several of these patients. However, re-examination of the cases reveals that five patients with complete and four with partial section did indeed show all or various degrees of postoperative hemiapraxia, agraphia and astereognosis of the subordinate hand. Similarly, a closer inspection of the case histories in these and subsequent studies by Akelaitis reveals that the majority of the patients displayed postoperative hemiplegia and various praxic disturbances of the non-dominant limbs. The symptoms were well documented but, because of their transient nature, were not considered indicative of a hemispheric disconnection. Furthermore, the fact that bilateral co-ordination of highly complex motor skills such as typing, playing the piano, etc., was not disrupted by complete callosal section in some patients did not warrant, in the view of the authors, the interpretation of callosal involvement in these functions. As a consequence, the role of the cerebral commissures in cerebral dominance of motor control and bilateral co-ordination was overlooked in these studies.

The failure to attribute postoperative motor disturbances to callosal disconnection also extended to two cases who exhibited "diagnistic dyspraxia," a term coined by Akelaitis (1945) to describe the most spectacular symptom of motor disconnection in which the two hands and feet tend to act at cross-purposes. Rather, these symptoms were attributed to different psychiatric and degenerative diseases (case 1) and epileptic personality traits (case 2), neglecting the similarity of the symptoms in the two patients. Although these manifestations are rare, they have occasionally been reported in the recent literature (Bogen, 1985; Spencer et al., 1987; Wilson, Reeves, Gazzaniga, & Culver, 1977). Evidently, these symptoms are very irritating to the patient. It is therefore not surprising that the two patients studied by Akelaitis showed increased distress which, together with the "schizoid" nature of the symptoms, was erroneously taken for the cause of the condition.

A psychological, rather than neurological, interpretation was also given to explain the phenomenon of the alien hand ("main étrangère"), a temporary inability of the patient to recognise the "disconnected" non-dominant hand as his own (Akelaitis, 1944). This symptom, together with diagnistic dyspraxia, has since been assumed to result from a combination of factors, namely the removal of transcallosal inhibition from the motor centres of the subordinate hemisphere and a temporary postoperative weakness and hypoesthesia resulting from the retraction of the right hemisphere during surgery (Spencer et al., 1987). In fact, both explanations had been considered by Akelaitis et al. (1942) to account for the hemiparesis and apraxia of the non-dominant limbs seen immediately after the surgery. Once again, however, the transient character of the praxic symptoms dissuaded the authors from attributing the observation to the division of callosal connections.

Akelaitis further touched upon the concept of cerebral plasticity by considering the possibility that the recovery or preservation of praxis and graphia seen in some patients may be attributable to the age at surgery (Akelaitis et al., 1942). This interpretation has been confirmed by the findings of recent studies which have shown that callostomised children show few praxic disturbances after the surgery and recover more rapidly than adult patients (Lassonde, Sauerwein, Geoffroy, & Décarie, 1986). In fact, the recruitment of ipsilateral motor connections was correctly considered as a possible explanation for the recuperation of hemiapraxia and agraphia. This hypothesis was, however, not deemed tenable in the light of contrary evidence from the electrophysiological studies of Penfield and Boldley (1937). The latter had failed to obtain ipsilateral motor responses during cortical stimulation of more than 100 patients. The possibility of the integrative function of subcortical structures was also discussed, whereas the use of other commissures was rightfully dismissed on the basis of their lack of connectivity with the motor centres.

An accurate explanation was also offered in relation to the results of a study of the grasp reflex (Akelaitis, Risten, & Van Wagenen, 1943). This reflex, which is usually observed in conjunction with a lesion to the frontal motor cortex, was thought at the time to result from the removal of transcallosal inhibition. Testing this hypothesis in twenty-five callosotomised patients, Akelaitis and collaborators found that this pathological reflex was elicited only in the three patients who showed preoperative frontal damage (atrophy, Pick's disease). Two of the patients were hemiplegics. The authors linked the appearance of the grasp reflex to perioperative trauma and to an interruption of transcallosal inhibition. Forced grasping of the non-dominant hand has now been observed in a number of contemporary studies (Botez & Bogen, 1976; Spencer et al., 1987). It occurs in conjunction with hemiparesis and sometimes micturition defects. The symptoms are thought to arise from parasagittal compression of the non-dominant hemisphere during surgery and/or cortical diaschisis from severing the connections between the two supplementary motor areas (Spencer et al., 1987). The question of whether or not the callosal section is instrumental in the production of this symptom has not been satisfactorily answered so far (Brion & Jedynak, 1975).

VISUAL FUNCTIONS

Field effects, gnosis, stereopsis, and complex functions involving language and spatial orientation were studied in the visual modality (Akelaitis, 1941b, 1942a). The author correctly reasoned that, after callosotomy, presentation to the temporal visual hemifields projecting directly to the ipsilateral hemisphere would reveal asymmetries in perception and identification of visually presented stimuli. On the other hand, no sensory loss in the visual fields was expected, and this was confirmed by perimetry in 24 cases (Akelaitis, 1942a). Study of visual gnosis consisted of lateralised presentation of common objects, colours, and letters in the visual half-fields. Since most patients had at least partial sparing of the splenium, the studies focus on eight cases with complete callosal section. The results are somewhat difficult to interpret because of the presence, in several of the cases, of preoperative gnostic deficits in the left visual field. Nevertheless, closer inspection of the reports reveals that at least one patient with complete callosotomy (case 1 in Akelaitis, 1941b) showed difficulties in identifying stimuli in the left visual field that were not present before surgery. This result points to a visual disconnection deficit similar to those found in later studies (e.g. Gazzaniga, 1970; Gazzaniga, Bogen, & Sperry, 1965; Sperry et al., 1969). In contrast, one patient in whom the anterior commissure was divided one year after complete calosotomy (case 1 in Akelaitis, 1944) showed no disconnection symptoms in the visual modality after either operation. Bilateral representation of speech was ruled out by Akelaitis since the patient had become aphasic and hemiplegic during the development of an abscess in the left frontal lobe.

Among the visual studies, a series of investigations conducted by two of Akelaitis' collaborators (Bridgman & Smith, 1945; Smith, 1947) deserves special attention. The studies are noteworthy not only for the well-controlled methodology and analysis of the data but also for the relevance of the results. In the first study, Bridgman and Smith (1945) investigated the role of the corpus callosum in stereopsis and apparent movement (phi-phenomenon) in 13 cases operated on by Van Wagenen and Herren (1940). Both midline fusion and stereopsis (convergent and divergent) were explored pre- and postoperatively. Although the authors noticed some difficulties in stereopsis, the results were not related to the absence of callosal input, mainly because no other deficits were detected. Similar but better-controlled studies have recently been conducted in callosotomised and callosal agenesis patients and they confirm the initial assumption that the corpus callosum is involved in midline stereopsis (Hamilton, Rodriguez, & Vermeire, 1987; Jeeves, 1991; Mitchell & Blakemore, 1970).

In the second paper, Smith (1947) gathered pre- and postoperative data on simple and complex crossed and uncrossed response times to visual, auditory and tactile stimuli. All possible hand–field combinations were explored. A postoperative deficit was noted only in terms of a general slowness, most pronounced in stimulus–response situations involving the non-dominant hand. No crossed–uncrossed differences (CUDs) were detected but the authors were unaware that, in fact, their methodology was confounded by spatial compatibility factors. Recent studies in normals (Anzola, Bertolini, Buchtel, & Rizzolati, 1977; Berlucchi, Crea, DiStefano, & Tassinari, 1977), as well as in acallosal and callosotomised patients (DiStefano, Sauerwein, & Lassonde, 1992), have shown that spatial compatibility between stimulus and response in choice reaction time experiments tends to override anatomical stimulus–response relationships.

LANGUAGE FUNCTIONS

Following the same line of reasoning as in the visual studies, Akelaitis (1943) set out to investigate the effect of callosotomy on language functions in the disconnected hemispheres. A total of 24 patients with various degrees of callosal section (15 partial, 9 complete or nearly complete) were asked to identify objects, letters, and digits presented unilaterally in the tactile and visual modes.

Temporary agraphia, tactile alexia and astereognosis for small objects were observed in four patients (cases 13, 14, 21, 24). In these four patients, the body of the callosum and the anterior part of the splenium had been divided. These deficits were clearly indicative of interhemispheric disconnection but, because of their transient nature, they were once more attributed to other factors such as epilepsy and/or cortical damage. Similarly, when stimuli were presented visually, two patients (cases 15 and 17) had more difficulties identifying letters in the left visual field. Again, the findings were ignored in the absence of deficits in the remaining 22 patients, most of whom had partial sparing of the splenium.

Akelaitis was aware that his negative results in the visual modality were at variance with previous findings by Trescher and Ford (1937) and he attributed this discrepancy to the presence of concomitant damage in Trescher and Ford's patient. However, the divergent results may also be ascribed to methodological differences. The description of Akelaitis' methods is vague. It appears from the reports that in many cases a motor rather than a verbal response was used to identify the stimuli in each visual field. Furthermore, no tachistoscope was employed at the time. Although stimulus presentation appears to have been well lateralised, no mention is made of the exposure time. It is probable that the latter exceeded that commonly used in tachistoscopic studies (between 100 and 150msec.). In fact, using exposure times of $\frac{1}{2}$ to 1 second, Maspe (1948) found no difficulties in object naming and matching in either visual field in two subjects with splenial section without cortical damage. However, both patients displayed alexia for short words in the left visual field. Prior to these findings, the notion of a specialised involvement of different parts of the corpus callosum had already been announced by Akelaitis. Indeed, he had argued correctly that, in many of his cases, sparing of some fibres in the "tip of the splenium" could have allowed for interhemispheric exchange of visual information.

Another explanation, advanced by Akelaitis on several occasions, was that cerebral reorganisation in terms of bilateral representation of speech could account for the preserved verbal functions in the non-dominant hemisphere. This hypothesis was confirmed in two of the patients who were retested twenty-seven years later by Goldstein and collaborators (Goldstein & Joynt, 1969; Goldstein et al., 1975) with more sophisticated methods. Both patients were in fact able to identify objects in the left hand by touch alone and to name tachistoscopically presented stimuli in the left visual field. They were, however, impaired on more complex tasks such as intermodal matching (visuo-tactile matching) and intermanual transfer of tactuo-motor learning. The latter result is of particular interest, because a previous study of nine of Akelaitis' patients by one of his collaborators (Smith, 1951) had revealed similar deficits in intermanual transfer of a maze learning task. Although the significance of these results was overlooked at the time, the findings are important, showing that the inability to transfer newly learned material is one of the most persistent sequelae of callosal section.

Finally, mutism is another transient disturbance that was first described by Akelaitis (1942a, case 1) and that has been found in subsequent split-brain studies (e.g. Bogen, 1985). This problem has been linked to the compression of the supplementary motor regions during surgery (Ross, Reeves, & Roberts, 1984; Sussman, Gur, Gur, & O'Connor, 1983). According to the detailed description supplied by Akelaitis (1942a), the ligation of two large veins feeding into the longitudinal sinus in the retraction of the hemispheres may have been responsible for this symptom.

TEMPORAL–SPATIAL GNOSIS

This investigation (Akelaitis, 1942b) was inspired by a number of clinical studies which had shown that a posterior callosal lesion might induce disorientation. Twenty-six patients with partial or complete callosotomy were tested for their ability to localise a sound source and orient themselves with respect to personal (own body) as well as extrapersonal (environment) space. In addition, time gnosis, rhythm, music appreciation and visual synthesis were studied. No changes in temporal or spatial perception were found. However, one patient (case 9) who used to play the steel guitar reportedly lost "all sense of rhythm in music" (p. 922) following section of the posterior part of the genu and the body of the corpus callosum. The latter observation is interesting in the light of recent findings suggesting that rhythm and melody may be processed in different hemispheres (Peretz, 1990; Peretz & Kolinsky, 1993). In fact, many of the tests used in this Akelaitis' study have only recently been known to address the functions of the right hemisphere, again indicating the original and innovative character of Akelaitis' work.

CONCLUSION

In conclusion, the detailed studies of the first large series of split-brain cases by Akelaitis have provided a rich source of information from which later investigators have frequently drawn. It is also evident that the author and his collaborators approached the study with the correct hypotheses and employed largely appropriate methods. The fact that some of the findings were negative or that positive findings were not recognised as such cannot simply be attributed to the lack of proper techniques. Many other factors such as the particular pathologies of the patients, the age at seizure onset and at surgery, and the regression of the symptoms over time, tended to mask some of the disconnection deficits that are known to us today. Furthermore, differences in patient selection and surgical procedure have to be taken into account when comparing the results of Akelaitis' cases to later commissurotomy and callosotomy patients.

Criteria for patient selection vary among surgical centres. However, it seems that the patients operated on by Van Wagenen and Herren exhibited a much larger variety and a greater severity of concomittant pathologies than those operated on in the 1960s and later. The preoperative presence of left hemianopia, dyspraxia or hemiplegia in 50% of the patients precluded the affirmation of the unilaterality of postoperative disconnection deficits. This may explain, in part, why not a single case studied by Akelaitis showed conclusive evidence of the split-brain syndrome in *all* modalities although all disconnection deficits were demonstrated across various cases. While alexia in the left visual field was present in some patients, by far the most consistent transient symptoms in patients with complete callosal section were dyspraxia, agraphia, and astereognosis of the non-dominant hand, even though their significance was often overlooked.

Yet another difference between these first patients and later series is that no uniform surgical procedure was employed in the former. Although Van Wagenen and Herren were experienced neurosurgeons who had published more than 20 papers between 1927 and 1940, they were navigating in uncharted waters when they first proceeded to section the corpus callosum in epileptic patients. Being well aware of the experimental nature of the surgery, they adopted a rather conservative approach by preserving those parts of the callosum that were not thought to be directly involved in interhemispheric propagation of the seizures, given the location of the primary lesion. If necessary, additional portions of the corpus callosum were divided in a subsequent operation. Thus, the extent of the callosotomy and the number of operations performed on a single patient varied considerably among the cases. Only one-third of the patients underwent complete callosotomy, two of them in two stages. Evidently, in the absence of appropriate neuroimaging techniques, completeness of callosal section was based solely on the surgeons' report. Therefore, the possibility cannot be excluded that the negative results in some of Akelaitis' studies were attributable to the presence of residual callosal fibres carrying information between the hemispheres.

It is then in this light that Akelaitis' contribution has to be evaluated. In interpreting his data, Akelaitis took a neuro-functional approach, making full use of findings from clinical and experimental studies that would apply to his cases. His discussions of cerebral plasticity and alternative mechanisms of interhemispheric communication are as relevant today as they were then. All of these potential compensatory mechanisms are frequently evoked to explain the absence of disconnection symptoms in callosal agenesis patients (e.g. Jeeves, 1986). Finally, it is largely owing to these pioneer studies that the role of the corpus callosum moved from the "mental" to the physiological domain. In this respect, Akelaitis' investigations have laid the foundation for subsequent experimental work on the functions of the cerebral commissures.

REFERENCES

Akelaitis, A.J. (1941a). Psychobiological studies following section of the corpus callosum. *American Journal of Psychiatry, 97*, 1147–1158.

Akelaitis, A.J. (1941b). Studies on the corpus callosum: II. The higher visual functions in each homonymous field following complete section of the corpus callosum. *Archives of Neurology and Psychiatry, 45*, 786–796.

Akelaitis, A.J. (1941c). Studies on the corpus callosum: VIII. The effect of partial and complete section of the corpus callosum on psychopathic epileptics. *American Journal of Psychiatry, 98*, 409–414.

Akelaitis, A.J. (1942a). Studies on the corpus callosum: V. Homonymous field defects for color, object and letter recognition (homonymous hemiamblyopia) before and after section of the corpus callosum. *Archives of Neurology and Psychiatry, 48*, 108–118.

Akelaitis, A.J. (1942b). Studies on the corpus callosum: VI. Orientation (temporal–spatial gnosis) following section of the corpus callosum. *Archives of Neurology and Psychiatry, 48*, 914–937.

Akelaitis, A.J. (1943). Studies on the corpus callosum: VII. Study of language functions (tactile and visual lexia and graphia) unilaterally following section of the corpus callosum. *Journal of Neuropathology and Experimental Neurology, 2,* 226–262.

Akelaitis, A.J. (1944). A study of gnosis, praxis and language following section of the corpus callosum and the anterior commissure. *Journal of Neurosurgery, 1,* 94–102.

Akelaitis, A.J. (1945). Studies on the corpus callosum: IV. Diagnistic dyspraxia in epileptics following partial and complete section of the corpus callosum. *American Journal of Psychiatry, 101,* 594–599.

Akelaitis, A.J., Risten, W.A., Herren, R.Y., & Van Wagenen, W.P. (1942). Studies on the corpus callosum: III. A contribution to the study of dyspraxia and apraxia following partial and complete section of the corpus callosum. *Archives of Neurology and Psychiatry, 47,* 971–1008.

Akelaitis, A.J., Risten, W.A., & Van Wagenen, W.P. (1943). Studies on the corpus callosum: IX. Relation of the grasp reflex to section of the corpus callosum. *Archives of Neurology and Psychiatry, 49,* 820–825.

Anzola, G.P., Bertolini, G., Buchtel, H.A., & Rizzolati, G. (1977). Spatial compatibility and anatomical factors in simple and choice reaction time. *Neuropsychologia, 15,* 295–302.

Berlucchi, G., Crea, F., DiStefano, M., & Tassinari, G. (1977). Influence of spatial stimulus-response compatibility on reaction time of ipsilateral and contralateral stimuli. *Journal of Experimental Psychology: Human Perception and Performance, 3,* 505–517.

Bogen, J.E. (1969). The other side of the brain: I. Dysgraphia and dyscopia following cerebral commissurotomy. *Bulletin of the Los Angeles Neurological Society, 34,* 73–105.

Bogen, J.E. (1985). The callosal syndrome. In K.M. Heilman & E. Valenstein (Eds.), *Clinical neuropsychology.* New York: University Press.

Bogen, J.E., & Vogel, P.J. (1975). Neurologic status in the long term following cerebral commissurotomy. In F. Michel & B. Schott (Eds.), *Les syndromes de disconnexion calleuse chez l'homme.* Lyon: Hôpital Neurologique.

Botez, M.I., & Bogen, J.E. (1976). The grasp reflex of the foot and related phenomena in the absence of other reflex abnormalities following cerebral commissurotomy. *Acta Neurologica Scandinavia, 54,* 453–463.

Bridgman, C.S., & Smith, K.U. (1945). Bilateral neural integration in visual perception after section of the corpus callosum. *Journal of Comparative Neurology, 83,* 57–83.

Brion, S., & Jedynak, C.P. (1975). *Les troubles de transfert interhémisphérique.* Paris: Masson.

Campbell, A.L., Bogen, J.E., & Smith, A. (1981). Disorganization and reorganization of cognitive and sensorimotor functions in cerebral commissurotomy: Compensatory roles of the forebrain commissures and cerebral hemispheres in man. *Brain, 104,* 493–511.

Collier, J. (1930). Localization of function in the nervous system. *British Medical Journal, 1,* 55.

DiStefano, M.R., Sauerwein, H.C., & Lassonde, M. (1992). Influence of anatomical factors and spatial compatibility on the stimulus–response relationship in the absence of the corpus callosum. *Neuropsychologia, 30,* 177–185.

Ferguson, S.M., Rayport, M., & Corrie, W.S. (1985). Neuropsychiatric observations on behavioral consequences of corpus callosum section for seizure control. In A.G. Reeves (Ed.), *Epilepsy and the corpus callosum.* New York: Plenum Press.

Gazzaniga, M.S. (1970). *The bisected brain.* New York: Appleton-Century-Crofts.

Gazzaniga, M.S., Bogen, J.E., & Sperry, R.W. (1965). Observations on visual perception after disconnexion of the cerebral hemispheres in man. *Brain, 88,* 221–236.

Gazzaniga, M.S., Bogen, J.E., & Sperry, R.W. (1967). Dyspraxia following division of the cerebral commissures. *Archives of Neurology, 16,* 606–612.

Geoffroy, G., Lassonde, M., Delisle, F., & Décarie, M. (1983). Corpus callosotomy for control of intractable epilepsy in children. *Neurology (Cleveland), 33,* 891–897.

Goldstein, M.N., & Joynt, R.J. (1969). Long-term follow-up of a callosal-sectioned patient: Report of a case. *Archives of Neurology, 20*, 96–102.

Goldstein, M.N., Joynt, R.J., & Hartley, R.B. (1975). Long-term effects of callosal sectioning: Report of a second case. *Archives of Neurology, 32*, 52–53.

Hamilton, C.R., Rodriguez, K.M., & Vermeire, B.A. (1987). The cerebral commissures and midline stereopsis. *Investigative Ophthalmology and Visual Sciences, 28*, 294.

Jeeves, M.A. (1986). Callosal agenesis: Neuronal and developmental adaptations. In F. Lepore, M. Ptito, & H.H. Jaspers (Eds.), *Two hemispheres—one brain*. New York: Alan Liss.

Jeeves, M.A. (1991). Stereo perception in callosal agenesis and partial callosotomy. *Neuropsychologia, 29*, 19–34.

Lassonde, M., Lepore, F., & Ptito, M. (1987). Les fonctions calleuses. In M.I. Botez (Ed.), *Neuropsychologie clinique et neurologie du comportement*. Montréal: Presses Universitaires de Montréal et Masson.

Lassonde, M., Sauerwein, H., & Geoffroy, G. (1991). Long-term neuropsychological effects of corpus callosotomy in children. *Journal of Epilepsy, 3 (Suppl.)*, 279–286.

Lassonde, M., Sauerwein, H., Geoffroy, G., & Décarie, M. (1986). Effects of early and late transection of the corpus callosum in children. *Brain, 109*, 953–967.

Ledoux, J.E., Risse, G.L., Springer, S.P., Wilson, D.W., & Gazzaniga, M.S. (1974). Cognition and commissurotomy, *Brain, 100*, 87–105.

Liepmann, H. (1905. Die linke Hemisphäre and das Handeln. *Münchener Medizinische Wochenzeitschrift, 52*, 2322, 2375.

Maspe, P.E. (1948). Le syndrome expérimental chez l'homme de la section du splénium du corps calleux: Alexie visuelle pure hémianopsique. *Revue Neurologique, 80*, 100–113.

Mingazzini, G. (1922). *Der Balken*. Berlin: Springer.

Mitchell, D.E., & Blakemore, C. (1970). Binocular depth perception and the corpus callosum. *Vision Research, 10*, 49–54.

Penfield, W., & Boldrey, E. (1937). Somatic motor and sensory representation in the cerebral cortex of man as studied by electrical stimulation. *Brain, 60*, 389.

Peretz, I. (1990). Processing of local and global musical information by unilateral brain-damaged patients. *Brain, 113*, 1185–1205.

Peretz, I., & Kolinsky, R. (1993). Boundaries of separability between melody and rhythm in music discrimination: A neuropsychological perspective. *Quarterly Journal of Experimental Psychology, 46A* (2), 310–325.

Ross, M.K., Reeves, A.G., & Roberts, D.W. (1984). Post-commissurotomy mutism. *Annals of Neurology, 16*, 114.

Sauerwein, H.C., & Lassonde, M. (1994). Cognitive and sensori-motor functioning in the absence of the corpus callosum: Neuropsychological studies in callosal agenesis and callosotomized patients. *Behavioural Brain Research, 64*, 229–240.

Smith, K.U. (1947). Bilateral integrative action of the cerebral cortex in man in verbal association and sensori-motor coordination. *Journal of Experimental Psychology, 37*, 367–376.

Smith, K.U. (1951). Learning and the associative pathways of the human cerebral cortex. *Science, 114*, 117–120.

Smith, K.U., & Akelaitis, A.J. (1942). Studies on the corpus callosum: I. Laterality in behavior and bilateral motor organization in man before and after section of the corpus callosum. *Archives of Neurology and Psychiatry, 45*, 519–543.

Spencer, S.S., Gates, J.R., Reeves, A.R., Spencer, D.D., Maxwell, R.E., & Roberts, D. (1987). Corpus callosum section. In J. Engel (Ed.), *Surgical treatment of the epilepsies*. New York: Raven Press.

Sperry, R.W. (1968). Hemisphere deconnection and unity in conscious awareness. *American Psychologist, 23*, 723–733.

Sperry, R.W., Gazzaniga, M.S., & Bogen, J.E. (1969). Interhemispheric relationships: The neocortical commissures—Syndromes of hemispheric disconnection. In P.J. Vinken, & G.W. Bruyn (Eds.), *Handbook of clinical neurology (Vol. IV)*. Amsterdam: North-Holland.

Sussman, N.M., Gur, R.C., Gur, R.E., & O'Connor, H.J. (1983). Mutism as a consequence of callosotomy. *Journal of Neurosurgery*, *59*, 514–519.

Trescher, J.H., & Ford, F.R. (1937). Colloid cyst of the third ventricle. Report of a case— Operation removal with section of the posterior half of corpus callosum. *Archives of Neurology and Psychiatry*, *37*, 959–973.

Van Wagenen, W.P., & Herren, R.Y. (1940). Surgical division of commissural pathways in the corpus callosum. *Archives of Neurology and Psychiatry*, *44*, 740–759.

Wilson, D.H., Reeves, A., Gazzaniga, M.W., & Culver, C. (1977). Cerebral commissurotomy for control of intractable seizures. *Neurology*, *27*, 708–715.

Zaidel, D., & Sperry, R.W. (1974). Memory impairment after commissurotomy in man. *Brain*, *97*, 263–272.

22 Speech from the Isolated Right Hemisphere? Left Hemispherectomy Cases E.C. and N.F.

Chris Code
Brain Damage and Communication Research, School of Communication Disorders, University of Sydney, Australia.

INTRODUCTION

The last decade has seen enormous growth in research which shows that the right hemisphere does a great deal. The final dogma of the dominance model is the notion that, while the left hemisphere may not control all language processing, what it does do that the right cannot do is *speak*. The importance of the hemispherectomy cases E.C. and N.F. is that they demonstrated most clearly what earlier, but less carefully studied, hemispherectomy patients had suggested for some years, that the isolated right hemisphere was capable of producing speech. In this chapter we consider the contribution that the hemispherectomy cases E.C. and N.F., described by Smith and Burklund (1966), have made to our understanding of the role of the right hemisphere in speech production. We look firstly, and briefly, at the role of the right hemisphere in language in general. We then look at hemispherectomy and consider the reports of speech production in E.C. and N.F. Finally, we contrast the two cases and consider the significance and limitations of their contribution.

LANGUAGE PROCESSING IN THE RIGHT HEMISPHERE

After some 30 years of research it now appears certain that the right cerebral hemisphere in human beings is involved in language processing (for reviews see Chiarello, 1988; Code, 1987; Joanette, Goulet, & Hannequin, 1990). However, for 100 years, since the earliest days of modern neuropsychology, it was considered impossible for the right hemisphere to possess any language functioning at all (see Bogen, 1969).

The question currently concerns the extent and quality of right hemisphere involvement in language. The significant barrier to answering questions concerning extent and quality results to a large extent from the population and methodological differences between studies. Studies have examined normal subjects, stroke patients, head-injured patients, hemispherectomies, and commissurotomies, in groups and as single cases. Investigators have used a range of methodologies which have included examination of lesion sites, cerebral bloodflow and metabolism, electric activity, and the effects of anaesthetising the hemispheres. A variety of behavioural methods that are thought to measure "lateral preference" for a wide range of language material have developed. These methods have been used to determine the contribution of the left and right hemisphere to language processing by examining and measuring laterality effects in the auditory, visual and tactile modalities; and by measuring eye and eyebrow movements, finger tapping, and degree of lateral mouth opening during speech. There is incompatibility and lack of agreement between studies and a poor replication record (Code, 1987). Thus, the data from these studies is mainly inconclusive. A further complication is that it is clear that there are significant individual differences in cognitive style and response to experimental tasks (Segalowitz & Bryden, 1983), brain organisation and representation of language (Ojemann, 1979), and cerebral circulation (Hart, Lesser, Fisher, Schwerdt, Bryan, & Gordon, 1991).

Bearing these caveats in mind, what does the research tell us about the right hemisphere's role in language processing in the normal brain? The study of aphasic symptomatology over the last 100 years or so confirms that damage to the left hemisphere for the great majority of right handers and most left handers results in impairments of those aspects of language which can be characterised through a formal unit-and-rule generative linguistic model. Aphasic individuals have problems at the strict linguistic levels of phonology, morphology, syntax, and lexical semantics. In comparison, the right hemisphere's involvement appears to be in features of language processing not covered by straight linguistic processes. Viewed thus, underlying the syntactic, morphological, and phonological processing associated with the left hemisphere, is a serial, analytical, segmental processing mode. In contrast, some have suggested that the right hemisphere's fundamental processing mode is holistic and parallel (Bradshaw & Nettleton, 1981; Wapner, Hamby, & Gardner, 1981). Thus left hemisphere damage produces problems in context-free linguistic processes (e.g. syntax, phonology) whereas right hemisphere damage effects context-dependent complex linguistic entities like verbal jokes, metaphors, narratives, indirect speech acts, as well as semantic discrimination and intonation (for reviews see Code, 1987; Joanette et al., 1990).

Not everyone is happy with dividing the contributions of the left and right hemispheres to mental activity in terms of an analytic–holistic dichotomy (see Bradshaw & Nettleton, 1981, and accompanying commentaries), although the fact remains that much of the research in the area is concerned with testing the predictions of this model and variants of the model. A dimension for examining hemispheric differences in speech production has been the notion of propositionality in language. Hughlings Jackson's (1874) observations of left- and right-hemisphere damaged patients convinced him that language could be contrasted in terms of whether it was propositional or nonpropositional or automatic. For Hughlings Jackson (pp. 81–82): "the right hemisphere is the one for the most automatic use of words, and the left the one in which automatic use of words merges into voluntary use of words—into speech."

While not a central area of study in psycholinguistics, the notion that language can be distinguished in terms of propositionality has been utilised by a number of writers since Hughlings Jackson (Code, 1987, 1991, 1994; Goldman-Eisler, 1968; Goldstein, 1948; Head, 1926; Van Lancker, 1987; Wray, 1992). Nonpropositional language does not entail straight linguistic, unit-and-rule analysis and synthesis. Its hallmarks are its automatic and invariant nature in such activities as reciting verse, singing, listing days of the week, counting, and use of everyday idioms and fillers like "Good morning," "sort of," "like," "by the way." Such formulaic language probably does not engage components of a generative grammar, but such utterances are probably processed as single lexical items, as complete "sealed units."

But the right hemisphere does appear to have some rudimentary straight linguistic competence. It appears to be able to differentiate affirmatives and negatives and comprehend concrete nouns, adjectival phrases and object definitional phrases, but it cannot process active versus passive, future tenses, or distinguish singular from plural. Assessing the right hemisphere of split-brain subjects on standardised tests has indicated that it has a vocabulary roughly equivalent to a 13-year-old child, but its syntactic competence may be around the 5-year-old level. Although it may have this auditory comprehension ability, the right hemisphere appears to possess little or no facility for processing phonological and phonetic information (Code, 1987; Searleman, 1977).

The right hemisphere has some abilities to process lexical-semantic information. Right-hemisphere damaged patients have impairments in the understanding of connotative but not denotative meaning (Brownell, Potter, & Michelow, 1984; Gardner & Denes, 1973), and problems in comprehending the meaning of individual words (Gainotti, Caltagirone, & Miceli, 1983). But the right hemisphere does not appear able to make judgements of semantic relatedness involving picture–word matching (Hart et al., 1991).

Wapner et al. (1981) have summarised the findings from a series of studies with right-hemisphere damaged subjects which looked at complex nonliteral aspects of language. They concluded that the left hemisphere handles the context-free, componential domains of syntax, phonology, etc., while the right deals with non-componential, context bound, nonliteral, complex features of language, such as understanding jokes, metaphors, and stories; using contextually bound discourse, integrating complex linguistic information and appreciating indirect speech acts (Bottini, Corcoran, Sterzi, Paulesu, Schenone, Scarpa, Frackowiak, & Frith, 1994; Bryan, 1989; Code, 1987; Wapner et al., 1981).

Finally, although it appears that the left hemisphere too is involved in processing prosody and emotional aspects of language, there is now extensive evidence that the right hemisphere is closely involved in the processing of various features of prosody (Ross, 1983), emotional prosody and emotional language (Ley & Bryden, 1981). There are close relationships between the processing of music and prosody, and the right hemisphere is engaged in the processing of both (Code, 1987).

Evidence from E.E.G. studies with epileptic subjects who have ictal speech automatisms, which are automatic utterances occurring during epileptic seizures, suggests that over half of subjects use the right hemisphere in their production of the utterance (Hécaen & Angelergues, 1960; Kawai & Ohashi, 1975; Serafetinides & Falconer, 1963). The speech automatisms and recurring utterances commonly observed in Broca's-type aphasia (Code, 1987, 1991, 1994) may, as Hughlings Jackson claimed in 1874, be the products of the right hemisphere. Patients who have undergone the radical surgical procedure of a left hemispherectomy are also capable of remarkable levels of speech and this speech can only come from the remaining right brain.

HEMISPHERECTOMY: THE BACKGROUND

The Operation

The term hemispherectomy is used widely and sometimes rather loosely. Strictly, the term describes the surgical procedure to remove an entire cerebral hemisphere and should be reserved for this purpose. Hemidecortication describes the removal of only the neocortex while leaving intact subcortical nuclear masses such as components of the basal ganglia and the thalamus. The distinction is more than pedantic and becomes important where discussion of the role of remaining brain in cognition is concerned, especially as subcortical areas are known to be involved in language processing (Crosson, 1984; Vallar, Cappa, & Wallesch, 1992; Wallesch, Kornhuber, Brunner, Kunz, Hollerbach, & Suger, 1983).

Hemispherectomy and hemidecortication are radical surgical procedures performed either on adults with large life-threatening neoplastic tumours, or on children to reduce the effects on congenital infantile hemiplegia. In some cases patients do not survive more than a few days. The hemispherectomy operation entails a brutal insult to the brain which, notwithstanding the effects of the removal of half of the brain, can have a massive effect upon the patient's cognitive and behavioural functions. Burklund's (1972) description of the operation vividly illustrates the dramatic and radical nature of the procedure. The surgeon exposes the entire hemisphere (pp. 9–10):

> the carotid, middle, cerebral, and anterior cerebral arteries were identified, clipped, and divided. All of the bridging veins from the surface of the cortex to the superior longitudinal were either coagulated or clipped and divided. The corpus callosum was then sectioned in its entire length exposing the interior of the lateral ventricle. The foramen of Monro was identified and an incision from its anterior superior border to the stria terminalis was made. The choroid plexus was coagulated and removed from the floor of the lateral ventricle, and an incision was made in the line of the stria terminalis posteriorly; this continued anteriorly and medially to include the anterior and dorsomedial nuclei of the thalamus, and it entered the posterior border of the foramen of Monro. The incision was extended into the depths of the brain posteriorly with the electrosurgical unit attempting to stay in the internal capsule posteriorly. The posterior cerebral artery was encountered, clipped and divided distal to the branch of the geniculate ganglion. The incision anteriorly was continued adjacent to the stria terminalis until the anterior and posterior cuts joined and the entire cerebral hemisphere, including all of the basal ganglia and the anterior dorsal portions of the thalamus, was removed.

It is significant to note that, unlike the commisurotomy subjects studied so intensely in the last 30 years (see Chapter 21), there is no reason to suspect a neurological abnormality in early life which may have interfered with the "normal" establishment and balance of hemispheric specialisation for language or any other aspect of cognition.

Right Hemisphere Speech in Previous Left Hemispherectomies

While Goltz (1888) was responsible for the earliest experimental hemispherectomies in mammals, and Burckhardt (see Chapter 20) was engaged in the early development of psychosurgery, it was Dandy (1928) who was apparently the first to perform the operation on a human being. Goltz removed the left hemisphere of a dog and claimed that, as well as normal movement, the animal showed essentially the same "personality" and only slightly reduced "intelligence." (We will pass over the question of how Goltz assessed personality and intelligence in the dog!) Dandy's (1928) case was a right hemisphere removal and it was not until Zollinger (1935) that a left hemisphere was removed in a human being.

When it is that language, or any other cognitive functions for that matter, becomes firmly lateralised is still unclear. Many feel, following Lenneberg (1967), that puberty is crucial and that there is significant plasticity until then. However, lateralisation may not be complete until adulthood (Teuber, 1975) and lateralisation may even be a process that develops into old age (Brown & Jaffe, 1975). The evidence from childhood hemispherectomy is equivocal, to say the least (Code, 1987) and we shall consider only the adult left hemispherectomies in this chapter.

Since Zollinger (1935) there have been relatively few left hemispherectomies in adults and the detail and care of recording much of the language impairment in most reports is disappointing. Zollinger's case (A.C.) was a 43-year-old right-handed woman who, following surgery which left the medial part of the thalamus and a small portion of the globus pallidus, retained (p. 1063) "an elementary vocabulary which was partially increased by training," but comprehension is not mentioned. Specific speech elements mentioned by Zollinger include "all right" to all questions several hours after surgery, but we are not told if this response was used appropriately. In the three days following surgery A.C. was able to say "yes" and "no", "thank you," and "sleep," "goodbye," and "please." On the third day A.C. is reported (p. 1060) to have shown "a more accurate use of words." A.C. survived just 17 days.

Crockett and Estridge (1951) reported on G.S., a male patient whose surgery spared half the globus pallidus, a third of the caudate nucleus, and all of the thalamus. This hemidecorticate was able to say "yes" and "no" some hours after surgery, although it is not clear if these were appropriately used. Two weeks later G.S. was able to say, "No, I don't want any" and "Put me back to bed." Apparently, a few more simple words were added until about one month post-surgery when he began to deteriorate and could utter only "caw" and "aw-caw", as well as "yes" and "no." The patient died four months later and autopsy revealed a recurrence of the tumour involving the pons and the basic pendunculi.

Hillier (1954, p. 720) describes a 15-year-old boy who underwent left hemidecortication "sparing as much of the basal ganglia as possible." Sixteen days after the operation he said "mother", "father", "nurse," and other words. The patient was discharged at one month and he was said to have normal auditory comprehension and daily improvement in vocabulary. He survived for 27 months and before his death he is described by Hillier as being slightly euphoric and as having an improving "motor" aphasia and anomia.

More recently Patterson, Vargha-Khadem, and Polkey (1989) have reported results of detailed investigation of the reading abilities of N.I., described (p. 42) as "a total left hemispherectomy." N.I., right handed before she became ill, suffered massive left-hemisphere damage secondary to Rasmussen's encephalitis starting at age 13 years and lasting for over 30 months before operation. While not an adult at onset of symptoms, and only 15 years' old at surgery, the investigation of her reading in particular was very detailed. The neurological disease process left her with a dense right hemiplegia, a complete right homonymous hemianopia and severely aphasic. A sodium amytal test was carried out prior to surgery and, although results were inconclusive (p. 41), "speech arrest coincident with the onset of hemiparesis was only evident when the right hemisphere was inactivated." This indicates that the right hemisphere had already taken over speech production *before* the hemispherectomy was carried out. So while results from N.I. cannot provide much information on the speech production capabilities of the normal adult right hemisphere, the results of the detailed investigation are worthy of summary here.

Following surgery, N.I. presented as predominantly anomic and deep dyslexic. She had significant problems in virtually all aspects of reading. There was clear impairment of grapheme to phoneme translation and reading of words was predominantly accomplished through the semantic system. She had some ability to read high frequency content and function words, no apparent reading of high or low imageability nouns or verbs or regular or irregular nouns. N.I. had more success with common concrete nouns (35%), animal names (70%), colour names (90%), and number words (100%). Patterson et al. comment on the striking similarity between this error pattern and that of acquired deep dyslexia. This provides support for a right hemisphere hypothesis for deep dyslexia, first put forward by Coltheart (1980). The features of deep dyslexia are semantic errors (semantic paralexias), derivational errors like "true" for "truth," visual errors, errors on function words, and errors reading non-words requiring an intact grapheme to phoneme route (see Chapter 14 in this volume).

N.I.'s speech production showed clear evidence of propositional speech. Her naming was far superior to her reading, and despite her anomia her spontaneous speech was well supplied with function words. Despite her severe aphasia, the anomic flavour of her speech production appears to make her very different to typically globally aphasic patients with massive left-hemisphere damage. While N.I.'s right hemisphere shows significant propositional speech production abilities, what seems most plausible is that there was significant reorganisation taking place over the period between first becoming ill and the surgical intervention. The sodium amytal results support this view.

Smith and Burklund's Cases E.C. and N.F.

There have been two adult left hemispherectomies where the cognitive examination was sufficiently careful to allow inferences on the role of an isolated hemisphere in cognitive functions and the surgery was sufficiently radical to allow us to conclude that only the right hemisphere could account for the patient's speech. These were the hemispherectomy cases E.C. and N.F. reported by Smith and Burklund. E.C. was the first left hemispherectomy studied where the standard of testing and reporting is high. As well as this, E.C. was a complete hemispherectomy. But despite the complete absence of a left hemisphere E.C. had significant, if limited speech.

E.C. was a 47-year-old male who in November 1964 was experiencing attacks of speechlessness and right-sided signs. In March, 1965 Burklund removed a neoplasm from the left sensori-motor area. A moderate "expressive" aphasia was evident but there was little evidence of receptive difficulties. The neoplasm recurred and E.C. underwent a complete hemispherectomy in December, 1965, some 12 months following the emergence of the original symptoms. The description of the operation (Smith, 1966, p. 467) confirms that the hemispherectomy was indeed complete in an attempt to ensure entire removal of any malignant material: "The corpus callosum was split lateral to the anterior cerebral artery, all branches of the artery being coagulated and divided. After cutting through the thalamus posteriorly and the basal ganglia anteriorly, the entire hemisphere was removed in one piece ... The isocortex, all four left cerebral lobes, limbic forebrain and basal ganglia were completely removed."

Following the operation, E.C. exhibited a right hemiplegia and hemianopia with severe receptive and expressive aphasia. At this time his attempts at speech were mostly unsuccessful (p. 468): "He would open his mouth and utter isolated words, and after apparently struggling to organise words for meaningful speech, recognised his inability and would utter expletives or short emotional phrases (e.g. 'Goddamit')."

In support of Smith and Burklund's reports on E.C., Zangwill (1967) was able to examine the patient about 18 months after surgery. He observed such speech as "yes,", "no," "don't know"—always used appropriately, and the emotional expressions "No, God damn it, that's...," "Yes, but I cannot," "God damn it, yes," and "Oh my God!" He could repeat some words, occasionally name objects and colours, but with semantic paraphasic errors ("pencil" he called "pen", "red" he called "black"). He made errors in "automatic speech" also. He was able to count to 20 with some errors. He could read some object and colour words, but could not even read a simple sentence. Moreover, writing was very impaired and he was only able to print his name. Zangwill (1967, p. 1017) concludes that:

> The general impression made upon me by this patient was very much like that of a case of severe motor aphasia and right hemiplegia from left-sided cerebrovascular accident. There was a typical severe motor aphasia, though with some retention of emotional and automatic utterance; good oral comprehension; evidence of insight into the speech defect, and almost total absence of paraphasia or jargon.

Furthermore, E.C. exhibited occasional, and exceptional utterances which Zangwill considered (p. 1018) "as essentially propositional." Zangwill was convinced that E.C.'s right hemisphere was sustaining the language he observed, perhaps in association with remaining subcortical structures.

In 1977, Burklund and Smith described another left hemispherectomy, N.F. This case is interesting for several reasons. Firstly, while N.F. showed similar recovery from the operation as E.C. and was also right handed and male in his forties (age 41 years), he showed a more rapid recovery of language than E.C. N.F. began to experience episodes of right hemiparesis and speechlessness five years before Burklund performed his first surgery. The first operation was an "inferior subtotal left frontal lobectomy with removal of gross neoplasm" (Burklund & Smith, 1977, p. 628). The entire frontal operculum was included in the resection. Recovery of speech was rapid, although there was some dysarthria and "some difficulty expressing words, especially names" at discharge. Eighteen months after the left lobectomy there was recurrence of the neoplasm in the left frontal area with extension into the temporal lobe and the right frontal lobe.

Burklund performed a left hemispherectomy at this time leaving some left thalamus but including some right frontal cortex and occlusion of both anterior cerebral arteries. N.F. was very ill following the operation, but nonverbal response to simple verbal commands was appropriate and prompt. Dysarthric, but appropriate, speech emerged on the third post-operative day. During the early post-surgical period, N.F. had problems focusing attention and showed fatigue during formal testing. This is reflected in his performance at one month post-surgery where he was able to repeat words and phrases but be unable to repeat the same utterances a few moments later. At this time he was able to respond "yes" and "no" appropriately and sing the words and melody of *Jingle Bells*. Spontaneous, apparently propositional, speech was observed about one month post-surgery when he asked a nurse, "You got a match?" Three weeks after this he responded with, "Well, it was OK," when asked if he liked his breakfast. However, he was not able to name objects, read object names, copy his name or simple designs, or write single letters to dictation at this time. There was progressive if erratic improvement in both verbal and nonverbal response to testing for a further nine months.

Eight months post-hemispherectomy, formal testing on the Minnesota Test of Differential Diagnosis of Aphasia showed just one error out of thirty-two in repeating phrases, no errors in automatic speech like counting and reciting days of the week, and two errors in completing eight sentences. Two months later he was able to repeat four digits forward and three backwards, five errors from thirty-two in matching words to objects and eight from thirty-two matching printed to spoken words. Writing was slower to recover but by six months post-surgery he could print letters, his name and concrete words (e.g. cat, bus, dog, banana) but with frequent errors in spelling. He was able to spell single words to dictation and his name with a letter board, but made errors on words of more than four letters. The types of error he made in reading are not detailed.

N.F. survived for 18 months following hemispherectomy. Burklund and Smith (1977, p. 632) concluded: "The rapidity and degree of recovery of verbal and nonverbal neuropsychological responses following 'dominant' hemispherectomy appear contradictory to cortical localisation theory."

Table 22.1 presents a summary of the reported utterances of E.C. and N.F.

THE SIGNIFICANCE OF E.C. AND N.F.

People who have had an entire hemisphere or even a substantial amount of one cortex removed constitute an exceptional group, to say the least. While this makes their study of particular interest for neuropsychology, it also raises problems when comparing the findings from these individuals to others and attempting to generalise findings from these individuals to the normal population in general.

The contribution of hemispherectomy cases to neuropsychology addresses two basic questions: the lateralisation of function in the developing brain and the lateralisation of function in the mature adult brain. Hemispherectomy on children is usually performed to reduce the effects of infantile hemiplegia. Neuropsychological studies with these children have addressed the question of the lateralisation of functions in the developing brain. Basser's (1962) review of the childhood hemispherectomy cases had a substantial effect upon notions of lateralisation development in children. Lenneberg (1967) based much of his argument for cerebral plasticity in the maturing brain on Basser's review. However, re-evaluation of Basser's study (Satz & Bullard-Bates, 1981; St James-Roberts, 1981) highlighted deficiencies in the quality of reporting data, reliance on anecdotal evidence, and failure to control test procedures. However, there

TABLE 22.1

Summary of the Utterances Produced by E.C., N.F., and the Other Adult Left Hemispherectomy Cases in the Literature

E.C.	N.F.	Other cases
yes, no, don't know; *Goddamit!;* *No, God damn it, that's …;* *Yes, but I cannot;* *God damn it yes;* *Oh my God!*	*yes, no.*	*yes, no;* *thank you, sleep, goodbye,* *please;* *"caw", "aw-caw";* *mother, father, nurse.*
Automatic speech with errors.	Error-free automatic counting, days of week.	
Repetition.	Almost error-free repetition of words/phrases; 4 digits forwards and 3 backwards.	
Reading single nouns.	Errors matching printed to spoken words. Could write name, and words *cat*, *bus*, *dog*, *banana* with errors. Words and melody of *Jingle Bells*. Some errors matching words to objects.	
Naming with some semantic paraphasias.	*You got a match?* *Well, it was OK.*	*No, I don't want any.* *Put me back to bed.*

are still remarkable reports of normal and indeed superior development of cognition following left hemispherectomy. Smith and Sugar (1975) reported the superior development of language and intelligence 21 years after a left hemispherectomy following surgery at age 5 years 6 months. Studies of children with hydrocephalus report the development of superior adult intellectual capacities, including completion of university education, despite severe hydrocephalus occupying as much as 95% of the cranial cavity (Berker, Goldstein, Lorber, Priestley, & Smith, 1992; Lorber, 1983). Such reports testify to the plasticity of the developing brain.

The major significance of the study of both N.F. and E.C. is that they have contributed to a reappraisal of the right hemisphere's contribution to language processing, particularly in speech production. Since the very early days of the development of contemporary neuropsychology, which is coincident with the birth of dominance theory (Bogen, 1969), it has been held that the right hemisphere cannot speak. Yet clearly in E.C. and N.F. it did. For N.F. language recovery was more rapid than for E.C. This may be attributed to the fact that, as Burklund and Smith suggest, he was some six years younger than E.C. It may also be because of the five-year onset in the neoplasm which may have caused the right hemisphere to become gradually more involved over time in left-hemisphere functions. In addition, there was a gap of 18 months between the initial left frontal lobectomy on N.F. and the fuller hemispherectomy. It could be argued that substantial shifting of language processing to the right hemisphere may have taken place during the intervening five years between onset of symptoms and the initial lobectomy and also the staging of the surgery, with 18 months between the first and second operation, may have increased any shift of function from left to right.

While we have known for some time that the young brain has significant plasticity, a comparison of E.C. and the staging of the surgery over time in N.F. allows us also to rethink the plasticity of the middle-aged brain and reappraise its abilities to reorganise. The conclusion appears to be that the older brain also has significant reorganisational abilities.

Other differences in N.F. and E.C. are worth noting. Specifically, dysarthria disappeared in E.C. early after surgery whereas it persisted in N.F. This may have been due to the excision of the right frontal area in N.F., as a persistent spastic dysarthria appears to require bilateral damage, at least in cerebrovascular accident (C.V.A.) (Darley, Aronson, & Brown, 1975). However, Burklund and Smith (177) pointed out that, in cases of bifrontal lobectomy, dysarthria appears to clear quickly following surgery.

Burklund and Smith (1977) showed that while language processing was seen to recover dramatically following left hemispherectomy in E.C. and N.F., the contrasting finding of recovery in nonverbal cognition following right hemispherectomy is not observed. Why does language recover relatively well following removal of the left hemisphere compared to the recovery of nonverbal processing following right hemisphere removal? It may be related to the holistic processing capacity claimed for the right hemisphere (Bradshaw & Nettleton, 1981). The right hemisphere may therefore be more flexible and able to reorganise to take on the analytical and sequential language processing of the left. In contrast, the claimed analytic processing mode of the left hemisphere (Bradshaw & Nettleton, 1981) may be more rigid and not capable of coping with processing of perception and visuospatial activities which require holistic mechanisms.

What these cases appear to confirm is that the right hemisphere can indeed speak, at least in the absence of a left hemisphere. But does that mean that for others the right hemisphere can speak? Without more solid physiological evidence, we must ask in what ways the speech of E.C. and N.F. are like the speech of people who have not had their left hemispheres removed. A further issue is the degree of propositionality in the speech of the left hemispherectomy subject. Utterances like "You gotta match?" and "Well, it was okay," while certainly sentences, would appear to be situation specific. Such utterances may be propositionally produced in some circumstances but relatively automatically produced in others. For a smoker the first utterance may be a very formulaic expression and not at all uniquely generated. So while it appears that the right can be engaged in speech production, the evidence does not permit us to claim that the adult isolated right hemisphere is capable of generating propositional speech. The nonpropositional utterances of left hemispherectomy patients, and the lexical speech automatisms of aphasic patients, may have originally been generated by a left hemisphere system in early development. The processing of automatic and nonpropositional speech by the right hemisphere may be part of a task-sharing metasystem. There is no overlearnt, familiar, formulaic, automatic speech during the period when the child is learning to speak. At this time for the child all speech is newly generated by the left hemisphere's linguistic system. Even counting and days of the week will acquire their morphological and phonological framework, including syllabification perhaps, during this early developmental period. With time and with overuse these utterances, like others which are overlearnt and familiar, will not require left hemisphere processing. Left hemisphere processing will have become redundant, and the utterances may be passed to the right hemisphere holistic speech lexicon in order to extricate the left hemisphere to allow it more space to process the most demanding and exacting of human activities, the creation and generation of novel language for the expression of semantic states.

The left hemispherectomy evidence also makes a contribution to understanding the role of the right hemisphere in the recovery of language and speech in aphasia. The notion that following left-hemisphere damage the right hemisphere is involved in the spontaneous recovery of aphasia is not a new idea and takes more than one form. One variant of the idea is that some or even all of the symptoms that characterise aphasia—agrammatism, paraphasia, speech automatisms, paralexia, etc., are produced by an intact right hemisphere and not by a damaged left. There is little direct evidence for this view. Right hemisphere hypotheses have been developed for some kinds of speech automatisms (Code, 1987, 1991, 1994) and some of the features of acquired dyslexia (Coltheart, 1980; Landis & Regard, 1988; Weniger, Kitteringham, & Eglin, 1988) and repetition in transcortical motor aphasia (Berthier, Starkstein, Leiguarda, Ruiz, Mayberg, Wagner, Price, & Robinson, 1991). Patterson et al.'s (1989) hemispherectomy case N.I., discussed earlier, is also helping in the reappraisal of the right hemisphere's contribution to reading. As there is little direct evidence from unilaterally left-hemisphere damaged patients yet available, inferential evidence from other populations has been sought. Table 22.1 shows some evidence of semantic paraphasia, a common feature of aphasia, from the right hemisphere of E.C. Table 22.2 shows some nonpropositional and automatic aphasic speech automatisms and recurring utterances (from Code, 1982). There are clear parallels that can be drawn between these utterances and the speech produced from the right hemispheres of E.C. and N.F. Particularly interesting are the emotionally charged expletives of E.C. It is also of interest to note that the "caw" and "aw-caw" of Crockett and Estridge's case G.S. is the only nonlexical utterance reported from a left hemispherectomy, and this emerged when the patient was beginning to deteriorate. Evidence suggests that if the right hemisphere becomes involved in recovery from aphasia it is a function of severity of aphasia and as a function of time since onset (Cappa & Vallar, 1992; Code, 1987).

The strongest variant, identified as the lateral shift hypothesis (Code, 1987), claims that following damage to the left hemisphere, perhaps to some control mechanism, the right hemisphere is released from the inhibition of the dominant left and there is a shift in control from left to right. Related to this is the notion that linguistic abilities which have been latent can emerge from the right hemisphere following damage to the left (Moscovitch, 1973). This view holds that the level of recovery we observe in aphasia is less than it should be compared to the apparent abilities of the right hemisphere in commisurotomy and left hemispherectomy cases. The left hemisphere in aphasic patients is inhibiting a possible compensatory system in the right. Little is certain in this area, but there are strong indications from a range of studies that the involvement of the right hemisphere in aphasic individuals varies as a function of severity and time since onset: the more severe the aphasia and the more time has elapsed since the damage then the more involved the right hemisphere appears to be (Cappa & Vallar, 1992; Code, 1987; Weniger et al., 1988). It was noted above that substantial shifting of

TABLE 22.2
Selected Lexical Speech Automatisms
and Nonlexical Recurring Utterances
(from Code, 1982)

Lexical speech automatisms

I can't	*I can talk*
I can try	*I said*
I want	*I want to*
bloody hell	*fucking hell*

Nonlexical recurring utterances

/tu tu tu uuuu/	/wi wi wi/
/bi bi/	/di di/
/ta ta/	/du du du/

language processing to the right hemisphere in N.F. during the five-year period between onset of symptoms and surgery may have underlain his superior (compared to E.C.) recovery of language and speech.

E.C. and N.F. are classic cases in neuropsychology in that they have suggested new directions. Their major contribution is that they have made us question entrenched neuropsychological dogma. They made us query some of the most established and ingrained doctrines of the dominance theory: namely the view that the right hemisphere is incapable of speech production. The abilities of these subjects also show us that some of the symptoms of aphasia observed following left-hemisphere damage may not be products of damaged left-hemisphere mechanisms but may represent intact right hemisphere functions.

ACKNOWLEDGEMENTS

I am grateful to Joseph Bogen, Aaron Smith, Yves Joanette, and John Hodges for useful correspondence during the writing of this chapter.

REFERENCES

Basser, L.S. (1962). Hemiplegia of early onset and the faculty of speech with special references to the effects of hemispherectomy. *Brain, 85*, 427–460.

Berker, E., Goldstein, G., Lorber, J., Priestley, B., & Smith, A. (1992). Reciprocal neurological developments of twins discordant for hydrocephalus. *Developmental Medicine and Child Neurology, 34*, 623–632.

Berthier, M.L., Starkstein, S.E., Leiguarda, R., Ruiz, A., Mayberg, H.S., Wagner, H., Price, T.R., & Robinson, R.G. (1991). Transcortical aphasia: Importance of the nonspeech dominant hemisphere in language repetition. *Brain, 114*, 1409–1427.

Bogen, J.E. (1969). The other side of the brain: II. An appositional mind. *Bulletin of the Los Angeles Neurological Societies, 34*, 135–162.

Bottini, G., Corcoran, R, Sterzi, R., Paulesu, E., Schenone, P., Scarpa, P., Frackowiak, R.S.J., & Frith, C.P. (1994). The role of the right hemisphere in the interpretation of figurative aspects of language: A positron emission tomography activation study. *Brain, 117*, 1241–1253.

Bradshaw, J.L., & Nettleton, N.C. (1981). The nature of hemispheric specialization in man. *Behavioral and Brain Sciences, 4*, 51–91.

Brown, J.W., & Jaffe, J. (1975). Hypothesis on cerebral dominance. *Neuropsychologia, 13*, 107–110.

Brownell, H.H., Potter, H.H., & Michelow, D. (1984). Sensitivity to lexical denotation and connotation in brain-damaged patients: A double dissociation? *Brain and Language, 22*, 253–265.

Bryan, K. (1989). *The right hemisphere language battery*. London: Whurr Publishers.

Burklund, C.W. (1972). Cerebral hemisphere function in the human: Fact versus tradition. In W.L. Smith (Ed.), *Drugs, development, and cerebral function*. Springfield, IL: C.C. Thomas.

Burklund, C.W., & Smith, A. (1977). Language and the cerebral hemispheres. *Neurology, 27*, 627–633.

Cappa, S.F., & Vallar, G. (1992). The role of the left and right hemispheres in recovery from aphasia. *Aphasiology, 6*, 359–372.

Chiarello, C. (Ed.). (1988). *Right hemisphere contributions to lexical semantics.* New York: Springer-Verlag.

Code, C. (1982). Neurolinguistic analysis of recurrent utterances in aphasia. *Cortex, 18,* 141–152.

Code, C. (1987). *Language, aphasia and the right hemisphere.* Chichester: Wiley.

Code, C. (1991). Speech automatisms and recurring utterances. In C. Code (Ed.), *The characteristics of aphasia.* Hove, U.K.: Lawrence Erlbaum Associates Ltd.

Code, C. (1994). Speech automatism production in aphasia. *Journal of Neurolinguistics, 8,* 135–148.

Coltheart, M. (1980). Deep dyslexia: A right hemisphere hypothesis. In M. Coltheart, K. Patterson, & J. Marshall (Eds.), *Deep dyslexia.* London: Routledge & Kegan Paul.

Crockett, H.G., & Estridge, N.M. (1951). Cerebral hemispherectomy. *Bulletin of the Los Angeles Neurological Societies, 16,* 71–87.

Crosson, B. (1984). The role of the dominant thalamus in language: A review. *Psychological Bulletin, 3,* 491–517.

Dandy, W.E. (1928). Removal of right cerebral hemisphere for certain tumors with hemiplegia: A preliminary report. *JAMA, 90,* 823–825.

Darley, F.L., Aronson, A.E., & Brown, J. (1975). *Motor speech disorders.* Philadelphia: Saunders.

Gainotti, G., Caltagirone, C, & Miceli, G. (1983). Selective impairment of semantic-lexical discrimination in right-brain-damaged patients. In E. Perecman (Ed.), *Cognitive processing in the right hemisphere.* London: Academic Press.

Gardner, H., & Denes, G. (1973). Connotative judgements by aphasic patients on a pictorial adaptation of the semantic differential. *Cortex, 9,* 183–196.

Goldman-Eisler, F. (1968). *Psycholinguistics: Experiments in spontaneous speech.* London: Academic Press.

Goldstein, K: (1948). *Language and language disturbances.* New York: Grune & Stratton.

Goltz, F. (1888/1966). On the functions of the hemispheres. In G. von Bonin (Ed.), *Some papers on the cerebral cortex.* Springfield, IL: C.C. Thomas.

Hart, J., Lesser, R.P., Fisher, R.S., Schwerdt, P., Bryan, R.N., & Gordon, B. (1991). Dominant-side intracarotid amobarbital spares comprehension of word meaning. *Archives of Neurology, 48,* 55–58.

Head, H. (1926). *Aphasia and kindred disorders of speech.* Cambridge: Cambridge University Press.

Hécaen, H., & Angelergues, R. (1960). Epilepsie et troubles du langage. *Encephale, 49,* 138–169.

Hillier, W.F. (1954). Total left cerebral hemispherectomy for malignant glioma. *Neurology, 4,* 718–721.

Hughlings Jackson, J. (1874/1958). On the nature of the duality of the brain. In J. Taylor (Ed.), *Selected writings of John Hughlings Jackson (Vol. 2).* London: Staples Press.

Joanette, Y., Goulet, P., & Hannequin, D. (1990). *Right hemisphere and verbal communication.* New York: Springer-Verlag.

Kawai, I., & Ohashi, H. (1975). Total speech disturbance and cerebral dominance. *Studia Phonologica, 9,* 40–44.

Landis, T. & Regard, M. (1988). The right hemisphere's access to lexical meaning: A function of its release from left-hemisphere control? In C. Chiarello (Ed.), *Right hemisphere contributions to lexical semantics.* New York: Springer-Verlag.

Lenneberg, E. (1967). *The biological foundations of language.* New York: John Wiley.

Ley, R.G., & Bryden, M.P. (1981). Consciousness, emotion, and the right hemisphere. In G. Underwood & R. Stevens (Eds.), *Aspects of consciousness: Vol. II. Structural Issues.* London: Academic Press.

Lorber, J. (1983). Is your brain really necessary? In D. Voth (Ed.), *Hydrocephalus in frühen Kindersalter*. Stuttgart: Enke.

Moscovitch, M. (1973). Language and the cerebral hemispheres: Reaction-time studies and their implications for models of cerebral dominance. In P. Pliner, L. Krames, & T. Alloway (Eds.), *Communication and affect: Language and thought*. New York: Academic Press.

Ojemann, G.A. (1979). Individual variability in cortical localization of language. *Journal of Neurosurgery*, *50*, 164–169.

Patterson, K., Vargha-Khadem, F., & Polkey, C.E. (1989). Reading with one hemisphere. *Brain*, *112*, 39–63.

Ross, E.D. (1983). Right hemisphere lesions in disorders of affective language. In A. Kertesz (Ed.), *Localization in neuropsychology*. London: Academic Press.

Satz, P., & Bullard-Bates, C. (1981). Acquired aphasia in children. In M.T. Sarno (Ed.), *Acquired aphasia*. New York: Academic Press.

Searleman, A. (1977). A review of right hemisphere linguistic capabilities. *Psychological Bulletin*, *84*, 503–528.

Segalowitz, S.J., & Bryden, M.P. (1983). Individual differences in hemispheric representation of language. In S.J. Segalowitz (Ed.), *Language functions and brain organization*. London: Academic Press.

Serafetinides, E.A., & Falconer, M.A. (1963). Speech disturbances in temporal lobe seizures: A study of 100 epileptic patients submitted to anterior temporal lobectomy. *Brain*, *86*, 333–346.

Smith, A. (1966). Speech and other functions after left (dominant) hemispherectomy. *Journal of Neurology, Neurosurgery and Psychiatry*, *29*, 467–471.

Smith, A., & Burklund, C.W. (1966). Dominant hemispherectomy. *Science*, *153*, 1280–1282.

Smith, A., & Sugar, O. (1975). Development of above normal language and intelligence 21 years after left hemispherectomy. *Neurology*, *25*, 813–818.

St James-Roberts, I. (1981). A reinterpretation of hemispherectomy data without functional plasticity. *Brain and Language*, *13*, 31–53.

Teuber, H.L. (1975). Recovery of function after brain injury in man. In R. Porter & D.W. Fitzsimons (Eds.), *Outcome of severe damage to the nervous system* (Ciba Foundation Symposium 34). Amsterdam: Elsevier.

Vallar, G., Cappa, S., & Wallesch, C.-W. (Eds.) (1992). *Neuropsychological disorders associated with subcortical lesions*. Oxford: Oxford University Press.

Van Lancker, D. (1987). Nonpropositional speech: Neurolinguistic studies. In A.W. Ellis (Ed.), *Progress in the psychology of language (Vol. III)*. Hove, U.K.: Lawrence Erlbaum Associates Ltd.

Wallesch, C.-W., Kornhuber, H.H., Brunner, R.J., Kunz, T., Hollerbach, B., & Suger, G. (1983). Lesions of the basal ganglia, thalamus, and deep white matter: Differential effects upon language functions. *Brain and Language*, *20*, 286–304.

Wapner, W., Hamby, S., & Gardner, H. (1981). The role of the right hemisphere in the apprehension of complex linguistic materials. *Brain and Language*, *14*, 15–33.

Weniger, D., Kitteringham, V., & Eglin, M. (1988). The variability of right-hemisphere reading capacities in global aphasia. In C. Chiarello (Ed.), *Right hemisphere contributions to lexical semantics*. New York: Springer-Verlag.

Wray, A. (1992). *The focusing hypothesis*. Amsterdam: John Benjamin.

Zangwill, O. (1967). Speech and the minor hemisphere. *Acta Neurol. Psychiatr. Belg.*, *67*, 1013–1020.

Zollinger, R. (1935). Removal of left cerebral hemisphere: A report of a case. *Archives of Neurology and Psychiatry*, *34*, 1055–1064.

23 H.M.: The Medial Temporal Lobes and Memory

Alan J. Parkin
Laboratory of Experimental Psychology, University of Sussex, Brighton, U.K.

The adverse effects of medial temporal lobe damage on memory have been known since the last century (see Parkin & Leng, 1993) but, for most psychologists, this fact remained largely unknown, and thus of little consequence, until the mid-1950s. There were a number of reasons for this. First, papers describing the effects of temporal lobe damage were mainly confined to the neurological literature and many appeared in languages other than English. Second, the intellectual climate of psychology in the first half of the century was not one in which the intriguing consequences of this form of damage might have been appreciated. During this period psychology was dominated by behaviourism and even those behaviourists who chose to look at humans used paradigms that stressed input–output relationships rather than making any attempt to specify the structural organisation and internal processes of human memory.

Things changed dramatically towards the end of the 1950s. Chomsky revealed the paucity of Skinner's account of language, imagery re-emerged as a valid construct for experimental investigation and, most important for our present purpose, William James' ideas about the nature of human memory resurfaced. Co-extensive with this was the emergence of what would now be termed cognitive neuropsychology and, as one of its main attractions, were the intriguing studies of temporal lobectomy patients carried out by Brenda Milner and her colleagues.

TEMPORAL LOBECTOMY

In the 1950s Brenda Milner worked in association with the neurosurgeon William Scoville who practised what he later described as "frankly experimental" neurosurgery for the relief of intractable epilepsy. Epilepsy most commonly has a temporal lobe focus and Scoville's approach was to excise that part of the temporal lobe in which the epicentre of the epileptic seizure was located. In 1957 Scoville and Milner reported a series of patients who had undergone temporal lobectomy. From the point of view of the patients' epilepsy the operations were successful, but they also had a disastrous consequence in that several of the patients presented a severe loss of memory. Among these was one man, H.M., who went on to be one of the most famous neuropsychological patients ever—someone who would be the subject of many scientific papers and whose case history would appear in textbooks of psychology all over the world.

CASE H.M.

H.M. was born in 1926 and his development was unremarkable until, at the age of seven, he was knocked down by a bicycle and rendered unconscious for about five minutes. At age 10 he suffered his first epileptic seizure, and his first grand mal seizure occurred when he was 16. By the time H.M. had left high school and taken a job as a motor winder he was having ten petit mal seizures per day and one major seizure each week. H.M.'s quality of life deteriorated to a point where both surgeons and family decided that a neurosurgical operation was the only hope of relieving the illness.

The operation is described in detail by Scoville and Milner (1957; see also Corkin, 1984) but, briefly, it involved exposure of the tips of the temporal lobes which were then retracted to allow examination of the uncus, amygdala, and hippocampus as possible epileptic foci. The medial half of each tip of the temporal lobe was then resected and, using suction, grey and white matter comprising the prepyriform gyrus, uncus, amygdala, hippocampus, and parahippocampal gyrus were removed bilaterally. The temporal neocortex was spared.

Corkin reports that H.M. was free of grand mal seizures for periods as long as a year and that the petit mal seizures he still suffered did not disturb him noticeably. However, as an unanticipated side-effect, H.M. had developed one of the most profound and pure anterograde amnesias ever discovered.

EXPERIMENTAL INVESTIGATIONS OF H.M.— SHORT-TERM VERSUS LONG-TERM STORAGE

The case of H.M. is perhaps unique within the neuropsychological literature because of both the depth to which his memory loss has been investigated and the extent to which the nature of his impairments have provided data consistent with the current *zeitgeist* in human memory research.

In *Principles of Psychology*, James (1890) had advocated a dualist account of memory in which he drew a distinction between the form of memory underlying our conscious experience, which he termed primary memory, and that representing the "genuine past"—secondary memory. James' seminal distinction had attracted little attention during the behaviourist era because the concept of primary memory was inextricably linked to the notion of consciousness—the *bête noire* of the behaviourists. However, with mentalistic concepts once again becoming respectable, experimental psychologists began to examine whether the distinction between primary and secondary memory had any psychological reality.

The early 1960s saw a massive explosion in experimental memory research aimed at demonstrating the plausibility of the primary/secondary memory distinction which, with the advent of computer-based analogies of humans as information processors, became transformed into the distinction between short-term and long-term storage. The pinnacle of this endeavour was Atkinson and Shiffrin's (1968) *Human Memory: A proposed system and its control processes*, in which the authors described an extensive series of experiments concerned with exploring the mechanisms of short- and long-term store. An interesting feature of this work is that the authors did not feel any need to show, experimentally, that the basic dichotomy was valid. They assumed this (p. 97) on the basis of "what is perhaps the single most convincing demonstration of a dichotomy in the memory system: the effects of hippocampal lesions reported by Milner."

It is not difficult to see why the reports emanating from Milner's laboratory were manna from heaven to the early proponents of the short-term/long-term storage dichotomy. In her own words:

> Bilateral surgical lesions in the hippocampal region ... produce a remarkably severe and persistent memory disorder. Patients ... seem largely incapable of adding new information to long-term store. This is true whether acquisition is measured by free recall, recognition, or learning with savings. Nevertheless, the immediate registration of new input ... appears to take place normally and material that can be encompassed by verbal rehearsal is held for many many minutes without further loss ... Interruption of rehearsal ... produces immediate forgetting of what went before ... and ... material that cannot be categorized in verbal terms decays in 30 seconds. Material already in long-term store is unaffected by the lesion, except for a certain amount of retrograde amnesia. (As cited by Atkinson & Shiffrin, 1968, p. 97.)

Much of Milner's account stems from her own observations of H.M. and those provided by one of her early students, Prisko. On tests of digit span and block span H.M.'s performance has been borderline normal but his performance deteriorates markedly as soon as his measured capacity is exceeded by as little as one item. Wickelgren (1968) tested H.M. on the probe recognition task in which individual digits are presented at a constant rate followed by a probe digit. The subject's task is to report the digit that came after the probe in the sequence. This technique was used extensively as a means of investigating forgetting in short-term store (e.g. Waugh & Norman, 1965) and Wickelgren's study showed that H.M.'s short-term forgetting curve was entirely within normal range.

In contrast, H.M.'s inability to commit information to long-term memory is legendary. In her review of H.M.'s case in 1984, Suzanne Corkin noted (p. 255) that he "still exhibits a profound anterograde amnesia, and does not know where he lives, who cares for him, or where he ate his last meal. His guesses as to the current year may be off by as much as 43 years... In 1982 he did not recognise a picture of himself that had been taken on his 40th birthday in 1966." However, some facts have managed to become stored although they defy any theory which relates memory strength purely to exposure. Thus, although unable to say anything at all about what Watergate meant, despite watching T.V. news every night, he had learned that Howard Cosell was the newsreader. Moreover, he had also learned the edifying fact that the T.V. character Archie Bunker called his son "Meathead."

On more formal laboratory measures H.M.'s anterograde loss was equally evident. On the Wechsler Memory Scale (W.M.S.) H.M.'s initial memory quotient (M.Q.) was 67 (average 100, SD 15)—this is extremely low, even for patients considered amnesic, especially when one takes into account probable inflation from his normal digit span and presumably good mental control. He also failed to recall anything about the Rey–Ostereith figure despite copying it accurately only minutes earlier. Indeed, whether the material was words, paired associates, abstract patterns, common objects, maze solutions, or locations, H.M.'s forgetting of these kinds of material was almost total.

In the early 1970s the short-term/long-term storage account came under threat from the levels of processing framework. Briefly it was argued that memory might be more fruitfully studied by examining the relationship between the "depth" to which information was processed during acquisition and the subsequent retention performance (Craik & Lockhart, 1972). This led naturally to a questioning of the presumed wisdom of regarding amnesia as some breakdown between the mechanisms of short- and long-term storage. Instead it was proposed that amnesia might be better understood as a deficit in the initial level of processing of information. In an overlooked review of evaluating theories of amnesia, Stern (1981) considered various lines of evidence against the levels of processing approach but, such is the compelling nature of H.M.'s memory loss, he felt that the final word should be left to Milner (1970, p. 37):

[H.M.] was able to retain the number 584 for at least 15 minutes, by continuously working out elaborate mnemonic schemes. When asked how he had been able to remember the number for so long, he replied: "It's easy. You just remember 8. You see, 5, 8, and 4 add to 17. You remember 8, subtract it from 17 and it leaves 9. Divide 9 in half and you get 5 and 4, and there you are: 584: Easy." A minute or two later, H.M. was unable to recall either the number 584 or any of the associated complex train of thought; in fact he did not know that he had been given a number to remember.

This anecdote, it was thought, was all one needed to be convinced that a whole mass of experimental data supporting the levels approach to amnesia could not be right.

H.M. AND THE EPISODIC–SEMANTIC DISTINCTION

In 1972 Endel Tulving introduced a new seminal distinction when he distinguished between episodic and semantic memory. Although these concepts have undergone some modification since the initial proposal (Tulving, 1985) the basic idea remains the same: episodic memory refers to our long-term store of autobiographical incidents and semantic memory describes our general knowledge about how the world functions.

In defining amnesia, psychologists have often relied on the discrepancy between a patient's M.Q. and their I.Q. as measured by the Wechsler Adult Intelligence Scale (W.A.I.S.). By these criteria amnesia was defined as any I.Q.–M.Q. discrepancy greater than 20 points. H.M.'s I.Q. was 122, thus giving him one of the largest I.Q.–M.Q. discrepancy scores ever observed (Parkin & Leng, 1993). Not only did this emphasise H.M.'s amnesia, but it was also a powerful argument for the dissociability of episodic and semantic memory: The argument being that W.M.S. provided a measure of episodic memory and that W.A.I.S. measured general intelligence—semantic memory.

H.M.'s case was at the forefront of several theoretical analyses of amnesia which attempted to describe amnesia within the episodic–semantic framework (Kinsbourne, 1981; Parkin, 1982). However, a later study of H.M. provided an important challenge to the episodic–semantic dissociation. Gabrieli, Cohen, and Corkin (1988) studied the ability of H.M. to acquire new vocabulary and found him completely incapable of doing so— a finding which complemented clinical observation of H.M. possessing a vocabulary more or less frozen in the 1950s with only a handful of words acquired since his operation (these included ayatollah and rock 'n' roll). This is one of the most detailed and extensive studies of an amnesic trying to acquire new vocabulary and his failure to do so has been used as a powerful argument for the interactivity of the putative episodic and semantic systems.

PROCEDURAL MEMORY

Following on from Tulving's initial distinction between episodic and semantic memory was the need to distinguish a third form of memory: procedural memory. This form of memory was defined as knowledge that was not accessible to conscious description and could thus only be expressed by action. Investigators keen to argue for the separability of procedural memory had to look no further than the extensive investigations of H.M. In 1966, Milner reported that H.M. showed a completely normal learning curve on the mirror drawing task and, a little later, Corkin (1968) showed that H.M. learned at a comparable rate to normals on the pursuit rotor, bimanual, and tapping tasks. She also observed the development of "testing habits" whereby H.M. would become increasingly familiar with the testing procedures (knowing how to turn the equipment on, etc.) even though he denied any conscious recollection of having undertaken any of the tasks before. The selective preservation of procedural memory has now been observed in many amnesic patients but the purity of the preservation in H.M. has rarely been equalled.

EXPLICIT AND IMPLICIT MEMORY

The distinction between explicit and implicit memory was formulated by Schacter and Graf (1986; see also Schacter, 1987). This distinction defines different memory systems or processes in terms of the conditions prevailing at retrieval. Explicit memory was defined as any memory test which required subjects to recollect a specific event (e.g. a word list they had been shown). In contrast, implicit memory referred to any test which assessed a subject's memory for a previous event in some indirect fashion. Put another way, an implicit test of memory is any one in which the subject can attempt performance without necessary reference to a previous event whereas, for explicit memory, access to a previous event related memory is the *sine qua non* of performance.

H.M.'s remarkable procedural memory abilities are, of course, examples of implicit memory because the tasks involved meet the criterion outlined at the end of the last paragraph. However, memory researchers do not usually regard motor skill learning as a measure of implicit memory in that they often choose to regard this form of learning as some specialised form of motoric memory. However, if one turns to the more typical domain of implicit memory, we again find that H.M. provides us with remarkable evidence of selective preservation.

Milner, Corkin, and Teuber (1968) evaluated H.M. on the Gollin (1960) incomplete pictures task. In the task he was shown a degraded picture and asked to identify it. If identification failed he was shown increasingly informative versions of the picture until he recognised it. Retention was tested by re-presenting the picture in its most degraded form and seeing whether any savings in identification were observed. H.M. showed clear evidence of savings, i.e. identification of previously exposed stimuli on the basis of a less informative picture than needed at the outset. This study predates many others which have used picture completion as a means of evaluating and establishing the separable status of implicit memory in normal children and adults (e.g. Parkin & Streete, 1988; Russo & Parkin, 1993).

Another widely used measure of implicit learning has been the Tower of Hanoi task. The minimum solution to this problem involves 31 moves and, although a little slower than controls (perhaps suggesting that explicit memory can facilitate this task to some extent), H.M. needed only 16 attempts to reach and maintain a minimum move solution (Cohen, 1984). Within the nonverbal domain, Gabrieli, Milberg, Keane, and Corkin (1990) have also shown that H.M. shows priming for novel patterns.

H.M. AND THE "TWO-AMNESIAS" DEBATE

One of the intriguing features of the amnesic syndrome is its association with two underlying pathologies: The midline diencephalic nuclei or the medial temporal lobe. Following a preliminary study by Lhermitte and Signoret (1972), in which it was suggested that temporal lobe amnesia (as observed in survivors of herpes simplex encephalitis) produced more rapid forgetting than amnesia associated with diencephalic lesions, the issue of whether there are two forms of amnesia has become an important issue (Parkin & Leng, 1993). Again investigations of H.M. were at the heart of this matter because, prior to the advent of M.R.I. scanning, H.M. was one of the few accessible patients with a known medial temporal pathology.

Huppert and Piercy (1979) presented data purporting to show that H.M. forgot information more rapidly than Korsakoff patients with a diencephalic pathology. This study set in train a flurry of activity trying to associate temporal lobe pathology with rapid forgetting (e.g. Kopelman, 1985; Martin, Loring, Meador, & Lee, 1988; Parkin, 1992; Squire, 1981). As is often the case with recognition memory, the data on rapid forgetting have become more complex because, in H.M.'s case at least, the rapidity with which he forgets seems determined by the manner in which he is tested (Freed & Corkin, 1988; Freed, Corkin, & Cohen, 1987). None the less, the rapid forgetting debate is one more example where observations on H.M. were sufficient to motivate a considerable research enterprise.

The two-amnesias argument has also hinged on the nature of retrograde amnesia with the suggestion that diencephalic pathology, at least as shown in Korsakoff's syndrome, involves a severe impairment of both anterograde and retrograde memory whereas in temporal lobe disturbance there is a

marked dissociation between the two. Again the extensive assessments of
H.M.'s remote memory, in association with the detailed neuropathology,
have meant that H.M. has been at the forefront of the argument. Central to
the argument has been the claim that H.M.'s retrograde impairment is
limited to about two years—this has been used by some as a crucial piece of
evidence supporting the idea that consolidation is a relatively long-term
process thus allowing a severe anterograde amnesia to be associated with a
relatively short period of retrograde amnesia (Squire, Cohen, & Nadel,
1984).

Milner's initial reports suggest that H.M.'s retrograde amnesia did extend
back only a few years but later studies (Marslen-Wilson & Teuber, 1975)
suggest a more extensive deficit. This issue is probably one where H.M.'s
data will perhaps become less important as the following anecdote (Corkin,
1984, p. 256) concerning H.M.'s high school reunion suggests:

A number of his classmates remembered him and greeted him warmly: one
woman even gave him a kiss. As far as we could determine, however, H.M. did
not recognize anyone's face or name. But he was not alone in this respect. We
met a woman who claimed that she too did not know anyone in the room.
Clearly she and H.M. were exceptions in this regard, but her comments remind
us that as people age they also forget.

H.M.: AN OVERVIEW

From the above we can see that data from H.M. has been extremely
prominent in supporting many of the ideas in modern memory research and,
perhaps more than any other case, his data, and the reactions to them, show
how compelling single case data can be. The reasons for H.M.'s substantial
influence are many. Undoubtedly important was timing. H.M. appeared
during a crucial phase in the development of experimental psychology, at a
time when theory development constructed new ideas amenable to the
dissociative framework provided by the emerging field of cognitive
neuropsychology. However, timing was not all because patients given
equal initial prominence, such as the intra-nasal penetrating head injury case
N.A. (Teuber, Milner, & Vaughan, 1968), did not have the same eventual
impact.

H.M.'s prominence can be attributed to a number of additional factors.
First there was the purity of his condition. Within the literature on human
amnesia it is difficult to find a patient with a purer amnesia[1] who so reliably
exhibited dissociations consistent with current experimental frameworks.[2]
Second, sound knowledge about his lesion meant that studies of H.M. could
be incorporated into investigations concerned with structure–function
relationships. A third factor is H.M.'s placid nature—one of "the most
striking characteristics is that he rarely complains about anything ... is

always agreeable and co-operative to the point that if ... asked to sit in a particular place he will do so indefinitely" (Corkin, 1984, p. 251)—which has enabled many hundreds of hours of experimenting to be carried out (for a more extensive memoire of H.M. see Ogden & Corkin, 1991).

Finally we must not rule out luck. It was extremely fortunate that H.M. turned up in Montreal and underwent investigation by Brenda Milner and the many other excellent researchers at her laboratory. This has ensured, to the current day, that investigations of H.M. have taken full account of recent developments in neuropsychology. One can only heave a huge sigh of relief that H.M. did not end up elsewhere in 1953 because, without him, one can argue that the progress of human memory research might have been slower and the outcome different.

NOTES

1. While it is true that H.M. presents an outstandingly pure amnesia he is not free from other deficits. He has a well-established olfactory deficit (Eichenbaum, Morton, Potter, & Corkin, 1983) and is also known to have difficulty interpreting and reporting internal states (Hebben, Corkin, Eichenbaum, & Shedlack, 1985).
2. To say that H.M.'s data have merely confirmed existing ideas about memory is perhaps misleading. There is at least one finding, that obtained by Sagar, Gabrieli, Sullivan, & Corkin (1990), that causes problems for current theories of memory. Briefly, these authors showed that although H.M. could correctly make temporal order judgements for pairs of stimuli he could not, under comparable exposure conditions, show any evidence of recognising. Similarly, he also made accurate frequency of presentation judgements about items he appeared incapable of recognising!

REFERENCES

Atkinson, R.C., & Shiffrin, R.M. (1968). Human memory: A proposed system and its control processes. In K.W. Spence & J.T. Spence (Eds.), *The psychology of learning and motivation (Vol. 2)*. New York: Academic Press.

Cohen, N.J. (1984). Preserved learning capacity in amnesia: Evidence for multiple memory systems. In N. Butters & L.R. Squire (Eds.), *Neuropsychology of memory*. New York: Guilford.

Corkin, S. (1968). Acquisition of motor skill after bilateral medial temporal lobe excision. *Neuropsychologia, 6*, 255–265.

Corkin, S. (1984). Lasting consequences of bilateral medial temporal lobectomy: Clinical course and experimental findings in case HM. *Seminars in Neurology, 4*, 249–259.

Craik, F.I.M., & Lockhart, R.S. (1972). Levels of processing: A framework for memory research. *Journal of Verbal Learning and Verbal Behavior, 11*, 671–684.

Eichenbaum, H., Morton, T.H., Potter, H., & Corkin, S. (1983). Selective olfactory deficits in case HM. *Brain, 106*, 459–472.

Freed, D.M., & Corkin, S. (1988). Rate of forgetting in HM: 6 month recognition. *Behavioral Neuroscience, 102*, 823–827.

Freed, D.M., Corkin, S., & Cohen, N. (1987). Forgetting in HM: A second look. *Neuropsychologia, 25*, 461–471.

Gabrieli, J.D.E., Cohen, N.J., & Corkin, S. (1988). The impaired learning of semantic knowledge following bilateral medial temporal lobe resection. *Brain and Cognition*, 7, 157–177.

Gabrieli, J.D.E., Milberg, W., Keane, M.M., & Corkin, S. (1990). Intact priming of patterns despite impaired memory. *Neuropsychologia*, 28, 417–427.

Gollin, E.S. (1960). Developmental studies of visual recognition of incomplete objects. *Perceptual and Motor Skills*, 11, 289–298.

Hebben, N., Corkin, S., Eichenbaum, H., & Shedlack, K. (1985). Diminished ability to interpret and report internal states after bilateral medial temporal resection: Case HM. *Behavioural Neuroscience*, 99, 1031–1039.

Huppert, F.A., & Piercy, M. (1979). Normal and abnormal forgetting in organic amnesia: Effect of locus of lesion. *Cortex*, 15, 385–390.

James, W. (1890). *Principles of psychology (Vol. 1)*. New York: Holt.

Kinsbourne, M. (1981). Episodic–semantic distinction. In L. Cermak (Ed.), *Human memory and amnesia*. Hillsdale, NJ: Lawrence Erlbaum Associates Inc.

Kopelman, M. (1985). Rates of forgetting in Alzheimer-type dementia and Korsakoff's syndrome. *Neuropsychologia*, 23, 623–638.

Lhermitte, F., & Signoret, J.L. (1972). Analyse neuropsychologique et differenciation des syndromes amnesique. *Revue Neurologique*, 126, 161–178.

Marslen-Wilson, W.D., & Teuber, H.-L. (1975). Memory for remote events in anterograde amnesia: Recognition of public figures from newsphotos. *Neuropsychologia*, 13, 353–364.

Martin, R.C., Loring, D.W., Meador, K.J., & Lee, G.P. (1988). Differential forgetting in patients with temporal lobe dysfunction. *Archives of Clinical Neuropsychology*, 3, 351–358.

Milner, B. (1966). Amnesia following operation on the medial temporal lobes. In C.W. Whitty & O.L. Zangwill (Eds.), *Amnesia*. London: Butterworth.

Milner, B. (1970). Memory and the medial temporal regions of the brain. In K.H. Pribram & D.E. Broadbent (Eds.), *Biology of memory*. New York: Academic Press.

Milner, B., Corkin, S., & Teuber, H.-L. (1968). Further analyses of the hippocampal amnesic syndrome: 14-year follow-up study of HM. *Neuropsychologia*, 6, 215–234.

Ogden, J.A., & Corkin, S. (1991). Memories of HM. In W.C. Abrahams, M.C. Corballis, & K.G. White (Eds.), *Memory mechanisms: A tribute to G.V. Goddard*. Hillsdale, NJ: Lawrence Erlbaum Associates Inc.

Parkin, A.J. (1982). Residual learning capability in organic amnesia. *Cortex*, 18, 417–440.

Parkin, A.J. (1992). Functional significance of etiological factors in human amnesia. In L.R. Squire & N. Butters (Eds.), *Neuropsychology of memory* (2nd ed. pp. 122–129). New York: Guilford.

Parkin, A.J., & Leng, N.R.C. (1993). *Neuropsychology of the amnesic syndrome*. Hove, UK: Lawrence Erlbaum Associates Ltd.

Parkin, A.J., & Streete, S. (1988). Implicit and explicit memory in young children and adults. *British Journal of Psychology*, 79, 361–369.

Russo, R., & Parkin, A.J. (1993). Age differences in implicit memory: More apparent than real. *Memory and Cognition*, 21, 73–80.

Sagar, H.J., Gabrieli, J.D.E., Sullivan, E.V., & Corkin, S. (1990). Recency and frequency discrimination in case HM. *Brain*, 113, 581–602.

Schacter, D.L. (1987). Implicit memory: History and current status. *Journal of Experimental Psychology: Learning, Memory and Cognition*, 13, 501–518.

Schacter, D.L., & Graf, P. (1986). Effects of elaborative processing on implicit and explicit memory for new associations. *Journal of Experimental Psychology: Learning, Memory and Cognition*, 12, 432–444.

Scoville, W.B., & Milner, B. (1957). Loss of recent memory after bilateral hippocampal lesions. *Journal of Neurology, Neurosurgery and Psychiatry*, 20, 11–21.

Squire, L.R. (1981). Two forms of amnesia: An analysis of forgetting. *Journal of Neuroscience*, *1*, 635–640.

Squire, L.R., Cohen, N.J., & Nadel, L. (1984). The medial temporal region and memory consolidation: A new hypothesis. In H. Weingartner & E.S. Parker (Eds.), *Memory consolidation*. Hillsdale, NJ: Lawrence Erlbaum Associates Inc.

Stern, L.D. (1981). A review of theories of human amnesia. *Memory and Cognition*, *9*, 247–262.

Teuber, H.-L., Milner, B., & Vaughan, H.G. (1968). Persistent amnesia following after stab wound to the base of the brain. *Neuropsychologia*, *6*, 25–29.

Tulving, E. (1972). Episodic and semantic memory. In E. Tulving & W. Donaldson (Eds.), *The organisation of memory* (pp. 382–404). New York: Academic Press.

Tulving, E. (1985). How many memory systems are there? *American Psychologist*, *40*, 386–398.

Waugh, N.C., & Norman, D.A. (1965). Primary memory. *Psychological Review*, *72*, 89–104.

Wickelgren, W.A. (1968). Sparing of short-term memory in an amnesic patient: Implications for a strength theory of memory. *Neuropsychologia*, *6*, 235–244.

24

Gail D.—Poizner, Klima, and Bellugi's (1987) Deaf Agrammatic Signer: Form and Function in the Specialisation of the Left Cerebral Hemisphere for Speech and Language

John L. Bradshaw
Department of Psychology, Monash University, Clayton, Australia.

There is a continuous tradition of tool-making and tool-using behaviours back through the early hominids, to *Homo habilis* of two million years ago (Bradshaw & Rogers, 1993); that taxon, moreover, is known from the pattern of successive flaking in the manufacture of its stone tools to have been dextral like ourselves (Toth, 1985). Indeed, tool using is common among our nearest relatives, the chimpanzees; they also appropriately select and trim branches and twigs (Brewer & McGrew, 1990) for a particular purpose, and even coach their young in the proper deployment of tools (Boesch, 1991). Praxis therefore probably antedates language, though it is probably no evolutionary accident that both functions share closely adjacent structures in the left sides of the human brain.

Language, of course, is not co-extensive with speech; the latter, the auditory-aural route, is one of several alternative channels available to us for communication. Pantomime and gesture are means to which we have recourse when stressed, in a foreign country, misunderstood, or aphasic. Many of our apparently innate gesticulations (e.g. beckoning, begging, touching, offering, patting, comforting, grimacing) are shared with our chimpanzee cousins, again suggesting a long tradition and a common ancestry. Language however is unique to humans. There are palaeoneurological indications that it might have been present in some form in *Homo habilis*, from surface structures present on the endocasts of ancient skulls (Tobias, 1987). Nevertheless, it may not have been until the time of anatomically modern humans at around 100,000 to 200,000 years ago that the peripheral physiology of the supralaryngeal tract permitted realisation of a full range of speech sounds (Lieberman, 1989; though see Duchin, 1990).

We appear to have an innate, species-specific drive to acquire speech. This may occur against great odds, in the face of sensory deficit and in the presence of imperfect models, as long as the appropriate stimulation is available before the end of a critical period in the first few years of life (Fromkin, Krashen, Curtiss, Rigler, & Rigler, 1974; and see later). In the event of profound early deafness, alternative communicatory channels may be developed, via signing; where such deafness is familial a unique private language may be evolved between siblings, with its own syntax. Alternatively, pre-existing sign languages such as American Sign Language (A.S.L.) may be taught. These are true independent languages, and not merely grafted upon a "host" speech such as English. Like Creole languages, they are of interest in their own right for the study of how languages may evolve ab initio (Bickerton, 1990). However, they are doubly interesting for the neuropsychologist because they close the circle between praxis and speech, those two great left-hemisphere functions whose independence or relatedness is such a matter of debate. Thus, with A.S.L., language is realised through the hands, and we can determine, via experiments of nature such as the effects of circumscribed brain lesions, whether or not language, qua sign language, can exist independently of gesture and pantomime, and praxis. If so, we can then ask whether it is by chance or necessity that all three faculties, language (broadly), pantomimic gesture, and manual praxis share closely adjacent left-hemisphere structures. Thus, for example, is the common denominator a left-hemisphere specialisation for fine motor control and/or temporal sequencing (Bradshaw & Nettleton, 1981)? Alternatively, is there an ancestral left-hemisphere propensity for oral communicatory behaviour, e.g. in birds (Nottebohm, 1979) and mice (Ehret, 1987)? Is it itself perhaps a consequence of an even earlier right-hemisphere mediation of emotional, agonistic, and spatial behaviours evident still in the chick (Rogers, 1989) and rat (Denenberg, 1984; see Bradshaw & Rogers, 1993)? Until recently, all our knowledge of language has come from studying its spoken form; it has long been assumed that the organisational properties of language are inseparably connected with the sounds of speech, and that hearing and speech development are necessary precursors for normal cerebral lateralisation.

There is a long tradition of research with individuals who are neurologically normal, though profoundly deaf from birth. Is auditory stimulation necessary per se, or sequenced auditory information, or speech in particular, before the expiry of a critical period in the first few years of life, for the proper development of lateralisation for language and non-language or visuospatial functions in their respective hemispheres? The general view has been that such individuals are indeed abnormally lateralised, with reduced or even reversed behavioural asymmetries. A proper and timely interaction of environmental factors or events and genetically hard-wired predispositions is increasingly a commonplace in developmental neurobiology; however, the human brain has for several million years exhibited profound morphological asymmetries in the speech-related areas (Holloway & de LaCoste-Lareymondie, 1982), asymmetries which today are evident even in the foetus (Chi, Dooling, & Gillies, 1977).

Neuropsychology can only ever go so far with normative studies; the other side of its experimental coin relates to the effects of localised lesions on behaviour. The availability of such a patient as Gail D. provides a unique research opportunity. She was the youngest in a family of five, and though she was born deaf of a hereditary condition with two similarly deaf siblings, her parents and other siblings could hear. The two deaf older siblings provided a sign-language environment for her before she went to school; indeed, she learned A.S.L. from her older sister. This signing environment was maintained throughout her schooling, where A.S.L. was in fact the primary language used, as she attended a residential institution for deaf children. She graduated with a vocational degree and later was active in a local association for the deaf, and was fluent in colloquial A.S.L. She married a deaf classmate and had three children, all deaf and similarly fluent in A.S.L., and aged between nine and fourteen at time of testing. This was eight months post stroke at the young age of thirty-seven. The stroke involved most of the frontal convexity on the left, including Broca's area, together with anterior portions of the superior and middle temporal gyri. The parietal lobe was spared except for the bottom of the postcentral gyrus. There were also small patchy lucencies in the white matter underlying the angular gyrus, and the left internal capsule, putamen, and claustrum were similarly involved (Poizner, Klima, & Bellugi, 1987). Subsequently, she seemed to follow A.S.L. conversations eagerly, but rarely participated; she could no longer formulate full statements, and her meagre signs, e.g. "yes" and "no," often seemed at variance with her intentions, as judged by her head gestures.

As a classic case, Gail D. provided control of handedness, locus and occasion of lesion, duration of deafness, early acquisition of signing, exclusivity in its use, and so on. Such questions could now be addressed as whether language is committed to the left hemisphere irrespective of the modality whereby it is made manifest, its relationship to gesture, pantomime and praxis, and whether hearing and speech are necessary prerequisites for the development of normal patterns of cerebral asymmetry, left and right.

It should be emphasised that A.S.L. is a living language, not a manual pantomime or merely derived from e.g. English. It is visuogestural, involving space and movement, but like spoken language has a grammar and a sequential and segmental structure analogous to the phonemes and syllables of spoken languages. Like them, it employs rules of recursiveness and a similar formal structuring, and has been passed down the generations (Bellugi, Poizner, & Klima, 1989; Poizner et al., 1987). Indeed, babbling by hearing and by deaf infants raised in an A.S.L. environment shows close parallels in development and in time course and structure for both spoken and signed languages (Petitto & Marentette, 1991).

Poizner et al. (1987) studied several A.S.L.-signing patients with left and right hemisphere lesions. However, Gail D., with her unique combination of features (mentioned previously), enabled the authors to address such specific questions as is A.S.L. with its visuospatial organisation more bilaterally represented than spoken English, and if not is it represented in the left or right hemisphere? Is A.S.L. parasitic upon the neural structures evolved for spoken English? If so, is any left-hemisphere specialisation based upon structures involved in sequential processing, praxis, gesture, or symbolic communication? Do sign aphasias dissociate from apraxia? Is left-hemisphere specialisation for language tied to function rather than form? Does a lack of auditory experience, and use of a spatial language, affect the development of the functional organisation of the brain of deaf signers for nonlinguistic visuospatial or configurational processing? How does right hemisphere damage affect A.S.L. and/or configurational processing? (These latter issues of course could only be addressed via Gail D.'s right-lesioned colleagues.)

Gail D., previously effortless and fluent in her signing, after her anterior left-hemisphere stroke resembled a Broca's aphasic. Her signing was effortful, agrammatic, and limited to single uninflected signs. Its content was almost exclusively referential and open class, i.e. nouns and verbs, without grammatical inflections or closed-class items. Her comprehension was comparatively normal which seemed odd, given the extensive nature of her lesion; as Poizner et al. (1987) observe, this may in fact have been a consequence of the medium (A.S.L., instead of English). Poizner et al. (1987) note, also taking into account findings from their other left- and right-lesioned signers, the strong parallels between the different forms of aphasic impairment in signed and spoken language. This is the case despite the superficial antithesis between the two systems, spatial and phonological; both systems require left and only left hemisphere injury for the manifestation of deficits. Moreover the basic contrast between anterior (Broca's) and posterior (Wernicke's) aphasia seems also to hold up in A.S.L., and the same structures may mediate both modes of communication. However, they also note that Karen L., with inferior parietal damage in the left hemisphere, though with both major spoken-language areas intact (i.e. Broca's and Wernicke's) nevertheless has marked loss of sign comprehension; this language deficit would probably not be predicted from her lesion in a hearing subject, though it is an area known to be involved in higher-order spatial analysis.

Gail D., with damage to her premotor regions and anterior corpus callosum, alone among her left- and right-lesioned colleagues demonstrated ideomotor apraxia. She produced and initiated movements on command only with considerable difficulty. Because the other aphasic signers with left-hemisphere damage were spared such symptoms, Poizner et al. (1987) differentiate between the linguistic, symbolic, and motoric aspects of hand movement. They argue instead for a dissociation between the capacities for using the linguistic gestures of sign language and for producing and initiating communicative and nonlinguistic gestures, e.g. miming. While others (Selnes, Rubens, Risse, & Levy, 1982) have claimed a double dissociation between spoken language aphasia and apraxia, it is significant that in this series of patients both language and skilled action are overtly expressed by the upper limbs. (We shall shortly also see how, in other patients, right hemisphere damage may dramatically impair general spatial functions, without affecting the visuospatial aspects of signing, as long as the latter involves communication.) Praxis is probably mediated by parietal and frontal interconnectivities in the left hemisphere which between them share the visuokinesthetic and the more strictly motor aspects of learned and skilled motor activities. Poizner et al. (1987) therefore conclude that linguistically relevant signing can break down independently of disorders of movement and gesture. They note that such a separation between linguistic and nonlinguistic function is all the more striking when the same modality mediates gesture and linguistic symbol.

Such a position contrasts with that of Kimura (1982), who claims a common underlying basis for disorders of gesture and language, with the latter a consequence of a more primary left-hemisphere disorder of movement control. It also contrasts with the positions of, for example, Goldstein (1948), that both apraxia and aphasia stem from an underlying left-hemisphere deficit in the capacity to express and comprehend symbols (and see also Brown, 1977). Indeed Corina, Vaid, and Bellugi (1992) subsequently used the concurrent-task paradigm (decrement in left- or right-hand tapping performance) to infer hemispheric specialisation for various tasks in the normally hearing and deaf A.S.L. signers. The tasks included shadowing speech, sign language, arbitrary motoric gesture, and symbolic gesture. They argued that if language lateralisation derives from the special characteristics of a left-hemisphere linguistic (speech or signing) system, speech and signing should give the same patterns of right-hand/left-hemisphere interference. (They did.) If motoric factors were important, sign and nonlinguistic manual gestures should show the same patterns. (They did not.) Finally, if symbolisation were important, sign and symbolic gesture should show the same patterns. (Again, they did not.) The functional separability of sign and gesture after left-hemisphere damage is further supported by Corina, Poizner, Bellugi, Feinberg, Dowd, and

O'Grady-Batch (1992); their deaf signer with global sign aphasia after left-hemisphere damage could nevertheless substitute symbolic gestures (pantomime), and similarly comprehend them.

We previously touched upon an apparent dissociation between loss of spatial functions in and out of a linguistic (signing) context. Poizner, Bellugi, and Klima (1989; and see also Bellugi et al., 1989) noted that their right hemisphere damaged deaf signers experienced left spatial neglect, together with impaired configurational processes and impaired ability to demonstrate the spatial relationships between objects; however, there was no impairment in signing even where space had a syntactic function. Poizner, Bellugi, and Klima (1990) reported a similar functional dissociation between the control of affective (emotional) and linguistic facial expressions in a right-hemisphere damaged deaf signer. Facial expressions are of course important both for conveying emotion and, in A.S.L., as a grammatical feature. The patient experienced severely attenuated emotional expression, with sparing of linguistic facial expressions. Another similar right-hemisphere dissociation occurs between the recognition of facial identity and facial expression (Bowers & Heilman, 1984; Etcoff, 1984; Ley & Bryden, 1979; Pizzamiglio, Zoccolotti, Mammucari, & Cesaroni, 1983). Finally, the fact that Gail D., and other deaf signers with left-hemisphere damage were aphasic for sign but showed normal asymmetries for nonlanguage visuospatial processing is evidence that auditory experience is not essential for the development of nonverbal hemispheric specialisation. See later, however, for contrary findings with non-clinical deaf signers.

The following general conclusions are drawn from the work on clinical populations of deaf signers, including Gail D. (see Bellugi et al., 1989; Poizner et al., 1987), and a Wada study (Damasio, Bellugi, Damasio, Poizner, & Van Gilder, 1986) where a hearing signer became aphasic in both English and A.S.L. after an amytal injection to the left carotid. Hearing and speech are not necessary for the development of hemispheric specialisation. There is a left-hemisphere dominance for sign language and a right-hemisphere dominance for spatial functions of a non-sign nature in signers, and the fact that grammatical information in A.S.L. is conveyed spatially does not alter this complimentary specialisation. The components of sign language (e.g. the lexicon and grammar) can be selectively impaired, reflecting a differential breakdown of A.S.L. along linguistically relevant lines exactly parallel to what obtains with spoken language, and an overall modular organisation. The left hemisphere has an innate predisposition for language, regardless of modality, spoken or signed. (Haglund, Ojemann, Lettich, Bellugi, & Corina, 1993, in an intraoperative electrostimulation and micro-electrode recording study of an A.S.L. user and native English speaker, did find a dissociation between closely adjacent cortical sites essential for the two modalities.) A straight dichotomy therefore between language and visuospatial functions is an oversimplification, given the interplay in signing between visuospatial and linguistic relationships within the same system, and the fact that unilaterally injured deaf signers show a dissociation between the two uses of space in A.S.L.; these are of course the representation of spatial relationships and the representation of syntactic relationships. As we saw, Corina, Poizner et al. (1992) and Corina, Vaid, & Bellugi (1992) excluded a superior motoric or symbolic capacity in the left hemisphere as the substrate of human cerebral asymmetry. They concluded instead in favour of a superior communicative/linguistic capacity. We have earlier (Bradshaw & Nettleton, 1981) argued in favour of an underlying left-hemisphere superiority in terms of analytic, sequential, time-dependent processing. Poizner and Tallal (1987) reported that deaf signers had an entirely normal capacity to process rapidly varying visual signals, and a normal pattern of hemispheric asymmetry, despite a lack of auditory experience. However, Marcotte and Morere (1990) dispute the position of Poizner and Tallal (1987) that it is early linguistic experience (of whatever modality) that is crucial for the unfolding of left-hemispheric language specialisation. In their dual task paradigm to assess language lateralisation in normal hearing and deaf adolescents, they found that it was a matter of whether or not subjects have had auditory–oral experiences before three years of age; there was an atypical hemispheric representation of language in the event of profound deafness only if it occurred before then (see also Fromkin et al., 1974).

We shall shortly address the rest of the extensive literature on lateral asymmetries in clinically normal individuals who became deaf at or some time after birth, but note that anomalous lateralisation in the early deaf is in fact a common finding. Others who also implicitly reject the Poizner–Bellugi–Klima thesis that early linguistic experiences are critical, invoking instead early sequential auditory experiences, include Craig and Gordon (1988) and McKee and Gordon (1987). From an evolutionary standpoint, this is our own current position (Bradshaw & Rogers, 1993); an early right-hemisphere superiority for spatial and emotional processing, present in birds and rats, preceded or co-occurred with a left hemisphere mediation of communicative, species-specific signals, present in birds, mice and at least some non-human primates like the macaque. Whether or not a predisposition for fine, time-dependent, sequential processing preceded (as we believe, and see also Bianki, 1988) or was a consequence of a developing communicative capacity is yet to be determined.

The main conclusion from clinical experiments such as those with Gail D. is that the left hemisphere is, and remains, dominant for the mediation of language, irrespective of its modality; this is the case even with visuospatial signs and individuals who have never been exposed to spoken speech. This conclusion is of course compatible with the evidence of morphological asymmetries in the speech-related areas of the brains even of the foetus (Chi et al., 1977). However, it contrasts with a long tradition that functional asymmetries develop (Lenneberg, 1967), and require exposure to adequate and appropriate sensory stimulation before a critical period has elapsed (Fromkin et al., 1974). Of course, there is also a long tradition, especially in the visual modality (Blakemore, 1978), and in the area of birdsong development (Nottebohm, 1979), that proper anatomical and functional development requires an interplay of both genetic hard-wiring and timely environmental input. Nor in fact may environmental modifications of neural connectivities and function be restricted to infancy. Merzenich (1987) has shown in the monkey that a region in the parietal cortex topographically mapping somatosensory information from a finger can subsequently respond to stimulation of adjacent fingers if that finger is lost. Even more dramatically, Pons, Garraghty, Ommaya, Kaas, Taub, and Mishkin (1991) found in adult macaques years after section of sensory nerves from the forelimbs, at the point of entry into the spinal cord, that the parietal zone originally responding to the limb now responded to facial stimulation; the area that was now newly responsive to the face was over 1cm beyond the original face-responsive zone. Neville (1988) likewise found that visual evoked potentials differ in deaf and hearing adults; the brain regions subserving auditory processing in hearing subjects respond to visual stimulation in the deaf.

Laterality studies with visual materials have long reported reduced or reversed asymmetries in those who have never been exposed to spoken language. There is a similar tradition (Bryden & Saxby, 1986; Hahn, 1987; Witelson, 1985) that normally hearing children are not "fully lateralised" until puberty. One could even argue (Stoel-Gammon & Otomo, 1986) that because deaf infants babble differently, being unable to hear their own efforts, this itself affects subsequent language development. One problem is that the populations are often not homogeneous in early linguistic experience, onset and severity of hearing loss, auditory or signing experiences at various stages of development, age at testing, etc. Indeed, at any age the early stages of acquiring a new language or script may be associated with (temporarily) abnormal laterality patterns (Bradshaw & Nettleton, 1983, Chapter 8). Another problem relates to a possible publishing bias preferentially to report work which shows differences between populations, in this case anomalous lateralisation in the deaf (or young, or left handed, or illiterate, or bilingual...). This is not the place to review in detail the reported patterns of behavioural lateralisation in the clinically normal long-term deaf (see e.g. Boshoven, McNeil, & Harvey, 1982; Gibson, 1988; Marcotte & LaBarba, 1985; Sanders, Wright, & Ellis, 1989; Szelag & Wasilewski, 1992). Suffice it to say that most studies (with visually presented letters or words, static or moving signs, nonverbal patterns or faces, tactile presentations, E.E.G. or concurrent task measures) find that the deaf show different laterality patterns from the hearing. Where signs have been visually presented to one or other visual field, in some cases only the deaf have shown a right-field/left-hemisphere superiority (e.g. Neville, 1988). This suggests that the linguistic function of a signal may be more important than its form. In other cases only dynamic (moving) rather than the more unnatural static versions have provided (with deaf subjects) a right-field/left-hemisphere superiority (e.g. Poizner, Battison, & Lane, 1979). Indeed Emmorey and Corina (1993) found that both deaf signers and hearing English speakers gave a right-field/left-hemisphere superiority to dynamic signs and English words respectively, as long as the items were abstract. However, A.S.L. signers showed a significant left-field/right-hemisphere superiority for imageable items, while for such material English speakers exhibited no asymmetries. The authors conclude that such an apparent difference in brain laterality may reflect differences in the role of imagery in the two languages.

Gail D., together with her handful of other left- or right-hemisphere damaged deaf signers, has provided the focus for current thinking on the roles of neural hard-wiring and modifying environmental factors with respect to the cerebral organisation of language. Lenneberg's (1967) position was, firstly, that at birth both hemispheres are capable of language, though the capacity of the right decreases with maturation, and secondly that left-hemisphere language lateralisation requires exposure to an appropriate linguistic environment. However, as we have seen, morphological asymmetries are present even before birth (Chi et al., 1977). With appropriate testing infants can demonstrate a double dissociation, i.e. a left-hemisphere superiority for speech and a right-hemisphere superiority for non-speech signals (Best, Hoffman, & Glanville, 1982; Entus, 1977; Glanville, Best, & Levenson, 1977; though see Vargha-Khadem & Corballis, 1979). Moreover, there is in fact little real evidence of lateralisation increasing with age (Bryden & Saxby, 1986; Hahn, 1987; Witelson, 1985). Any such apparent effect could merely reflect an increase of cognitive capacity, an unfolding of latent abilities, a change in information-processing strategies, or even a reduction in the capacity for plastic reorganisation of the brain in the face of insult. The left hemisphere certainly seems to have an innate predisposition for language, though it is also sensitive to environmental influences, which if abnormal (e.g. through deafness) might modify how language is manifested. Thus, the third of the following four graded propositions may be preferred:

1. Language lateralisation is totally innate, and needs no environmental influences to develop.

2. Language lateralisation is genetically determined, unfolding after any exposure to language.
3. Language lateralisation is innate, but may require appropriate language exposure to develop normally.
4. Language lateralisation is not innate, and needs appropriate exposure to environmental influences.

Nevertheless it is likely that the dispute about the possibility or extent of a right-hemisphere contribution to language functions in the congenitally and profoundly deaf will continue, with claims and counter-arguments similar to those in the parallel dispute on language lateralisation in early versus late bilingualism (Harris, 1992; Johnson & Newport, 1989; Paradis, 1989; Zatorre, 1989). In both cases, population non-homogeneity, particularly concerning familiarity with the chosen medium and age of acquisition, may be major determining variables.

REFERENCES

Bellugi, U., Poizner, H., & Klima, E.S. (1989). Language, modality and the brain. *Trends in the Neurosciences, 12*, 380–388.

Best, C.T., Hoffman, H., & Glanville, B.B. (1982). Development of infant ear asymmetries for speech and music. *Perception and Psychophysics, 31*, 75–85.

Bianki, V.L. (1988). *The right and left hemispheres: Cerebral lateralization of function.* New York: Gordon & Breach.

Bickerton, D. (1990). *Language and species.* Chicago: University of Chicago Press.

Blakemore, C. (1978). Maturation and modification in the developing visual system. In R. Held, H.W. Leibowitz, & H.-L. Teuber (Eds.), *Handbook of sensory physiology: Vol. VIII. Perception* (pp. 377–436). New York: Springer.

Boesch, C. (1991). Teaching among wild chimpanzees. *Animal Behaviour, 41*, 530–532.

Boshoven, M.M., McNeil, M.R., & Harvey, L.O. (1982). Hemispheric specialization for the processing of linguistic and nonlinguistic stimuli in congenitally deaf and hearing adults: A review and a contribution. *Audiology, 21*, 509–530.

Bowers, D., & Heilman, K.M. (1984). Dissociation between the processing of affective and nonaffective faces: A case study. *Journal of Clinical Neuropsychology, 6*, 367–379.

Bradshaw, J.L., & Nettleton, N.C. (1981). The nature of hemispheric specialisation in man. *Behavioral and Brain Sciences, 4*, 51–91.

Bradshaw, J.L., & Nettleton, N.C. (1983). *Human cerebral asymmetry.* Hillsdale, NJ: Prentice-Hall.

Bradshaw, J.L., & Rogers, L.J. (1993). *The evolution of lateral asymmetries, language, tool use and intellect.* New York: Academic Press.

Brewer, S.M., & McGrew, W.C. (1990). Chimpanzee use of a tool set to get honey. *Folia Primatologica, 54*, 100–104.

Brown, J. (1977). *Mind, brain and consciousness.* New York: Academic Press.

Bryden, M.P., & Saxby, L. (1986). Developmental aspects of cerebral lateralization. In J.E. Obrzut & G.W. Hynd (Eds.), *Child neuropsychology (Vol. 1)* (pp. 73–94). New York: Academic Press.

Chi, J.G., Dooling, E.C., & Gillies, F.H. (1977). Left–right asymmetries of the temporal speech areas of the human foetus. *Archives of Neurology, 34*, 346–348.

Corina, D.P., Poizner, H., Bellugi, U., Feinberg, T., Dowd, D., & O'Grady-Batch, L. (1992). Dissociation between linguistic and nonlinguistic gestural systems: A case for compositionality. *Brain and Language, 43*, 414–417.

Corina, D.P., Vaid, J., & Bellugi, U. (1992). The linguistic basis of left hemisphere specialization. *Science, 255*, 1258–1260.

Craig, H.B., & Gordon, H.W. (1988). Specialized cognitive function and reading achievement in deaf adolescents. *Journal of Speech and Hearing Disorders, 53*, 30–41.

Damasio, A., Bellugi, U., Damasio, H., Poizner, H., & Van Gilder, J. (1986). Sign language aphasia during left-hemisphere amytal injection. *Nature, 322*, 363–365.

Denenberg, V.H. (1984). Behavioral asymmetry. In N. Geschwind & A.M. Galaburda (Eds.), *Cerebral dominance: The biological foundations* (pp. 114–133). Cambridge: Harvard University Press.

Duchin, L.E. (1990). The evolution of articulate speech: Comparative anatomy of the oral cavity in *Pan* and *Homo. Journal of Human Evolution, 19*, 687–697.

Ehret, G. (1987). Left hemisphere advantage in the mouse brain for recognizing ultrasonic communication calls. *Nature, 325*, 249–251.

Emmorey, K., & Corina, D. (1993). Hemispheric specialization for A.S.L. signs and English words: Differences between imageable and abstract forms. *Neuropsychologia, 31*, 645–653.

Entus, A.K. (1977). Hemispheric asymmetry in processing of dichotically-presented speech and nonspeech stimuli by infants. In S.J. Segalowitz & F.A. Gruber (Eds.), *Language development and neurological theory* (pp. 63–73). New York: Academic Press.

Etcoff, N.L. (1984). Selective attention to facial identity and facial emotion. *Neuropsychologia, 22*, 281–295.

Fromkin, V., Krashen, S., Curtiss, S., Rigler, D., & Rigler, M. (1974). The development of language in Genie: A case of language acquisition beyond the critical period. *Brain and Language, 1*, 81–107.

Gibson, C. (1988). The impact of early developmental history on cerebral asymmetries: Implications for reading ability in deaf children. In D.L. Molfese & S.J. Segalowitz (Eds.), *Brain lateralization in children: Developmental implications* (pp. 591–604). New York: Guilford.

Glanville, B.B., Best, C.T., & Levenson, R. (1977). A cardiac measure of cerebral asymmetries in infant auditory perception. *Developmental Psychology, 13*, 54–59.

Goldstein, K. (1948). *Language and language disturbance*. New York: Grune & Stratton.

Haglund, M.M., Ojemann, G.A., Lettich, E., Bellugi, U., & Corina, D. (1993). Dissociation of cortical and single unit activity in spoken and signed languages. *Brain and Language, 44*, 19–27.

Hahn, W.K. (1987). Cerebral lateralization of function—from infancy through childhood. *Psychological Bulletin, 101*, 376–392.

Harris, R.J. (1992). *Cognitive processing in bilinguals*. Amsterdam: Elsevier.

Holloway, R.L., & de LaCoste-Lareymondie, M.C. (1982). Some preliminary findings on the palaeontology of cerebral dominance. *American Journal of Physical Anthropology, 58*, 101–110.

Johnson, J.S., & Newport, E.L. (1989). Critical period effects in second language learning: The effect of maturational state on acquisition of English as a second language. *Cognitive Psychology, 21*, 60–99.

Kimura, D. (1982). Left hemisphere control of oral and brachial movements and their relation to communication. *Philosophical Transactions of the Royal Society of London, B298*, 135–149.

Lenneberg, E.H. (1967). *Biological foundations of language*. New York: Wiley.

Ley, R.G., & Bryden, M.P. (1979). Hemispheric differences in processing of emotions and faces. *Brain and Language, 7*, 127–138.

Lieberman, P. (1989). The origins of some aspects of human language and cognition. In P. Mellars & C. Stringer (Eds.), *The human revolution: Behavioral and biological perspectives on the origins of modern humans* (pp. 391–414). Princeton: Princeton University Press.

Marcotte, A.C., & LaBarba, R.C. (1985). Cerebral lateralization for speech in normal and deaf children. *Brain and Language, 26*, 244–258.

Marcotte, A.C., & Morere, D.A. (1990). Speech lateralization in deaf populations: Evidence for a developmental critical period. *Brain and Language, 39*, 134–152.

McKee, D., & Gordon, H.W. (1987). Analysis of specialized cognitive functions in deaf and hearing signers. *Society for Neuroscience Abstracts, 13*, 47 (abstract).

Merzenich, M.M. (1987). Dynamic neocortical processes and the origins of higher brain functions. In J.-P. Changeux & M. Konishi (Eds.), *The neural and molecular bases of learning* (pp. 337–358). Chichester: Wiley.

Neville, H.J. (1988). Cerebral organization for spatial attention. In J. Stiles-Davis, M. Kritchevsky, & U. Bellugi (Eds.), *Spatial cognition: Brain bases and development* (pp. 327–421). Hillsdale, NJ: Lawrence Erlbaum Associates Inc.

Nottebohm, F. (1979). Origins and mechanisms in the establishment of cerebral dominance. In M.S. Gazzaniga (Ed.), *Handbook of behavioral neurobioology: Vol. 2. Neuropsychology* (pp. 295–344). New York: Plenum.

Paradis, M. (1989). Bilingual and polyglot aphasia. In F. Boller & J. Grafman (Eds.), *Handbook of neuropsychology (Vol. 2)* (pp. 117–140). Amsterdam: Elsevier.

Petitto, L.A., & Marentette, P.F. (1991). Babbling in the manual mode: Evidence for the ontogeny of language. *Science, 251*, 1493–1496.

Pizzamiglio, L., Zoccolotti, P., Mammucari, A., & Cesaroni, R. (1983). The independence of face identity and facial expression recognition mechanisms: Relationship to sex and cognitive style. *Brain and Cognition, 2*, 176–188.

Poizner, H., Battison, R., & Lane, H. (1979). Cerebral asymmetry for American Sign Language: The effects of moving stimuli. *Brain and Language, 7*, 351–362.

Poizner, H., Bellugi, U., & Klima, E.S. (1989). Sign language aphasia. In F. Boller & J. Grafman (Eds.), *Handbook of neuropsychology (Vol. 2)* (pp. 157–172). Amsterdam: Elsevier.

Poizner, H., Bellugi, U., & Klima, E.S. (1990). Biological foundations of language: Clues from sign language. *Annual Review of Neuroscience, 13*, 283–307.

Poizner, H., Klima, E.S., & Bellugi, U. (1987). *What the hands reveal about the brain.* Cambridge, MA: MIT/Bradford.

Poizner, H., & Tallal, P. (1987). Temporal processing in deaf signers. *Brain and Language, 30*, 52–62.

Pons, T.P., Garraghty, P.E., Ommaya, A.K., Kaas, J.H., Taub, E., & Mishkin, M. (1991). Massive cortical reorganisation after sensory deafferentation in adult macaques. *Science, 252*, 1857–1860.

Rogers, L.J. (1989). Laterality in animals. *International Journal of Comparative Psychology, 3*, 5–25.

Sanders, G., Wright, H.V., & Ellis, C. (1989). Cerebral lateralization of language in deaf and hearing people. *Brain and Language, 36*, 555–579.

Selnes, O.A., Rubens, A.B., Risse, G.L., & Levy, R.S. (1982). Transient aphasia with persistent apraxia. *Archives of Neurology, 39*, 122–126.

Stoel-Gammon, C., & Otomo, K. (1986). Babbling development of hearing-impaired and normally hearing subjects. *Journal of Speech and Hearing Disorders, 51*, 33–41.

Szelag, E., & Wasilewski, R. (1992). The effect of congenital deafness on cerebral asymmetry in perception of emotional and nonemotional faces. *Acta Psychologica, 79*, 45–57.

Tobias, P.V. (1987). The brain of *Homo habilis*: A new level of organisation in cerebral evolution. *Journal of Human Evolution, 16*, 741–761.

Toth, N. (1985). Archaeological evidence for preferential right handedness in the Lower and Middle Pleistocene, and its possible implications. *Journal of Human Evolution, 14*, 607–614.

Vargha-Khadem, F., & Corballis, M.C. (1979). Cerebral asymmetry in infants. *Brain and Language, 8*, 1–9.

Witelson, S.F. (1985). On hemisphere specialization and cerebral plasticity from birth: Mark II. In C.T. Best (Ed.), *Hemispheric function and collaboration in the child.* (pp. 33–85). New York: Academic Press.

Zatorre, R.J. (1989). On the representation of multiple languages in the brain: Old problems and new directions. *Brain and Language, 36*, 127–147.

Postword: The Future of Neuropsychology— Deconstructing the Past

John C. Marshall
Neuropsychology Unit, University Department of Clinical Neurology, The Radcliffe Infirmary, Oxford, U.K.

There is a fairly widespread tendency in the teaching of psychology to ignore the discipline's past. How many students have recently been required to read G.T. Fechner's *Elemente der Psychophysik* (1860), William James' *The principles of psychology* (1890), or Kurt Koffka's *Principles of Gestalt psychology* (1935)? For that matter, how many professors have more than a nodding acquaintance with the history of psychological inquiry? I am tempted to assign the primary responsibility for such constricted vision to science-envy. The "real" sciences (physics and chemistry) are held to be progressive and cumulative. Thomas Kuhn notwithstanding, there is accordingly (the argument goes) little point in learning about past error when there is so much current "truth" to acquire.

The notion that one should teach psychology from (only) the latest textbook and the last five years' worth of papers in the experimental journals seems, then, to stem from delusions of (scientific) grandeur: Insofar as Wilhelm Wundt (for example) did or wrote anything of interest, the gold (it is believed) will have been seamlessly incorporated into the overall scientific edifice and the dross washed away. True, our current psychology may not be complete, or even fully accurate, but it is not so false that there is any reason to look at the (even worse) errors of our predecessors. To consult the original sources would merely be a waste of precious time (they say). Now it *may* be the case that all psychologists are nowadays so clever and knowledgeable that it is pointless for them to read what Franz-Joseph Gall or Karl Buhler once wrote ... but I would not bet on it.

It might be thought that we *neuro*psychologists are less disposed to living in the specious present than many of our colleagues in other domains of psychological science. Most of us can, after all, recite the litany of our illustrious forebears: Gall, Charcot, Déjèrine, Liepmann, Goldstein ... etc. Indeed, we could hardly forget the giants who became eponymously associated with a disease (Alzheimer, Parkinson, Pick...), an aphasia (Broca, Wernicke...), or a syndrome (Anton, Balint...).

And yet ... we should not become too pleased with ourselves, for neuropsychologists suffer (in common with our medical colleagues) from what I can only call "Adam's-syndrome". The very act of *naming* a neuropsychological disorder (especially when the name looks Greekish or Latinate) seems to confer "reality" upon the referent. This unthinking reification takes place with (what appear to be) purely descriptive expressions (e.g. ideational apraxia), with syndromes, and (above all) with disease entities; that is, we believe too readily that the objects of our inquiries are given, that the existence of (for instance) "Broca's aphasia" or "the amnesic syndrome" is beyond doubt. We fail to see that such categories are theoretical constructs devised by fallible scientists, not God-given entities that we have been invited to explore. Because we do not read the primary literature of the past we forget that people constructed the symptom-complexes that figure in the textbooks of the present.

It is our job to evaluate the theoretical constructs that have been handed down to us (and those that we ourselves create). And it is thus an empirical (and theoretical) issue whether or not Wernicke's aphasia (or deep dyslexia) is a natural kind. The way forward may indeed be to refine, extend, and add further content to the construct of Wernicke's aphasia. But equally it may be the case that the symptom-complex should be *deconstructed* and replaced by an entirely different constellation of signs and symptoms that permits greater insight into the underlying reality of how language is represented in the human brain.

How, then, can we convince ourselves that even the most basic (foundational) categories of neuropsychology are not actually engraved on tablets of stone (the Moses syndrome)? And that radical redescription is always a possibility (to be taken seriously).

Strangely enough, it would appear that the way forward can be facilitated by looking back. For, of course, Paul Broca did not "discover" Broca's aphasia, and neither did Reszö Balint "discover" Balint's syndrome. Rather, these investigators described individual cases (or case series) of a cognitive disorder that they found notable *for some reason or other*. It is invariably instructive to see what those reasons were *at the time*. It is equally instructive to observe that what we mean by, for example, Broca's aphasia bears very little in common with anything that Broca himself could have "seen" or conjectured when originally examining the cases. Similarly, the conceptual relationship between "Pick's disease" then and now is by no means obvious (Hodges & Gurd, 1994).

On second thoughts, then, it is not so strange that history can free us to create the future: Those who know no history are indeed doomed to repeat it. And some of those repetitions are extremely bizarre. For example, the persistence of the notion that "dementia" is an entity (medical, psychological, sociological, or whatever) remains both tragedy and farce.

The editors and authors of *Classic cases in neuropsychology* are accordingly to be warmly congratulated for providing us with a relatively painless way of beginning a long-overdue process of reappraisal. All the chapters should enable us to see more clearly why we are where we are and, more importantly, should help us to move to better positions; positions, that is, that are theoretically more revealing and more useful practically to the care of patients.

It is particularly good that the volume includes cases ancient *and* modern. There is always a temptation to draw a line between studies of purely "historical" interest and studies of current value. It is too easy to believe that criticisms of "them" could not apply to "us". The format of the present volume forces one to see how strictures that relate to 19th-century syndromes apply with equal force to more recent constructs. For example: What exactly is the relationship between Paterson and Zangwill's 1944 concept of unilateral neglect and both earlier (Poppelreuter, 1917/1990) and later studies of disorders of spatial cognition (Halligan & Marshall, 1992)? Are Warrington and Shallice (and their collaborators) correct in advancing the construct of "category-specific aphasia" (Warrington & Shallice, 1984), or does the true generalization still elude us? Were Marshall and Newcombe (1973) moving in the correct direction when they made G.R. a case of the (then new) syndrome of "deep dyslexia"? G.R. was *not* an example of "deep dyslexia" when he was originally described in 1966, just as Balint's cases were not (at the time) cases of "Balint's syndrome". The patterns that the major behavioural neurologists of the distant past (thought they) saw were sometimes misleading. Some patterns that we see escaped our predecessors. How many of those latter patterns will our successors find equally misleading?

The Taoist cook was greatly admired by his employer Prince Wen Hui because of his great skill in cutting up the ox. The cook disclaimed skill in cutting but acknowledged skill in finding the natural joints. We, like the cook in Chuang Tzu's parable, seek to cut (cognitive and biological) nature at its joints. But the determination of natural kinds in the cognitive neurosciences is fraught with conceptual difficulties that go way beyond any problems that the Taoist cook may have experienced. Yet those difficulties will be better overcome if we remember and learn from neuropsychology's past. History is both then and now.

REFERENCES

Fechner, G.T. (1860). *Elemente der Psychophysik*. Leipzig: Breitkoff und Hartel.

Halligan, P.W., & Marshall, J.C. (1992). Left visuo-spatial neglect: A meaningless entity? *Cortex, 28*, 525–535.

Hodges, J.R., & Gurd, J.M. (1994). Remote memory and lexical retrieval in a case of frontal Pick's disease. *Archives of Neurology, 51*, 821–827.

James, W. (1890). *The principles of psychology*. London: Macmillan.

Koffka, K. (1935). *Principles of Gestalt psychology*. New York: Harcourt, Brace & World.

Marshall, J.C., & Newcombe, F. (1973). Patterns of paralexia: A psycholinguistic approach. *Journal of Psycholinguistic Research, 2*, 17–199.

Paterson, A., & Zangwill, O.L. (1944). Disorders of visual space perception associated with lesions of the right cerebral hemisphere. *Brain, 67*, 331–358.

Poppelreuter, W. (1917/1990). *Disturbances of lower and higher visual capacities caused by occipital damage* (Trans. J. Zihl). Oxford: Clarendon Press.

Warrington, E.K., & Shallice, T. (1984). Category specific semantic impairments. *Brain, 107*, 829–854.

Cases Index

Names Index

Subject Index